Contents

Contents		5
List of Figures and Pictures		9
List of Appendices		11
Glossary		13
Band, club, festival, and label names with translation		19
Acknowledgements		27
Foreword by Yngvar B. Steinholt		31
Introduction		**33**
1	**Theory**	**41**
	1.1 Scenes	42
	1.2 Cultural flow	48
	Migration	53
	1.3 "That kind of Russian melody": Identities and band images	56
	Collective identities	58
	Music and identity	60
	Post-colonial perspective	62
2	**Methodology**	**69**
	2.1 The ethnographer's position and impact	73
	My impact and how I was perceived	77
	My musical impact	82
	2.2 Concluding remarks	84
3	**The St. Petersburg scene**	**87**
	3.1 Social networks	88

		Svoboda	91
		Fans	97
		Band promotion	98
		Art direktors – Booking managers	100
	3.2	Social hubs	102
		Clubs	103
		Practice rooms	108
		Recording and distribution	111
	3.3	Discursive scene boundaries	114
		Underground – Commercial	115
		Popsa	118
		Moscow and Marijuana: The St. Petersburg – Moscow rivalry	124
		That shit: The *russkii rok*-discourse	133
		The musicians' perception of *russkii rok*	136
	3.4	Concluding remarks	142
4	The musical embedding of St. Petersburg		145
5	Reggae and ska in St. Petersburg		153
	5.1	Style indicators of reggae and ska	156
	5.2	*"We're not Rastamen, we're reggae-people"*: Reggae in St. Petersburg	158
	5.3	*"And that word grooves"*: Ska in St. Petersburg	167
		Ukra-Ska Pung I: Svoboda and ska	170
	5.4	Concluding remarks	174
6	Russian perceptions of Ukraine		177
	6.1	*Ukra-Ska Pung II*: Svoboda and Ukraine	181
		"As folklore as it gets": Svoboda and Ukrainian coloring	184
		Svoboda's *russkii rok* legacy	189

Soviet and Post-Soviet Politics and Society (SPPS) Vol. 101
ISSN 1614-3515

General Editor: Andreas Umland,
Kyiv-Mohyla Academy, umland@stanfordalumni.org

Editorial Assistant: Olena Sivuda, *Drahomanov Pedagogical University of Kyiv*, SLS6255@ku-eichstaett.de

EDITORIAL COMMITTEE*

DOMESTIC & COMPARATIVE POLITICS
Prof. **Ellen Bos**, *Andrássy University of Budapest*
Dr. **Ingmar Bredies**, *University of Regensburg*
Dr. **Andrey Kazantsev**, *MGIMO (U) MID RF, Moscow*
Dr. **Heiko Pleines**, *University of Bremen*
Prof. **Richard Sakwa**, *University of Kent at Canterbury*
Dr. **Sarah Whitmore**, *Oxford Brookes University*
Dr. **Harald Wydra**, *University of Cambridge*
SOCIETY, CLASS & ETHNICITY
Col. **David Glantz**, *"Journal of Slavic Military Studies"*
Dr. **Marlène Laruelle**, *Johns Hopkins University*
Dr. **Stephen Shulman**, *Southern Illinois University*
Prof. **Stefan Troebst**, *University of Leipzig*
POLITICAL ECONOMY & PUBLIC POLICY
Prof. em. **Marshall Goldman**, *Wellesley College, Mass.*
Dr. **Andreas Goldthau**, *Central European University*
Dr. **Robert Kravchuk**, *University of North Carolina*
Dr. **David Lane**, *University of Cambridge*
Dr. **Carol Leonard**, *University of Oxford*
Dr. **Maria Popova**, *McGill University, Montreal*

FOREIGN POLICY & INTERNATIONAL AFFAIRS
Dr. **Peter Duncan**, *University College London*
Dr. **Taras Kuzio**, *Johns Hopkins University*
Prof. **Gerhard Mangott**, *University of Innsbruck*
Dr. **Diana Schmidt-Pfister**, *University of Konstanz*
Dr. **Lisbeth Tarlow**, *Harvard University, Cambridge*
Dr. **Christian Wipperfürth**, *N-Ost Network, Berlin*
Dr. **William Zimmerman**, *University of Michigan*
HISTORY, CULTURE & THOUGHT
Dr. **Catherine Andreyev**, *University of Oxford*
Prof. **Mark Bassin**, *Södertörn University*
Prof. **Karsten Brüggemann**, *Tallinn University*
Dr. **Alexander Etkind**, *University of Cambridge*
Dr. **Gasan Gusejnov**, *Moscow State University*
Prof. em. **Walter Laqueur**, *Georgetown University*
Prof. **Leonid Luks**, *Catholic University of Eichstaett*
Dr. **Olga Malinova**, *Russian Academy of Sciences*
Dr. **Andrei Rogatchevski**, *University of Glasgow*
Dr. **Mark Tauger**, *West Virginia University*
Dr. **Stefan Wiederkehr**, *BBAW, Berlin*

ADVISORY BOARD*

Prof. **Dominique Arel**, *University of Ottawa*
Prof. **Jörg Baberowski**, *Humboldt University of Berlin*
Prof. **Margarita Balmaceda**, *Seton Hall University*
Dr. **John Barber**, *University of Cambridge*
Prof. **Timm Beichelt**, *European University Viadrina*
Dr. **Katrin Boeckh**, *University of Munich*
Prof. em. **Archie Brown**, *University of Oxford*
Dr. **Vyacheslav Bryukhovetsky**, *Kyiv-Mohyla Academy*
Prof. **Timothy Colton**, *Harvard University, Cambridge*
Prof. **Paul D'Anieri**, *University of Florida*
Dr. **Heike Dörrenbächer**, *Naumann Foundation Kyiv*
Dr. **John Dunlop**, *Hoover Institution, Stanford, California*
Dr. **Sabine Fischer**, *EU Institute for Security Studies*
Dr. **Geir Flikke**, *NUPI, Oslo*
Dr. **David Galbreath**, *University of Aberdeen*
Prof. **Alexander Galkin**, *Russian Academy of Sciences*
Prof. **Frank Golczewski**, *University of Hamburg*
Dr. **Nikolas Gvosdev**, *Naval War College, Newport, RI*
Prof. **Mark von Hagen**, *Arizona State University*
Dr. **Guido Hausmann**, *University of Freiburg i.Br.*
Prof. **Dale Herspring**, *Kansas State University*
Dr. **Stefani Hoffman**, *Hebrew University of Jerusalem*
Prof. **Mikhail Ilyin**, *MGIMO (U) MID RF, Moscow*
Prof. **Vladimir Kantor**, *Higher School of Economics*
Dr. **Ivan Katchanovski**, *University of Ottawa*
Prof. em. **Andrzej Korbonski**, *University of California*
Dr. **Iris Kempe**, *Heinrich Boell Foundation Tbilisi*
Prof. **Herbert Küpper**, *Institut für Ostrecht Regensburg*
Dr. **Rainer Lindner**, *CEEER, Berlin*
Dr. **Vladimir Malakhov**, *Russian Academy of Sciences*

Dr. **Luke March**, *University of Edinburgh*
Prof. **Michael McFaul**, *US National Security Council*
Prof. **Birgit Menzel**, *University of Mainz-Germersheim*
Prof. **Valery Mikhailenko**, *The Urals State University*
Prof. **Emil Pain**, *Higher School of Economics, Moscow*
Dr. **Oleg Podvintsev**, *Russian Academy of Sciences*
Prof. **Olga Popova**, *St. Petersburg State University*
Dr. **Alex Pravda**, *University of Oxford*
Dr. **Erik van Ree**, *University of Amsterdam*
Dr. **Joachim Rogall**, *Robert Bosch Foundation Stuttgart*
Prof. **Peter Rutland**, *Wesleyan University, Middletown*
Prof. **Marat Salikov**, *The Urals State Law Academy*
Dr. **Gwendolyn Sasse**, *University of Oxford*
Prof. **Jutta Scherrer**, *EHESS, Paris*
Prof. **Robert Service**, *University of Oxford*
Mr. **James Sherr**, *RIIA Chatham House London*
Dr. **Oxana Shevel**, *Tufts University, Medford*
Prof. **Eberhard Schneider**, *University of Siegen*
Prof. **Olexander Shnyrkov**, *Shevchenko University, Kyiv*
Prof. **Hans-Henning Schröder**, *University of Bremen*
Prof. **Yuri Shapoval**, *Ukrainian Academy of Sciences*
Prof. **Viktor Shnirelman**, *Russian Academy of Sciences*
Dr. **Lisa Sundstrom**, *University of British Columbia*
Dr. **Philip Walters**, *"Religion, State and Society," Oxford*
Prof. **Zenon Wasyliw**, *Ithaca College, New York State*
Dr. **Lucan Way**, *University of Toronto*
Dr. **Markus Wehner**, *"Frankfurter Allgemeine Zeitung"*
Dr. **Andrew Wilson**, *University College London*
Prof. **Jan Zielonka**, *University of Oxford*
Prof. **Andrei Zorin**, *University of Oxford*

* While the Editorial Committee and Advisory Board support the General Editor in the choice and improvement of manuscripts for publication, responsibility for remaining errors and misinterpretations in the series' volumes lies with the books' authors.

David-Emil Wickström

CKING ST. PETERSBURG

cultural Flows and Identity Politics n Post-Soviet Popular Music

th a foreword by Yngvar B. Steinholt

Soviet and Post-Soviet Politics and Society (SPPS)
ISSN 1614-3515

Founded in 2004 and refereed since 2007, SPPS makes available affordable English-, German- and Russian-language studies on the history of the countries of the former Soviet bloc from the late Tsarist period to today. It publishes approximately 15-20 volumes per year, and focuses on issues in transitions to and from democracy such as economic crisis, identity formation, civil society development, and constitutional reform in CEE and the NIS. SPPS also aims to highlight so far understudied themes in East European studies such as right-wing radicalism, religious life, higher education, or human rights protection. The authors and titles of all previously published manuscripts are listed at the end of this book. For a full description of the series and reviews of its books, see www.ibidem-verlag.de/red/spps.

Note for authors (as of 2009): After successful review, fully formatted and carefully edited electronic master copies of up to 250 pages will be published as b/w A5 paperbacks and marketed in Germany (e.g. vlb.de, buchkatalog.de, amazon.de) and internationally (e.g. amazon.com). For longer books, formatting/editorial assistance, different binding, oversize maps, coloured illustrations and other special arrangements, authors' fees between €100 and €1500 apply. Publication of German doctoral dissertations follows a separate procedure. Authors are asked to provide a high-quality electronic picture on the object of their study for the book's front-cover. Younger authors may add a foreword from an established scholar. Monograph authors and collected volume editors receive two free as well as further copies for a reduced authors' price, and will be asked to contribute to marketing their book as well as finding reviewers and review journals for them. These conditions are subject to yearly review, and to be modified, in the future. Further details at www.ibidem-verlag.de/red/spps-authors.

Editorial correspondence & manuscripts should, until 2011, be sent to: Dr. Andreas Umland, ZIMOS, Ostenstr. 27, 85072 Eichstätt, Germany; e-mail: umland@stanfordalumni.org

Business correspondence & review copy requests should be sent to: *ibidem*-Verlag, Julius-Leber-Weg 11, D-30457 Hannover, Germany; tel.: +49(0)511-2622200; fax: +49(0)511-2622201; spps@ibidem-verlag.de.

Book orders & payments should be made via the publisher's electronic book shop at: www.ibidem-verlag.de/red/SPPS_EN/

Authors, reviewers, referees, and editors for (as well as all other persons sympathetic to) SPPS are invited to join its networks at www.facebook.com/group.php?gid=52638198614
www.linkedin.com/groups?about=&gid=103012
www.xing.com/net/spps-ibidem-verlag/

Recent Volumes

92 *Philipp Casula, Jeronim Perovic (Eds.)*
Identities and Politics During the Putin Presidency
The Discursive Foundations of Russia's Stability
With a foreword by Heiko Haumann
ISBN 978-3-8382-0015-6

93 *Marcel Viëtor*
Europa und die Frage nach seinen Grenzen im Osten
Zur Konstruktion ‚europäischer Identität' in Geschichte und Gegenwart
Mit einem Vorwort von Albrecht Lehmann
ISBN 978-3-8382-0045-3

94 *Ben Hellman, Andrei Rogachevskii*
Filming the Unfilmable
Casper Wrede's 'One Day in the Life of Ivan Denisovich'
ISBN 978-3-8382-0044-6

95 *Eva Fuchslocher*
Vaterland, Sprache, Glaube
Orthodoxie und Nationenbildung am Beispiel Georgiens
Mit einem Vorwort von Christina von Braun
ISBN 978-3-89821-884-9

96 *Vladimir Kantor*
Das Westlertum und der Weg Russlands
Zur Entwicklung der russischen Literatur und Philosophie
Ediert von Dagmar Herrmann
Mit einem Beitrag von Nikolaus Lobkowicz
ISBN 978-3-8382-0102-3

97 *Kamran Musayev*
Die postsowjetische Transformation im Baltikum und Südkaukasus
Eine vergleichende Untersuchung der politischen Entwicklung Lettlands und Aserbaidschans 1985-2009
Mit einem Vorwort von Leonid Luks
Ediert von Sandro Henschel
ISBN 978-3-8382-0103-0

98 *Tatiana Zhurzhenko*
Borderlands into Bordered Lands
Geopolitics of Identity in Post-Soviet Ukraine
With a foreword by Dieter Segert
ISBN 978-3-8382-0042-2

99 *Кирилл Галушко, Лидия Смола (ред.)*
Пределы падения – варианты украинского будущего
Аналитико-прогностические исследования
ISBN 978-3-8382-0148-1

100 *Michael Minkenberg (ed.)*
Historical Legacies and the Radical Right in Post-Cold War Central and Eastern Europe
With an afterword by Sabrina P. Ramet
ISBN 978-3-8382-0124-5

Bibliografische Information der Deutschen Nationalbibliothek
Die Deutsche Nationalbibliothek verzeichnet diese Publikation in der
Deutschen Nationalbibliografie; detaillierte bibliografische Daten sind im
Internet über http://dnb.d-nb.de abrufbar.

Bibliographic information published by the Deutsche Nationalbibliothek
Die Deutsche Nationalbibliothek lists this publication in the Deutsche Nationalbibliografie;
detailed bibliographic data are available in the Internet at http://dnb.d-nb.de.

Cover Picture: The band Svoboda performing at the music festival *Okna otkroi!* (Open the windows!) on July 2nd, 2005 in St. Petersburg. © Fedor Naumov, 2005.

Photographs in the book block: © David-Emil Wickström

Second, Revised and Expanded Edition

∞

Gedruckt auf alterungsbeständigem, säurefreien Papier
Printed on acid-free paper

ISSN: 1614-3515

ISBN-13: 978-3-8382-0100-9

© *ibidem*-Verlag
Stuttgart 2014

Alle Rechte vorbehalten

Das Werk einschließlich aller seiner Teile ist urheberrechtlich geschützt. Jede Verwertung außerhalb der engen Grenzen des Urheberrechtsgesetzes ist ohne Zustimmung des Verlages unzulässig und strafbar. Dies gilt insbesondere für Vervielfältigungen, Übersetzungen, Mikroverfilmungen und elektronische Speicherformen sowie die Einspeicherung und Verarbeitung in elektronischen Systemen.

All rights reserved. No part of this publication may be reproduced, stored in or introduced into a retrieval system, or transmitted, in any form, or by any means (electronic, mechanical, photocopying, recording or otherwise) without the prior written permission of the publisher. Any person who does any unauthorized act in relation to this publication may be liable to criminal prosecution and civil claims for damages.

Printed in Germany

		Svoboda's multifaceted band identity	192
	6.2	Excursion: Ukrainian popular music and Ukrainian nationalism	194
		Ruslana's *Kolomyika*	195
		"*Preserving the cultural heritage*": Band identity construction based on traditional music, history, and politics	199
		"*Ethnic sounds of the mountain people*": Ruslana's Ukrainian anchoring and questions of representation	201
	6.3	Concluding remarks	204
7		**Popular music and ideas of the Russian nation**	**207**
	7.1	*Russkii* vs. *Rossiskii*: Russian national identities	208
	7.2	*Nashe Radio*: Made in Russia?	211
	7.3	Popular music and the ruling elite	213
		Boris Grebenshchikov and the government	213
		Rock 'n' Roll Cross: Kinchev and the Church	216
	7.4	Nationalism and nostalgia	219
		Gazmanov's *Sdelan v SSSR*	219
		Piligrim's *Slava Rossii*	222
		Nostalgia	224
	7.5	Concluding remarks	225
8		***The Russendisko-scene***	**229**
	8.1	Boundaries	232
		Auditorium: German speaking audience	232
		Eastblok Music	235
		Radio Schum	237
		Boundary: Russian speaking audience	238
		Crossing	239
	8.2	Concluding remarks	243

| 9 | The post-Soviet emigrant community in Germany | 247 |

9.1 The post-Soviet emigrant community in Germany – a diaspora? 249
9.2 *"Who are these guys from Svoboda?"*: The flow of music to Berlin 254
9.3 The *Russendisko's* music 257
      "Russian popular music" – a new sound? 260
9.4 Asymmetries in the flow 262
9.5 Concluding remarks 266

| 10 | Post-Soviet popular music in Germany | 269 |

10.1 *Kasatchok Superstar*: The European Russian folklore lineage 270
      Apparatschik 273
      Russkaja 275
      Irrational East: Russians as an exoticized *Other* 277
10.2 *"False Russians"*: The stereotyped strike back 278
10.3 The bigger picture: *Ost Klub* and *Balkanisierung* 281
10.4 Concluding remarks 284

Concluding words and outlook 285

Appendices 291
References 335

List of Figures and Pictures

Figures

1	Network diagram I – Group-networks in St. Petersburg	89
2	Network diagram II – Svoboda's musical network	93
3	Wave form excerpt of *Mama anarkhiia*	173
4	Beginning of the first verse of Ruslana's *Kolomyika*	195
5	The trumpet and tsymbaly part (intro) in Ruslana's *Kolomyika*	197
6	Sonogram of the first bars of Ruslana's *Kolomyika*	198

Pictures

1	Flyer for the release party of the compilation *Russkii Andegraund vol. 1* (Orlandina, 20.12.2006)	44
2	Svoboda	91
3	Denis Vashkevich	96
4	Flyer from Markscheider Kunst (*Red Club*, 23.09.2005)	99
5	Markscheider Kunst	104
6	Entrance to Svoboda's rehearsal room at *Bania 43*	109
7	Plaque from the Soviet record label *Melodiia* at the entrance to *Antrop-studio*	112
8	*Piterskii Andegraund* (Piter's underground)	119
9	Viktor Tsoi's grave at the Bogoslovskoe cemetery (St. Petersburg)	134
10	Cover of Billy's Band's album *Parizhskie Sezony*	150
11	View from where the canal Moika flows into the canal Fontanka	151
12	Reggistan	155
13	Dr. I-Bolit (aka Andrei "Rastaman" Kunitsyn)	162
14	Flyer from *Den' Rozhdenia Boba Marli* (*Red Club*, 05.02.2006)	164
15	Svoboda's business card	170
16	Flyer from *RaSKAlbas* (*Staryi Dom*, 01.04.2005)	172

17	Flyer from Svoboda's Nestor Makhno-concert (*Roks Club*, 26.10.2007)	182
18	Graffiti *Rossia dlia Russkikh* (Russia for Russians)	210
19	*Bolschoi Don Kosaken* concert poster	272
20	Apparatschik	274
21	Russkaja's *Kasatchok Superstar* promotion sticker	276
22	Flyer from a *Balkanisierungsparty* featuring SkaZka Orchestra (*Supamolli*, 15.02.2008)	282

List of Appendices

A	Short biographies of people interviewed	291
B	Selected lyrics	297
C	Quotes in their original language	311

Glossary

Art direktor – booking manager. The person in charge of booking bands in clubs.

Bardovskaia pesnia, also *avtorskaia pesnia* – bard song, authored song. A musical genre associated with singers like Bulat Okudzhava and Vladimir Vysotskii. Its roots are in songs from the Soviet penal camps and the urban pre-revolutionary genres *gorodskoi romans* (city ballad) and *blatnaia pesnia* (underworld song) as well as European singer-songwriters like Jacques Brel, Georges Brassens, Wolf Biermann, and Mikis Theodorakis (Steinholt 2005, 103ff; Hufen 2010).

Bit – cf. *rok*.

Blatnaia pesnia, blatniak – underworld song, today often referred to as (*russkii*) *shanson*. Cf. *bardovskaia pesnia*.

Blizhnee zarubezh'e – Near Abroad, a term used in Russia for the former Soviet republics.

Bratan – bro, buddy, brother, mate. Used as a strong acknowledgement of male friendship.

Casatschok/Kasatchok – a Cossack folk dance in 2/4 (Lehmann 2008).

Chastushki (Pl., Sg. *Chastushka*, from *chasto* – rapid) – a widespread vocal-instrumental genre whose songs often have humorous (and obscene) lyrics. The musical accompaniment has traditionally been balalaika and accordion. The lyrics are in part based on proverbs and folk sayings arranged around a fixed meter (normally 8+7+8+7 syllables) and grouped around short, single-stanza couplets (mostly 4 lines) which usually are rhymed. *Chastushki* with satyrical lyrics have been most widespread both for expressing socio-political thoughts as well as through their didactical nature (Kovalev 2004; Frolova-Walker et al. n.d.). *Chastushki* are not limited to traditional music, they have also been used in popular music ranging from *estrada* (e.g. Alla Pugacheva and Maksim Galkin) to rock (e.g. Splin and Sektor Gaza) as well as for short ditties at weddings and other events (also without music).

Estrada – small stage. Used for officially approved popular music in the Soviet

Union (Steinholt 2005, 15, Fn. 14). MacFadyen (2002, 3) defines it as Soviet popular/light entertainment "that includes pop music but also applies to modern dance, comedy, circus arts, and any other performance not on the 'big,' classical stage."

Format – the stylistic direction of a club or radio station.

Gastarbaiter – guest-worker. Normally used for transmigrants from the former Soviet Union – at times with a negative connotation.

Horilka – Ukrainian for vodka. In Russia *horilka* can also mean vodka with red chili peppers (and honey), usually marketed as a Ukrainian speciality.

I-Bolit (or *Aibolit*) – Ouchhurts. A Russian/Soviet children's poem written by Kornei Chukovskii (aka Nikolai Vasil'evich Korneichukov) about Aibolit, a doctor who cures animals.

Khokhol – topknot/tuft of hair; uncultured (Ukrainian) oaf (colloquial). While a common Russian designation for somebody from Ukraine, the word's original meaning topknot/tuft of hair refers to the hair style of the Cossacks (Kappeler 2003, 197). Even though commonly used in St. Petersburg it can also have negative connotations like "uncultured oaf" (Bilaniuk 2005, 115).

Kievan Rus' – a loose conglomeration of medieval city-states (or principalities) which emerged in the late 9th and early 10th centuries with Kiev as its original center and at times main force. Looked upon as the historical foundation of the Russian Federation.

Kolomyika – a dance, instrumental, and a vocal music genre from the Carpathian mountains (Hrytsa n.d., Olha Kolomyyets, pers. comm., 24.09.2007).

Kommunalka, acronym for *kommunal'naia kvartira* – a communal housing system typical for the Soviet Union (and still a reality in post-Soviet Russia) where families were allocated rooms in big apartments together with others, mostly strangers. The families shared the kitchen and bathroom. Unlike the German concept of *Wohngemeinschaft* where some extensively scrutinize potential co-residents, the families were placed in the *kommunalka* by chance (cf. Virtual'nyi muzei :::: Kommunal'naia kvartira n.d. for a virtual tour of a *kommunalka*).

Korporativnaia/Firmennaia vecherinka – company/corporate party. A private party usually organized by a company for their employees, especially common in December. These events often book musicians or bands to provide entertainment for the guests.

Kuchka – acronym for *moguchaia kuchka*, the mighty handful. A term often applied to a group of St. Petersburg based composers active during the middle and second half of the 19th century. Grouped around the composer Mili Balakirev, the other composers were Aleksandr Borodin, Tsezar' Kiui, Modest Musorgskii, and Nikolai Rimskii-Korsakov. The music critic Vladimir Stasov was also close to the group and helped provide an ideological basis to the *Kuchka's* composition.

Kvartirniki – concerts in an apartment which were common in the Soviet Union.

Leningradskii rok-klub – Leningrad Rock Club (LRK). The first rock organization in the Soviet Union, founded in 1981 (cf. Steinholt 2005).

Magnitizdat – magnetic publishing. A way to copy records and record music of radios in private. These were multiplied and then circulated within informal networks in the Soviet Union (cf. Steinholt 2005, 38f).

Marshrutka, acronym for *marshrutnoe taksi* (fixed route taxi) – normally a private owned mini-bus which functions as public transportation with slightly higher prices and faster than public transportation.

Mat – Russian curse words.

Natsional'nost – translatable both as ethnic group or nationality. In Russia the term also includes Judaism since Jews are considered an ethnic group.

OBeRIu, Ob"edinenie real'nogo iskusstva – Association of Real Art. A group of St. Petersburg based poets linked to the post-revolutionary avant-garde of the late 1920s and 1930s. The group was founded by Danil Kharms and Aleksandr Vvedenskii.

Piter – a commonly applied (endearing) abbreviation for St. Petersburg used by its inhabitants.

Popsa, popsnia – a (derogatory) word for pop, often used in opposition to rock music.

Portvein – port wine is a common symbol for Leningrad rock of the 1980s.

Radio Fritz – based in Babelsberg/Potsdam it is part of Rundfunk Berlin-Brandenburg (RBB), the public broadcasting corporation for Berlin and Brandenburg.

Radiomultikulti – a state-owned Berlin based radio station promoting a multicultural Berlin from 1994 to 2008.

Rok – fate; rock. Due to its original Russian meaning fate, *rok* was first used in the 1970s as a synonym for rock. In the Soviet Union rock 'n' roll was originally considered a jazz subgenre and with Beatlemania in the 1960s the term *bit* (beat) was used instead (Steinholt in press).

Rossiskii – Russian. This adjective encompasses all citizens of Russia. It does not mean Russian in an ethnic meaning which is instead covered by the word *russkii*.

Russendisko – in its normal meaning in Germany, *Russendisko* refers to a discotheque for emigrants from the post-Soviet countries. Through the activities of Yuriy Gurzhy and Wladimir Kaminer it has, however, become a synonym for their fortnightly event and the music they play.

Russian Empire – a poly-ethnic empire which existed from 1552 until 1917 with Moscow and later St. Petersburg as its capital.

Russkii – ethnic Russian. Cf. *Rossiskii*.

Russkii rok – Russian rock, also Russian fate. A style within Russian rock music which is closely associated with the groups active in the 1980s and where the lyrics play an important role.

Russlanddeutsche – cf. *Spätaussiedler*.

(Russkii) Shanson', blatnaia pesnia, blatniak – songs which are associated with the criminal world and/or Odessa. Cf. *bardovskaia pesnia*.

Slabye doli – weak syllables / accents, reference to the off-beat accents in reggae and ska.

Solianka – a Russian vegetable-meat soup, *solianka* can also be used to refer to a mix of different things (e.g. a concert).

Spätaussiedler, also *Russlanddeutsche* and *Wolgadeutsche* – descendants of Germans who emigrated to, inter alia, Russia, Rumania, Hungary, and Ukraine in the 18th and 19th century. The term also refers to those displaced from what is now Western Poland due to the second World War. The German state has allowed for their repatriation based both on the imagined blood-lineage as well as the persecution of ethnic Germans in former Eastern Europe.

Starovery – old believers. A group of Russian-Orthodox Christians who in the 17th century disagreed with the church reforms by Patriarch Nikon and subsequently broke with the mother church.

Stiob – a special Russian form of subtle irony delivered with a straight face which is quite common and can be very ambiguous and provocative.

Tel'niashka – blue and white striped shirts worn by Russian sailors.

Vokal'no-Instrumental'nyi Ansambl' (VIA) – Vocal-Instrumental Ensemble. A system for professional musical groups organized under the trade union houses and palaces of culture. By becoming officially sanctioned the groups had to conform to certain requirements like cutting their hair, wearing uniforms, playing optimistic and positive music, and having the songs go through a curator (Steinholt 2005, 21f).

Vyshivanka – a shirt with embroidery, widely used in Ukraine.

Wolgadeutsche – cf. *Spätaussiedler*.

WOMEX – World Music Expo, an international trade fair aimed at the world music market.

Zagranpasport, acronym for *zagranichnyi pasport* – foreign passport. Russian citizens have two passports – an internal one (*vnutrennii pasport*) which includes their registration, in other words, where they live, as well as draft information and a foreign passport (*zagranichnyi/zagranpasport*) which is only needed for travel abroad. Getting one is a bureaucratic hassle thus many people do not have one.

ZhEK – acronym for *Zhilishchno-ekspluatatsionnye kontory*, Housing and Maintenance Department.

Band, club, festival, and label names with translation

This list contains the most commonly mentioned names of bands, festivals, recording studios, labels, and clubs in this book. Names not immediately comprehensible to an anglophone speaker have a translation.

Bands

5'Nizza – acronym for *Piatnitsa*, Friday.

7B.

Ackee Ma-Ma Urban Reggae Band – Ackee is the fruit of the African tree *Blighia sapida*, Ma-Ma refers to mother (the band was called *Ackee Wa-Wa* before the lead singer gave birth to her first child).

Affekt.

Afrodisiac.

Akvarium – Aquarium.

Alisa – named after the main character of Lewis Caroll's "Alice in Wonderland".

Amsterdam Klezmer Band.

Apparatschik – Machine Operator, in German (and Russian) it has a slight derogatory meaning for a state or party functionary, who within the bureaucracy of Stalinist-influenced states promotes the Party line (Scholze-Stubenrecht and Wermke 1996, 121).

Ariia – Aria.

Auktsyon – Auction, with a deliberate misspelling to avoid confusion between the band's concerts and an auction (*auktsion*).

Avia – acronym for *Anti-VIA* (cf. p. 17), hence accent on the *i* rather than the first syllable as in the prefix *avia-*.

Bacchus – the Latin name of the Greek god *Dionysus*.

Banana Gang.

Barocco Flash.

Batareia – Battery.

Beshenye Ogurtsy – The Rabid Cucumbers.

Bi-2.
Billy's Band.
Blestiashchie – The Shining Ones.
Bloody Kalinka – *Kalinka* refers to the plant *Viburnum opulus* (Snowball Tree) and is the refrain to the well-known eponymous Russian song written by Ivan Petrovich Larionov.
Boney M.
Boni' Nem – Boni the Dumb, pun on the German band Boney M.
Brat'ia Grim – The Brothers Grim.
Brigadnyi Podriad – Brigade Contract
BroSound.
Chaif – "The title of the band combines the word chai (tea) and kaif (pleasure, high)" (Beumers 2005, 222).
Chizh i Kompaniia – The Siskin and Company.
Con Brio – With Fire.
Cosmonautix.
Crossing – Refers to the meeting of two cultures embodied by the band members home country (former Soviet Union) and place of residence (Berlin/Germany).
DDT.
Deadushki – Dead Ears.
Dekabr' – December.
DiaPositive.
Distemper.
DJ Schum – DJ Noise.
Dobranoch' – Good Night.
Dr. Bajan – Dr. Accordion.
Dschinghis Khan – Genghis Khan.
Dusty Hills.
Dva Samoleta – Two Airplanes.
Dzha Divizhn – Jah Division, pun on the band Joy Division.
EAV – acronym for *Erste Allgemeine Verunsicherung,* First General Uncertainty.
Elektricheskie partizany – The Electric Partisans.
Froglegs.

Gogol Bordello.
Grazhdanskaia Oborona – Civil Defence, reference to primary school lessons.
Greendzholi – Green Jolly.
Haydamaky – an 18th century partisan movement mainly consisting of Orthodox peasants and Cossacks based in Right-Bank Ukraine. They carried out insurrections targeted against Polish landowners, Jews, and clerics from the Roman-Catholic and Uniate / Ukrainian Greek-Catholic Church.
Iu-Piter – refers to the planet Jupiter as well as a reference to St. Petersburg (Piter).
Iva Nova – *Ivanova* is a common Russian female surname.
JD & the Blenders – JD are the initials of the group's vocalist, Jennifer Davis.
Kalinov Most – Kalinov Bridge.
Kino – Movie.
KOLKhUi – acronym for *Koldovskie Khudozhniki*, The Bewitching Artists. *Khui* is also Russian *mat* (curse word) for penis.
Korol' i Shut – The King and the Jester.
Kukryniksy – an acronym based on Mikhail Vasil'evich **Ku**priianov, Porfirii **Ni**kitich **Kry**lov, and **Nik**olai Aleksandrovich **S**okolov a collective of three influential Soviet caricaturists.
Leningrad – the Soviet name for St. Petersburg.
Lia Minor – A-Minor.
Liapis Trubetskoi – a character from Il'ia Il'f and Evgenii Petrov's book "*Dvenadtsat' stul'ev*" (The Twelve Chairs).
Liube – no direct translation, could be based on the origin of the group's founder who is from the Moscow suburb Liuberets.
Mad Heads XL.
Male Factors.
Markscheider Kunst – *Markscheider* is a old German technical term for a mine surveyor and *Kunst* is German for art. According to the band's narrative some of the band's founding members studied geology in St. Petersburg, hence the name.
Mashina vremeni – Time Machine.
Mata Khari – Mata Hari, aka Margaretha Geertruida Zelle MacLeod.
Multfilmy – Cartoons.
Mumii Troll' – Mumintroll, Moomins.

Nado podumat' – Have to Think.
Nautilus Pompilius – the Latin name of the chambered nautilus.
Nochnye Snaipery – The Night Snipers.
NOM – acronym for *Neformal'noe Ob'edinenie Molodezhi*, The Non-Formal Youth-Association, a Soviet bureaucratic term for rock bands and other youth groupings.
Novokain – trade name for a local anesthetic based on procaine.
Okean El'zy – Elza's Ocean.
Optimystica orchestra – *Optimystica* is a word play both alluding to optimistic as well as mystical.
Pallada – from the Greek goddess *Afina Pallada* (Pallas Athena).
Perkalaba – Perkalab is a river and a village in the Carpathian mountains.
Piknik – Picnic.
Piligrim – Pilgrim.
Pilot.
Pinches Tiranitos – Petty Tyrant.
Port(812) – 812 refers to St. Petersburg's telephone area code.
Porto Franco – Free Port.
PTVP – acronym for *Poslednie Tanki V Parizhe*, The Last Tanks in Paris.
Raggapop.
Rammstein – a German city known for its US air force base.
Raznye Liudi – Different People.
Red Elvises.
Reggistan – alludes to Reggae and a common suffix for Central-Asian countries (-stan).
Respublika Dzha – The Republic of Jah.
Rok-gruppa – Rock Group.
Rot Front – The Red Front.
Ruslana – a Russian female name.
Russkaja – Russian.
Schum – Noise.
Sektor Gaza – Sektor of Gas.
Severnye Vrata –The Nothern Gates.
Simba Vibration.

S.K.A. – besides alluding to the musical style ska, S.K.A. is an acronym for *Soiuz Kommercheskogo Avangarda*, The Union of Commercial Avant-garde.
Skalariak.
Skal'pel' – Scalpel.
SkaZka Orchestra – The Story Orchestra.
Smyslovye Galliutsinatsii – Meaningful Hallucinations.
S.O.K. – while the acronym can be translated as juice, S.O.K. is short for *S"esh' oba Kuska*, Eat Both Pieces.
Spitfire.
Splin – Spleen, Longing.
St. Petersburg Ska-Jazz Review.
Stanok – Machine.
Strannye Igry – Strange Games.
Streetboys.
Svinokop – Pig Cop (Ivanov 2005).
Svoboda – Freedom.
t.A.T.u. – acronym for *Ta liubit Tu*, She Loves Her.
Tantsy Minus – Dances Minus.
Televizor – Television.
Tequilajazzz.
Timati – a male name.
Traund.
Tsentr – Center.
Uma2rman – Uma Thurman.
Uniquetunes.
Va-Bank" – *Ka-Boom*.
Verka Serdiuchka – stage name of the Ukrainian actor Andrii Danylko.
VIA Gra – a wordplay not only referring to the potency medicine but also to VIA (cf. p. 17). Finally, *gra* can be seen as a shortening of *igra*, Russian for game.
VIA Samotsvety – The Gems.
VIA Volga-Volga.
Volkov Trio – Volkov's Trio.
Vopli Vidopliasova (VV) – The Cries of Vidopliasov.
Zapreshchionnye barabanshchiki – The Banned Drummers.

Zdob si Zdub – onomatopoetic for the sound of a drum.
Zemfira – first name of the female singer Zemfira Ragazanova.
Zoopark – Zoo.
Zvuki Mu – The Sounds of Mu (Mu as in the mythic Kingdom of Mu and as an abbreviation for *Muzyka*).

Clubs and festivals

10 klub.
90 Grad – 90 degrees.
A-lounge.
ArktikA – Arctic.
Art klinika – Art Clinic.
B2.
BKZ Oktiabr'skii – Big Concert Hall October.
Cafe Zapata – Refers to the Mexican revolutionary Emiliano Zapata Salazar.
City Club.
Club Rodina – Club Motherland (cf. p. 230, FN 201).
Club SSSR – Club USSR.
Deep Sound.
DK Lensoveta – The Leningrad Soviet's House of Culture.
Donauinselfest – Donau-island party.
Dzhambala – Wordplay based on the mythical *Shambhala* where *Sha-* is replaced by *Dzha-* (Jah).
Fish Fabrique – Fish Factory.
GEZ-21 – acronym for *Galereia Eksperimental'nogo Zvuka-21*, Gallery of Experimental Sound 21.
Griboedov – surname of the Russian writer Aleksandr Sergeevich Griboedov.
Hühnermanhattan – Chicken-Manhattan.
Kamchatka – a peninsula in the Russian Far East.
KGB Bar.
Mankhetten – Manhattan.
Moloko – Milk.
Mudd Club.

Okna Otkroi! – Open the Windows!
Orlandina – female version of the name Orlando.
Ost Klub – East Club.
Pereval – Passage.
Pivnoi Festival' – Beer Festival.
Platforma – Platform.
Port – Port, Harbor.
Postgarage – Postal Garage.
Purga – Snowstorm, Blizzard.
RaSKAlbas – the word alludes to *kolbasit'sia* meaning to party, chill out, and have fun while emphasizing ska as the musical common denominator.
Red Club.
The Red Lion.
Rossi's.
Russendisko – Russian Discotheque (cf. p. 229, FN 197).
S-club.
SK Iubileinyi – Sport Complex Anniversary.
Stary Dom – Old House.
Tacheles – from "*Tacheles reden*", to do some frank talking.
TaMtAm.
Tanzwirtschaft Kaffe Burger – Dance-cafe Cafe Burger.
Vo100ok [Vostok] – East.
Wild Side.
Zorro.

Recording studios and labels

Antrop – acronym for Antrop's director, Andrei Tropillo.
Bomba Piter – The Bomb of Piter (St. Petersburg).
Comp Music Ltd.
Dobrolet – Good Flight.
Eastblok Music.
Gala Records.
Grand Records.

Kap-kan.
Melodiia – Melody.
Misteriia Zvuka – The Mystery of Sound.
Real Records.
Space X.
ShSS.

Acknowledgements

This project started in 2001, while I was working on my master's thesis on Norwegian traditional vocal music in Bergen. There I became acquainted with Yngvar Steinholt, who was working on his Ph.D. on the Leningrad Rock Club. Through his work and then through my partner, I started listening to Soviet and Russian popular music. After returning to Germany in 2003, I decided to learn Russian and look for a research topic for a possible dissertation examining the processes of a more and more interconnected world. Since Germany had become a hub for Russian popular music through the *Russendisko* in Berlin, exploring popular music in St. Petersburg and how it flowed to other places seemed to be an interesting topic. After receiving a one-year grant, I left Berlin almost head over heels for St. Petersburg and started my fieldwork (and simultaneously several intensive formal and informal Russian language courses) in autumn 2004 and thus the research which provides the basis for my dissertation and, subsequently, this book.

This research project has over its many years been aided by numerous generous people: First of all, I would like to thank all the musicians and other people within the St. Petersburg scene and post-Soviet music scene in Germany and Austria – especially Matthias Angerer, Dmitrij Baburin, Dmitrii Bekker, Andrei Burlaka, Sergei Chernov, Elena Danilova, Dima Dobrovol'skii, Sergei Efremenko, Evgenii Fedrov, Ekaterina Fedorova, Sergej Fiedler, Nikolai Fomin, Artur Gorlatschov, Anton Gornung, Yuriy Gurzhy, Victor Harder, Tat'iana Iatsenko, Andrei Ivanov, Dmitrii Ivanov, Steffen Jamowitsch, Andrei Kagadeev, Dima Kalchert, Alexander Kasparov, Dmitrii Khramtsov, Evgenii Kiselev, Elena Kolganova, Nikolai Kopeikin, Oleh Kovtun, Viktor Kultashov, Nikolaj Leinweber, Inka Lishenkevich, Svetlana Loseva, Anton Lukanin, Ilja Matuschinski, Billy Novik, Elena Novikova, Olaf Opitz, Roman Parygin, Anastasia Postnikova, Aleksandr Rudenko, Armin Siebert, Sergej Stehr, Andrei Tropillo, Denis Vashkevich, Aleksandr "Nevskii" Vladimirov, Oleksandr Yarmola, Mikhail Yaroshevskiy, and Elena Zhornik – without your help this book would never have been written!

Outside the "field" I have also been helped by conversations with numerous people without whom this work would not have been what it is. Here my gratitude goes to (and I apologize to those I might have left out) Stephen Amico, Stephen Blum, Matthias Bodenstein, Markus Bogisch, Giacomo Bottà, Anna Brixa, Thomas Burkhalter, Nataliya Chumak, Iurii Domanskii, Neil Edmunds, Steven Feld, Eva Fock, Ivan Gololobov, Florian Grammel, Anca Giurchescu, Agathe Hahn, Adriana Helbig, Lillian Helle, Terje Helland, Harald Huber, Sverker Hyltén-Cavallius, Ol'ha Kolomyyets', Tamara Lönngren, Sergio Mazzanti, Susan McClary, Ol'ga Nikitina, Don Niles, Tobias Ohnewald, Evelyn Radke, Maria Sonevytsky, Martin Stefanov, Martin Stokes, Jane C. Sugarman, Serhy Yekelchyk, Mark Yoffe, the faculty and the administrative personnel at the Section for Musicology at the University of Copenhagen – especially my phd colleagues Axel Teich Geertinger, Sanne Krogh Groth, Mads Klitgård Hansen, Jens Hjortkjær, Anja Mølle Lindelof, Bjarke Moe, Ingeborg Okkels, Henrik Smith-Sivertsen, and Jan Andreas Wessel – as well as the faculty at the Institute for Folk Music Research and Ethnomusicology at the University of Music and Performing Arts in Vienna – especially Gerlinde Haid, Ursula Hemetek, and Hande Saglam and the participants of the *DissertantInnenkolleg*.

This gratitude also goes to the *Deutscher Akademischer Austauschdienst* (DAAD) for funding my fieldwork in St. Petersburg 2004/2005 as well as the University of Copenhagen, where I was employed from 2006 to 2010. Furthermore, the Norwegian University Center in St. Petersburg as well as the Institute for Folk Music Research and Ethnomusicology at the University of Music and Performing Arts in Vienna were so kind to have me as a visiting scholar and provided me with a stimulating working environment. Finally, Christian Kaden's research seminar at the Humboldt-Universität zu Berlin gave me an inspiring platform to present and discuss my findings.

Some parts of the book draw on the previously published articles (Wickström 2007, Wickström 2008, and Wickström and Steinholt 2009). I would like to thank the journals *Musik og Forskning* (University of Copenhagen), *Yearbook for Traditional Music* (ICTM), and *Popular Music and Society* (Taylor and Francis) for allowing me to draw on my articles here.

My academic advisors provided me with crucial theoretical, empirical, and methodological stimuli and critique and I would like to thank Morten Michelsen, Annemette Kirkegaard (both University of Copenhagen), and Yngvar Bordewich Steinholt (University of Tromsø). I would also like to thank Christian Kaden

(Humboldt-Universität zu Berlin) and Thomas Solomon (University of Bergen) who together with Yngvar were my initial advisors before I arrived at the University of Copenhagen. Here I would also like to thank Martin Stokes (Oxford University), Hans Weisethaunet (University of Oslo), and Erik Steinskog (University of Copenhagen) for being good opponents at my dissertation defense as well as the editor of the series *Soviet and Post-Soviet Politics and Society* Andreas Umland and the anonymous reviewer for their comments during the publishing process.

Finally, a big thanks goes to Bengt-Arne Wickström for language corrections, Judith Wickström-Haber for proofreading, and to Anastasia Kozhevnikova for transcribing most of the interview excerpts from my Russian to correct Russian.

Second edition
This book is an revised and expanded version of *Okna otkroi! – Open the windows! Scenes, transcultural flows, and identity politics in popular music from Post-Soviet St. Petersburg* (Wickström 2011) – which was a revised version of the eponymous dissertation publicly defended on September 25th, 2009 at the University of Copenhagen. Besides revising the text I have included two new subchapters in this edition: In chapter 6.2 I examine the Ukrainian singer Ruslana and juxtaposes her approach to that of the St. Petersburg based band Svoboda. In chapter 8.1 I expand the discussion of boundaries in Germany in relation to the Russian speaking audience by examining the Berlin based band Crossing.

I would like to thank the ibidem-team – especially Valerie Lange, Christian Schön, and Andreas Umland – for the opportunity to revise the first edition, Yngvar B. Steinholt for writing a new foreword, and Judith Wickström-Haber for once again proofreading the manuscript.

Technicalities
If not otherwise noted, all interview excerpts, quotes from books, lyrics, and other material have been translated into English by me. Unless it is a short phrase, the original language can be found in Appendix B. "Selected lyrics" (p. 297) and Appendix C. "Quotes in their original language" (p. 311). Song titles etc. are translated on first mention unless the word resembles its English equivalent or is a proper name. Interview excerpts in the original language have not been grammatically corrected so the quotes reflect what was said (this especially applies to interviews done in English). Any grammar mistakes in the English *translations*, however, are

mine. Unless otherwise noted, all emphases in quotes are by the respective author, not my own. All photographs and transcriptions are, unless otherwise noted, mine.

I use the Library of Congress' (1997) romanization tables for Russian and Ukrainian in the book's main body, but omitted ligatures and umlauts. The only exceptions are other transcription systems used in written correspondence by my consultants, official spelling of names and words in languages other than Russian or Ukrainian (e.g. Haydamaky, Wladimir Kaminer, and Yuriy Gurzhy), and where the original script is important.

When referring to people I interviewed or with whom I interacted on a daily basis I normally use the form I used to address them (mostly the first name or, very common in Russia, the diminutive form of the first name). When there are two people with the same first name in the same paragraph then I add the surname for clarity. If a person's statement can be damaging or compromising to that person I leave out his/her name and use an anonymous word like "acquaintance" or "musician" instead.

Foreword

If an invitation to write the foreword for a good book is an honour, it is a rare honour to be invited to write a new, improved foreword to its upgraded and improved edition. With the addition of the chapter on the Ukrainian pop star Ruslana, the current edition now shows the full span of David-Emil Wickström's study. This book has come into being as the result of a meticulous work process, characterised by a brave disregard for disciplinary boundaries and formal institutional-bureaucratic demands. It has been a privilege to follow the development of Wickström's research from project sketch in the early 2000s, via a sparsely-funded pilot fieldwork, into an impressive doctoral thesis, and, finally, into this book.

The popular music scene in St Petersburg – Leningrad in Soviet times – has for the past 30 years attracted a fair amount of attention from western academics. Most research has centred on the Russian rock scene in the transition period from the late 1980s until the early 1990s. This book is one of few approaches to look at the generations that followed in the wake of *russkii rok*, and who, it will appear, don't always relate to their older colleagues with humble respect. It is an important contribution to the field of post-Soviet popular music studies and brings scholars in touch with the living organism of Russian contemporary culture: mentality, humour, social affinities, activism, intellectualism or anti-intellectualism, aesthetics, notions of the everyday, nostalgia, patriotism, religion, and complex relationships with the near and far abroad.

The author has put the qualitative methods of ethnomusicology, including participant observation, to full use. This has enabled a focus on the contemporary music scene and its recent development, and despite the years that have passed since the extensive fieldwork, its relevance for studies of contemporary Russian popular music remains unquestionable. The enduring relevance is partly a consequence of the work's emphasis on music production, which in principle changed little since the study was conducted. In discussing the cultural-historical context, the author has also taken a cautious position in relation to post-colonial perspectives, carefully considering the extent of their relevance to the post-Soviet space.

The concept of cultural flows has enabled, for the first time in the field of Russian popular music studies, a proper discussion of notions of 'Russian-ness' (and also certain aspects of 'Ukrainian-ness') by effectively contrasting the notions of St Petersburg performers with notions cultivated by emigrants in marketing their music for non-Russian audiences. Here, the author's insistence upon learning the language and properly examining the cultural and historical context has paid off. This is reflected in detail, such as in the analyses and treatment of songs and their contextual cues, as well as in the general discussions, effectively introducing the reader to key features and particularities of contemporary Russian, and Ukrainian, popular music and to their encounters with western audiences.

As these words are written, the newsfeeds report of yet another failed government attempt to clear central Kiev from demonstrators. A re-issue of this important research with the added chapters on popular music and nationalism in the Ukraine could hardly have been better timed. Here is plenty of food for thought for scholars with interests in the contemporary post-Soviet space, from Slavonic studies to Ethnomusicology. Приятное читание!

Dr. Yngvar B. Steinholt
Tromsø University

Introduction

> Beautiful on the left,
> Beautiful on the right
> Today Bundes,
> Yesterday Warsaw
> Where else will the devil lead me?
>
> On Nevskii it's cold
> In the port a raid
> On Nevskii it's cold
> On Nevskii it's cold
>
> *Krasivo sleva* (Markscheider Kunst 2001 – Russian: p. 301)

When discussing the song *Krasivo sleva* Markscheider Kunst's vocalist and lyricist Sergei "Efr" Efremenko said that he was inspired to write the song while traveling in Switzerland and Germany (*Bundes* being here an abbreviation for *Bundesrepublik Deutschland* – the Federal Republic of Germany). At the same time the song is about *Piter* as St. Petersburg is called by its inhabitants:

> "'On Nevskii it's cold / In the port a raid' – that takes us home, that is, it is, most probably, a comparative element. Of course, it relates to Piter, naturally, I probably wrote everything about Piter. Probably, all the songs are about Piter and about Piter's inhabitants."
>
> (Efremenko 2005 – Russian: p. 321)

For Efr the song's second verse takes the group "home" again to the St. Petersburg realities: It is cold on the city center's main parade street, *Nevskii prospekt* (Nevskii Avenue), and the police are raiding the port which is one of the city's main revenue sources – as an entry and departure point for both tourists and goods.[1] This verse also evokes two of the city's unpleasant sides: cold, almost arctic winters and an inquisitive police force with sticky palms. Still, the city is Efr's home and central to both his personal as well as his professional life.

Other musicians, like Aleksandr "Sasha" Rudenko (Svoboda), Tat'iana "Tania" Iatsenko (Ackee Ma-Ma U.R.B., short Ackee Ma-Ma), Andrei Kagadeev (NOM), and Billy Novik (Billy's Band) also stressed the importance of St. Petersburg for

---

1. St. Petersburg is Russia's largest tourist center, with about 3 million visitors during my fieldwork in 2004 (Stolyarova 2005). The city is also an important economic and transportation hub, linking the Russian inland navigation (including river cruises to Moscow) with the Baltic Sea.

themselves both personally and in their creative work. While not necessarily reflected in the songs lyrically or musically, the city itself provided these musicians with inspiration to write and compose – thus stressing the importance of their *home*.

After the collapse of the Soviet Union in 1991 and the tumultuous 1990s this home is for some not only manifested spatially but also temporally in the form of *nostalgia* for a lost home, for a period of (perceived) stability and pride as in a "pristine" medieval Russia (untainted by European influences) or the more recent Soviet Union. While these expressions can, at times, be perceived as chauvinist nationalism – especially by neighboring countries – they provide a source of inspiration in a search for a new identity in a post-Soviet reality by drawing on a nostalgically colored past.

The lyrics also point to this home's complexities. The groups live in the city, which possesses a vibrant music scene. Since, however, the city itself cannot provide a satisfactory income for most groups, they frequently go on tour to earn a living. Here large post-Soviet emigrant communities living in Germany, Israel, and the United States – in part through the connection to their country of origin – play an important role, providing an initial market for groups from St. Petersburg (among other places) to perform for. In Germany this market has expanded to include non-Russian speakers through the fortnightly event *Russendisko*, run by two emigrants from respectively Russia and Ukraine. At the same time, St. Petersburg attracts many foreign students, some of whom are musicians, who also influence the music played in the city. Markscheider Kunst is a good example of where the musical style has been influenced by ska and other Caribbean, Latin-American, and African musics (in part due to their former Congolese vocalist Seraphim Selenge Makangila).

The ethnomusicologist Martin Stokes (1997b, 17) notes that "musics are seldom stable in contexts of social change" and St. Petersburg offers a good case in point. This book focuses on the result of these changes by examining the above mentioned issues, namely the meaning of place, transcultural flows, nationalism, and nostalgia. Here special attention is given to the music production in post-Soviet St. Petersburg from the perspective of local groups, the processes that enable Markscheider Kunst and other groups to tour Central Europe as well as how the groups respond to social and cultural changes in their creative work. The aim is to provide a better understanding of popular music's role in society especially in its relation to music, migration, and transcultural flows. These findings also help to give a deeper understanding of cultural processes in the second decade after the fall of the Soviet Union.

St. Petersburg, Russia's second largest city with officially 4.576 Million inhabitants during my fieldwork in 2006 (Ofitsial'nyi portal Administratsii Sankt-Peterburga 2008),[2] was chosen since, as Russia's *okno v evropu* (window towards Europe), it has played a major role in the country's cultural development: Through its proximity to Europe, through early efforts to import artists from Europe (e.g. court musicians, touring theatre/opera troops), and by being home to some of the most important and influential Russian composers and writers of the 19th and 20th centuries, the city has emerged as one of Russia's cultural centers. This is one of the reasons that St. Petersburg is considered the cultural capital of Russia. The city's role as an international metropolis has also left traces on the local popular music – especially what was labeled by those I talked to as (and which is the focus of this study) rock and alternative music.[3]

This is in part based on the fact that St. Petersburg – or Leningrad as it was called then – had emerged as the center for Soviet rock music by the 1980s. While there were several reasons for this – amongst them Leningrad being home to the first official rock organization in the Soviet Union, the *Leningradskii rok-klub* (Leningrad Rock Club, LRK), founded in 1981 – St. Petersburg has now taken on the role of the "rock city" in contrast to Moscow, which in the Soviet Union was the center for *estrada* (officially approved popular music). This opposition is part of a broader rivalry between the cities, which has its roots in the fact that St. Petersburg was founded in 1703 as an alternative to Moscow.

Extensive research on Russian and Soviet art music has been done, however, popular music has been somewhat neglected. In addition to chapters touching on popular music in books on Soviet/post-Soviet (youth) culture (e.g. Stites 1992; Pilkington 1994; Pilkington et al. 2002; Beumers 2005; Zhuk 2010) and numerous articles (cf. Wickström 2013 for a continuously updated bibliography on post-So-

---

2. Although unofficially the number is probably 5-6 million due to migrants from the former Soviet Union living there illegally.
3. Regarding the use of musical labels when discussing popular music and different styles like ska, reggae, and punk, my approach has been pragmatic by – when possible – applying the definitions of the bands, musicians, and other actors I talked to.

viet popular music), there have been some full length monographs and edited books on the topic. Most of these have been focused on *rock* music in the Soviet Union and the early 1990s (Ryback 1990; Ramet 1994; Cushman 1995; Steinholt 2005; Gavrikov 2007; Radke 2008; Domanskii 2010; Eriomin 2011; Nikitina 2011), however there have also been monographs on Belarusian popular music (Survilla 2002), punk in Russia (Gololobov et al. 2014), Hip Hop in Ukraine (Helbig 2014), the blues in Russia (Urban and Evdokimov 2004), *Russkii shanson* (Hufen 2010), as well as a trilogy on Russian *estrada* (MacFadyen 2001, 2002, 2003).[4] Besides Iurii Domanskii's 2010 monograph *Russkaia Rok-poeziia* (Russian rock-poetry) Russian language publications on the subject are even sparser (Gavrikov 2007; Eriomin 2011; Gavrikov 2011; Nikitina 2011), mainly centered around the (almost) annually appearing anthology *Russkaia Rok-poeziia* co-edited by Domanskii (Tverskoi gosudarstvennyi universitet n.d.). As the title of both the monograph as well as the anthology already hints at, the publications are primarily focused on the lyrics and their poetic quality.

There are also many Russian-language publications directed at a Russian fan market. These, which primarily cover rock in Russia, consist of encyclopedias (e.g. Trofimov 2003; Burlaka 2007c) and books written by music critics as well as journalists (e.g. Troitsky 1987; Smirnov 1994; Chernin 2006; Kozyrev and Barabanov 2007a, 2007b, 2007c).

The academic focus of research on popular music in the Soviet Union and Russian Federation has thus primarily been on rock as a genre and Leningrad during the Soviet Union as a spatial and temporal location. What is termed pop or *estrada* is more or less overlooked as is also popular music from other areas than Leningrad/St. Petersburg and Moscow (the exception being Ryback 1990; Ramet 1994; Survilla 2002; Zhuk 2010). Despite the fact that these publications are on popular music, they do not necessarily discuss music. Criticizing previous approaches for focusing too much on the lyrics, Steinholt's (2005) book attempts to put the focus back on the music.

---

4. The arrest and trail of three members of Pussy Riot (Mariia Alekhina, Ekaterina Samutsevich, and Nadezhda Tolokonnikova) after their performance of *Punk Prayer* at the Cathedral of Christ the Saviour has resulted in an academic interest in the band and questions related to the case (e.g. Gololobov and Steinholt 2013; Gololobov 2013; McMichael 2013; Shaw 2013; Steinholt 2013; Strukov 2013; Tochka 2013; Voronina 2013).

While my work does not do justice to Russia's geography (being more a continuation of the studies of Leningrad rock music in the 1980s) it seeks to balance the discussion between lyrics and music. Following Cushman (1995) and Steinholt (2005), I pay attention to musicians and other actors involved in the production of contemporary popular music.

My focus on music production and the transcultural flows between St. Petersburg and Berlin, including the link to emigrant populations, offers a new approach within the study of post-Soviet popular music, however, within ethnomusicology this approach is more common. Here I have primarily been stimulated by the writings of the ethnomusicologist Thomas Solomon on Turkish language hip-hop in Germany and Turkey (e.g. Solomon 2003, 2004, 2006, 2008) as well as more general writings on music, identity, and transcultural flows (e.g. Slobin 1993; Lipsitz 1994; Stokes 1997a; Taylor 1997; Monson 1999; Slobin 2003; Turino 2003; Stokes 2004; Sugarman 2004; Turino 2004).

Hence, by using the group Svoboda as a point of departure, this book focuses primarily on popular music production in St. Petersburg and how the music is embedded in transcultural flows. Here I specifically examine the relationship to the post-Soviet emigrant community in Berlin (Germany) focusing on the event *Russendisko*. Central questions are

- What are the conditions for popular music production in St. Petersburg? How do social networks, social hubs, and discourses influence the production? How do the conditions affect a group's creative work?
- What are the processes involved in the flow of music? Who is involved in the flows? What happens when music is embedded in a new location? How is the music appropriated? What impact does a new location have on the music's promotion? What filtering processes are present? What are the power relations?
- How do bands position themselves within the market? What strategies are employed in constructing band images? How do band images reflect local discourses? How do band images participate in and become entangled with broader discourses around local, regional, and national identities.

These questions not only help to give a snapshot of popular music production in St. Petersburg of the 2000s but also show what changes have emerged since the fall of the Soviet Union – especially through the transition to a market economy which had several consequences for Soviet popular musicians.

At the same time, these questions put in doubt some of the broader assumptions from previous research on Soviet popular music (e.g. Cushman 1995) which conceptualizes the Soviet rock musicians as people being outside Soviet society. Another aspect is the link between youth and popular music, often assumed within popular music studies, which does not hold water here. Finally, these questions show that the processes labeled globalization are not necessarily idiosyncratic coincidences as theorized by Appadurai (1996) and within ethnomusicology, amongst others, adopted by Slobin (1993). Instead, I argue for transcultural flows following certain paths of migration (Hannerz 1992; Hannerz 1996).

Before discussing these issues, the next chapter outlines my theoretical frame by discussing theories related to *(musical) scenes, transcultural flows*, and *identity* followed by a discussion of my methodology in chapter 2. Due to my role as the groups Svoboda's and Con Brio's trumpet-player, this section especially focuses on my dual role as a participant-observer and active musician. That discussion is followed by the book's main body which consists of two overarching parts:

The first part consists of chapters 3 through 7 and focuses on popular music in St. Petersburg. It starts by examining popular music production in St. Petersburg from a *scene* perspective, as theorized by Will Straw (1991, 2004) and others in chapter 3. The discussion is here loosely structured around the group Svoboda's experiences. By tracing the *social networks*, *hubs*, as well as *underlying discourses* relevant to Svoboda, an overview of music production in the St. Petersburg rock scene is given.[5] This chapter (as well as chapter 8 for Berlin) also provides the ethnographic foundation for the following discussions. Chapter 4 extends the scene discussion by focusing on how St. Petersburg is represented in the discussed groups' creative work. At the same time the chapter functions as a critique of music carrying an inherent meaning.

Drawing on Ulf Hannerz's theorization of transcultural flows (1992, 1996) chapter 5 traces some of the flows to and from St. Petersburg. Here the focus is on the flow of music aided by media and people within the frames *form of life* and *market* to both St. Petersburg and Berlin. Since influences from ska were quite

---

5. As I will return to in chapter 1 and 3 rock is here discussed from a broad perspective since the St. Petersburg scene is very heterogenous. While the latter discussions focus to a large extent on ska(-punk) and reggae I deliberately keep this broad focus in order to strengthen my argument that the music that flows to Berlin is just a small selection – filtration – of the general St. Petersburg music production.

prominent in the music heard at the *Russendisko* in Germany the discussion centers around the presence of ska and its related sibling, reggae in St. Petersburg. Bands playing within these two idioms often overlapped, hence the discussion also includes how reggae is perceived.

The following two chapters focus on identity constructions, specifically how bands primarily from St. Petersburg create a band image and market themselves. Here the focus is on how these constructions relate to concepts of collective identities – specifically how groups assert their origin (from St. Petersburg/Russia) as partially discussed in chapter 4 and ideas of Russian national identities. One notion of Russian national identity is that Russia, Ukraine, and Belarus historically belong together. Inspired by post-colonial theory, the relationship to Ukraine is thus given special attention in chapter 6: By drawing on clichés of Ukraine, Svoboda follows a Russian tradition of belittling and patronizing Ukraine. I then juxtapose Svoboda's approach to Ruslana's, a Ukrainian singer appropriating a Ukrainian ethnic minority. Chapter 7 rounds off the St. Petersburg part by focusing on how various Russian groups represent ideas of the Russian nation in their creative work.

The second part, which is made up of chapters 8 through 10, shifts the focus to Germany and specifically, the *Russendisko* in Berlin. By discussing the *Russendisko*, whose music contains a high percentage of St. Petersburg groups, chapter 8 moves the scene approach away from a geographically bound area to a multi-local and virtual music production. Here the focus is both on the *Russendisko* itself as well as related events in Germany.

The link between St. Petersburg and Berlin is Svoboda since their songs have been played at the *Russendisko*. Chapter 9 focuses on the flow of post-Soviet music to Berlin. An important connection between the two cities which has provided the basis for the *Russendisko* is the massive emigration from the former Soviet Union to Germany after 1990 which is also briefly discussed.

While the focus in chapter 9 is on the flow of music, the final chapter examines how band identities shift when promoted to a primarily non-Russian speaking audience within the *Russendisko*-scene and what I label the *Russian folklore lineage*. At the same time the *Russendisko* in both Germany and Austria seems to be part of a broader musical focus on *the East* – especially linked with music from the

Balkans. Using an interview with the owner of the Viennese *Ost Klub*, the *Russendisko*-scene discussion is rounded off within this broader perspective.

1   Theory

> Vitia: "You'll sort things out with the melody, no problem? In short, that [imitates trumpet] – is not necessary."
> David-Emil: "You yourself demonstrated that."
> Vitia: "I never sang [imitates trumpet] Like it's, you know... That kind of Russian melody was there also the very first time. In short, play [it] as it is. And that [imitates trumpet] also, not 'grr.'"
> (Con Brio and Kultashov 2005 – Russian: p. 325)

Since Svoboda's guitarist was traveling, Viktor "Vitia" Kultashov, Svoboda's former guitarist was subbing in an upcoming concert. Due to some last minute cancelations only Vitia and I (at the time Svoboda's trumpet-player) showed up at the rehearsal room. Since we were both there we decided to use the time to jam, which resulted in Vitia inviting me to join his project Con Brio. Two months later he called and I started to rehearse with the group on August 24, 2005.

Describing his group's style, Vitia stressed that the main aim was not to sound like *russkii rok* (Russian rock – cf. p. 133ff), not even to sound Russian as the opening quote from my third rehearsal with Con Brio demonstrates. Instead he imagined a kind of popsy jazz-like sound:

> "Melody and chords which are used in this music, they have, I feel, never been used in russkii rok and what has been used in russkii rok, is not used in our project, all those usual melodies. Probably, we differ through the jazz sound. It is not jazzy like if you take jazz which is improvised jazz, there is no solo. Here it is namely some jazz chords, some jazz notes."
> (Kultashov 2006 – Russian: p. 325)

This obsession about not sounding like *russkii rok* (or anything Russian) was not only demonstrated during that rehearsal, but was a continuing theme within the band discourse.[6]

This short field anecdote is interesting on several levels: It taps into both the *russkii rok*- as well as the *popsa* (pop)-discourse, two central discourses amongst

---

6. During another rehearsal Vitia said that one of the songs we had played sounded like an American *popsa*-song. He added, that was good as long as it did not sound like a Russian one. He was also very proud, because he was playing the chords as in *russkii rok*, but they did not sound like *russkii rok*. At yet another rehearsal the band played one of the songs with a beat of straight quarter notes on the drums and a reggae rhythm on the guitar (accents on 2 and 4). The band members commented after the song that it was the "Russian" way of playing it.

the musicians I talked to in St. Petersburg and discussed in chapter 3. Vitia's comments show how he and Con Brio use these two issues to position Con Brio within a certain stylistic frame – building a certain band identity, which argues for why the band is unique within the local scene and can thus be used in marketing. It also points to one way (musical) meaning is exchanged and transmitted – through conversations between two (or more) musicians. While seemingly a very local discourse, this exchange is an example of one of the ways music flows to new locations based on personal exchange. Finally, on a methodological level (which I will return to in chapter 2) it highlights how my role as an active band-member participant observer "learning to perform" (Baily 2001), gave me access to discussions which would not have been open to people just sitting in on a rehearsal and listening.

In other words, this example points to the three overarching theoretical areas of the following discussions: the (local) organization of musical practice, which will be explored through the concept of *scenes*, how music travels through time and space connecting scenes, which will be discussed within the frame of *transcultural flows*, and, finally, how bands both position themselves and are perceived within the scenes – aspects of *identity*. These three theoretical frames thus provide the tools to describe post-Soviet popular music production in both St. Petersburg and Berlin, as well as how these two locations are connected and embedded within a broader flow of popular music.

1.1 Scenes

Despite a growing celebration of attending concerts virtually (e.g. opera productions from the *Bayreuther Festspiele* streamed live over the internet), musical practice remains a very local phenomenon. Band rehearsals happen in certain venues, concerts in others, and band members tend to live in a fixed location. Thus an exploration of musical practice in an interconnected world should start at the local level, exploring how musical practice is organized.

One of my aims is to examine how particular musical practices such as popular music in St. Petersburg or the *Russendisko* in Berlin work to produce a sense of community within the conditions of metropolitan music life. The popular music and urban studies scholar Will Straw with his theorization of *cultural scenes* (1991,

2004) offers a concept which can be used to delimit musical practice in a certain location while at the same time leaving the boundaries open to explore connections to other locations.

As an analytical tool "*[s]cene* designates particular clusters of social and cultural activity without specifying the nature of the boundaries which circumscribe them" (Straw 2004, 412), in other words, delimiting one's research object while leaving the boundaries to some extent fluid. The building of musical alliances and the drawing of musical boundaries are negotiated through forms of communication which enable those processes (Straw 1991, 373). In St. Petersburg these alliances can be seen in the relationship between musicians, clubs, and fans. These alliances also create the boundaries – which groups are allowed to play in which clubs, what bands do the fans accept, and on what premise. It is thus important to chart the relations within the scene in order to uncover the social alliances as well as different discourses.

Within popular music studies, "scene" – originating as a geographical delimitation of musical practice (e.g. alternative rock – Cohen 2001; Shank 1994) – has been broadened to include genres of cultural production and loosely defined social activities (Cohen 1999; Straw 2004). This makes the concept of scene a useful tool in both examining popular music locally and as a genre of cultural production, anchored locally originally, but sustained through transcultural flows (discussed below) to other localities. This makes a theorization of the *Russendisko*, originally a fortnightly event in Berlin playing music from the post-Soviet sphere and musically linked to the St. Petersburg scene, possible.[7]

The cultural studies scholar Lawrence Grossberg raises an important point when he writes:

> "[A] scene is characterized by a particular logic which may, in a sense, transcend any particular musical content, thus allowing the scene to continue over time, even as the music changes. This also means that very different musics [sic] may exist in very similar scenes".
>
> (Grossberg 1994, 46)

---

7. While it can be argued that a *scene*-approach moves the emphasis away from focusing on the life-worlds of the actors – which could provide a more rounded portrait of these individuals – the latter approach would at the same time both limit the comparative approach of this study due to space concerns and lead to distractions not necessarily relevant to the topic which would have to be explained. Furthermore, my methodology was aimed at a broad description of the scene, which means that for some musicians my material would not suffice to give a balanced account of their world views.

While St. Petersburg as a rock scene has been around since at least the 1970s, the music played has changed. While active groups share some common discourses today, the musical styles they play vary. Furthermore, the economic basis and infrastructure have changed significantly since 1981 when the LRK was established. The major watershed here was the collapse of the Soviet Union and the resulting transition from a union-based cultural sector to a free-market economy (resulting in 70-80% of the LRK-groups disbanding by 1992 – Wickström and Steinholt 2009).

Picture 1: Flyer for the release party of the compilation *Russkii Andegraund vol. 1* (Orlandina, 20.12.2006).

One way to approach scenes is from a marketing perspective (e.g. Seattle scene) as done by Olson (1998), who draws on Grossberg's above mentioned quote. This is a step I do not want to take for two reasons: Popular music from St. Petersburg has not, until now, been marketed as something derived from a scene (as the Seattle scene). Musicians in St. Petersburg pointed to a continuing rivalry between Moscow and St. Petersburg, portraying Moscow as the pop city contrasted to St. Petersburg as the rock city, but this seems to be more of a locally bounded (and historical) discourse than an actively used marketing ploy. When marketed in Berlin, the music is either promoted as Russian (or Ukrainian), creating national entities, or as Eastern European, creating supra-national entities (cf. chapter 10). This is also to some extent reflected in Russia – cf. Picture 1, advertising the first volume of a compilation of *Russkii Andegraund*, Russian underground groups (not the "local underground" from St. Petersburg or Moscow – Various Artists 2006b).

Secondly, and more importantly, I want to use *scene* as an analytical tool to analyze music produced in St. Petersburg from the musicians', not a marketing or consumption, point of view. In other words, the *production* side. By production I do not primarily mean the *music industry* consisting of recording studios, record labels, music publishers, and distribution networks which aid in producing and promoting an album. While my research in part focused on established groups within the scene, these were not necessarily well known or "famous" outside the scene. Being released on a label was one of the major goals of many musicians I talked to, but it was not part of their daily production activities and thus I only briefly discuss this for St. Petersburg. These groups were more focused on *rehearsing* and *performing* as well as *promoting* their bands. These three activities, which aimed at building a broad enough appeal which then could result in recording an album make up my working definition of production and loosely structure the St. Petersburg scene discussion in chapter 3. Furthermore, this focus enables me to show the complexities of the discourses from the musicians' perspective. While musicians strategically position themselves and their groups in conversations, letting the musicians speak makes it possible to explore their opinions and conditions of work. As positioning tools these utterances have to be read critically, but at the same time they give a more nuanced view of popular music in St. Petersburg.

My ethnography is inspired by Sara Cohen's (2001) exploration of music production in Liverpool – my aim is to describe the activities, show what dynamics, problems, and discourses musicians in St. Petersburg face and through using the concept of scenes, offer a frame to chart these issues. Here I distance myself from the term *subculture*, probably most influentially applied by Dick Hebdige (1993) in his account of British youth culture in the 1970s.[8] While *scene* in some

---

8. While the book has been enormously influential, its focus on style as a semiotic battlefield

instances has been used as an updated version of subculture focused around a major theme or issue (e.g. Hitzler et al. 2005), I want to apply the term broadly – namely to rock.

Used as a stylistic marker "rock" (Russian: *rok*) is often applied in a broad sense both orally as well as in published material by musicians and critics in St. Petersburg: The music critic Andrei Burlaka's three volume *Rok Entsiklopediia* (Rock encyclopedia – Burlaka 2007c) on popular music from St. Petersburg covers a broad range of groups with diverse styles. This broad approach is also applied to the CD compilation *My iz Pitera – Obzor piterskogo roka* (We are from Piter – Survey of Rock from Piter – Various Artists 2003a) which in two places clearly states *Pochuvstvuite nastoiashchii piterskii ROK!* (Feel real Piter ROCK!). This definition of rock, however, includes groups which have labeled themselves rock, punk, ska-punk, and ska. This use of rock for a broad range of popular music styles was not only used in CD promotions and by music critics, but was also reflected in how those I talked to defined their music in opposition to "pop".

Inspired by Keightley's (2001) use, rock is here thus not seen as a musical genre but as a larger *musical culture*. Keightley's definition looks at both rock and pop as segments of what he calls the popular mainstream. Within this musical culture there are different sounds and styles. My approach has initially been guided by clubs, where for example Svoboda performed, rather than following specific styles. The general label was that those clubs hosted "alternative music" or "rock".[9] Music production in St. Petersburg is, however, not rigidly divided among different (sub-)styles, it is more inclusive, with these clubs also hosting other styles of music (e.g. heavy metal, diy-punk, ska-punk, reggae). Hence a more open approach is needed – a concept with fluid boundaries – which "scene" allows for. In

---

of resistance and the compartmentalization of society (in other words, fixed boundaries between the different subcultures) does not reflect the field I encountered. Hebdige discusses a social and economic context specific to Britain in the late 1970s which is neither comparable to the Soviet Union of the same time nor to contemporary Russian society. Neither does this study cover youth culture – unless youth culture includes an audience which predominantly consists of people in their 20s and musicians that are in their 30s. In general the link between popular music and youth culture is outdated (cf. Keightley 2001; Hesmondhalgh 2005).

9. Both the terms *alternative* as well as *rock* have been used by the musicians to designate the scene I discuss here. My use here is, in compliance with the term "scene", more a general label with very fluid boundaries than a (practically impossible) generalization of the music itself.

other words, chapter 3, discussing the St. Petersburg scene, focuses on groups ideologically united under rock as musical culture. This enables me to look at, for example, the boundaries *underground* vs. *commercial* as two ends on the same continuum.

Any dynamic concept depends on the perspective. Since the focus here is on production, I will chart the scene from the perspective of Svoboda, where I was involved as a trumpet-player. Being a semi-professional band, Svoboda provided a good example of the issues bands trying to make a commercial breakthrough were involved in. Using the relationships emanating from Svoboda, the narrative portrays some of the clusters of social and cultural activities present and some relevant boundaries within the St. Petersburg rock scene. Musically that means that besides a general musical overview, three styles central to the band's musical idiom – reggae, ska-punk, and *russkii rok* – play a central role in the discussions following chapter 3.

Even though the St. Petersburg scene is geographically bounded, there are connections to other localities and events like the *Russendisko*, geographically based in Berlin, but musically linked to, amongst other places, St. Petersburg. In other words, music from St. Petersburg is drawn on to create a music scene in Berlin (as well as Germany and Austria) targeting a non-Russian speaking audience and with a musical common denominator.

Here the popular music scholar Andy Bennett's (2004, 223) distinction between *local*, *translocal*, and *virtual scenes* is productive: When discussing translocal scenes he stresses that the global flow of people strongly characterizes these scenes. This is also the case in the following discussions, where many different participants facilitate the exchange of music to/at the *Russendisko* as well as the DJs touring with the concept in Europe. This characteristic comes in addition to what Bennett calls the "global mobility of particular local styles" (Bennet 2004, 230) as well as the ability of scene members to interact thanks to new communication technology (e-mail, chat-programs, internet forums, file-sharing services etc.), which also plays an important role in the *Russendisko*-scene.

While Bennett's trichotomy is productive as an analytic tool, the levels overlap with each other, something that Straw accounts for better in his definition:

"*Scene* invites us to map the territory of the city in new ways while, at the same time, designating certain kinds of activity whose relationship to territory is not easily asserted."

(Straw 2004, 412)

While the St. Petersburg scene-discussion is focused on local groups and their social networks, hubs, and discourses, I will, due to the nature of the original event, trace the *Russendisko*-scene from the perspective of the *Russendisko's* concept and its two main motors, Yuriy Gurzhy and Wladimir Kaminer. As I argue in chapter 9, due to the DJs filtering of groups, the music played at the *Russendisko* is based on a certain set of recognizable styles. This makes it more interesting to focus on the *Russendisko's* music and related events playing similar music than to focus on a broad overview of post-Soviet popular music in Germany.

My aim with the scene-discussion is twofold. First, to provide an ethnography of St. Petersburg (chapter 3) and the *Russendisko*-scene (chapter 8) which serves as the foundation for the following discussions. On a theoretical level, I will show how the concept of scenes from a production perspective can be applied to a geographically bounded area (St. Petersburg) as well as to a translocal concept which has its center in Berlin, Germany, but whose relationship to territory is more ambiguous being also physically translocal.

1.2 Cultural flow

When exploring translocal scenes, one central question is what local meanings these flows take on. As the ethnomusicologist Keila Diehl writing about music in the Tibetan refuge community says:

"Yet, the flow is, as I have said, not a free-for-all. What gets grabbed out of the torrent by whom, what is done with it, and what this *means* to the grabber and his or her family and friends: this is where the global and the local come together and seem to preserve a place for ethnography for a while longer."

(Diehl 2002, 11)

Diehl points to two important aspects here: First, that the flows are rooted in human agency, which carries an element of selection with it. Secondly, that music can adopt new meanings when it is localized. As I will return to, the images drawn upon within local ska(-punk) and reggae groups in St. Petersburg remain recognizable as originating in Jamaican ska and reggae and retain an imaginary link to an idealized Jamaica (Rastafarianism, music, national symbols). The filtration in

St. Petersburg, created through the transcultural flow, however, demonstrates a local music tradition which not only draws on these globally accessible styles, but also a local Russian tradition.

The flows can thus be examined on two levels: One level is the process of flow – how music is transported over time and place (in other words a separation between production, mediation, and consumption) while another level explains how "deterritorialized" music is "grabbed out of the torrent", localized in its new environment. The former is discussed in chapter 5 and 9. While those chapters also, to some extent, discuss the latter, this is done more extensively in chapters 4, 6, 7, and 10.

When discussing how meaning and meaningful forms arise in local contexts, the social anthropologist Ulf Hannerz (1996, 69) argues that cultures are "shaped and carried by people in varying social constellations, pursuing different aims". He points out that cultural production and circulation in social relationships operate within four frames: *form of life*, *state*,[10] *market*, and *movement*.[11] These four frames involve different agents which manage meaning and which have different motives and dimensions of interaction. In the following discussion, the frames *form of life*, which refers to everyday communication and interaction between people, and *market*, which involves the commodification of meaning and people relating to each other as buyer and seller, are important. Hannerz argues that

> "a large part of world city cultural process [can be viewed] in both its local and its transnational facets, in terms of an interplay of cultural currents within and between these organizational frames [form of life, market]."
>
> (Hannerz 1996, 132)

---

10. Some early globalization theorists like Arjun Appadurai (1996) and Ulrich Beck (1997) argue that globalization is linked to the demise of the nation-state and its influence. While it can be argued that the nation-states are more dependent on other states as well as transnational companies and much focus has been on the local and its relationssship to other locations and/or global flows, recent research (e.g. Cloonan 1999; Stokes 2004; Biddle and Knights 2007) has readdressed the role of the national level within popular music. I will return to the *state* in chapter 7 when I discuss nationalism and how *russkii rok* is being appropriated by church and state for their means.
11. Describing the frame *movement* Hannerz (1992, 49) writes: "We often describe these entities as 'social movements,' yet even when their ultimate concern is with the distribution and use of power or material resources, they are often very much movements in culture, organizations for 'consciousness raising,' attempts to transform meanings." This frame, while important within societies, does not directly play a major role in the processes described here and will thus not be discussed further.

This includes music production, which to a large extent operates within these two frames.[12] One major difference between these two frames is that cultural production and distribution in the form of life frame is more or less symmetrical, while the market frame is more deliberate and asymmetric (Hannerz 1996, 69).[13] Musicians interact on a daily basis both with each other and with visiting groups. They exchange ideas, participate in projects and draw on each other's musical (and other) resources. This is, in other words, a symmetrical form of interaction. At the same time, the musicians are part of a market, selling commodified meaning (e.g. music) both live at concerts and medialized, as recordings. This is more asymmetric or one-sided (from group to audience/consumers).

The sum of these frames makes up culture, which, according to Hannerz, should be studied through the concept of *cultural flow*:
> "the cultural flow consists of the externalizations of meaning which individuals produce through arrangements of overt forms, and the interpretations which individuals make of such displays".
>
> (Hannerz 1992, 4)

The concept combines a cognitive and discursive approach to culture. His use of the metaphor *flow* – similar to a river – stresses that culture is perceived as a structure (the sight of a river in the distance), but is fully dependent on process (through the constant flow of water the river is never the same):
> "the flow occurs in time and has directions. As a whole, it is endless; externalizations depend on previous interpretations, depending on previous externalizations."
>
> (Hannerz 1992, 4)

In other words, while in part drawing on previous cultural products culture is in constant development. Hannerz goes on to argue that the study of culture through cultural flow should pay attention to the dimensions *ideas and modes of thought*, *forms of externalization*, and *social distribution*.

---

12. The state plays an indirect role here being important e.g. through subsidizing music schools, tolerating concert venues and through state sponsored music events, which in Russia at times tend to have a political implication e.g. the festivals *Slava Rossii, Slava Moskve* (Hail Russia, Hail Moscow) and *Ia vybiraiu Rossiiu – Rossiia – vpered!* (I vote for/choose Russia – Russia – ahead!).
13. The use of symmetric/assymetric refers to the organizational features present in the frames mentioned – the characteristics of cultural management in social relations present in the flow of meaning. These dimensions include aspects of access and power present in the interaction. Where a more symmetric approach entails equal access on each end, an asymmetric approach means that one side dominates the exchange of meaning (cf. Hannerz 1992, 46,55ff).

One way in which meaning and meaningful forms are externalized and distributed in society is through media, which enables people to communicate with one another without being in each other's presence.[14] This implies both a *spatial* separation in the production and consumption of forms of meaning, as well as a *temporal* separation, since meaning can be stored (records, CDs, MP3-files etc.) for later use. This separation is essential to the functioning of radio and discotheques in general and is specifically the case in the *Russendisko*, where the material is primarily stored on CDs.[15] The impact of media also implies a broadening of the concept of relationships (from a face-to-face to a detached one) and contributes "greatly to making the boundaries of societies and cultures fuzzy" (Hannerz 1992, 30).

Lundberg et al. (2003, 68ff) offer a model to look at transcultural flows of music based on *mediaization*. Arguing that music's form, use, and function mostly is affected by *mediaization* they focus on the relationship between music and technology.

This model offers a good way to examine how music both flows to St. Petersburg, becomes localized, and then flows from the city to, for example, Germany and the *Russendisko* there. Two terms Lundberg et al. (2003) apply which are important in this context are *de-mediaization*, mediated music that has been adopted locally and is performed in a local context, and *re-mediaization*, local (de-mediaized) music adapted to local (musical/stylistic) conventions which is recorded and made available through a medium on a regional, national, or transnational level.

Even though cultural flows are, to a great extent, mediated through the increasing mobility of *media*, the human component and its increasing mobility also play an important role, as I will demonstrate in my role as an involuntary manager for Svoboda in Berlin, discussed in chapter 9. These are the two components Hannerz (1996, 19) and Appadurai (1996, 3) identify as particularly important in changing the cultural organization in the late 20th century.[16]

---

14. The distribution mainly operates through the market frame – either the official or unofficial market (e.g. p2p-networks, piracy), but also the form of life frame (exchange between friends).
15. This is also important when both in- and outbound travel is restricted as it was in the Soviet Union. Here medialized music available on the radio or through home copied music (*Magnitizdat* – cf. Steinholt 2005, 38f) circulating within informal networks was important.
16. Appadurai argues further that these two contribute to *imagination as social practice* being "a

Criticizing the term *globalization*, the social-anthropologist Thomas Hylland Eriksen (2003, 4) argues that "[w]hether it is ideas or substances that flow, or both, they have origins and destinations, and the flows are instigated by people." To his critique Hylland Eriksen (2003, 4) adds that

> "[t]he ideational and institutional framework of the flows may be 'placeless' or global in principle (the Internet is, and so [...] [is] the global salmon market), but their instantiation necessarily involves situated agents and delineated social contexts".

This is an important point, since even though media is available, it first becomes accessible through human interaction (either face-to-face human contact, virtual chatting, or surfing the net).

Thus, the musical flows operate on different levels of interaction between media and human agency. This is valid for musicians in St. Petersburg, the *Russendisko*, and for the Berlin based record label *Eastblok Music* – besides using the Internet and buying CDs (stronger focus on media), the actors travel to Central-Europe, respectively to Russia (stronger focus on human agency) and also rely on people who go abroad to collect new material for their work (equal focus on both aspects).

While arguing for agency as an important aspect of transcultural flows, Hylland Eriksen hints at a problem of using the term "global" which reflects my reluctance to use the term: Most processes described here are European phenomena mainly following migration paths between certain nodes – in other words, these transcultural flows are a regional phenomenon. Here transcultural implies on the one hand supranational flows, but at the same time does not imply that these operate on a global level

These processes, however, are not limited to certain individuals within the elite, they are (becoming) mass-phenomena, fueled both by the increasing amount of travel by individuals (for leisure, studies, and business) and by *migration* due to economic or political reasons creating migrant communities (like inhabitants of the former Soviet Union in Berlin). These movements heavily contribute to transcultural flows and the formations of translocal and virtual networks.

---

form of negotiation between sites of agency (individuals) and globally defined fields of possibility" (1996, 31).

1.2.1 Migration

Within a post-Soviet context St. Petersburg is a migration center, attracting not only musicians to study and perform there but primarily (unskilled) workers from other regions and CIS-states, due to better working conditions. The city has had this function as a node within a transnational network attracting migrants since its foundation and these flows of people enable an influx of cultural flows which have also affected the music scene.

While the term *migrant*, defined by the Merriam-Webster Online Dictionary (n.d.) as "a person who moves regularly in order to find work", emphasizes the fact that the person involved left his/her home country/country of prior residence, it both implies a temporary residence in one or several new host countries and lacks the emphasis and connection to their (original) home. The terms *emigrant* (somebody leaving his/her country of residence/home) and *immigrant* (somebody who takes up a residence in a new country) bring more accuracy, however they still lack an explicit reference to the person's origin, an important question for this study. The terms *transnationalism* and *transmigrant* may be used to specify this relationship:

> "Transmigrants are immigrants whose daily lives depend on multiple and constant interconnections across international borders and whose public identities are configured in relationship to more than one nation-state. [...] Transnational migration is the process by which immigrants forge and sustain simultaneous multi-stranded social relations that link together their societies of origin and settlement."
> (Schiller et al. 1995, 48)

In other words, people maintain strong personal (and at times also professional) ties to their point of origin in the new setting, traveling back and forth across national boundaries. This moves the focus away from immigrants being static residents trying to adopt to a new context and stresses their links to the country they came from, in other words, their agency. This definition fits well with migrants living in St. Petersburg like Svoboda's vocalist Sasha (from Ukraine) or my brother-in-law Dzhon (from Armenia) who works within the construction sector in St. Petersburg. Both have ties to their respective country of origin where they still have family, go back to visit and, as in Dzhon's case, sends money back "home" to his relatives in Armenia. Thus, what both have in common and share with a majority of transmigrants from the republics of the former Soviet Union is that the ties they maintain are *bidirectional*: between St. Petersburg and their country of origin.

Placed within a global music market, St. Petersburg belongs to the periphery with more flows of foreign music entering the country than escaping from it. However, within Russia it is a center of rock music, attracting musicians from the former Soviet Union to perform, but also to relocate and live in the city as a cursory look at the line-ups of local St. Petersburg bands shows.[17] This dual role makes the city interesting as a meeting point where local musicians pick up on music from live concerts abroad and, more commonly, through media (de-mediaization) and rework it based on their listening biography (Feld 1994a), musical interests, and marketing interest. This interaction happens on the form of life level with musicians interacting with other musicians – some from St. Petersburg and some from other places. The music that emerges – or in Lundberg's terms, is re-mediaized in St. Petersburg does not only remain there, but is also disseminated both nationally (e.g. on radio, internet, and tours) as well as internationally (e.g. to the *Russendisko* in Berlin). The discussions in chapters 5 and 9 focus on one example of these flows, the de-mediaization of reggae and ska in St. Petersburg and its re-mediaization in the *Russendisko* in Berlin. Besides placing these flows to Berlin (*Russendisko*) within a historic context, I also want to stress that the flows in this case follow paths of migration. This offers a more nuanced perspective on global cultural flows than Appadurai's non-isomorphic paths with different flows (or scapes) in disjuncture with each other – making the flows unpredictable (Appadurai 1996) – something I will return to in the discussions.

The second example is Germany, which has, together with the United States and Israel, due to political and historical circumstances, become one of the prima-

---

17. Svoboda's line-up was mixed – the musicians came from Kandalaksha (Province of Murmansk), Krasnodar (Southern Russia), Zhdanov (now Mariupol', South-Eastern Ukraine) and Shostka (North-Eastern Ukraine). Also established bands did not only consist of locals: Markscheider Kunst included musicians from the Ural mountains, Kirov, and Congo as well as an Israeli citizen: "In the current line up those who moved here are [...] our guitar-player, the second Volodia [...] he was a DJ, arrived, was born in the Ural, has lived here for already 20 years, in Piter. Or our trumpet-player, Sania. [...] He was born in Kirov and moved here to study the trumpet at the Institute of Culture, and landed in the group with us. He's been here in Piter about 4-5 years. [...] Seraphim [Selenge] Makangila came from Congo. And Vadia Iagman, who used to play the trumpet with us, is a citizen of Israel." (Efremenko 2005 – Russian: p. 321) This is not only limited to these two groups, many musicians as well as groups (e.g. Mata Khari from Dzerzhinsk and BroSound from Surgut) in the city have moved there. Besides labor migration, musicians also moved to the city to study at the local conservatories and music colleges.

ry destinations of post-Soviet emigration. This community, commonly referred to as "Die Russen" (the Russians), sports ties both to the former Soviet Union as well as to groups of post-Soviet migrants in other places. One way to group this community is through the term *transmigrants,* which stresses a strong tie between host and home-land (Schiller et al. 1995). This term, however, does not really include the transnational network beyond the home and host country, which is an important aspect of this community – especially among the musicians I talked to.

The concept of *diaspora* seems more suitable to describe the emigrants in Germany. Originally used to describe the expulsion of the Jews from the biblical Land of Israel, the term has been widely used to describe any community dispersed from their homeland, including religious groups, ethnicities, and imagined supranational communities (e.g. African-Americans).[18]

Living in a host country, the post-Soviet emigrants have a common origin, the former Soviet Union, and common points of reference like language (Russian), socialization, and official Soviet popular culture. Furthermore, they maintain contact both to friends and family back in the former Soviet Union as well as people dispersed across the world. Another common denominator of the emigrants who came after 1990 is that they left on their own – they were not forced to leave by the government or systematically persecuted.[19] This gives them the possibility of traveling between their host- and home country without fears of repercussions from the authorities.

Diasporas challenge national boundaries and as Yuriy Gurzhy's statement on page 257 demonstrates, the music promoted at the *Russendisko* comes from a transnational network of residents in and emigrants from the former Soviet Union.

While at first glance the concept of diaspora seems apt to grasp the network of (primarily) Russian-speaking inhabitants, the term, especially when applied from

---

18. During the last two decades writings on diaspora have surged. Besides the journal *Diaspora* some seminal works on diaspora are Hall (1990), Clifford (1994), and Tölölyan (1996). Within ethnomusicology important contributions include Slobin (2003), Turino (2003, 2004), and Solomon (2006).
19. However, the socio-economic situation in Russia during the 1990s as well as the current anti-semitic and anti-protestant sentiments provided a strong motivation. This choice of leaving out of their own free will is also reflected in the fact that some emigrants have returned to Russia, especially since the conditions of life in Russia have improved and the adaptation to the host country has proven harder than expected.

outside the community, hides the fact that this group is not homogenous. It consists of both different ethnicities as well as religions. Tölölyan argues that the notion of diasporas only emerging from homogenous groups

> "emphasizes the preservation and/or non-discontinuous evolution of a single, previously available identity, and tends to overlook the possibility that quite loosely related populations possessed of many different, locally circumscribed identities in their homelands, but regarded as 'one' in the hostland, can be turned into a diaspora by the gaze of that hostland."
>
> (Tölölyan 1996, 13)

This previous homogenizing identity is *Russen*, used both by the emigrants as well as by people living in Germany:

> "Schum is a radio show about 'Russian' music [...]. 'Russian' in quotation marks since for most Germans (and often for the Russians themselves) all russophone people are 'the Russians'. And so we also play Ukrainian, Moldavian, Belarusian, Jewish music and collect them under the term 'Russian.'"
>
> (Schum n.d. – German: p. 314)

This quote, taken from the website of the monthly Radio show *Schum*, based in Halle, reflects the overarching use of the term "Russian" to designate the russophone emigrant community.[20] This both allows for questions of what ethno-religious groups the migrants are made up of as well as if the term diaspora at all is applicable to this (heterogenous) community (questions that will be discussed in chapter 9). On a more general level these issues touch on how the emigrants perceive themselves and how they are perceived by their host society. This leads to the third theoretical complex, identities.

1.3   "That kind of Russian melody": Identities and band images

As the opening Con Brio example demonstrated, identities are a way of representing one's self in contrast to something one is not. An identity can also be based on a notion of one's self – which is both influenced by the person's life history and cultural background as well as being made up of conscious choices: In the above example Vitia has a clear idea of what *russkii rok* is through listening and having played songs within that tradition. Thus he can clearly define his taste in music and band style in opposition to *russkii rok*. Another central point here is that

---

20. This use of "Russian" as a homogenous category was also reflected through the answers I got in interviews done in Germany.

identities are relational: They are made up both in negation to what one is not and at the same time through elements of perceived similarities with other (collective) identities and – focusing on personal identities – how a person is seen by others.[21] An identity is, at the same time, based on an accumulating biography. This, in turn, is based on experiences which shape a person and his/her habits. In the ethnomusicologist Thomas Turino's words: "Identity is the representation of selected habits foregrounded in given contexts to define self to oneself and to others by oneself and by others" (Turino 2004, 8).[22] Here an added element appears – identities represent one's self towards others but at the same time also construct a coherent representation of one's self for oneself (cf. DeNora 2000, 62f).

Turino draws on *habits* as the basis for identity – which is used to represent one's self to others – but which in sum also make up the person's *individual subjectivity*. This subjectivity is shaped through different habits accumulated over a person's life and "the ongoing interaction between particular subjects and objective conditions in which they [the particular subjects] find themselves." (Turino 2004, 8) The individual subjectivity (and thus also identities as a select representation of those) is influenced by social factors (such as other people, groups, school/education, and government institutions), and is in constant development.

Identity is thus a *representation* of a person's selected habits, not the person's subjectivity itself. The selection of habits used to promote an identity depends on the context and can touch even assumed fixed constitutive elements such as a person's biological sex and name. While the creation of an identity can be a conscious choice, it is first when in interaction with others that it turns meaningful and is accepted (or not).

---

21. These perceived similarities are etymologically anchored in the originally medieval latin *identitas* which root is *idem*, "the same".
22. The cultural studies scholar Stuart Hall, drawing on psychoanalysis (Lacan) and discourse theory (Foucault), has a similar model which is, however, based on the *subject*, not self: "Identities are thus points of temporary attachment to the subject positions which discursive practices construct for us [...]. Identities are, as it were, the positions which the subject is obliged to take up while always 'knowing' (the language of consciousness here betrays us) that they are representations, that representation is always constructed across a 'lack', across a division, from the place of the Other, and thus can never be adequate – identical – to the subject processes which are invested in them." (Hall 1996, 6) Here as in Turino's model, identities are representations of the subject – however the process shaping these representations are to a higher degree formed by power relations in society which are expressed in the discourses.

This personal approach to identities can also be adopted to official band identities where the band's image (which here is used as a synonym for band identity) is a selection and a representation of the band's "subjectivity": In Svoboda's case the band constitutes and markets itself as not being Russian, but Ukrainian, thus differentiating itself from other popular music groups in St. Petersburg. This identity as a Ukrainian group is accepted in St. Petersburg because Sasha speaks Russian with a Ukrainian accent. In addition, the songs are in what the audience perceives as Ukrainian. Ukrainian speakers, however, are very quick to point out that Sasha's Ukrainian is not "pure", that he is a native Russian speaker. While this, due to the country's bilingual reality, does not exclude him from being Ukrainian, he and thus Svoboda are not perceived as Ukrainian at the level of other groups which sing in (more proficient) Ukrainian. There is also a discrepancy between an intended band image that is promoted (theory) and the resulting performance (practice) which can encompass other identities as well (displaying other representations of the band's "subjectivity") – not all of which are part of the promoted band image but which still affect the band's overall image.

The problematic stance when applying identity is balancing a too essentializing approach (predetermined identities) with an overly fluid approach, where identities are strategically chosen depending on the needs of the individual. By basing subjectivities and identities on habits, Turino presents a good balance between those two poles. On the one hand, habits change over time (some more, some less) taking into account that the representation of those habits – one's identity – also changes. On the other hand, some habits are also hard to change, as, for example, a person's playing style or language use, especially traces of "otherness" expressed by accent or differing dialects.

1.3.1 Collective identities

While being a part of a person's personal identity, shared identities can also function as a basis for creating groups. These *collective identities* are based on identities shared with other individuals who form part of that collective. Collective identities can span from tangible day-to-day (or face-to-face) interactions as, for example, people living in the same house, with the same job/education, to more abstract entities such as ethnicity, citizenship, (supra-)nationality or religion.

Drawing on Aristotle, the Scandinavian cultural studies scholar Stephan Michael Schröder differentiates between two forms of collective identities. The first, which he calls a *kollektive Identität ersten Grades* (collective identity in the first degree – Schröder 1996, 582), is based on a group or community which can still be directly experienced. These group identities emerge through an individual's interaction with others and are based on communal experiences. This communal experience is based on one or more shared or overlapping identities, which function as a synecdoche for the collective. These can be more rigid, such as family, or more voluntary, like clubs frequented or music-making in a band.

Svoboda constitutes a collective identity based on the music played. The musicians joined the group in order to play and help create Svoboda's music. Furthermore, they have a common interest in performing for an audience, they both have a common spoken (Russian) as well as a musical language (popular music, ska, punk). The musician's personal identities, however, vary since each musician's subjectivity is based on different musical habits. While it could be argued that Svoboda is Sasha's band and thus he determines the collective identity based on his personal identity, this is also not quite accurate, since the musical style of the band has been colored by the instrumentalists. I will return to this when discussing Svoboda's style in chapters 5 and 6, especially the *russkii rok*-influences. Here a distinction should to be made between the *collective identity of the musicians (or participants)* and the *band identity/image* which constitutes a mediated identity. In Svoboda's case this image is both made up of Sasha's background (Ukraine) as well as the musical style the group plays – determined in part by the rhythm, melody, and harmony (ska, punk) and in part by the instrumentation (horn section).

The second collective identity Schröder terms *diskursiv-kollektive Identität* (discursive-collective identity) or short *DiKoIdentität* (Schröder 1996, 582). This one is more abstract, where the community is not directly, but indirectly and symbolically experienced. This identity is not fixed, but changes as it is exposed to different forms of power, hence the term discursive. Furthermore, while the key symbols constituting the *DiKoIdentität* might be clear, their interpretation is not as fixed – both due to this identity's discursive nature as well as due to the fact that the symbols can be interpreted and decoded in different ways.

Applying the *DiKoIdentität* to national identity, Schröder argues that the individuals are *not part of*, but symbolically *take part/participate in* the nation.[23] Here

---

23. This is similar to participating in Benedict Anderson's *imagined community* where an individual participates in the same imagined community as other – mostly unknown – individ-

he specifically criticizes an essentialized primordially given national identity and argues instead that national identities should be conceptualized as something voluntary to actively participate in, something which is continuously evolving – a discursive formation which is continuously being reexamined.

Another form of *DiKoIdentitäten* is ethnic groups[24] which

"are to be understood in terms of the construction, maintenance and negotiation of boundaries, and not the putative social 'essences' which fill the gaps within them. Ethnic boundaries define and maintain social identities, which can only exist in 'a context of opposition and relativities'"

(Stokes 1997b, 6, drawing on Chapman, McDonald, and Tonkin)

The drawing of boundaries based on differences to other groups (cf. Barth 1998) is legitimated by rallying around certain symbols and origin myths which define the specific ethnic group in opposition to other ethnic groups.

The distinction outlined here has been between a *kollektive Identität ersten Grades* where the individual is (physically) *part of* a specific community or group and thus actively contributes to its development and *DiKoIdentitäten* which individuals *participate in* which makes it harder for the individual to shape and change the identity and symbols used. However, both forms of identity involve elements from the other so these collective identities should be seen as belonging to a continuum: While musicians are physically part of a band actively contributing to the music played, they, at the same time, participate, in a performance drawing on certain symbols – some which they themselves have chosen, but also some which have become a "naturalized", unreflected part of the music activities (line-ups primarily consisting of at least a drummer, vocalist, guitarist, and bass-player, participating in certain discourses etc.).

1.3.2 Music and identity

From the level of personal identities via a collective level to the level of *DiKoIdentitäten*, music plays an important role in constructing and maintaining identities. The sociologist Tia DeNora aptly shows the role music plays as building material for self-identities (personal identities) and its role in "mobiliz[ing] and hold[ing] on to a coherent image of 'who one knows one is.'" (DeNora 2000, 63)

---

uals sharing a common notion of the nation: "It is imagined because the members of even the smallest nation will never know most of their fellow-members, meet them, or even hear of them, yet in the minds of each lives the image of their communion." (Anderson 1991, 6)

24. In Russia the term *natsional'nost'* is used – which can be translated both as ethnic group or nationality.

1 Theory

Music can take on this role because it does not carry an inherent meaning (cf. chapter 4). Any meaning is created by the listeners themselves while experiencing the music. This means that, as the ethnomusicologist Jeffrey Summit points out, music is "a deep vessel, a form of expressive culture that can combine and hold many expressions of identity" (Summit 2000, 17). He adds that due to music's nature it is possible to both blend and layer components like language, text, tune, rhythm, vocal timbre, and instrumentation enabling different meanings and associations.

Inspired by Pierceian semiotics, Turino takes this argument a step further and argues that musical performances are a rich semiotic field based on the interplay of various components:

> "As in all art, because of the nature of the artistic frame, and because of the absence of strict grammars determining iconic and indexical semiotic combinations, music contains tremendous room for the creation of new coherent forms from pre-existing icons and indices."
>
> (Turino 2004, 17)

Decoding the signs (icons, indices, and symbols[25]) depends on the individual experience of the listener, his/her listening biography and interpretive moves (cf. Feld 1994a). DeNora describes how music helps to revive and relive past memories and thus is an essential part of producing the individual's self over time:

> "It [music] serves also as a means of putting actors in touch with capacities, reminding them of their accomplished identities, which in turn fuels the ongoing projection of identity from past into future. Musically fostered memories thus produce past trajectories that contain momentum."
>
> (DeNora 2000, 66).

These memories can include constructing a place. Stokes points to the power musical events (in a broad sense – from listening to CDs to performances) have in

> "evok[ing] and organis[ing] collective memories and present[ing] experiences of place with an intensity, power and simplicity unmatched by any other social activity."
>
> (Stokes 1997b, 3)

He goes on to point out that these places (similar to identities) are constructed in oppositions, including social and other differences as well as hierarchies of moral and political order.[26]

---

25. To avoid confusion with Saussure's definition of symbol the musicologist Philip Tagg (1999, 4) employs the term *arbitrary sign* instead of *symbol*.
26. Stokes draws on the sociologist Anthony Giddens' (2000, 18) distinction between place and space (a separation which sets in with modernity).

Criticizing the approach that music *symbolizes* social boundaries Stokes argues that music aids in transforming social space as well as that music itself can act as a container for other social activity. This in turn provides a unique experience for the listener making

> "music socially meaningful not entirely but largely because it provides means by which people recognize identities and places, and the boundaries which separate them."
>
> (Stokes 1997b, 5)

This shift is important since it points to how music is not only used by individuals to negotiate their social mobility (class) but also the aesthetic power that music conveys, which, in the worse case, can lead to physical violence.

With this in mind it is also possible to see how music functions as a communal activity and can thus be symbolically employed by social actors (like ethnic and other groups) in constructing their (collective) identities. Stokes sets the frame for the following discussion by asking

> "how music is used by social actors in specific local situations to erect boundaries, to maintain distinctions between us and them, and how terms such as 'authenticity' are used to justify these boundaries".
>
> (Stokes 1997b, 6)

1.3.3 Post-colonial perspective

A productive lens to use when examining identity constructions and discourses in St. Petersburg and the former Soviet Union – especially how the boundaries/borders are errected – is that of a post-colonial perspective.

While the literary scholar Edward Said (1994), in his seminal book *Orientalism – Western Conceptions of the Orient*, focused on how the representation of the colonies in the Near and Middle East is fashioned by a European discourse of the Other, post-colonial studies have extended their field to include African and other so called developing countries. The term *post-colonial* functions as a

> "designation for critical discourses which thematize issues emerging from colonial relations and their aftermath, covering a long historical span (including the present.)"
>
> (Shohat 1992, 101)

This is also one of the problems since the concept glosses over a wide variety of different forms of coloniality and independence as well as temporalities (the prefix "post" also masking continuing influences), keeping the term very vague.[27]

---

27. In a detailed critique of the term, Shohat (1992, 107) writes: "[T]he term 'post-colonial' posits no clear domination, and calls for no clear opposition. It is this structured ambiva-

One of the foci of post-colonial studies starting with Said's *Orientalism* has been on power relations and how the colonized have been represented (or *orientalized*) and thus domesticated by the colonizers. This has been done by depicting the colonized as *passive* and *feminine* (in opposition to the active and masculine colonizers). Through such an approach (based on a Foucaultian discourse analysis) strategies of domestication and power-relations can be uncovered (I will return to the question of representation in chapter 6). This focus has been broadened to not only examining the colonizers but also how the colonized resisted these ascriptions.

Another area of study which has become especially prominent in ethnomusicology and popular music studies looks at what is most commonly labeled *hybridity*.[28] The term allows for a

> "negotiation of the multiplicity of identities and subject positionings which result from displacements, immigrations and exiles without policing the borders of identity along essentialist and originary lines."
> (Shohat 1992, 108)

First used for cultural products resulting from coloniality and now often used in combination with immigrant communities or diasporas, the term is also used within popular music – especially within the music industry category *world music* (cf. Frith 2000 on the origin of the genre). Here hybridity refers to cultural products which draw on and blend different (local) styles. The term is often used in opposition to *authenticity*, central to the popular music and rock discourse. This, despite the fact that music, being hybrid through drawing on local or traditional musics, can also be a sign of authenticity within the world music discourse. (Stokes 2004, 59; Solomon 2006). While the term has enabled important contributions to research on popular music I prefer not to use it since music and musicians have always been influenced by its/their surroundings (all music is in this sense hybrid) and writers using the term tend to celebrate a positive multicultural cos-

---

lence of the 'post-colonial,' of positing a simultaneously close and distant temporal relation to the 'colonial,' that is appealing in a post-structuralist academic context. It is also this fleeting quality, however, that makes the 'post-colonial' an uneasy term for a geopolitical critique of the centralized distribution of power in the world." She concludes her critique by arguing for a context sensitive approach to the researched subject: "In sum, the concept of the 'post-colonial' must be interrogated and contextualized historically, geopolitically, and culturally." (Shohat 1992, 111)

28. This has been strongly influenced by Homi Bhabha's (1990, 1994) writings on the *third space*.

mopolitan approach to music, overlooking the fact that this is not always the case (e.g. the Ukrainian case studies discussed in chapter 6.2 and Wickström 2008 show a nationalistic approach).[29]

Returning to the post-Soviet sphere, David Chioni Moore (2001) criticizes the fact that post-colonial theory has primarily been used for what has been referred to as *first* and *third world countries*, overlooking, however, the *second world countries*. He argues for broadening the scope further, stressing that the Soviet and post-Soviet sphere can be examined from a colonial and then post-colonial perspective with Russia in the role of the (former) colonizer. This would include not only the former Soviet Republics, but also the countries in Central and Eastern Europe. Placing the Russian Empire's land acquisition in a wider context, he argues that their colonial expansion in the 19th century was linked to a mimicry of British and French colonial aspirations – as a way to "join" Europe. At the same time he argues that the motives for Russian imperialism were also revenge for, and/or a return to, the land conquered by the Mongols in the 13th century (Moore 2001, 120). The latter period has, for some, remained a national trauma until today (cf. Alisa's *Seeds of the horde* and *Basurman's yoke* in *Nebo Slavian* – p. 218). Here Russia's position as a country somewhere between Europe and Asia is important to keep in mind – a country whose modern roots go back to the Russian 19th century debate between the *Westeners* and *Slavophiles*.[30] Discussing the countries of Central and Eastern Europe (mostly part of the Warsaw Pact), he argues that this could be called a *reverse-cultural colonization*, where not the colonized, but the colonizer is orientalized.[31]

---

29. For some seminal works on the circulation of music, identity, hybridity, world music, and questions of representation cf. Slobin 1993, Feld 1994b, Lipsitz 1994, Mitchell 1996, Taylor 1997, Erlmann 1999, Born and Hesmondhalgh 2000b, Feld 2000a, Feld 2000b, Brusila 2003, Stokes 2004, Solomon 2006.
30. This refers to two movements emerging in the early 19th century shaped through Romantic nationalism and possible paths for Russia's future: The *Westernizers* looked towards Europe as a model for Russia's progress. They were inspired by Tsar Peter I's and subsequent European orientated reforms and called for liberal changes. The *Slavophiles* condemned the European influences brought by Tsar Peter I's reforms. They glorified a mythic untainted pre-Petrine era, focusing on the Orthodox religion and on Russian "original" values linked to the village community (*mir*) on which Russia's social order was based (in opposition to European individuality). These ideals were used to argue that the basis of Russia's civilization was a special case and thus needed its own path.
31. He links this to a Russian inferiority complex towards Europe. Thus, the claiming of Poland, Hungary, and Eastern Germany should be seen as Russia claiming trophies, not as countries

Chioni Moore's argument is in line with a theorizing of Russia as a polyethnic empire and explains the Russian Federation's current attempt to guard its influence in the former colonies. While the concept of *nationalism* would also be productive in explaining the developments, the post-colonial perspective adds a crucial layer of interdependence which I think is important in the analysis, since it allows for understanding reactions in the respectively other country.

This approach is not only reflected on a governmental level, but also within popular music. One example is the radio station *Nashe Radio's* (Our Radio) definition of Russian music including bands from Belarus and Ukraine discussed in chapter 7. Another example evolves around Svoboda's use of perceived Ukrainian elements discussed in chapter 6. As I argue here and elsewhere (Wickström 2008), Ukrainian bands like Haydamaky and Ruslana use local traditional music – as "an exaggerated desire for authentic sources" (Moore 2001, 118) – in their creative work, while in Russia Svoboda appropriates Ukrainian elements as exotica.

While I believe this is a productive approach when examining the relationship between Russia and Ukraine, the Slavic studies scholar Andreas Kappeler's (1992, 14) caution of applying a set of terms originally conceived for another reality to Russia, as well as Shohat's (1992) call for a context sensitive approach, should not be neglected. While Russia (or the Tsar dynasty and Moscow) has been the ruling faction, the area which encompasses today's Ukraine has – while under Russia's rule – not been subject to the same kind of exploitation which has been seen by other colonial powers like Great Britain and France.[32] Kappeler (1992) also shows how the Tsar employed different techniques of ruling and co-optation which varied depending on the region in the Russian empire. This makes it hard to conceptualize Russian colonialization as one, coherent strategy (also pointed out by Moore 2001). Furthermore, while Ukraine now is formally independent, thus

---

needing civilizing through Russia. Furthermore, he argues that the Central European countries saw Soviet-Russia as Asians, in other words as savages – which the Soviet Union exploited at times of tension in Europe by stationing Central Asian troops in those countries (Moore 2001, 121).

32. Due to its geographical location the country that constitutes Ukraine today has been part of the Russian, Ottoman, and Habsburg empires as well as the Polish-Lithuanian commonwealth. Thus, Ukraine's position as a country divided between Russia and Europe has a long history and strong socio-cultural ties to both Russia and Poland exist. Due to its history Ukraine is both religiously (Ukrainian-orthodox, Uniate/Ukrainian Greek-Catholic) as well as linguistically heterogenous (Russian, Ukrainian).

post-colonial in a temporal meaning, applying the term conceals the fact that the country still remains within Russia's sphere of influence: This influence is both economic (as the disputes over gas starting winter 2005/06 have shown) and cultural – being both part of the same founding myth as Russia – the *Kievan Rus'* – as well as the languages Russian and Ukrainian linguistically belonging to the same family (the East Slavic languages). The language issue is especially contentious as a ground of post-colonial struggle: the increased use of Ukrainian after Ukraine's independence can also be perceived as a signal of exclusion for the Russian speaking population of Ukraine, some of whom have relocated to Russia partly because of a feeling of alienation (amongst them Sasha from Svoboda).[33] Finally, Ukraine also faces Russian influence geographically with Russian politicians like Moscow's former major Iurii Luzhkov (re)claiming Sevastopol on the Crimean peninsular.[34] Ania Loomba (2005, 12) points to an important distinction to keep in mind when she writes that

"[a] country may be both postcolonial (in the sense of being formally independent) and neo-colonial (in the sense of remaining economically and/or culturally dependent) at the same time."

This situation is also one of the reasons for the Orange Revolution in 2004, which pitted the more Western-European-oriented politicians Viktor Iushchenko and Iuliia Tymoshenko, who were supported by groups like Haydamaky, Vopli Vidopliasova (VV), and Ruslana against the Russian-favored candidate Viktor Ianukovych and the outgoing president Leonid Kuchma.[35]

This post-colonial struggle[36] between the former colonial power Russia / the Soviet Union and Ukraine is present in St. Petersburg, among other places,

---

33. Cf. Wanner (1996) for an analysis of the second *Chervona Ruta Music Festival* (1991) in Zaporizhzhia (East Ukraine) in relation to a bourgeoning Ukrainian nationalism. Wanner highlights how ethnic Ukrainians who were Russian socialized were alienated by the cultural performance of Ukrainian nationalism at the festival.
34. The predominantly Russian speaking Crimean peninsular was "given" to Ukraine by Nikita Khrushchev in 1954. This was resented by some Russians I talked to who said that it belonged to Russia.
35. While I do not want to reproduce the Eastern vs. Western Ukraine reduction of the Orange Revolution and the following political conflicts and intrigues propagandized in European and Russian media, one issue was staked around Ukrainian national identities and language politics in a post-Soviet world.
36. Another arena for this struggle is the *Eurovision Song Contest* where both Ukraine (Greendzholi's *RAzom NAs BAhato* – Together we are many! – in 2005 and Verka Serdiuchka's *Dancing Lasha Tumbai* in 2007) as well as Georgia (Stephane and 3G's *We Don't Wanna Put In* in 2009) have taken shots at Russia (cf. Wickström 2009b).

through Svoboda's band image and activities discussed in chapter 6. It, however, loses its context once recontextualized within the *Russendisko* in Germany.

Drawing on the theoretical triad *scenes, transcultural flows,* and *identity* enables me to locate Svoboda's musical activities within a social network in St. Petersburg and discuss what (local) meanings their creative work has. At the same time it demonstrates how the music flows to Berlin and is ascribed a different meaning there. In other words, while the concept of scenes enables me to chart the local infrastructure and how the different agents interact with each other it is limited in describing what local meaning is present. The concept of identity allows for that discussion. The concept of transcultural flows together with Hannerz's culture concept bridges the scene and identity theory by not only uncovering how meanings are exchanged on a local level but also by demonstrating how music flows through time and space – thus explaining how meanings can diverge in different locations.

While hinting at it, this chapter has not discussed one aspect of the opening example – my presence and role in the research process. This is the topic of the following chapter which focuses on my research methodology.

2 Methodology

We were in the middle of our three song set performed at the St. Petersburg rock festival *Okna otkroi!* (Open the windows!) on July 2nd, 2005.[37] Despite some technical difficulties with the vocalist Sasha's microphone during our first song, *La-la* (La-La), the sound on the stage in front of the Kirov stadium was perfect and the audience was dancing – clearly enjoying our music. Fedia, the trombone-player and I were playing our parts during the second refrain of Svoboda's cover of the Soviet cult-group Kino's hit *Mama anarkhiia* (Mother Anarchy). Accompanied by Prokhor's distorted power chords on the guitar, Fomich's booming bass, and Misha on the drums, we were mentally preparing for our solo which immediately followed the refrain when, instead, Sasha started singing. I quickly lowered my trumpet and danced along – acting like nothing happened. Fedia's reaction was, however, somewhat slower and he managed to play the first couple of notes before glaring at Sasha with an annoyed expression on his face. Sasha just continued singing and patted Fedia's back in reassurance that it was nothing to be worried about. While Fedia vented his frustration after the concert, this mistake, as well as the fact that Sasha mixed the lyrics of the second and third verse, was not commented on by our fans and was – aside from ridiculing Sasha during rehearsals – not given much further notice within the band.

Besides showing how unnoticeable small blunders are, this short fieldwork anecdote offers a good entry point into the group this study is closely linked to as well as the methodological issues surrounding this project – especially my own experience which includes questions linked to my role both as a researcher and a participant-observing musician.

At the time of the above mentioned performance, Svoboda consisted of Fedor "Fedia" Naumov (trombone), Roman "Fomich" Ushakov (bass), Mikhail "Misha" Nefedov (drums), Prokhor Ivanov (guitar), and the band leader Aleksandr "Sasha" Rudenko (vocals). The group was active within the St. Petersburg scene during my 18 month stay from 2004 until 2006: during my 9 month tenure with the band we

---

[37]. The performance can be viewed on Youtube (Svoboda 2009a).

played 33 concerts ranging from small clubs to big festivals not only in the city but also in Moscow and Lodeinoe pole.

Andrei Ivanov, one of my first contacts in St. Petersburg and the *art direktor* (booking manager) of the reggae club *Dzhambala*, introduced me to the group in March 2005. Svoboda offered me an ideal way to participate in the St. Petersburg scene as a musician in order to "learn to perform" (Baily 2001), to observe, and experience the life of a musician in St. Petersburg first hand. The band was a good choice, since it was (more or less) established within the scene, having played for about a year. Moreover, the group's ambition was to become professional, in other words, to live from their earnings, thus this also provided a way to follow the hardships involved.[38]

In addition to *experiencing* the city's musical life from a musician's perspective, the group also provided an introduction to a post-Soviet geopolitical reality, namely the complex Russian-Ukrainian relationship. By marketing itself as a *Ukrainian* ska-punk band drawing on Sasha's country of origin, the group incorporated Russian clichés of Ukraine, which were aimed at a Russian speaking audience. At the same time, the band was firmly rooted in a Soviet and Russian rock tradition, referred to as *russkii rok* (Russian rock) while the group's rhythm, harmony, and timbre drew on elements from ska, reggae, grunge, and punk. This complexity is probably most clearly expressed in the previously mentioned *Mama anarkhiia*: Being a cover of a *russkii rok*-anthem from 1986 (Kino 1986), it had been rhythmically adapted to the band's ska-punk idiom and included not only lyrics translated into Ukrainian but also Ukrainian cliché terms (I will return to the song in chapters 5 and 6).

Through my activities in Svoboda, I was also invited to participate in the budding project Con Brio, mentioned in the previous chapter, which enabled me to observe how a band started up and how its members created the band's repertoire.

These two groups enabled me to experience the dynamics of being a musician in St. Petersburg. Even though two bands are not necessarily a representative selection, I argue that the musicians active in these groups share experiences, problems, and a general approach to music making with other bands in a similar ca-

---

38. I use the term *professional* to indicate that the musicians' aim is to be full time musicians and to make a living through musical activities. The term in no way whatsoever reflects on the musicianship or quality of performance.

reer-stage and style/idiom in St. Petersburg. These observations also provided me with material to address in interviews I conducted with other musicians in St. Petersburg and my experience also overlapped with those of other musicians.

These activities, furthermore, facilitated the more observational parts of my research, whose main aim was to *observe* popular music production, while focusing on semi-professional bands from a qualitative research perspective.

My interview strategy in St. Petersburg was based on four points: Musicians from groups that were established and quite successful in the St. Petersburg scene, central actors (critics, producers, journalists etc.) within the music scene, groups and people I became acquainted with through my musical activities, and the two mentioned groups I was involved in as a trumpet-player and their fans. While the "successful" groups and central people were selected based on my observations in the field and on recommendations people gave me, the groups and people I became acquainted with were approached with an element of chance. This, to some extent, also reflects how new musicians would establish themselves in a new location. My strategy was chosen both to examine groups I thought were interesting as well as to uncover new interesting groups through a certain element of chance. Furthermore, the groups I got to know through my musical activities tended to be upward striving, but not yet as successfully established, so this contributed to a more balanced account of the scene.

My point of departure for the ethnographic interviews as well as participant observation was viewing culture as something that emerges from communication between people and which is in constant development. Through this interaction *meaning* and *meaningful forms* are produced (here I draw on the anthropologist Ulf Hannerz's use which I discussed in more detail in the previous chapter). Special attention is paid here to those meanings and meaningful forms which are embedded in music and which are externalized and distributed through media. The general approach is to examine music as *cultural and social practice* through what is normally referred to as fieldwork.

While fieldwork in a Malinowskian tradition as long term habitation in a single locale has been central to ethnomusicology (Cooley and Barz 2008) this has, in the last decades, changed in part due to an increasingly interconnected world, where both specific cultural products lose their local anchoring in a global cultural exchange through delocalization (e.g. the worldwide commodification of reggae and ska) and where global commodities are relocalized and transformed, gaining new meaning (e.g. the appropriation of ska in St. Petersburg). Our research objects[39] migrate, maintain contact with people in different localities, and exchange ideas within a transnational network. Therefore, research in one location cannot always satisfy or exhaust the topic of study.[40]

Russia has experienced several waves of emigration during the last 100 years, especially after what Russia's current president Vladimir Putin called *"krupneishei geopoliticheskoi katastrofoi veka"* (the largest geopolitical catastrophe of the century – Putin 2005), the fall of the Soviet Union, which created large emigrant communities in, inter alia, Germany, USA, and Israel. Through my combined role as a researcher and as Svoboda's trumpet-player, I experienced this first hand: After I had contacted the *Russendisko*-DJs to interview them for my dissertation, they started including Svoboda's demo in their playlists. This allowed for fieldwork in Berlin (in October 2005 and in July 2006) as well as short fieldwork stints in both New York and Vienna. The focus here was on people who were central in promoting post-Soviet music as well musicians somehow linked to the *Russendisko*.

This spatial delimitation of the field is also linked to a musical boundary: popular music, which is commonly referred to as rock (in a *broad* sense) or alternative music (discussed in the previous chapter and which I will return to in chapter 3) and more specifically, popular music locally created and perceived within the scene in St. Petersburg (linked to past and present clubs like *Moloko, TaMtAm, Platforma, Dzhambala,* and *Red Club*) as well as the *Russendisko*-scene in Berlin. The *Okna otkroi!*-performance is a case-in-point, being a festival including both lesser known bands like Svoboda as well as known bands. While playing in different idioms (rock, punk, ska-punk), the groups were united by being part of a popular musical culture sphere referred to as rock (Keightley 2001, 128). Besides following the trajectories of emigration, these musical products are interwoven within transcultural musical commodities, both adapting the commodities locally, appropriating music from each other, and feeding the products back into a

---
39. In this chapter's meta-discussion I use *research object* for the people I talked to in St. Petersburg and Berlin as a rhetorical strategy. In the remaining part of the book I use *consultant* instead since that word better reflects the agency of the people I interviewed and interacted with. They are not sterile objects, but living human beings who not only helped me but acted as consultants in my research.
40. For a more detailed discussion of these changes and new approaches defining "the field" cf. Gupta and Ferguson (1997).

transcultural web of music – which Lundberg et al. (2003, 70ff) discuss under the label *mediaization*. This is increasingly achieved through simplified circulation using the internet as a medium (besides more traditional distribution channels such as labels, record stores, and people who physically visit the locations).

To chart the fields, I primarily draw on two methodological tools: qualitative semi-structured interviews with actors within the popular music scene and participant observation. These tools, especially participant observation, raised some methodological challenges, which I will discuss below, specifically regarding different perspectives of reflexive participant observation: the researcher being reflexive about her/his actions, the impact of her/his presence, and the impact on the music.

2.1 The ethnographer's position and impact

While ethnographies have concentrated on describing the field, questions regarding the *politics of representation* and *ethnographic authority* emerged as an important issue during the late 1970s and during the 1980s. James Clifford (1986, 6) argues that the account of the field is partial or, as he calls it, "true fiction". It is "true fiction" since the account inevitably is made up by the researcher and there are always, even though unintended, exclusions from the narration. This can be due to the selection of research objects (who to include/exclude), the (shifting) focus of the research, and the general reduction of the reality that an ethnography entails. As Clifford Geertz points out

> "Cultural analysis is intrinsically incomplete. And, worse than that, the more deeply it goes the less complete it is. It is a strange science whose most telling assertions are its most tremulously based, in which to get somewhere with the matter at hand is to intensify the suspicion, both your own and that of others, that you are not quite getting it right. But that, along with plaguing subtle people with obtuse questions, is what being an ethnographer is like."
>
> (Geertz 1973, 29)

The focus on representation binds the researcher (subject) closer to the researched (object), taking into account that there is a close connection between the two and possible ethical implications in how the objects (who are equally subjects in their own right) are portrayed.

Another important issue which has gained prominence is the question of the researcher's *experience* as well as the "shadow" left in the field. In ethnomusicology the first prominent discussion was launched with the book *Shadows in the Field* (first published 1997, revised 2008). As Timothy J. Cooley, one of the editors, wrote in the first edition:

> "[W]e deliberately shift the focus of the resulting 'crisis' from *representation* (text) towards *experience* (fieldwork broadly defined). [...] [W]e wish to reframe the critical debate within postmodern social science to consider more meaningfully the aspects of the ethnographic process that position scholars though their fieldwork as social actors within the cultures they study."
>
> (Cooley 1997, 4)

This shift highlights the fact that not only is the description of the research object dependent on the researcher, the research object is also affected by the researcher. In other words, they are both social actors within the same culture. Discussing the relationship between subject and object, the anthropologist Kirsten Hastrup (1999, 146) argues that as researchers we are always part of what we study – the object cannot be studied without considering the subject (researcher). We thus have to be both conscious and reflexive of our choices. This includes examining our choices from the perspective of our research objects, in other words inverting the subject-object relation and making the researcher the object of focus.

This raises several questions: How are symbols and actions interpreted? What kind of communication is present? What perception of the researcher do the musicians and other actors have and what information are they sharing? When I share my knowledge with the local scene, how does this effect the outcome of the study? Linked to this is my experience: what is expected of me, what position I occupy, what politics underlie my actions and observations. It also touches on friendships (on both sides of the relationship) and underlying issues of power and desires connected to that. It affects the different identities or roles (Koning 1980) I had while living in St. Petersburg – as a researcher, as a (semiprofessional) musician, as a friend. This includes ethical issues (How do I, as an ethnographer, react to racist and anti-Semitic slurs? Do I conceal my Jewish identity? Do I defend migrants?), music-participational issues (How active am I in the production process in the band? How vocal am I on questions of musical quality?), marketing issues (Do I use my friends abroad to promote Svoboda? Do I create a web page for Svoboda?), and writing (When writing a CD-review of one of the groups or labels I interviewed, how does that affect my relation to that group or record label?).

The questions are delicate and shape the outcome, but are also an integral part of the research. An ethnographer inevitably carries along baggage that influences the study. This starts at such basic notions as gender/sex, musical and personal background, language knowledge, and personality. In my situation, the fact that I am a white European-American male probably helped me gain access to and acceptance within Svoboda and Con Brio.

Thus it is important that "ethnographers attempt reflexively to understand their positions in the cultures being studied and to represent these positions in ethnographies" (Cooley 1997, 17). This means, as Hastrup (1999, 150) points out, to attempt to look at oneself from the perspective of the objects – away from the first person to the second and third – in other words, becoming the research object. By ignoring both issues of representation as well as experience in the field (including the researcher's impact), the researcher runs the risk of essentializing the object's culture as something static because it withstands influences from outside and the object is not a thinking entity in itself.

Reflecting over her position in her fieldwork among Syrian Jews living in New York, the ethnomusicologist Kay Kaufman Shelemay highlights her role when she describes issues of transmission and the complex relationship between researcher and researched: "when the study of a tradition becomes part of the life of the tradition itself and relationships in the field deepen to a more interactional model" (Shelemay 2008, 149). She identifies three ways the researcher is implicated in the transmission process – preserving tradition, memorializing tradition, and mediating tradition.[41]

While my work also contributes to preserving, memorializing, and mediating popular music in St. Petersburg, the scope of how much my research will be implicated in future transmission processes remains to be seen. At the same time, through my activities as a musician in St. Petersburg, I am also a stronger part of the musical tradition transmitted than e.g. Shelemay, whose main goal was to understand, document, and maybe preserve the tradition, but not to actively take part in the music production itself.

---

41. While not to the same extent implicated in the transmission process as Shelemay, I was surprised to discover that my master's thesis (Wickström 2003), which focused on the Ragnar Vigdal tradition in traditional Norwegian vocal music and how it is performed by two contemporary singers, has been used as promotional material for a CD produced by Vigdal's grandchildren (Tonereise n.d.). Here my work was used to legitimate the Ragnar Vigdal tradition within Norwegian traditional music and, in extension, the CD-release.

My research focus differs since the main goal is not to document a "living" tradition per se, but to grasp aspects of and discourses around the musical production on the level of active bands within the St. Petersburg-scene and how they relate to transcultural flows, in other words: *How* their music becomes a commodity and is ascribed identities. I argue that the best way to do this is by actively participating in the music scene in order to experience these dynamics.

Following in the Mantle Hood tradition, Baily argues that "only as a performer does one acquire a certain essential kind of knowledge about music" (Baily 2001, 86). While an important part is acquiring musical skills and a profound knowledge of the musical culture explored, he also stresses that music making has social advantages and enables a more profound participant observation through the experiential dimension. While my learning as a band musician was primarliy focused on experiencing the life of a musician in St. Petersburg, and not so much in learning to master a new musical instrument, tonal system, or repertoire,[42] Baily's approach is also valid here. It enabled me to chart discourses around music which would not have been open to me as a non-playing participant observer (e.g. taking the role as a "fan" or "groupie") simply due to the fact that being a co-musician includes and ties one to a band in a much stronger way than mere observation does – as the opening anecdote regarding the skipped solo demonstrates. This includes observations on how songs were rehearsed, influences on the songs, information on how the band style was formed, life as an active performing musician, and the discourse around *russkii rok*, *popsa*, and *underground*. It also means that I have a bigger responsibility towards the band when leaving/winding down my fieldwork.

The decision to be an active musician entailed making some choices: since the band was active, striving to be professional, I had to make an effort to maintain a level of quality in my playing and be active in band-related matters (what parts I should play, issues of quality related to rehearsals and concerts). These issues became more important when I was, to a degree, dependent on the income after my DAAD-grant expired in October 2005.

---

42. This is not to imply that I was competent in the musical styles played, this was also something I had to acquire. However, this learning was primarily focused on learning my parts and the corresponding Russian/Soviet references, not so much technique, harmony, or a different tonal system.

At the same time, I consciously kept a distance to issues relevant to my research, using a stronger observer and less participatory stance – I did not question the use of songs in our repertoire or the musical style of the group, did not impose my views on democracy, civil society, or xenophobia, but tried to observe the discourse around these aspects which are part of their life (and my research aim).

The question that arises here is that through being too active, the researcher risks overlooking important aspects as well as influencing the results. While these are valid points, they do not take into consideration that any presence of the researcher has an impact on observations made and thus the outcome of the study: my mere presence in itself had an impact on the band, the internal dynamics, and how they dealt with me.

2.1.1 My impact and how I was perceived

As previously mentioned, being reflexive not only involves making choices but also being able to examine these choices and how they are perceived from the perspective of the research objects. This includes how the researcher's presence is perceived. Issues the researcher is aware of are not necessarily issues the research objects share and vice versa. Furthermore, how the researcher is perceived by the research objects – the ascribed identity – also determines the course of the research, reflexive decisions made by the researcher, and, finally, how the research objects are represented in the ethnography.

As discussed in the previous chapter, identities function within a social frame and constitute themselves in part based on identities shared with other individuals (e.g. taste in music, political views, religion, ethnicity, and place of residence): As a researcher doing fieldwork, I drew on certain habits to shape my *researcher identity* when presenting myself as an ethnomusicologist doing research on Russian popular music. The main habits used for this representation of myself were my formal education as an ethnomusicologist, my experience as a musician, as well as my social and language skills. Other factors influencing those habits also emerged as determining – e.g. the fact I had only studied Russian for a year before venturing to St. Petersburg (influencing my habit of speaking Russian and clearly marking me as a foreigner) and my slightly complicated personal history (which I for simplicity reduced to either saying I was from Norway or Berlin – depending on the circumstance).

Furthermore, my researcher identity was also shaped by the identities ascribed to me by those I interacted with in St. Petersburg. While these were based on shared identities the constituting elements were different. The ethnomusicologist Jos Koning argues that

> "[t]he research technique of musical participation induces informants to apply to the fieldworker those roles with which they are familiar and which seem to suit the fieldworker's behavior best. Therefore, the fieldworker's behavior is experienced by his informants as role behavior, and as such has consequences for the behavior of others."
>
> (Koning 1980, 428)

Koning discusses the discrepancy between the role (or identity) a researcher assumes (or tries to assume) and the roles (or identities) available in and ascribed to the researcher by the community – which are linked with specific expectations and actions on both sides. Here the fact that I was active as a trumpet-player in Svoboda ascribed to me the role of a musician. Since most of the brass-players I talked to had some kind of higher musical education, this identity somehow assumed that I had a conservatory education (which I never claimed to have) – ascribing to me a predefined identity based on other musicians' habits. Furthermore, since the concept of an ethnomusicologist studying popular music was not too common among the people I talked to, I was often introduced by others as a music critic – a role musicians were more accustomed to using for a person who interviewed musicians.

In other words, even though my research identity was built on identities shared with or known to others, these identities often took certain assumed habits as a basis for granted which I did not have and which were hard to rebut. While this did not lead to any major problems, it did at times result in some confusion about who I was, where additional clarification from my side was then needed.

Being a foreigner was probably the most defining element of how the group and fans perceived me, both in a positive but also, I think, in a negative sense. My identity as a foreigner was used in and after concerts to point out that I was not Russian and hence indirectly not one of them: during an interview with a television channel after the mentioned *Okna otkroi!*-performance Sasha cut off the question directed to me by saying I could not speak Russian since I was a foreigner. Svoboda's former bass-player tended to address me in terms of *gastarbaiter* (guest-worker, normally used for transmigrants from the former Soviet Union) and I am still not quite sure when it was used with negative, when with positive connotations.

On the other hand, the fact that I was a foreigner also generated much interest and has been used by Sasha as a sign of status as the following excerpt from Svoboda's website demonstrates:

> "In the beginning of 2005 David-Emil Wickström – trumpet / citizen of Austria and USA – enters the group. He arrived to study Russian, but, hitting upon Svoboda, also Ukrainian contemporary music"
>
> (Rudenko n.d. – Russian: p. 327)

Thus I was (and still am) used to position the group as something special within the St. Petersburg music scene – here my role is almost correctly ascribed (I was not involved in writing the text).[43]

This perception of me being a foreigner also involved expectations: Sasha wanted me to promote Svoboda and organize concerts abroad through contacts I have. His ambitions brought up the dilemma that I did not think the band was ready for touring abroad.

This is an ethical problem which arises within fieldwork. On the one hand, the researcher is deeply thankful for the help s/he gets from his/her research objects and would like to help. On the other hand, being an outsider can also bring in knowledge which can dampen these aspirations.[44]

My musical activities also defined my musical persona and how I was perceived. Not only did it positively impact on my playing and stage presence, but I was also to some extent a professional musician just based on the amount of concerts I played and I shared many of the experiences and responsibilities my fellow band mates had (e.g. rehearsing, how to get home after the concerts late at night).

---

43. This "role" has changed now that I am not in the group anymore. My last "official" status (which is purely representational) was "second trumpet and exclusive representative of Svoboda in Europe" (Rudenko n.d. – Russian: p. 327).
44. In my case I decided that I would hand out Svoboda's demo (Svoboda 2005) to potential contacts abroad and if they were interested I would function as a mediator. This resulted in the song *Marusia* being released on the *Russendisko* compilation *Ukraine do Amerika* (Various Artists 2008c) and being included in the movie *Russendisko* (released 2012) as well as the accompanying soundtrack (Various Artists 2012b). At the same time I was quite clear in telling Sasha that the band was not ready to go on tour (mainly due to quality issues and a too small repertoire), thus striking a balance between fulfilling the desires of the research object and advising the group on what should be done. Shelemay (2008, 146f) discusses similar negotiations where her authority as a researcher was used for issues within the Jewish community.

This together with my knowledge of music in St. Petersburg both contributed to uncovering aspects of popular music production in St. Petersburg as well as facilitated contacts I made both in St. Petersburg (e.g. joining Con Brio as a trumpet-player) and in Berlin (gaining access to the *Russendisko*-DJs and *Eastblok Music*).

Related to this is how involved one gets with one's research objects and how a professional distance is maintained, the "negotiation of human relations in the field" (Shelemay 2008, 149). Here issues of asymmetric power, underlying agendas and motives, as well as possible manipulation figure. In order to build rapport with the research objects, one has to establish contact and become friendly with them. But when this relationship matures, where are the boundaries between acquaintance and friendship?

Fieldwork is not a clear-cut division between subject and object where the subject is in total control, but a holistic whole, where both the researcher and the research objects are acting subjects who create meaning based on their social and cultural history and their own experiences. At the very least, the researcher has to, as a token of respect, take into consideration the results of his/her impact – including friendship. The ethnomusicologist Ruth Hellier-Tinoco concludes an article by saying that researchers have to regard

> "the field as an intrinsic element in our normal lives and the relationships within the field as requiring of us the same responsibility, reciprocity and commitment that we give to our 'normal' life relationships. [...] Whilst the field may or may not be our home, it is home for those people with whom we form relationships. We are all experiencing people, we are not play-acting: this is for real."
> (Hellier-Tinoco 2003)

That much said, as researchers we also have to ask ourselves why a person is friendly with us and critically reflect on the relationship and underlying politics. It also includes whether the research object/friend is well aware of the researcher's position. Andrei Ivanov, one of my first contacts in the field, and I became good friends during my stay in St. Petersburg. He was, and still is, well aware that I was in St. Petersburg to conduct fieldwork on Russian music and we discuss Russian popular music when we are together. But we also discuss other topics like German music, food, *bania* (sauna), and everyday experiences, and these topics overlap.

Asymmetric issues of power and desire are present in this relationship as well e.g. I gather information about Russian music and Andrei practices his German with me. Andrei has his idea of music in St. Petersburg and what should be studied (which mainly consists of his friends' groups), which does not always coincide with my research priorities. Here I have to be aware of his perception of music and listen to it, but not let it guide my research.

In Berlin my relations to both Yuriy Gurzhy from the *Russendisko* as well as Armin Siebert and Alex Kasparov from the record label Eastblok Music should be seen in light of the fact that they work with post-Soviet music so they also had a professional interest in me and my research as a possible way to find new groups.

Being so closely involved with Svoboda and Con Brio also means that I have to be reflexive on judging what material to use and be careful regarding compromising issues. This touches issues which would be considered problematic in a Northern European context, like homophobic, racial, and anti-semitic slurs, but which in Russia are a prominent part of the public discourse.[45] This has implications for representation, since such remarks can also color my perception of the individuals and how I portray them. However, due to the close relationship, it is also easier to see beyond such remarks than if I had only met the person once (especially since the use of *stiob*, a special Russian form of irony delivered with a straight face, is quite common, and can be perceived as very provocative).

Fieldwork experience is, however, not only limited to a researcher's public or official life, it also touches one's private life. All actions contribute to a deeper understanding of the culture one lives in. The fact that my partner is from St. Petersburg initiated this project, helped me practically come to St. Petersburg, and to understand different parts of the Russian language and culture. Spending time with my partner's friends and family also opened my eyes to different aspects of Russian popular music, which would not have emerged to such a degree had I limited myself to my research objects. This includes observations on the rise of consumer items like computers or new TVs, financed (mostly) through short term loans.[46] It also includes observations on how people socialize – mostly with a

---

45. This is not to say that these issues are absent in Europe where xenophobia, especially in the forms of anti-semitism and islamophobia are on the rise. Discrimination against minorities – like the Danish Mohammed caricature scandal in 2005 – is often hidden under the vail of freedom of expression where the majority decries (self-)censorship if criticized. However, freedom of speech does not mean that anything goes – respect for human dignity of the minorities remains – something often forgotten by the majority. In defense of Russia I want to note that during my four years in Denmark as well as my years living Norway, Austria, and Germany I have on several occasions been personally reminded of how the majority neglects both ethnic and religious minorities.
46. These short term loans, which have become increasingly popular in Russia during the last few years, enable the acquisition of consumer products like MP3-players, multimedia cell

TV running, playing (Russian) popular music (*popsa*/Russian pop) and *shanson*, styles not included in my research. In other words, I was able to experience the role of music in their lives (what kind of music they listen to on a daily basis, how they listen to music), generational, and social differences, including different value hierarchies when talking about music, and the daily routines, and problems of middle-class inhabitants of St. Petersburg. This is also participant observation, but a very intimate form, which is generally not that accessible to a foreigner with a limited research time frame. Even though I do not consider this part of my life in St. Petersburg a direct part of my research, the paths between private, and professional life cross, and these observations give an added dimension to help me understand and interpret my research material from a different angle, and place it within a broader context.

Finally, the researcher's imprint is also present in the written representation of the field – this book. Besides filtering, and reducing the material to the scope of a book, this includes both general research decisions (St. Petersburg, rock scene) as well as the previously mentioned aspects.[47] When writing the ethnography, an important aspect has been to let my research objects themselves "speak", especially when s/he voices a common opinion shared by other actors I have talked to, and/or my own observations.[48] This also applies to the use of song lyrics and musical material to demonstrate a point.

My imprint also touches the theoretical focus. It is, in part, colored by my personal background of moving and living in different countries, which has made me aware of different layers of identities (both personal and collective) and how these can be used to both include and exclude (e.g. nationalism).

2.1.2 My musical impact

Moving away from the interpersonal level, my presence in the field can also be heard. Besides the *Okna otkroi!*-performance, this also includes demo recordings

---

phones, TVs, and computers.
47. One example is an article Yngvar Steinholt and I co-authored about Russian popular culture (Steinholt and Wickström 2008) which was criticized by two of Steinholt's students for being written from the perspective of St. Petersburg and rock. This critique is justified to some extent since we both have done our primary research in St. Petersburg on rock music, and this thus colored the article.
48. Taking the musicians perspective into account the utterances also have to be critically examined especially regarding questions of self-promotion.

of both Svoboda (2005), and Con Brio (2006). Being an active musician in those two groups also implied that my playing to some extent influenced the groups' style. This both includes my personal trumpet sound as well as the parts themselves. When I joined Svoboda, their repertoire consisted of about 13 songs that drew on *style indicators* (cf. p. 156 and Tagg 1999) from ska (*Mama anarkhiia*) via reggea (*Ganzhubeilo* – Marijuana) to punk (*Super para* – Super Couple). The parts I played were, to a large extent, doubling the trombone and/or playing some of the guitar riffs. The arrangements were influenced by musical ideas that came up during the rehearsals as well as by the technical abilities and limitations in my playing: My jazz background and ability to improvise also colored the band's playing style and directly influenced two songs in our repertoire (*Detstvo* – Childhood – and *Pogoda* – Weather). I also added a harmony part to the song *Marusia* (diminutive of Mary – mainly by doubling the melody in the refrain, playing my part a third up) with the intention to make it sound more "folksy" and "Ukrainian". The harmony idea was also based on *my* notion of folk(lore) harmony, not necessarily Ukrainian practice. This was accepted by Sasha and the other bandmates. However, Sasha always retained the last word in terms of musical style, which resulted in some other suggestions I made regarding melody/harmonization not being accepted. The band's aesthetic foundation was thus quite solidified. During the period I played, we did not compose any new songs, so I was not involved in creating new trumpet parts from scratch, and I generally tried to be passive when it came to questions of composition and arrangements.

The style of the group is in constant development, depending on different musicians who have left "their" mark (cf. chapter 5 and chapter 6 for a more thorough discussion of the group's style and development) – including myself. The guitar sound changed when Prokhor Ivanov left and Sergei Klets entered the group. The same can be said of the horn section, where new arrangements were made (while the general structure of the riffs was retained) by Mikhail Kuril'chik, the trumpet-player who replaced me (pers. comm., 21.06.2006). Thus, the songs that were recorded in 2007 and 2008 – while structurally the same – *sound* quite different from what I played.

The situation in Con Brio was slightly different, since they were in the process of creating their repertoire – so here more creative input from my side was wanted. That said, Vitia already had the parts he wanted me to play thought out (including how it should sound), so I was limited, and when I tried to vary the parts I was usually directed to play it the way he wanted it.

In both cases I tried to remain passive as much as possible and primarily play what I was told to play. My research aim was to both observe the discourses in the band as well as to get an understanding of the style played (what references were used, how the band identity was constructed) as well as the internal band dynamics (power relations in the group, motivation of the band members). Since both bands' images were already quite solidified by Sasha and Vitia, my presence did not have any significant influence in that respect, neither did I comment on these issues.

2.2 Concluding remarks

In this description of my methodology, I have focused on the decisions I made and highlighted my positions in the field. Doing fieldwork neither as a student of a "master", nor as an observer, but as an active musician, enables possibilities in exploring the conditions for musicians in a certain locality: experiencing the general treatment at clubs, interacting with listeners and other musicians, and being a participant in the (creative) decisions making process during rehearsals and concerts. These observations are more restricted for non-performing researchers, since they are generally watching from the side, not directly involved with the different actors present and thus have a different status both within the group, as well as amongst the fans and club management. Doing research as a musician-participant-observer also has pitfalls – primarily that one's presence influences the music played, but also more general issues of asymmetric power structures that arise between the researcher and the researched have to be considered.

In general, a critical reflection on one's position also gives a clearer understanding of a study's limitations and boundaries. In my case, my work focused on musicians and not fans, discussed rock music, not music referred to as *popsa*, *estrada*, or *shanson*, and was geographically limited to primarily St. Petersburg. These decisions in turn also exclude, amongst others, a comparative study of Russian popular music geographically as well as genrewise.

A reflexive approach thus gives the reader the necessary perspective to understand the researcher's involvement and narrative focus – as in the following chapter structured around Svoboda's experience in St. Petersburg.

3 The St. Petersburg scene

> "Let's drink to our acquaintance!"[49]
> Andrei Ivanov, pers. comm., 22.10.2004

It was a nice Friday in October. I arrived a little early at the reggae club *Dzhambala* at Bol'shoi pr. 80 on Vasil'evskii Island. This was my third week in St. Petersburg and I was looking for a band to play in. Earlier that week I had called the local reggae musician Dr. I-Bolit (aka Andrei "Rastaman" Kunitsyn) with whom I had spoken during a previous visit that year at the now defunct club *Moloko*. Back then he said he was looking for a trumpet-player and that I should contact him once I had moved to the city.

I entered the club and asked for Andrei. I was promptly directed to a person who did not really resemble the Andrei I had spoken to a couple of months earlier, but I decided that my mind was just playing tricks on me. I introduced myself and was just going to ask about playing the trumpet when Andrei said *"Davai vyp'em za znakomstvo"* (Let's drink to our acquaintance)!

That evening did not end too well. After three shots of vodka I figured out that Andrei was not the Dr. I-Bolit I was supposed to meet. When Dr. I-Bolit finally arrived (wearing a top hat in the Jamaican tri-color and mentally in another dimension – cf. Picture 13, p. 162) he did not show any interest in my trumpet playing or having me in the band. The other Andrei, however, was continuing to offer me vodka and trying to speak German to me. I somehow managed the one hour ride back to my apartment in the Ozerki-region on foot, by subway, and *marshrutka* (fixed route taxi) before passing out and experiencing my first black out ever.

This shock emersion in Russian drinking culture was something I gradually learned to cope with during my stay in St. Petersburg. More importantly, Andrei Ivanov, who turned out to be *Dzhambala's art direktor*, and I became good friends and he eventually hooked me up with the group Svoboda which formed the basis for my research.

---

49. *Davai vyp'em za znakomstvo!*

This short fieldwork anecdote serves as an introduction to an important social hub in the St. Petersburg music scene, the club and, arguably its musically most influential person, the club's booking manager. This meeting was also formative in my fieldwork since it introduced me to one of my key consultants and thus also to Svoboda, the band I was active in as a participant observing musician.

In other words, this encounter was a key factor in enabling my access to the St. Petersburg music scene and its musical practice, whose description is this chapter's main aim. Drawing on my main fieldwork the chapter is written from Svoboda's perspective. The observations are combined with those of other, more established musicians and other agents outlining the St. Petersburg scene during my time in the city. This is done to broaden the discussion through pointing to shared experiences within the St. Petersburg scene.

I will start with a description of the network underlying the St. Petersburg scene and the important physical locations used for activities, before touching on some important common discourses within the scene. In order to anchor the discussion in a (post-)Soviet reality I will also give some historical context. By doing this I want to focus on the interconnectedness of musical activities in St. Petersburg and highlight the fluid boundaries. In addition, the historical context is necessary to grasp the specificity of the St. Petersburg scene in the 2000s. Besides showing similarities to other locations, this description also highlights what makes St. Petersburg unique.

3.1 Social networks

> "For me scene is a term, where you have many people who somehow think similarly, have a similar notion of music, and constantly exchange [this notion with each other]. So in Petersburg [...] you see somehow 10 Bands. If you look closer, there are about 20 musicians who play in 10 Bands."
>
> (Gurzhy 2005 – German: p. 312)

A key element of scenes – both in the colloquial use (as Yuriy Gurzhy's quote above) as well as in a theoretical use – is the building of musical alliances whose basis is a network of musicians and other actors within the cultural scene. Through the musicians' activities on the form of life level, they interact with other musicians, which, in turn, provides the basis for networks. Within these networks the musicians share information about new albums, concert venues, instruments, and gossip. These networks also support the groups providing them with backup musicians (or even replacements) as well as a pool of musicians and groups to draw on when organizing concerts and mini-festivals. This in turn provides a basis for shared experiences and ideas.

Figure 1: Network diagram I – Group-networks in St. Petersburg.

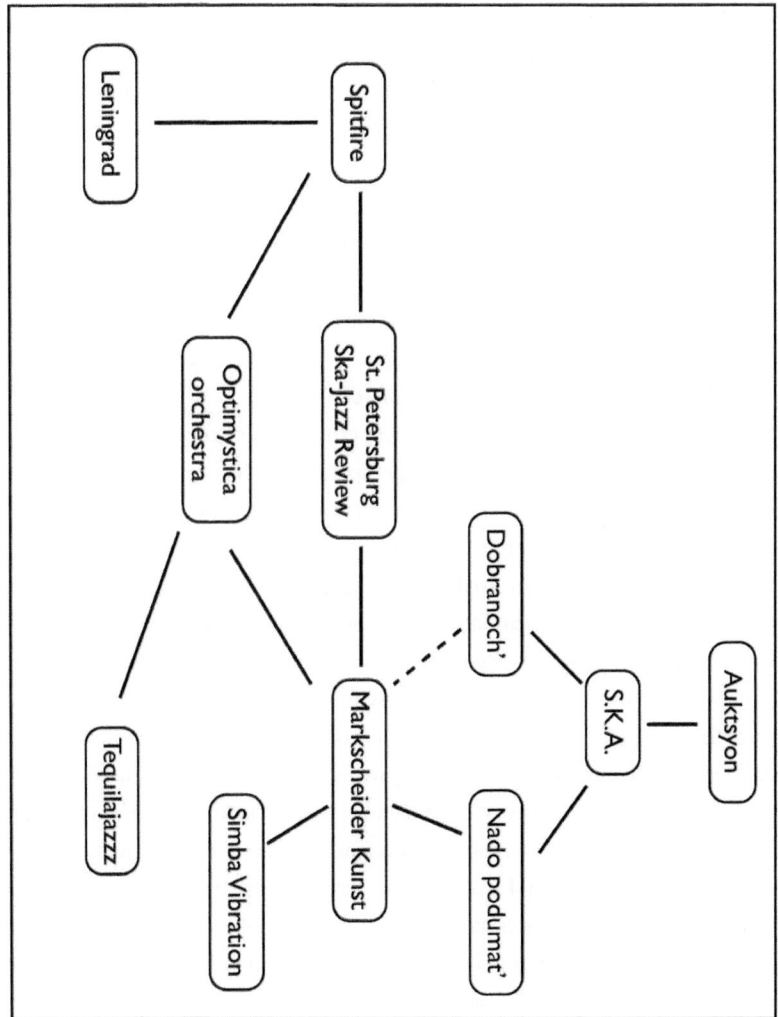

Several people I talked to in St. Petersburg stressed the vibrancy and quantity of groups in the city's music community as being an advantage. A closer look also uncovers networks and relationships between the groups, just as Yuriy's quote points out. These range from friends being used as guest-musicians both at concerts and on recordings to groups consisting of overlapping musicians.

One of the more well-known examples in St. Petersburg is the group Spitfire. In 2002, while remaining a separate group, the members also became a part of the group Leningrad. Furthermore, some musicians from Spitfire joined forces with musicians from Markscheider Kunst to create the group St. Petersburg Ska-Jazz Review. Both groups also participate in Evgenii Fedorov's (Tequilajazzz) side project Optimystica orchestra. In addition, the musicians often perform as guests on other groups' recordings. Former musicians from Markscheider Kunst have also started their own side projects, for example, the trombonist Ramil' Shamstudinov's Nado podumat' and the vocalist Seraphim Selenge Makangila's Simba Vibration. Nado podumat' also draws on musicians from S.K.A. and Dobranoch' (the violinist Dmitri Khramtsov used to play in Markscheider Kunst) – S.K.A also shares musicians with Auktsyon and so on (cf. Figure 1).

Such overlapping is not limited to these groups: Another, more historic example, is found with the members of the group Strannye Igry (cf. p. 168) who went on to play in Avia, NOM, and Deadushki. In other words, groups in St. Petersburg are closely connected, as Yuriy's statement implies.

While the musicians involved in these bands – some of whom appear in the following pages – provide an interesting case of how the groups are entwined in overlapping networks, they also belong to some of the most established groups in St. Petersburg. Because of this, I would like to refocus on the lesser known bands, since they are more representative of the overall scene. One such group is Svoboda. Here I will focus on four overlapping networks central to Svoboda and its musical activities: past and present band members, contacts to other bands, fans, and clubs. As the club discussion shows, musicians in St. Petersburg (as well as in other cities such as Berlin and Copenhagen) have different roles – besides playing music (and in some instances pursuing their day time job) they also occupy different roles within the scene e.g. booking, management, renting out practice space, running studios, and working as DJs. These jobs draw on the musician's network in the scene thus highlighting its importance.

Picture 2:   Svoboda. From left to right: Fedia, Prokhor, Sasha, me, and Fomich.[50] Picture taken in St. Petersburg in 2005.

3.1.1 Svoboda

Svoboda's vocalist Sasha is the center of the group. Originally from Eastern Ukraine, he moved to the city in 2000 (and became a Russian citizen around the same time). Besides vocational training as a cook, he has pursued studies as an ac-

---

50. An acquaintance of Prokhor was a fashion student who designed the outfits worn in the picture as her final exam at a fashion school (except for Prokhor we did not perform in them).

tor and director, first in Ukraine and later in Moscow. Another reason for leaving Ukraine in the mid 1990s was a feeling of alienation through the growing process of Ukrainization – coming from Eastern Ukraine he grew up speaking Russian (Rudenko 2006). Having founded the first version of Svoboda while at theatre school in Moscow, he revived Svoboda in St. Petersburg in 2003 and the group started to perform in 2004.

Despite being relatively new in the city, Sasha has actively built his network including musicians and other actors within the scene – amongst them Andrei who brought me to the band. When I joined the group as a trumpet-player in March 2005, the group already had a trombone-player and was – except for the drummer Misha – identical to the line up discussed in the methodology chapter (cf. p. 69).[51]

The turnover rate in the band was quite high. Konstantin "Shliapa" Panchuk, the drummer when I joined, was, by April 2005, replaced by Misha (but he remained a backup drummer since Misha primarily played the paid gigs). When I left the band in February, 2006 I was – besides Sasha – the last musician to remain from the line up when I started. Some musicians had been kicked out of the band due to poor playing, others decided to leave because of disagreements with Sasha, in order to pursue other projects, or because they had been drafted (cf. Figure 2 for Svoboda's band members and network). This kind of fluctuation was quite common and was also pointed out to me by other musicians. A reason for this is that many bands in St. Petersburg are centered around a singer-songwriter who then finds musicians to play in their project.[52]

After my departure the line up has remained more or less stable – both Sergei Liubarskii (trombone) and Mikhail Kuril'chik (trumpet), who replaced Fedia and me, as well as Sergei Klets (guitarist – joined end of 2005) and Sergei "Pankrat" Mishchenkov (bass – joined 2006, replaced Misha who replaced Fomich) were still active in the band when I returned for some additional fieldwork in 2008.[53]

---

51. In other words, the group consisted of a vocalist, a rhythm section (electric guitar, drums, and bass) and a horn section. After my departure, the horn section was extended to include a bass trombone. An accordion was included in the line up in 2008.
52. This is particularly evident with the LRK-groups still active like Akvarium, Televizor, Alisa, and DDT – they are all based around one front-person.
53. The line up has since changed again – in part because Sasha moved back to Ukraine around 2011.

Figure 2: Network diagram II – Svoboda's musical network.

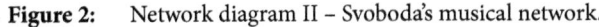

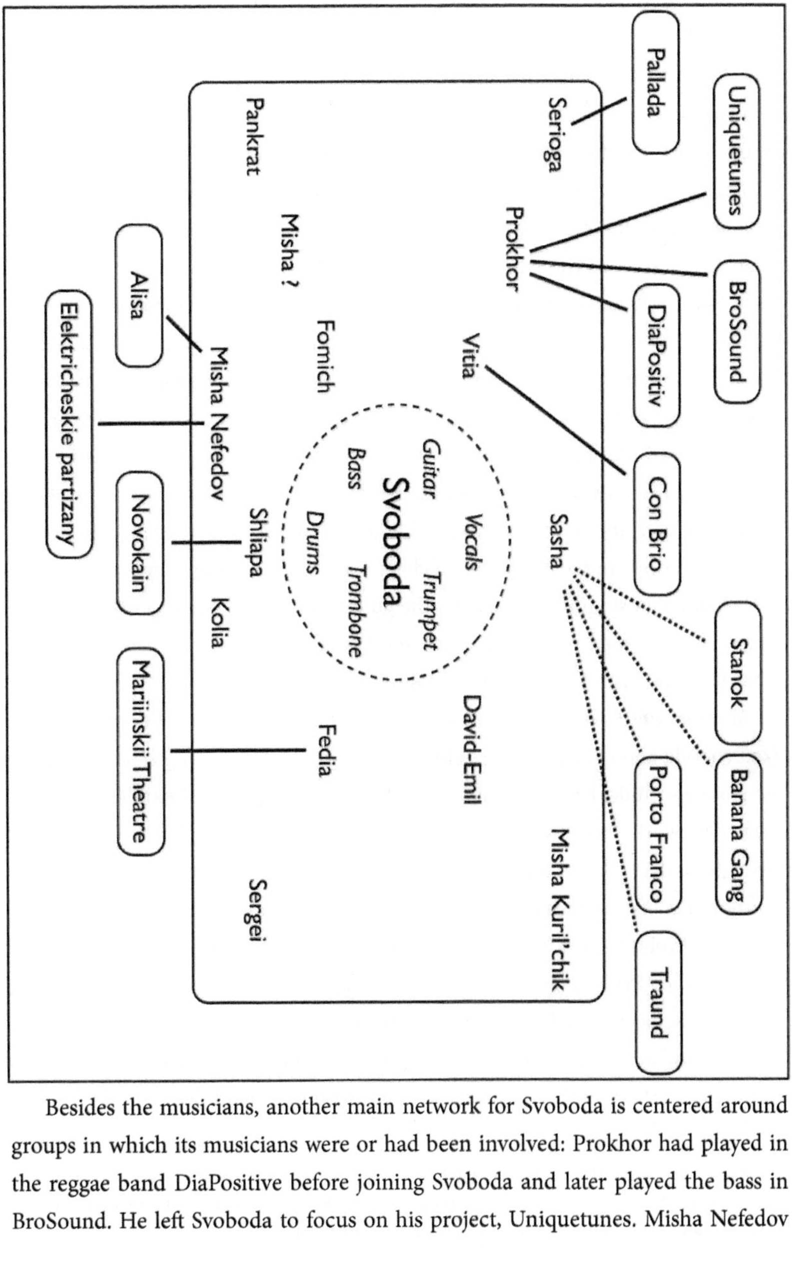

Besides the musicians, another main network for Svoboda is centered around groups in which its musicians were or had been involved: Prokhor had played in the reggae band DiaPositive before joining Svoboda and later played the bass in BroSound. He left Svoboda to focus on his project, Uniquetunes. Misha Nefedov had been the drummer in Alisa and in addition to Svoboda also played in Elektricheskie partizany. Finally, Shliapa was the drummer in Novokain, Sergei was active in the group Pallada while Fedia was part of the stage orchestra at the *Mariinskii Theatre* (St. Petersburg's main opera house).

Related to this is also the musical alliances maintained by (mainly) Sasha – groups who could be contacted if we were to organize a concert/festival and needed other bands as warm-up or to fill a festival set. These partially consisted of the Svoboda musicians' other bands, newly emerging bands, e.g. Traund (a punk band where the musicians were around 20 years old), bands playing similar music (e.g. Porto Franco, Banana Gang) or bands friendly with Sasha (e.g. Stanok).

Former Svoboda musicians were also part of these networks such as Viktor "Vitia" Kultashov. Answering an ad for a grunge band looking for a guitar-player, Vitia joined Svoboda as one of the founding members. He stayed for a year and helped prepare the program, then left after the first concert since he had found another, in his eyes, more promising group. When Svoboda's guitarist Prokhor, however, could not play in a concert, Vitia was called, which resulted in the rehearsal described in the beginning of chapter 1 and me joining Con Brio.[54]

Besides Vita singing and playing the guitar there was Zhenia on the bass and his brother Lesha on the drums. Vitia and the brothers had met through another project called Dusty Hills, which played heavy metal.

In other words, most of the immediate contacts were with other groups who, like Svoboda and Con Brio, were either starting out or becoming established. But there are also links between Svoboda and the more established bands mentioned in the "Network diagram I – Group-networks in St. Petersburg" (p. 89), especially through Sasha, who spent a lot of time talking to members of Spitfire and Leningrad – one of Sasha's main inspirational sources – with the aim of having them use Svoboda as a warm up band for their concerts. Through Prokhor and Andrei Ivanov Svoboda had contacts to the reggae groups active in St. Petersburg, including Reggistan and Ackee Ma-Ma (discussed in chapter 5) and the reggae club Dzhambala. These links were also audible since Svoboda often performed with reggae groups and Dzhambala was one Svoboda's main performance venues.

---

54. While Con Brio – the working name of the project – rehearsed twice a week, the group actually did not perform during my tenure. Instead, the time was used to prepare the repertoire and to record three of the songs to be used on a demo.

Sasha also pursued the music critic Andrei Burlaka, who was frequently seen at concerts. Burlaka knew most of the groups discussed here (including Svoboda). Another person Sasha spent a lot of time pursuing was the (legendary) record producer Andrei Tropillo, whose studio Sasha wanted to use for Svoboda's first album.[55]

Thus, as with the established bands, the more unknown bands also have overlapping networks to draw from in their musical activities. While I, in the following discussion, at times distinguish between Svoboda's network and those of established bands, which, besides those mentioned above, include Iva Nova, Billy's Band, and Severnye Vrata, there was a surprising overlap in opinions within the discourses mentioned in 3.3 "Discursive scene boundaries" (p. 114ff). This is why I choose to discuss them together and, if necessary, point out differences.

---

55. Being probably the most important rock recording engineer and producer in Leningrad of the 1980s, he is dedicated to promoting groups which embody the LRK spirit (Tropillo 2005) – both the "old" groups (which he also recorded in the 1980s like Kino, Zoopark, and Akvarium) as well as contemporary groups such as PTVP and Mata Khari. Furthermore, he is involved in festivals like the 2005 *Pivnoi Festival'* (26.06.2005) where Svoboda played on the stage he (co)-organized. Cf. Steinholt (2005) and McMichael (2009) for a discussion of his role in the 1980s.

Picture 3: Denis Vashkevich. Denis is proudly showing his posters of Konstantin Kinchev, Alisa's vocalist. Picture taken in St. Petersburg in 2006.

3.1.2 Fans

"[Denis ...] let me listen to those three songs and they fell on my soul – especially Otstoi [Trash]. Now, for some reason a song that stands out, but very merry because I recognize myself in that song. Just about every morning. [laughs]"

(Anton in Vashkevich and Lukanin 2006 – Russian: p. 318)

The fans, such as the quoted Anton Lukanin, make up an important band support network. While not necessarily musicians themselves they support the group by being present at the concerts and by dancing and vocally supporting the band – even at out-of-town concerts: Denis Vashkevich and Anton followed us to Lodeinoe Pole where we gave two concerts (03.-04.02.2006) and to Moscow where Svoboda performed at the club *B2* (14.09.2005). During the latter trip we benefitted from their network of friends. Denis contacted Iurii, a friend of theirs living in Moscow, where we stayed while waiting for the concert to begin. Iurii, in turn, called his friends and thus managed to organize some local fans. Svoboda was also hired to play at Denis' wedding.

While Denis and Anton were probably Svoboda's most dedicated fans, there were also other fans who regularly came to our concerts and supported the band morally by creating a positive atmosphere at the gigs.

The fans are a direct financial asset (by paying the cover charge at clubs, buying CDs and merchandise and thus contributing to the band's income). Dedicated fans are, however, equally important as indirect financial assets by knowing the songs and thus participating more profoundly and actively creating a good atmosphere in the audience. This adds to the band's reputation of being a good live band – which is important when promoting the group.[56] Sasha also recognized the importance of the dedicated fans by letting them participate in the performance, putting some of them on the guest list or trying to smuggle them into the concert venue.[57]

---

56. The quality of the performance often depended on our fans and their moral support: Both with them as well as people dancing and having a good time present we got energy from the audience which motivated us to play better and in a more concentrated way.
57. The most extreme example was cramming about 10 people in a small transporter when Svoboda played at *Okna otkroi!* (02.07.2005). Ironically Fomich, who was driving, had to bribe a police officer due to a traffic violation (too many people in the transporter) – however, Sasha managed to argue us through the concert security.

3.1.3 Band promotion

"Friday – last day at work and on Nashe Radio [...] they announce [...] 'Club Moloko: Brigadnyi Podriad.' [...] Called my at that time still future wife. 'Let's go?' – 'Well, let's go'. And Svoboda performed first."

(Denis in Vashkevich and Lukanin 2006 – Russian: p. 318)

In order to make the group visible to fans, promotion is very important: *Nashe Radio* (Our Radio – cf. p. 135f and 211ff), the radio station Denis refers to, is, together with *Radio Roks* (Radio Rock) and other stations, an important medium in announcing upcoming concerts.[58] Concerts are also listed in newspapers and magazines (e.g. *Fuzz, Time Out St. Petersburg, St. Petersburg Times*). However, most of the promotion was left to the bands.

Due to congested roads and constant traffic jams, the subway, which transported about 2.3 million passengers a day in 2005 (Ivanova 2008) and is the most reliable way to travel in the city, is an ideal location for band promotion. One of St. Petersburg's specialities is the long escalator ride down to the trains. This makes the escalators ideal places to advertise and they – as well as the subway cars – are plastered with stickers announcing concerts (as well as stickers inciting racial hatred[59]) – even though the cleaning personnel regularly scrape them off.

Besides stickers, word of mouth, and cellphone text-messages, forms of band promotion included posters and flyers for upcoming concerts. The flyers could be found at the clubs, record stores, and were also handed out by members of the bands. As also common in Western Europe, the fliers would sometimes give a discount on the cover charge (as in Picture 4) or draw attention to a reduced cover charge if the tickets were bought in advance.

The production of promotional material varied: sometimes the flyers were created by the clubs hosting the concerts (normally using a template with the club's

---

58. *Radio Roks* also hosts the program *Russkii rok* moderated by Zhenia Gliuk which features local bands.
59. Stickies proclaiming *Rossiia dlia Russkikh* (Russia for the ethnic Russians – cf. Picture 18, p. 210 for graffiti with that slogan) or displaying how Jews or people from the Caucasus are bound to take over Russia were common sights. There were also instances of sticker-dialogue. This was clearly seen after the brutal murder of the musician and anti-fashist Timur Kacharava on November 13th, 2005 by a group of Neo-Nazis. Following his assassination stickies commemorating him showing his profile with the writing *Timur – my pomnim* (Timur – we remember) appeared. Around January/February 2006 new stickies with his profile and *Timur – nam pokhui* (Timur – we don't give a fuck) started to surface in the subway.

logo and adding the names and/or logos of the performing band), sometimes by the band (or associates of the band with designer possibilities and capabilities). While most were either copied or printed on normal paper some, especially from clubs like *Red Club*, *Rossi's*, and *Moloko* were printed on sturdier, sometimes even glossy paper. Posters tended to be large versions of the flyers. While some clubs would hang up posters, this as well as distributing stickies and flyers was mostly left to the bands themselves to do, something Sasha often tried to delegate to Fomich and Fedia since they had cars.

Picture 4: Flyer from Markscheider Kunst (*Red Club*, 23.09.2005). The cover-charge with flyer was 200 rubles, without, 250.

Websites were also a way to promote bands, however this was not too common due to slow connection speeds (during my stay dial-up modem was the standard way to get connected) and musicians lacking computers. Those websites that existed were mostly very basic in the programming and layout, using free advertisement-financed site hosting, and primarily in Russian. While I designed and maintained Svoboda's site, it was not an important asset within St. Petersburg and in getting us booked there. The site did, however, help us get included in the *Russendisko* (cf. chapter 9).

The internet as a medium to promote the bands I was looking at first took off after I left St. Petersburg in 2006, especially through social networking sites like *myspace* and *vkontakte* (in contact) – Russia's answer to *facebook*. Today much band promotion has moved online, including downloadable flyers.

While the bulk of the promotion work rested on the bands themselves, the band's network – in particular the fans – was an important resource, affixing stickers around town and handing out flyers to their acquaintances convincing them to come.

3.1.4 *Art direktors* – Booking managers

While promotion was important, Sasha spent most of his time trying to get Svoboda booked to play concerts. He would try to talk to the management during concerts of other groups and after rehearsals he would sometimes go to new clubs. Here he would talk to the club's *art direktor*.

The *art direktors* tend to be (former) musicians They use their knowledge of the scene to book appropriate acts for the clubs they work for and to negotiate the pay.[60] They get a percentage of the earnings the evenings they book a band and sometimes a regular base salary.[61] *Dzhambala*, whose *format* (stylistic direction) is reggae, provides one example: Andrei Ivanov, the club's founding *art direktor*, is the reggae group Reggistan's vocalist, thus Reggistan was the house band during Andrei's tenure. Through Andrei's knowledge of the local scene he both knew which bands played what kind of music and got requests from new bands and musicians (like me) thus broadening his knowledge of active groups.[62]

In other words, the *art direktors* work as gate keepers, including the bands they like and fit the club's format. They also know which bands can profit from which kind of musicians and function as a pool of knowledge and gossip – in other words, important nodes within the network.

---

60. Similar to other European cities the musicians I talked to said that they either negotiated a flat fee (especially when the concert was during a weekday) or opted for a percentage of the money collected at the door when the concert was on one of the prime nights (Friday, Saturday) and they could expect many listeners. Common practice for Svoboda was to negotiate a flat fee.
61. Andrei got a base salary of 2500 rubels a week plus 25% of the door (with 25% going to the club and the remaining 50% going to the band) at the end of his tenure at *Dzhambala*. At the club *Vo100ok*, where he started working October 2008, his salary was a percentage of the door (pers.comm., 30.09.2008).
62. Other examples of clubs during my stay with musicians as *art direktors* are *Griboedov* (Dva Samoleta), *Stary Dom* (Korol' i Shut), *City Club* (Artur Kurnikov) and *Mankhetten* (Mata Khari). This practice seems to be common in Russia (regarding blues cf. Urban and Evdokimov 2004, 138).

Issues of power also play a role here, where *art direktors* can limit access to groups they find financially not viable, stylistically not fitting (and thus also financially risky) as well as groups they do not like because of personal differences. Since their salary is tied to the earnings/attracted clients, the *art direktors* have a personal financial incentive to book bands who can gather an audience. They are, however, also under pressure from the clubs' owners to attract people and revenue for the club (primarily through sales at the bar) and thus are at risk of losing their job if the management is not content with their work.

Returning to Andrei: he was fired from *Dzhambala* in January 2005 only to start working there again in September 2006 after the management changed. Due to low visitor numbers Andrei was given the sack by the new management in August 2008. Both times he was replaced by *Khvost* (Tail), a former ballet dancer, because he also entertained the audience with sketches and competitions – at least that was Andrei's version (pers. comm., 25.08.2008).[63]

This fluidity can also lead to the situation, where the *art direktor* who booked a band has changed club by the time the band is supposed to perform. This happened to Svoboda when we were supposed to play with a punk band in the newly opened *S-club* (27.01.2006): The *art direktor* with whom Sasha had spoken had left and the management decided that the punk band was not appropriate for the club (did not fit their *format*). Furthermore, they did not honor the agreement that there should not be a cover charge.

While established bands usually can draw on a vast network of musicians and fans, bands trying to establish themselves dedicate a lot of time to networking, as seen in Sasha's efforts described above – both establishing new contacts as well as maintaining and using existing ones. Social relations are a vital component for groups – not only in relation to staffing a band with musicians, but also for providing an audience at concerts and thus proving that a band is attractive when negotiating with clubs. Besides personally talking to different actors within the scene and thus introducing oneself, promotion is another central aspect of building

---

63. While I do not know his real name, his nickname *Khvost* is due to his pony tail. Svoboda played at a corporative party (*korporativnaia vecherinka*) at *Dzhambala* on December 29, 2005 with about 40 participants where Khvost was the master of ceremonies. Besides organizing a dancing competition (disco dancing) he also presented (his version of) Jamaican Christmas and explained the styles reggae and ska to the audience.

(new) relationships. It is within the networks that meaning and meaningful forms are exchanged and thus culture is created and distributed.

3.2 Social hubs

While social relations make up the backbone of scenes, there are certain social hubs where the scene is made visible and real (Cohen 1999, 241). These include concert venues as well as record stores, practice rooms, and recording studios – spaces of interaction between musicians and musical styles and where musicians interact with the audience/fans and people involved in the music business. For clubs the *art director* plays a key role as the link between network and institution. Not only are clubs social hubs, but they are also a central economic hub for the scene constituting the major income chance for groups in St. Petersburg, which also highlights the *art direktor's* role as a gate keeper.

It can help to frame important aspects and processes within scenes which are not too fluid (like clubs), while maintaining the clusters of social and cultural activities. Incorporating material, political, and economic prerequisites for performances, Lundberg, Malm, and Ronström's concept of *arena* uses metaphors from performances and the physical structure of the concert stage in order to describe the processes and actors involved. This allows for a differentiated analysis of the activities. They define *arenas* as "those 'places of performance' where social and cultural differences can be made visible and manifest." (Lundberg et al. 2003, 53). Here the previously discussed *art direktor* can be understood as a bouncer. S/he determines which bands have access to the *stage* – the performance area of the arena (a club). The *art direktors* themselves are less visible, working *backstage* where the performances are prepared. They wield much power by deciding which music is included and which does not fit the club's *format*. This music, not in focus within the arena, is part of the *offstage* – which I will return to when discussing the boundaries.

What makes St. Petersburg and Russia interesting within a global perspective is the transition to a capitalist economy which brought a shift in attitude regarding the arena, "clubs".

3.2.1 Clubs

"Now there are few. [...] The first club opened in summer 91, in the autumn some more clubs opened, mostly Rock 'n' Roll clubs and until, indeed, the middle of the 90s in Piter there were about 15 where it was possible to go. Some were open 3-4 times a week, some once or twice a week, some more often, some less. The peak of all this was reached in 97, but in 97 just about all the leading clubs closed. Then, [...] so to say, a new economic attitude started [...]: The landlords wanted a lot of easy money at once. Therefore within literally a half-year 6 of the leading clubs closed: Orlandina, the nearby Pereval, [...] Art klinika, TaMtAm, 10 klub, Wild Side, [...]. But Moloko appeared about a year after that and Griboedov."

(Burlaka 2005 – Russian: p. 316)

Besides *kvartirniki* (house concerts) the main venue for (rock) concerts during the Soviet Union was the LRK, hosting concerts and festivals (cf. Steinholt 2005). As Andrei Burlaka (2005) who has been active within the scene since the 1980s described in the quotation above, the first clubs (in the meaning of performance venue and not organization) opened in 1991 and the number increased until 1997. The pioneering and today most well-known of the first generation clubs was *TaMtAm* founded by Akvarium's former cellist Vsevolod "Seva" Gakkel (it operated from 1991 to 1996).

Around 1997 a decline in clubs set in. The sociologist Anna Zaytseva (2006) argues that some of them were pushed out by "commercial" companies – what Andrei Burlaka calls a "new economic attitude" – where the landlords wanted to earn money fast and easily. A major contributing factor was also the economic crisis in Russia, which peaked in 1998.

Around this time a new generation of clubs appeared, among them *Moloko* and *Griboedov* (both opened late 1996), which still were active during my fieldwork. Describing these second generation clubs, Zaytseva (2006) argues that the clubs appearing after 1998 were, in her words, commercially orientated, focusing on entertainment, professionalism, and aiming at a broader, wealthier audience.[64]

---

64. In the interview Burlaka (2005) referred to concert venues where people do not necessarily hang out, catch up on gossip, or meet acquaintances as "commercial" (e.g. the venues *Port*, *BKZ Oktiabr'skii*). These lack, in Burlaka's words, a micro climate which is essential to his definition of a "club". This should be read from his position both as a local music critic writing about St. Petersburg bands who mainly perform in smaller clubs and as someone who spent much time in *Moloko* – his main hangout (thus putting the club in a better light). Furthermore, this view is not necessarily shared by the more established bands since they depend on these venues to perform in.

Seen from an business perspective, the first generation of clubs emerging after the end of the Soviet Union were run by people mainly without the experience of how a capitalist economy worked. While traces of this can still be felt today – especially in the attitude of many clubs towards musicians as people who deliver goods to a set price[65] – clubs today focus not only on providing music but also on retaining financial stability and when the revenue is not right, new solutions have to be found, such as firing the *art direktor*, changing the *format*, and/or raising the prices (cover charge, bar).

Picture 5: Markscheider Kunst. The band performing at the club *Moloko* in St. Petersburg (26.03.2005).

Finding this balance still seems hard. For a city of its size, there are relatively few clubs in St. Petersburg compared to e.g. Berlin. Geographically most of the clubs are concentrated in the city center (with a few scattered around more remote parts of the city). Unlike major European cities, most concerts start early, around 21:00 and end around 23:00 so that the visitors can reach the last subway home before it stops running. Some clubs (e.g. *Fish Fabrique, Griboedov*), however, have concerts starting later or include both an evening and a night set.

The clubs I frequented during my fieldwork were located in a variety of settings: basement (boiler) rooms (*Kamchatka, Moloko, Mankhetten*), old bomb shelters (*Griboedov, Deep Sound*), the Research Institute of Arctica and Antarctica (*ArktikA*) and an old theatre (*Port*) just to mention the more obscure places. Some clubs (*Mankhetten, The Red Lion*) also doubled as tourist restaurants during the day.

---

65. Perks such as free beverages (bottled water, beer), food, as well as designated back stage areas for musicians common in my experience as a musician in Berlin, Copenhagen, and Vienna for musicians were not always provided and the management was also not always friendly. The club *Moloko* was a positive exception.

As these inventive locations suggest, the scene in St. Petersburg is very creative – partially to avoid complaints of noise and partially due to landlords' economic thinking. The scene is also very fluid – clubs open and close fast and while the life spans of some clubs amount to several years, some open and close within a year. The reasons range from economic (non-)viability to problems with city authorities such as experienced by *Orlandina*, which (re)opened March 29th, 2002 and closed January 31st, 2005 due to a decree by the Petrogradsky City Region.[66]

Another effect of this fluidity is that there generally is a lack of clubs to play in:

"Well there are few clubs in Piter, but a lot of groups. Petersburg is, in general a musical city – [there are] a lot more groups than in Moscow, despite the fact that Moscow is bigger. But because of that there are long lines [to perform] at clubs – concerts have to be organized in advance – 3 months, 2 months, because there are a lot of groups but no clubs."

(Katia in Fedorova et al. 2005a – Russian: p. 324)

The members of the group Iva Nova shared a common perception with other musicians in St. Petersburg that it is harder (and takes some advance planning) to play on desirable weekdays (Friday, Saturday) and in clubs with higher status and (normally) better pay. This especially applied to new or not too well known bands. This scarcity of performance venues also has an effect on the treatment the bands received and, more importantly, the money paid:

LenaN: "The problem is that there are few clubs. I don't know and little money and everything in Russia. That is, that concerts in Russia that's a fundamental problem. That there is never enough money for instruments, even for living."
Katia: "And therefore a lot of musicians work and music becomes a hobby" [...]
LenaN: "And since there are few clubs in Piter, that is they don't pay a lot. In Moscow it's, well, more or less ok. That is, we are saved only by European concerts where you can, well, earn a little money."

(Fedorova et al. 2005a – Russian: p. 324)

Both more established and (especially) beginning bands shared the common opinion that it was not practically possible to depend on popular music as a main source of income in St. Petersburg. Either musicians of the more established bands (e.g. Markscheider Kunst, Iva Nova, Leningrad, Billy's Band) went on tour in Central Europe to support themselves (cf. p. 128 and p. 254ff) or the musicians

---

66. Rumors are that the reason was the killing of Vu An Tuan, a Vietnamese student, on October 13th 2004 by local Skinheads in the same area as the club. Following the killing, the club was accused of being a local hangout for Neo-Nazis and thus closed. However, another more plausible rumor is that there were complaints by neighbors about noise from the club and that the space the club occupied was more profitable as office space. Orlandina reopened in a new location on March 15th, 2006.

(especially of the aspiring groups) had side jobs.[67] Most of Svoboda's and all of Con Brio's members had blue-collar daytime jobs or were still studying. Sasha tried to live off the group's earnings, but after I left, he started working (as a security guard, a messenger, and as a guard in a church).

The cover charge during my fieldwork normally ranged between 100 and 200 rubles ($3.50-$7.50) with the prices for more prominent local bands rarely exceeding 400 rubles ($15).[68] Svoboda's average pay for the whole band during my tenure was 1500-2000 rubels ($55-80) for an evening gig and 2000-2500 rubles ($80-100) for a night gig. Svoboda would sometimes play at the higher status clubs (*Moloko, Red Club*), new clubs (*Zorro, S-club*) or festivals (*Okna Otkroi!* 2005 and 2006) for considerably less or no money just for the exposure. One example is the *Pivnoi Festival*, (25. & 26.06.2005) where Svoboda partly played to be included in the record producer Andrei Tropillo's network.

One reason for not being able to depend on music as the main source of income is that the concert goers' disposable income is quite low:[69]

> "Most musicians also work somewhere else. In Petersburg it is very hard to earn money because the city itself is quite poor. Hence the audience can't leave a lot of money at the clubs. That is, the musician [or] club raises the prices, that means it lowers the amount of audience, that is, they won't get more money. [...] Hence it means that musicians don't get a lot of money either."
>
> (Burlaka 2005 – Russian: p. 317)

Drawing on his knowledge of the music scene Andrei Burlaka's comment that there is a delicate balance between the audiences' disposable income and the cover charge reflects the observations I made. The average price varied between the clubs and was in part linked to the target group: clubs like *Moloko, Deep Sound,*

---

67. Iva Nova's bass-player Elena Novikova (Fedorova et al. 2005a) pointed out that female musicians were doubly disadvantaged since they also had to take care of the house work and thus had less time to invest in music (or to have a side job). This made it harder to go on tour. Iva Nova experienced this first hand in line up changes since both Elena Novikova and their former vocalist Vera Ogareva left the group because they gave birth.
68. The ruble-dollar conversion is an approximation based on the exchange rates during my stay. During a visit in October 2008 the prices had risen considerably, ranging between 200 and 450 rubles for average groups, however reaching 1000 rubles for more prominent local bands.
69. The average monthly salary was $311 in 2004, $350 in 2005 and $650 in 2008 (Staff Writer 2005; Scherbakova 2006; Sharapova 2008). While this sum is quite low when seen in a European context it is important to keep in mind that the cost of living was also quite low at that time. Furthermore, young single people in their 20s normally live with their parents and it is quite common for married couples to live together with one of the spouses' parents.

Dzhambala, and *Orlandina,* which primarily targeted younger people and students, had lower prices (topping off at about 200 rubles) than clubs like *Platforma* and *Red Club* which targeted an older working audience where tickets could cost as much as 400 rubles.

Some groups managed to carve a niche, opening for other earning possibilities. Dobranoch's violinist Dmitri Khramtsov pointed out an advantage that his group had:

> "Firstly, the kind of music we play, it's a little different. On the one hand it's good, because we don't have competition. We are alone in this. On the other hand it's bad, because we don't have a sort of environment, in which we could exist. [...] Well, on the level of earnings not much, well, in principle, quite all right. [...] That is, compared with musicians who play in clubs as much as we do, we earn more money, because we also have other variants: we play at festivals and corporative events, which don't call such musicians, because they play alternative music, which is only in clubs for, don't know, for punks. [laughs] In that context, we have, of course, something to complain about, but we have an income. We have an income with music, that is some money and that's fine, that's good. Could be better of course, waiting for when... our disks also start to sell."
>
> (Khramtsov 2005 – Russian: p. 330)

Dobranoch's style is different from most of the groups I talked to since they play on acoustic instruments and since their repertoire is to a large extent based on klezmer and other Eastern and South-Eastern European traditional music. This limits their concert possibilities within the clubs mentioned, but also increases the possibilities for playing at festivals in Europe focusing on traditional and world music and at corporative events (*korporativnaia vecherinka*) in Russia.[70]

Finally, one thing repeatedly pointed out to me by established groups as a handicap was the lack of medium range clubs (300-600 listeners) to perform in. Severnye Vrata's vocalist Aleksandr "Nevskii" Vladimirov stressed the lack of such venues in combination with the financial aspect:

> "At our concerts somewhere between 300 to 600 people come [...]. Therefore, basically, it was always difficult for us on that level, because not a lot of places fit. Now, apart from that, one also has to consider that our audience – it is not made up of

---

70. Such private events are important within a Russian context: The Russian music critic Artem Troitskii estimates that Russian popular music artists within what he calls *popsa* earn 60-80% of their income at corporative events playing several times a week – making Russia in his words unique within the popular music business (Feoktistova 2008 for a summary and Russia.ru 2008 for the interview). According to a newspaper article, however, the rock groups DDT, Akvarium, and Mashina vremeni categorically refuse to play at such events despite a lucrative pay (Alekseenko and Prokhorova 2008).

the most well-off people. Therefore they don't go to a concert staged at a some very expensive place."

(Vladimirov 2005 – Russian: p. 320)

Severnye Vrata tended to perform in big clubs like *Port* and *Arktika*. These were not packed, but attracted considerably more people than a small club could fill. That made balancing ticket prices, expected income, and costs for the club difficult. While playing in even bigger venues would be possible, the fixed costs would exceed the revenue generated by the visitors. For other groups such as Markscheider Kunst, it is only profitable to play a few concerts a year in St. Petersburg in order to gather a big enough audience (Efremenko 2005). The lack of medium sized clubs also points to the scene's size since it is not financially viable to operate those clubs profitably: there is both a lack of a big enough audience base as well as sufficient (local) groups that can draw enough audience to fill those clubs.

Hence, St. Petersburg has an active club scene with many bands, however limiting factors are the lack of (medium-sized) clubs, a relatively small audience base as well as their financial limitations. While the clubs were the main public space for musicians to perform in and interact with the audience and other musicians, another social hub for the band was the the practice room where most of the creative work was centered.

3.2.2 Practice rooms

Located on the first floor of *Bania 43* (*Nab. reki Moiki* 82 – Picture 6), a Russian sauna still in use during my tenure with the band, the main place of Svoboda's day to day activities was their practice room. To get to the practice room one had to pass two courtyards and enter the building through a small narrow staircase. To the left was a functioning (male) *bania* and to the right a storage and repair area. Next to that area was Svoboda's room with a table and benches. On the wall there was a current calendar with Svoboda's gig dates. Behind that area there was a smaller room closed off by carpets and other material to isolate the sound. A decrepit drum set was in one corner together with guitar, bass, and vocal amplifiers, two microphones, and a Behringer mixer (the equipment belonged to Sasha, Fomich, Prokhor, and Shliapa).

In addition to us rehearsing there, non-band members including fans came by to drop off or pick up belongings like equipment and flyers, to talk to us, and to hang out and listen.

Thus the place had a triple function. Besides socializing, its primary use was for rehearsals. It was also used for storage.⁷¹ This was both for practical reasons as well as for private space limitations (e.g. Sasha did not have his own apartment).

When asked about the location Sasha explained that when he moved to St. Petersburg he lived close to the *bania* which he frequented when the warm water was switched off in his apartment.⁷² Through contacts there he managed to rent unused space in the *bania* to use as a practice room.

Picture 6: Entrance to Svoboda's rehearsal room at *Bania 43*. Picture taken in St. Petersburg in 2005.

While Svoboda was fortunate and it was easier for established groups, finding practice rooms in St. Petersburg is hard:

---

71. More established bands like Markscheider Kunst also used the space to store merchandise sold while on tour.
72. Warm water which is mainly provided by the city is normally switched off for maintenance work during a 3-4 week period in summer.

> Lena: "In general that [finding a practice room] is a very big problem. [...] For us this is currently not a problem, not at this time."
> Katia: "We have been going for a long time."
> LenaN: "It was always continuous resettlements, that's it. Generally, for musicians in Piter it is a problem, yes."
>
> (Fedorova et al. 2005a – Russian: p. 324)

In general there were two solutions: either renting a room on an hourly basis or finding a permanent place.

Con Brio turned to the former, renting a room once or twice a week and paying between 300 and 500 rubles for 3 hours. The other solution, especially for more established bands who rehearsed often was, like Svoboda, to find a permanent space where the groups could rehearse and leave their equipment (Svoboda paid 2000 rubles a month). Besides Svoboda's I encountered practice rooms in a corner of an Admiral's/Officers' club and the basement of an old movie theatre, now called the *Modern Art Foundation*. Andrei Burlaka (2005) pointed to other solutions like the documentary film studio, music clubs, as well as businesses, factories, and (research) institutes with spare rooms when I asked him about the rehearsal room situation in St. Petersburg. He added, however, that businesses and others were rethinking their strategies since it was possible to charge a higher rent when leasing out to stores. While the situation in St. Petersburg is not so much different from other European cities, these problems are, as Andrei Burlaka points out in part also historically rooted.

> "In the past each micro-region had a ZhEK. Yes, that organization which was responsible for the water pipes there, and the light. The so-called ZhEK – housing-operation office. It was a small representation of the authorities. Each had a small red corner, like a cultural center. There, as a rule, there was some kind of equipment, and there groups rehearsed. Of such clubs there were probably several hundred: 3-400 a city. That is, not in every, but in the 70s there were, yes, enough to cater to the number of groups. Well a lot rehearsed in those small red corners in the ZhEKs. And now they don't exist. Everything is closed."
>
> (Burlaka 2005 – Russian: p. 317)

As with the clubs discussed above, a shift has occurred due in part to the transition from the Soviet to post-Soviet economy – away from designated (and largely subsidized) practice rooms as a part of (cultural) institutions to available space in any institution to (negotiable) "market rates". These solutions (especially the *bania* and officers' club also show a willingness to capitalize on unused space in places normally not used as practice rooms.

To offset the costs, the bands renting permanent spaces often made these accessible to other bands showing one of the benefits of having an active social network: Sasha first shared Svoboda's practice room with Bacchus, another group where Fomich, Prokhor, and Shliapa played, and afterwards rented it out to other groups.

Thus, practice rooms are one of the places where the scene is made visible – a social hub. However, unlike the clubs a practice room is not a public space, it is more intimate with stricter access requirements – mostly limited to the band, close acquaintances, and at times invited people. Practice rooms are ideal locations for meeting strangers interested in the band, since during rehearsals the complete band is normally present and the space is not as intimate as a musician's apartment nor as noisy as a cafe.

3.2.3 Recording and distribution

The third major social hub for groups and another place where the scene becomes visible is the recording studio. While not so often frequented as the previously mentioned hubs, they are an important part of the creative output and can (indirectly) help acquire access to clubs and media by having an audible business card. Both for Svoboda, Con Brio, and other bands starting out, recording songs was considered an important first step in order to gain access to clubs as well as radio. The recording's main aim was thus promotion, not to earn money by selling CDs.

Just like the *art direktor*, the recording engineer acts as a node both within as well as beyond the scene. S/he knows what music is being recorded – at least in the studio – and thus what styles are popular. This relates to quality control by, for example, hinting at better phrasing, taking part in artistic choices, and correcting mistakes – both intonation as well as technical ones: While recording with Con Brio at the studio *Space X* (near *Baltiiskii Vokzal* – the Baltic station), the engineer commented on the playing as well as the singing and added a pitch corrector both to Vitia's vocal parts as well as to my trumpet part. The recording engineers are sometimes also musicians and have access to (potentially) better instruments than the groups' own. During the above mentioned recording session, Con Brio's bass-player was lent a better-sounding bass for the recording. The result was three polished and good-sounding tracks. The recording engineer is – similar to the *art direktor* (and other actors within scenes) – a person with several potential roles –

e.g. often being a musician and an engineer or, like Andrei Burlaka, a producer and a music critic.

Picture 7:   Plaque from the Soviet record label *Melodiia* at the entrance to *Antrop-studio*. Picture taken in St. Petersburg in 2005.

As in other cities, St. Petersburg offers a wide variety of recording and mastering possibilities (both analogue and digital), ranging from home studios in a person's apartment to full fledged studios with several sound-insulated rooms. Two examples of the latter used by the musicians I talked to are *Antrop*-studio run by Andrei Tropillo and located at a premise that used to belong to the state run *Melodiia* (cf. Picture 7) and *Dobrolet* studio at *DK Lensoveta*. Andrei Burlaka (2005) estimated that there were about 80 active studios in St. Petersburg.

The studios also double (to a lesser extent than clubs and practice rooms) as places of social interaction: After I interviewed Tequilajazzz's vocalist Evgenii Fedrov at *Dobrolet*-studio (02.02.2006) I met members of Markscheider Kunst and Spitfire at the studio. Markscheider Kunst had been recording there during the day and after I interviewed Evgenii, he rehearsed some songs for his project Optimystica orchestra with members of both bands in the studio.

While there were a significant amount of recording studios in St. Petersburg, record labels were more limited – the main labels based in St. Petersburg covering the not so well-known bands I looked at were *Antrop*, *Kap-kan* and *Bomba Piter*.[73] More well-known bands tended to be released by labels located in Moscow like *Grand Records*, *Gala Records,* and *Misteriia Zvuka*. Svetlana Loseva (2005) who briefly worked as the PR-manager for *Grand Records* touched on this when she said the big, powerful labels were in Moscow while the small ones were in Piter. Some groups like Dobranoch' released their albums on their own since it was too expensive to use a label.

A general problem mentioned by several people I talked to was distribution. This is reflected in the (lack of) availability of local groups' recordings in St. Petersburg: While the big chains like *Titanik*, *505,* and *Aisberg* (Iceberg) were spread about the city, they carried few albums of local groups.[74] They focused more on major non-Russian artists covering the main popular music genres and major Russian groups. This was especially a problem for lesser known bands on smaller labels, albums released without a label, and niche styles like the self-ascribed ones "pagan metal" (Sasha Nevskii) and "world music" (Dmitri Khramtsov) since these groups lacked a category to be filed in in the record stores.

---

73. *Bomba Piter* also regularly released a sampler called *Okhota* (Hunt, Desire) featuring little known and mostly not signed groups from Russia. The groups payed a fee (when Svoboda was invited to participate in 2006 it was 3000 rubles, about $110) to be included. The CD was sent out with the monthly popular music magazine *Fuzz* and was also distributed to radio stations and other interested companies.
74. The price for CDs in stores during my stay was around 100 rubles, sometimes less. The stores also offered MP3-CDs containing a collection of (all) albums from a certain group.

Instead, small stores like *Kailas, Dolina Bartanga,* and *Castle Rock* have a good selection of local groups including those playing niche styles. Furthermore, *Bomba Piter* as well as *Kap-Kan* records have their own outlets. The best possibility was, however, to buy records at the concerts of the respective groups. The performing groups usually had a table selling their releases, but sometimes people selling different recordings and even some smaller labels were present – as at a mini-punk festival at *Moloko* (19.09.2005) where amongst others, Dmitri "Sharapov" Ivanov, who runs the label *ShSS*, was selling various recordings and 'zines. In addition, some of the clubs had a limited selection of recordings for sale.

This last example also demonstrates that social hubs are a part of the *market frame* – the economic realities of the scene – by providing a space to perform and sell (and thus to earn money or goods) or a space to rehearse and record (and thus to spend money or goods). In other words, the scene's social hubs are part of the relevant local infrastructure for the bands I was involved in. This infrastructure, especially the performance venues, makes up a kind of physical and thus visible boundary of the scene. Besides the economic reality, the hubs provide a space where the groups interact within the *form of life frame* renewing their contacts with fans and other actors within the scene and thus maintaining and expanding their networks.

3.3 Discursive scene boundaries

Another set of boundaries determining which bands have access to the scene and to the physical stages depends on communication, perception, and shared taste. The *art direktors* at the clubs select groups based on a shared perception of whether the music fits into the clubs' *format*, of what kind of crowd the groups attract, and of personal favors. Similarly, musicians make conscious aesthetic choices when playing and recording – what musicians to include, what kind of music to play, and how to promote themselves.

While these choices can be minuscule, there is an overarching shared perception (or taste) of what makes the scene part of the cultural sphere labeled rock. This is linked to discourses with more fluid boundaries. The following section will focus on boundaries which are actively negotiated in the community and thus help delimit the scene. These boundaries are both flexible and imaginary, and appear in communication between the actors (form of life frame). They are, however, also audible and visible within the creative work, such as songs and CD-compilations – also doubling as a marketing tool, e.g. the compilation *Russkii Andegraund Volume 1* (Russian Underground Volume 1 – Various Artists 2006b) or *My iz Pitera* (We're from Piter – Various Artists 2003a), in other words within the market frame.

These discourses touch upon, among other things, the binary *underground* vs. *commercial/pop*, St. Petersburg vs. Moscow and the *russkii rok* legacy. Together they help create a sense of being situated within a quite diverse musical landscape (which points to a certain performance type – "self-composed serious" music performed live – which is in opposition to Moscow and which distances current musicians from the previous generation). Here actors participate in other projects which might not be musically similar to what they normally play, but which is considered part of the same scene. In short, it is a community of musicians who interact with each other.

These issues, especially the underground vs. commercial/pop, touch on similar discourses in other cities and – grouped under the heading "authenticity" – are a central topic in popular music studies (cf. Keightley 2001; Moore 2002; Weisethaunet and Lindberg 2010). What makes this topic complicated is that manifestations of authenticity are both relational and context sensitive. Instead of contributing to the general discussion on authenticity and how it is manifested per se, I will therefore in the following paragraphs explore how these discourses are anchored in St. Petersburg within the frame of Soviet and post-Soviet popular music.

3.3.1 Underground – Commercial

During a Svoboda concert at *City Club* (21.05.2005) a listener came up to me and praised the band for being honest towards its music unlike the very popular St. Petersburg group Leningrad, which he said primarily plays for money. As he put it, Leningrad was too "commercial". Nuancing this view a little, the *Russendisko* DJ, Yuriy Gurzhy, described Leningrad's musical location in these terms:

"This is again a cliché, but in my eyes the underground [...] is what is not [considered] mainstream. [...] Lately, however, [...] as the typical example of Leningrad [demonstrates] we see how the underground is finding its way into the mainstream, even though it, to some extent, is remaining underground."

(Gurzhy 2005 – German: p. 312)

This initiates one of the discourses negotiating the boundaries within the St. Petersburg rock scene as well as within scenes in other cities (e.g. Cohen 2001 discusses the tension between creativity and commerce in Liverpool): underground vs. commercial (or mainstream). Essentially a value judgement, the debate evolves around how "true", "honest" and "authentic" a group is to its listeners and how "creative" their material is. The listeners' judgements are based on how the bands promote themselves, how (physically) accessible they are to the listener, how dogmatic the bands are ideologically, how they create and produce songs, how established they are, and how the bands position themselves within the general music market. This has to be distinguished from the fact that most bands and clubs are commercial in the sense that they play or host concerts in exchange for (mostly) financial or material compensation and gain. The compensation received from concerts can, however, also influence the listener's value judgement. In other words, a group's position within these boundaries is fluid and relational and can thus easily change depending on the factors mentioned as perceived by the listener.

A frequent recurring definition by people in St. Petersburg was related to financial gain: Underground bands did not play for profit and thus could be free to stylistically do what they wanted to (in other words, art for the sake of art and artistic freedom). The following quote by Sharapov, Svinokop's vocalist and a music journalist, demonstrates this as well as the complexities quite well:

"A lot of that is rather evident. [...] Stadium rock is right [sic] and there are some bands who are playing in big clubs like Port and whatever, which are like indie bands, they have CDs released by the likes of Kap-kan Records which is an indie-label [...]. And then there are some underground bands that are doing their own thing, but they still don't mind getting paid for what they play, like a lot of bands that headline gigs at Moloko [...]. Then there are totally underground bands that don't even think of getting any money for [...] A lot of younger bands are like that but the thing is for some bands there's just no other way and some bands have conscious ideologically informed decisions to form their career. But sometimes it's just a combination of both. Some of my friends, they wouldn't want to play any kind of music that would bring any money."

(Ivanov 2005)

Sharapov's quote shows that being underground is partially a conscious choice and on a continuum. His statement also reflects his position, which is within the DIY-punk/noise scene, whose ideology is close to what he calls the "totally underground bands".[75]

For many musicians, including the more established ones, being underground also meant not being played on radio or TV because the style did not fit (being *ne-format*) or because the music lacked commercial potential (the ability to reach a broad audience as defined in the stations' target group and thus satisfy the advertisers). Mikhail Kozyrev (2007b, 53), the founding director of *Nashe Radio*, pointed to this in one of his books when he discussed Billy's Band's radio debut on *Nashe Radio*: They were briefly aired, but the group was not too well received in the bi-weekly listening tests and thus subsequently removed. I mention this since the group's vocalist Billy Novik (2005) argued that they were underground since they were neither played on radio nor TV – they were *ne-format*. For Billy "commercial bands" conform to one style, preferably that of the station's *format*, so they are played and can earn money. At the same time this should be viewed as a way to define his band as special, since it implies that they incorporate different styles and are thus interesting. He, in other words, uses the label as a marketing tool through positioning the band as an underdog within the popular music market (of those interviewed Billy's Band was one of the most successful in St. Petersburg).

The label *underground* is thus used as an ideological label indicating a non-financial art-for-the-sake-of-art-interest in music making, which, in part, is expressed in the lack of media coverage. At the same time the label functions as a marketing tool used to position a band as valuable and interesting in relation to the "commercial" bands.

---

75. The term "underground" is not only applied to music, but also to clubs, e.g. *GEZ-21* (Picture 8), *Moloko* (*Andegraundnyi muzykal'nyi klub* – Muzykal'nyi klub Moloko n.d.), and *Deep Sound* (*Podzemnyi klub DEEP SOUND* – Deep Sound Underground Club n.d.). Note how both a phonetic transliteration of the English word in cyrillic is used (*andegraundnyi*) as well as a translation (*podzemnyi*).

3.3.1.1 *Popsa*

> Popsa – the pink jaw of a hungry dog!
> Popsa – pink shit from the antlers to the tail![76]
> *Popsa* (Rok-gruppa 2003)

An often used antonym for underground (and at times synonym for "commercial" and "mainstream") is *pop* and its derogatory forms *popsa* and *popsnia*. The words generally had a negative connotation with musicians from the St. Petersburg scene as the refrain of the song *Popsa* demonstrates.[77] Summed up in the words of one of the vocalists as "Vse radi deneg!" (Everything for money – Il'ia Chert qtd. in Kozyrev and Barabanov 2007a, 134) *Popsa*'s lyrics primarily criticize the life style of *popsa* singers and the music's omnipresence in everyday life.

Linked with this idea of doing anything for financial gain, *popsa* was, by the musicians I talked to, musically given the attributes of lacking musical individuality and creativity, being hastily performed and of even being plagiarized.

The term as well as the dichotomy underground – pop/commercial is also applied to clubs. One of my aquaintances wrote the following while instant messaging with me:

> "And I like Arktika [the club], of course not the klub itself, but what they play – the club itself is kind of poppy [*popsoviy*], there at night they have disco[.] They combine two aspects of activity – apparently it doesn't pay to only have a metal-club here"
>
> (Electronic chat with Elena Zykova, 16.09.2005 – Russian: p. 322)

Here the club is defined by the music heard there, both the groups performing and the music played by the DJ, which in turn influences the target audience coming to the different events.

Elena's distinction between the music played and the venue itself also appeared when I interviewed Andrei Burlaka (2005): He drew a distinction between commercial and non-commercial venues as mentioned above in his critique of "commercial" clubs (cf. p. 103).

---

76. *Popsa – rozovaia past' golodnogo psa! Popsa – rozovaia drian' ot rogov do khvosta!*
77. Originally a song by the St. Petersburg punk band Brigadnyi podriad (2003) the song *Popsa* was covered with a few minor changes by the group Rok-gruppa, consisting of Iurii Shevchuk (DDT), Mikhail Gorshenev, Andrei Kniazev (both Korol' i Shut), Aleksei Gorshenev (Kukryniksy), Il'ia Chert (Pilot) and Aleksandr Chernetskii (Raznye Liudi) – all St. Petersburg based musicians. Musically the song is interesting since each singer has his characteristic and easily recognizable voice giving the song an unusual mix of different timbres.

Picture 8: *Piterskii Andegraund* (Piter's underground). Writing next to the club *GEZ-21's* entrance. Picture taken in St. Petersburg in 2005.

This should be seen from the perspective of a general rock-pop dichotomy which can also be found in European and US-American popular music. Keightley (2001, 111), discussing US-American popular music, argues that this division goes back to what he labels a "stratified mainstream" during the big band era but which develops fully with the emergence of rock. The division between rock and pop is influenced by a polemic against mass-society inspired by the US-folk

movement, however from a position within popular music (which Keightley refers to as "mainstream"). Showing the artificiality of this divide he writes:
> "Like rock itself, pop is not a musical style but a sphere of popular musical culture. From the rock perspective, pop is defined by its obliviousness to the broader social implications of musical production and consumption. 'Pop', of course, is that area of popular music said to be marked by ethical compromise and capitulation. [...] Pop is understood as popular music that isn't (or doesn't have to be, or can't possibly be) 'taken seriously'. Rock, in contrast, is mainstream music that is (or ought to be, or must be) taken seriously."
>
> (Keightley 2001, 128)

Thus rock and pop are two *perceived* ideological dogmas operating within an overarching popular musical cultural sphere. While this notion has been adopted in Russia as the previous discussion has shown, there is also a more specific Soviet twist to the story: the rivalry between state sanctioned *estrada* (while not a synonym of *popsa* the two are close) and non-sanctioned rock (the official existence of rock music in the Soviet Union was first recognized after 1985 – Steinholt in press).

The development of *bit* (beat) music and *rok* (rock) went through times of tighter and looser control and was primarily fueled by amateur bands consisting of members of the intelligentsia – it was not a Soviet working class phenomenon.[78] An attempt to gain more control over the bourgeoning Soviet beat- and rock-music wave was introduced in 1966 with the *Vokal'no-Instrumental'nyi Ansambl'* (VIA – Vocal-instrumental Ensemble) – a system for professional musical groups organized under the trade union houses and palaces of culture. By becoming officially sanctioned, the groups had to conform to certain requirements like cutting their hair, wearing uniforms, playing optimistic and positive music, and having the songs go through a curator (Steinholt 2005, 21f). While regarded with suspicion and disdain by the rock musicians at the time, the *VIA*-groups were able to incorporate some rock songs and thus they were positioned on a continuum between rock and *estrada* (Steinholt 2005, 25).[79] Amateur rock bands first got structural support with the LRK in 1981 and with maybe the exception of Mashina vremeni,

---

78. Steinholt (in press) points out that the term *rok* was due to its Russian literal meaning (fate) first used in the 1970s. Rock 'n' roll was in the beginning considered a jazz subgenre and with Beatlemania in the 1960s the term *bit* (beat) was used instead.
79. Steinholt (in press) also points out that even though the amount of amateur bands initially decreased, in the long run the introduction of the VIA system offered better accessibility to musical instruments and improved training due to musicians shifting between professional and amateur activities.

which became a VIA band in 1980, VIAs were looked down upon by most amateur rock bands. While this history also has traces of the rock-pop dichotomy where questions of authenticity play a major role (amateur beat/rock-bands being "serious"/"authentic" and the *VIAs* and *estrada*-acts being on a continuum of rising ethical compromise) the major difference is that amateur rock was not born out of official popular music as Keightley (2001) argues for rock in the USA. In the Soviet Union rock did not become a mass phenomenon until the mid- to late 1980s. Instead, the *VIAs* were the state's response to a growing number of amateur beat/rock-groups.

While there was a shared notion of "underground" being unknown, playing in small clubs for little money and not receiving air play on television/radio, the groups I talked to were, in general, conscious of the ambivalence between being underground and commercial/pop and that the underground was not necessarily a desirable place to remain. Underground bands were often associated with hobby musicians, both by more established bands as well as ambitious new-comers: Vitia whose aim was to earn money with Con Brio and thus not to remain underground, associated underground with playing as a hobby (Kultashov 2006). Here several musicians also stressed that being underground was a temporary or fluid state easily changeable to being pop/commercial, depending on popularity, perspective, media exposure, performance venues, and fate. Dmitri Khramtsov sums these views up well from the perspective of Dobranoch':

"In the sense that we sort of aren't such a widely-known band, that is we are not played on radio or television, in that respect we are underground. That is, we don't have any kind of task to resist somebody, I don't know, as if there were an official culture and we were unofficial, we have our own values – that is, we love this music and play it, it differs a little from pop music or something like what most people know, listen to. In that sense maybe [we are] underground. That is, we ourself, we don't want to be underground, because we are a kind of nonconformists or anything, I don't know, it's just that we play in clubs, in small ones – in that sense [we are] underground. Because that kind of music, 'world music', is not very widespread in Russia, that is, there's not a big market, that's why it stands a little close to such an underground music."

(Khramtsov 2005 – Russian: p. 330)

Here underground is linked to the band's lack of broad popularity and performing in small clubs, not based on a personal desire or ideological stance. In other words, this dichotomy is seen more as two poles on a continuum which depends on both musical and extra-musical factors.

A closer look at how the words *pop* and *popsa* are used also reveals some nuances between the words. Discussing the popular groups Akvarium, DDT, Splin, and Chizh Andrei Burlaka said about the style that:

> "[i]n principle it is rock, but understandable yes that it is popular art, it is already mass art. [...] Therefore we simply have here in Russia such an understanding as popsa, that is that low-class variety, thus there is a certain kind of distancing, but such, in all, in general there are people who play in stadiums. That is, generally, already pop-music. That is, it does not mean that it is bad, is that clear? Just that it is already mass art. That is you can't suppose that 10 000 people who came to a DDT concert in a sport-complex, that they all understand what Shevchuk sings about, that they all share his spiritual views, his quest. Just that it is becoming a figure for some already public fashion. The same can be said about Grebenshchikov as well."
> (Burlaka 2005 – Russian: p. 317)

When a little later I asked what *estrada* was Andrei answered:

> "Estrada? You mean, pop music? There is good pop-music, there is bad pop-music, everywhere there is good and bad. In rock music even a weak group tries to say something, tries to do something. In estrada, as we just discussed, there it is – just a conveyor."
> (Burlaka 2005 – Russian: p. 318)

While pop-music is here defined through mass-appeal, *popsa* has an added low status. The high status music (underground) is that which reaches and appeals to a limited audience (or select elite) and has a message.[80]

Another term used by several people I interviewed to describe rock music with mass appeal but which at the same time was not *popsa*, in Andrei Burlaka's words, it still tries to say something, was *pop-rok*:

> "Yes, pop-rock – there are such groups as Splin, Bi-2, 7B, Smyslovye Galliutsinatsii, well all those 7th wave or 8th – I mix them up now, but not important. [talks about next wave] Our popsa that is Meladze, Orbakaite – all those kinds of people."
> (Rudenko 2006 – Russian: p. 327)

Sasha distinguishes between the singer Kristina Orbakaite and the Meladze-brothers, whom he associates with *popsa* and the groups he labels *pop-rok* which emerged in the 1990s. Splin and Bi-2 were also given as examples of *pop-rok* by the music journalist Sergei Chernov (2006a) who added that the music played on

---

80. The Russian popular music critic Artiem Troitskii – using a different terminology – polemically differentiates between a soulless (*bezdushnaia*), stupid (*tupaia*), idiotic (*idiotskaia*) and empty (*bessoderzhatel'naia*) music as performed by Dima Bilan, Timati, and the group Blestiashchie and more sincere and comforting musicians like Tat'iana Bulanova, the Soviet *estrada* singer Alla Pugacheva, and the group Liube. His general argument is that due to the evolving economic crisis in Russia in 2008, Russian popular music will shift away from what he calls soulless performers to the more comforting musicians, since a newly unemployed audience will not want to see glamour but will want to be comforted.

Nashe Radio (cf. *russkii rok*-discussion below) was *pop-rok*. Here too media presence is used as a value criteria.

A distinction between *pop-rok/pop* and *popsa* often made in the interviews was linked to the production and performance of the music. A common understanding both with musicians as well as non-musicians and fans on how *popsa* is produced and performed is exemplified in the following statement by Sasha Nevskii:

> "In a European understanding a producer is a person, who is responsible for the quality of the sound on the album and who fulfills necessary requirements to make everything in the necessary sound, in the necessary format, and tries to reach this, accordingly, from the studio, from the musicians. In a Russian understanding a producer is some sort of 'daddy', who in general decides everything. [goes on about producers in Russia not interested in creative work, just interested in earning money] That is, they [producers] take some boys who sing popular songs, well but they do it badly. Well, where is the problem? Most important is that they have some kind of charisma and then it is possible to hire musicians for them, who play everything behind them, their vocals are corrected on the computer as prescribed, make an expensive music video, and everything is ok."
>
> (Vladimirov 2005 – Russian: p. 320)

The main points of criticism touch on production (taking a good looking person and have the person sing songs composed by somebody else with the aim of short-term profit), talent (performers cannot sing, their performances are lip-synched), looks (they target the sex appeal more than the intellect especially through scantily clad women – e.g. t.A.T.u., VIA Gra), and permanent rotation on TV/radio (they pay for their own rotation). This builds on a general notion within the scene that *popsa* artists are not ascribed any creative talent whatsoever. Even though cast as a Russian understanding, similar notions of producers and pop-production circulate in Germany and Denmark as well.[81]

By both assigning and being assigned to or claiming roots in the underground, bands negotiate their access to the cultural sphere *rock* and hence also to the St. Petersburg scene. In other words, the discussion surrounding *underground* and *commercial/pop* serves more to position the groups' and clubs' creative output than it reflects on the music played (in a way, all the bands I talked to in St. Petersburg were "commercial", simply because they aimed to earn money with their music – disregarding where they played or what they said). This is more important

---

81. This is also a gendered discourse in which pop/*popsa* is seen as female and effeminate – this is in part displayed through rumors that many of the male singers (e.g. Boris Moiseev, Valerii Leont'ev, and Filipp Kirkorov) are homosexuals.

for new groups than established bands – hence also Efr pointing out that Markscheider Kunst's "location" is for the listener to judge, not for him (Efremenko 2005).

The categories are thus dynamic and ever shifting – depending on factors such as where a band performs, whether they received air play, how accessible they were to fans etc. as the opening anecdote demonstrated. Despite this, while the boundary between underground and commercial/pop is fluid, there was still an outer, second boundary, often described as *popsa*, which was more fixed and from which the groups clearly distanced themselves. Here the distinction is not only limited to the lyrics and musical quality, but also the performance and production side: While *popsa* is considered to be some pretty model lip-synching to somebody else's songs, the St. Petersburg bands I interviewed identified themselves and their music through an act of composing and performing *their* songs *themselves*.

As mentioned, this discourse is not unique to St. Petersburg and Russia as even the "Russian" terms *underground* and *pop* hint at. Issues of authenticity have played a major role in popular music, especially since the emergence of rock, and function as a form for value judgement within the music market. Playing (rock) music is very competitive with musicians competing for access in clubs and media. How a band promotes itself plays an important role in St. Petersburg – especially due to the low club density and the relative lack of media promoting Russian rock music in the city. An added meaning also exists here since the city is considered the cradle of Russian rock implying that being within that rock tradition means that a group is somehow underground. This especially becomes clear when the discourse underground vs. commercial is placed within the city-rivalry with Moscow – this gives the discourse a specific local flavor.

3.3.2 *Moscow and Marijuana*: The St. Petersburg – Moscow rivalry

Ah-ah-ah, Moscow and Marijuana[82]
Moskva i mariuana (Ackee Ma-Ma u.r.b. 2005)

During a concert of the 'urban reggae' group Ackee Ma-Ma Urban Reggae Band at the St. Petersburg club *Red Club* (30.06.2005) the singer Tat'iana "Tania" Iatsenko invited the audience to sing the above mentioned refrain. An audience member

---
82. *A-a-a, Moskva i mariuana*

shouted something referring to the refrain to which the singer jokingly replied that the band also liked neither "Moscow" nor "Marijuana". When I asked about the lyrics Tania said that the song was a sarcastic song about Moscow:

> "I often travel with Boni' Nem to Moscow and I happen to socialize with Muscovites very often, and 'Moscow and Marijuana' is a bit of a sarcastic song because Muscovites – they very blindly follow fashion, that is with them: 'Oh, cocaine's a fashion' – everybody snorts. 'Oh, marihuana is a fashion' – everybody buys it and smokes in simply crazy amounts. And all my sarcasm about Moscow poured into that song. Well, and in general, marijuana is sold better there and in better quality than here."[83]
>
> (Iatsenko 2006 – Russian: p. 331)

Sharapov also mentioned the latest style in combination with DIY-Punk in Moscow: "pretty good punk scene [in Piter], the people are largely political and not all the bands are playing the latest Western trendy stuff which is often the case in Moscow" (Ivanov 2005). Depicting people from Moscow running after the latest fashion, in other words, the music following the latest styles and not being made for its *artistic* values as in St. Petersburg was a recurrent theme in the interviews I made. These comments point to an ongoing rivalry between the two cities, which Tequilajazzz's vocalist and bass-player Evgenii Fedrov put in the following way:

> "Well, the atmosphere which is here, the culture, which is here, it is very traditional, not as avant-garde as in Moscow. [...] Of course that has relevance. We live here. If that wasn't relevant, we would have moved to Moscow and become rich people. There is a lot of money in Moscow. Not here, but instead there are people here who think more about art than about money."
>
> (Fedrov 2006 – Russian: p. 329)

When talking to musicians like Evgenii in St. Petersburg, St. Petersburg is positioned as an alternative city, where the creative aspect of music is in the center and the groups are located in the underground. Groups in Moscow, on the other hand, aim to earn money, thus Moscow is seen as being a commercial city as well as the capital of *popsa*-groups. Discussing the difference between the two cities, Andrei Kagadeev (2004) said that groups from Moscow are more commercial, more professional, and good at business while groups from St. Petersburg are more honest, more creative, and sound rougher. Both Moscow's lack of creativity and focus on money were recurrent themes when talking to musicians in St. Petersburg. Other differences mentioned stressed that there were more groups in St.

---

83. She later on also jokingly referred to Moscow as Babylon – within Rastafarianism a place of decadence and sin (cf. p. 158ff for a discussion of the group and reggae).

Petersburg than in Moscow (Fedorova et al. 2005a; Efremenko 2005), that there was a greater stylistic freedom and mixing of styles (musical as well as fashion) in St. Petersburg (Burlaka 2005; Vladimirov 2005), that the musicians and lyrics were more serious (Burlaka 2005; Ivanov 2004), and that the St. Petersburg audience was more critical towards poorly playing groups (Ivanov 2004). *S-Club's art direktor* Evgenii Kiselev (2006) even went so far to say that in order to live in St. Petersburg one needs a certain character – brain and soul – to understand the city and its specificity – which also influences the creative work. This rivalry's roots can be traced to the cities' histories, the development of Soviet and post-Soviet popular music, as well as infrastructure.

As mentioned above and pointed out by musicians, St. Petersburg itself was founded as an (European) alternative to Moscow and became the capital of the Russian Empire. Moscow, however, remained important and was reinstated as the capital in 1918, thus elevating it to the capital of the Soviet empire. Today Moscow is the country's financial center. That lures many people to Moscow who want to try their luck. Culturally Moscow competes with St. Petersburg with several theaters, concert venues, and conservatories, making the city very attractive for musicians to move to.

While St. Petersburg is Russia's second city, being second hints at an inferiority complex expressed by inhabitants I talked to. St. Petersburg markets itself as a city of traditions (as Evgenii's quote above hints at) and so-called high culture, exemplified by the art museums *Gosudarstvennyi Ermitazh* (The State Hermitage Museum) and *Russkii muzei* (The Russian Museum) as well as the *Mariinskii Theatre*, the city's main opera house. While not the only cultural institutions in the city, these are three of the main destinations for visiting tourists. The *Mariinskii Theater's* predominant focus is the canon of Western art music – mainly 18th and 19th century European composers, Russian 19th century composers and ballet with only few forays into the 20th century. This focus on tradition for the sake of tradition was also pointed out by Evgenii who contrasted it with Moscow where "culture" is commodified to sell and serve the rich (Fedrov 2006).

Another reason for this rivalry is located within the the realm of popular music. While Moscow was important in the development of Soviet popular music, especially *estrada*, Leningrad in the 1980s became the main center of Soviet rock music as an alternative to *estrada*.[84] This was in great part due to the LRK – the first rock organization in the Soviet Union (cf. Steinholt 2005). One of the main traits of Soviet rock music – today also referred to as *russkii rok* (cf. below) – is its focus on the quality of the lyrics. Due to the fact that lyrics of officially sanctioned VIA- and *estrada* groups were supposed to be positive and optimistic and had to be officially approved, the lyrics were kept as uncontroversial as possible – accounting for the numerous *estrada* "songs about the weather" (Wickström and Steinholt 2009, 314). One way for the amateur bands to distance themselves from *estrada* was to focus on "serious" and "uncompromising" lyrics described by them with attributes like "depth", "spirituality", and "poetry". The above mentioned point that the lyrics of St. Petersburg bands are more serious should be seen within this context. This binary Moscow-pop vs. St. Petersburg-rock has remained until today:

> "If we talk just about music, then compared to [rock from] Piter rock from Moscow never existed. Piter – that is 'Kino', 'Akvarium', 'Alisa', 'DDT'. And Moscow – what's that? The remarkable 'Tsentr' and, of course, 'Zvuki Mu'. That's all."
>
> (Viacheslav Petkun in Kozyrev and Barabanov 2007b, 56 – Russian: p. 326)

Tantsy Minus' vocalist Viacheslav Petkun is originally from St. Petersburg, where he started his musical career, but moved to Moscow in the mid 1990s. By labeling some of the most well-known groups from the LRK as *Piter rock* he voices a common opinion heard in St. Petersburg by placing the rock lineage in St. Petersburg not Moscow. This was reflected in several comments made to me such as the following:

> "Piter remains as before, as I understand it, for the whole country, for Russia, or in general for the whole post-Soviet area, a certain cultural bulwark, because Moscow with all its contemporary 'Fabrika Zvezd' [Star Factory], talking in a more general sense, is understandable what that is. Anyway, for thinking people it can't but evoke sympathy, and in Russia there were always a lot of thinking people. Hence Piter as before remains such a city of hope, from which people still expect something real. [...] That is, there was always Moscow – that's commerce, Petersburg – that's spirituality."
>
> (Burlaka 2005 – Russian: p. 318)

This "soulful" (rock) music from St. Petersburg (in other words, music for the sake of music and nod to "high" culture) is juxtaposed with the music played in Moscow, which he links to *Fabrika Zvezd*, the Russian equivalent of *Star academy* – considered *popsa* and thus commerce. This link to the TV-show was also

---

84. People discussing Soviet popular music in general distinguish between three centers or "schools" of Soviet rock: the Leningrad, Moscow, and Sverdlovsk school (e.g. Radke 2002).

made by Andrei Ivanov (2004), who furthermore criticized producers in Moscow for "improving" the music of bands previously playing good music so it sells better and reaches a broader audience (in other words, making the bands more "commercial"). To him, current pop musicians are (bad) clones of Soviet *estrada*, implying that the music is uninteresting since it does not change (this is similar to Troitskii's differentiation, cf. p. 122, Fn. 80).

More importantly, Andrei, also links the difference between the two cities to the local infrastructure – a third root for this rivalry:

> "Yes, there are problems playing in St. Petersburg in the sense that, sorry to say, there are not that many clubs here, they are few. It is no secret that St. Petersburg, sorry to say, is a city which does not have that many financial resources, [...] even though it is really embarrassing that a lot of musicians, good musicians, good groups, travel to work in Moscow, because in Moscow there are a lot of clubs, in Moscow, in general, they pay good salaries, from which musicians, in principle, somehow can live."
>
> (Ivanov 2004 – Russian: p. 323)

As mentioned above, finding practice rooms is hard and the club density in St. Petersburg in relation to similar cities in Europe is quite low. Furthermore, the more prominent groups from St. Petersburg are released on Moscow based labels like *Misteriia Zvuka* (e.g. Leningrad 2003; Leningrad & the Tiger Lillies 2004; Akvarium 2006, 2008), *Gala Records* (e.g. Leningrad 2000, 2002; Markscheider Kunst 2004, 2008), *Real Records* (e.g. Various Artists 2000; Alisa 2005) and *Grand Rekords* (e.g. Billy's Band 2005; Alisa 2007b).

Another effect is that it is, for most bands, not possible to earn money playing primarily in St. Petersburg so the more established bands (e.g. Billy's Band, Dobranoch', Iva Nova, Markscheider Kunst) frequently travel to Moscow, where both the club scene and the pay (even with the travel costs) is better. Logistically this is no major problem, since there are several night trains between the two cities, some with low fares (~ 700 rubles – $ 25 round trip in 2005). Both the vocalist from Billy's Band as well as from Markscheider Kunst mentioned that it is possible to play several consecutive gigs in Moscow and the crowd will be different at each concert – something very hard to achieve in St. Petersburg. Billy was even contemplating moving to Moscow because traveling from Moscow was much easier. Markscheider Kunst spent a year living in Moscow in 1997, but returned since, as Efr put it, "it was better at home" (Efremenko 2005). Musicians including the above mentioned do not only travel to Moscow to play, but also tour other parts of Russia and also Europe – especially Germany – to earn money.[85]

Despite this, going on tour is also hard, because contacts abroad are needed as well as a *zagranpasport* (foreign passport). Furthermore, the travel costs are very high for Russians and their disposable incomes are low, limiting the amount of money that could be invested in tours.

Traveling to Moscow was, however, not always seen as positive. When I asked about musicians often going to Moscow to play, the musicians from Iva Nova gave the following reply:

> Katia: "There are those people who often, probably, work mostly in dives. [...] Many of the Petersburg bands, who often play in Moscow, [do] not all live in Piter, because they can't play [in Piter] often enough to live there. And those who perform often normally work in a bar or in dives."
> LenaN: "Who every day..."
> Katia: "Yes, that is work. Our work is a little different. There is a difference between a musician who only works in bars each time, well, every evening, like going to work everyday or three scheduled times a week, but we are in a different situation. We can't play that often, because a concert is conceptual. And we don't have to. Why? You only get tired from that as well. A lot relate to it in such a way: 'Ah, there's a dive, well.' That is not creative work, that is earning money. And therefore for such musicians maybe it is, of course, more convenient to leave for Moscow. Just to work. Many go away to Finland."
>
> (Fedorova et al. 2005a – Russian: p. 324)

Here two boundaries ("playing in bars" and "everyday") are linked together, both of which are projected against "creative" especially in Moscow, since the city offers such a possibility. Again Moscow is seen as a city which values money/quantity over creative work/quality, an argument they returned to later in the interview. It also points to a musical hierarchy and elitist approach, where people playing in dives and bars are seen as less creative and have lower status than people playing in clubs – a hierarchization I also encountered when talking to musicians in Berlin. The essence of this critique is that restaurant musicians primarily play covers (and not self-composed songs which are valued higher) as well as that the music is in the background – thus the guests are not primarily at the venue to lis-

---

85. According to Andrei Ivanov (pers. comm., 20.12.2004) some musicians spend the summer months on the Krim-peninsula (Ukraine) and other tourist-places playing "Schlager"/pop-music. After the season is over they live off the earnings during the rest of the year.

ten to the groups. In other words, the music is considered pure entertainment. So playing too often as well as playing background music was also at times seen as a way of becoming "commercial".

Regarding the musical qualities, this rivalry argument is, however, schematic and not really representative of all the music in the two towns. It is more concerned with elements of local patriotism. For example, groups playing covers of Western popular music in bars also exist in St. Petersburg. Furthermore, St. Petersburg is an attractive city for musicians, especially coming from other places than Moscow. Several groups I heard during my stay had formed in their home town and then moved to St. Petersburg, e.g. Mata Khari (from Dzerzhinsk), BroSound (from Surgut), DDT (from Ufa) and Svoboda (from Ukraine/Moscow). Some also see St. Petersburg as a stepping stone to Moscow.

In addition, most musicians readily admit that the rivalry is based on clichés and disregard it saying that there is no difference between the cities. As the violinist Dmitrii Khramtsov from the group Dobranoch' puts it:

> "About Piter they say that it is a creative city: 'Piter. We came to Piter. We strived...' For me it's hard to say because I was born here and for me here is nothing remarkable, I know everything here, so for me everything is monotonous. Piter has always been this way and I don't see anything that special about it. That is, compared to Moscow – I travel to Moscow only once a month to play, and I can't say that Piter is better than Moscow in any way, that there is no creativity in Moscow, only in Piter."
> (Khramtsov 2005 – Russian: p. 330)

Furthermore, people I talked to pointed out that life for artists and musicians living in Moscow was not easy: The Tomsk-born artist Nikolai Kopeikin (2005) who had lived in Moscow prior to moving to St. Petersburg said that for him living as an artist in Moscow was hard and that a second job/income was needed. Compared to Moscow the cost of living is lower in St. Petersburg and it is possible to survive only doing art, which for him makes life more relaxing – something Sasha Rudenko also mentioned:

> "And I liked it here. I understood that it is better to make music here than in Moscow. Here it is somehow, well I in the beginning did not believe it. They say the atmosphere here, here yes, here it is somewhat calmer, here the city is more musical. It's not for nothing that you can say that all the best groups are from here, from Piter. Who ever you'd take. Well, there are some in Moscow, but less. And here it is somehow more pleasant. Here's not a lot of space. Here everybody somehow knows each other. And Moscow – is huge. Well! No, it [Moscow] is a good city. But I did not fit in, did not succeed. [...] Therefore music, I feel, is better to do here, at least in the beginning. Moscow, I don't know, always wears me down. Moscow – is a city where the conflict between the little man and the megapolis is felt very strongly. In

> Piter that is somehow not felt so much. Here also the people are nicer, which is the most valuable, it is somehow softer. There in Moscow there is a lot of negativity as I saw it. I just left that behind."
>
> (Rudenko 2006 – Russian: p. 327)

While both St. Petersburg and Moscow are megapolises the pace in Moscow is, in my experience, noticeably more hectic, which can be felt in the overcrowded public transportation, permanent traffic jams, and a sheer abundance of people everywhere. Moscow's size also means that the distances people have to travel and thus time spent in travel to and from concert venues in the center to the outskirts where the residential areas tend to be, is greater than in St. Petersburg. In that sense St. Petersburg is, as Sasha claims, calmer.

An important point to note is Sasha's reference to people knowing each other, in other words a personal network which is the basis for a scene. Here Piter's relatively small scene makes the network more intimate than Moscow. Despite the fact that the pay compared to St. Petersburg is better, the cost of living in Moscow is also higher, making it harder to survive for a group just starting out. Besides the city being calmer and having a network of musicians and friends, other musicians I interviewed mentioned family, an apartment, and the fact that they grew up in St. Petersburg as reasons to remain in St. Petersburg. This reflects, in part, the fact that most of the established musicians I talked to are over 30 and more tied to the city due to family and children. Another factor is that it is hard to get an official residence registration for Moscow (as also for St. Petersburg).

Even though the cliché art vs. commercialism is maintained on the surface as an element of distinction between the two cities and the boundaries of the St. Petersburg scene, the lives of musicians in St. Petersburg are intertwined with Moscow. The musicians profit both from the lower cost of living in St. Petersburg and from the better pay in Moscow, where they often play. To some extent St. Petersburg remains a provincial city dwarfed by Moscow and is used by some musicians as a starting point before trying to make it big (and thus for some "becoming commercial") in Moscow. While there are other differences between Moscow and St. Petersburg like clubs and infrastructure influencing the choices of where to live, a comparison of musical qualities is beyond the scope (and desire) of this book.

A further limitation is how musicians in Moscow view their counterparts in St. Petersburg. Since doing extensive fieldwork in Moscow was beyond the scope of this book I do not have any data to point to except for my assumptions: As the capital, Moscow is the media center, it has good educational institutions, and a well-established music scene with a number of different clubs. In other words, the question is if the rivalry is less explicit in Moscow. Returning to Viacheslav Petkun's words:

> "Arriving from Piter, I understood that the antagonism of people living in Moscow towards people from Piter was much weaker than that of people from Piter towards people from Moscow. Because apart from Piter, people from Moscow also have antagonisms towards the rest of Russia. But in Piter in that sense it's easier."
> (Petkun in Kozyrev and Barabanov 2007b, 63 – Russian: p. 326)

As I have shown, these linked discourses (underground vs. commercial/pop, St. Petersburg vs. Moscow) are in part based on historical and infrastructural differences. An important part of the discourse, however, is relegated to the musicians' imagination of the *Other* (pop, Moscow) which is influenced by the factual differences. The musicians try to distance themselves from these ideas – especially since playing rock – even for the established groups – is from their perspective here perceived as coming from the underdog position. Compared to rock, *popsa* dominates the media and is heard more frequently in St. Petersburg's cafes, discotheques, and family events. By geographically relegating this other, often despised, music to Moscow, which is also perceived as dominating, the rock musicians in St. Petersburg can carve out and claim a space which they market as both geographically as well as musically special.

While there is one national radio station, *Nashe Radio*, that plays Russian language rock, the music aired on that station (including some of the more well-known St. Petersburg bands) was mostly labeled *pop-rok* by the musicians I talked to. This can be seen as a reclaiming of their music as having more worth since it has not been "commercialised" and thus been watered down through being played on the station (here the fact that the station was founded and is based in Moscow also helps). At the same time *Nashe Radio* also opens another discourse based on music labeled *russkii rok* – whose groups, through their exposure, have also been criticized by contemporary groups.

3.3.3 *That shit*: The *russkii rok*-discourse

> On the tape recorder the group "Kino" is playing
> You go: turn off that shit
> You'll go dim from all those oldies
> Shut up, that's my favorite song!
>
> O, gruppa krovi [blood group] on the sleeve[86]
> *Gruppa Krovi* (Leningrad 2000)

The song's protagonist sings about how one of the most popular 1980s LRK bands Kino's *Gruppa Krovi* (Blood group) is his/her favorite song – disdained by the antagonist as "oldies". After telling the antagonist to keep quiet the protagonist quotes the first line from Kino's refrain: *O, blood group on the sleeve* (Kino 1988). This song demonstrates quite well the different reactions towards a certain part of Soviet and Russian popular music. Referred to as *russkii rok* the style emerged during the late 1970s and developed during the 1980s. While today very popular with the last Soviet generation and teenagers, musicians I talked to had a more critical stance towards the music. The next section will discuss this in more detail uncovering another set of boundaries within the St. Petersburg scene.

One of the factors making Leningrad the major center of Soviet rock was the amateur groups linked to the LRK, e.g. Akvarium, Zoopark, the above mentioned Kino, Alisa, and Televizor. The organization gave the groups a possibility to perform and offered workshops. Nevertheless, the material conditions were not optimal, both considering equipment, available technology, and know-how as well as finances which to some extent influenced the performance quality. To compensate for the material problems, the groups put a stronger focus on the lyrics and certain styles which were more accessible for them to play under those conditions (Steinholt 2005, Steinholt, pers. comm., 16.10.2008). These *russkii rok*-groups[87] have remained influential and most of the vocalists still alive such as Boris

---

86. *V magnitofone igraet gruppa "Kino"*; *Ty govorish' mne: "Vykliuchi eto govno!"*; *Tebia lomaet ot vsiakogo star'ia*; *Zatknis', eto liubimaia pesnia moia! O, gruppa krovi na rukave*
87. Literally *Russian fate* – but *rok* is here used as an English borrowing. While being used as a synonym for the previously mentioned groups, the term itself is of more recent origin: The slavist Sergio Mazzanti (2007) has charted the use of *russkii rok* and argues, that as a label *russkii rok* was retroactively applied in the 1990s to define Soviet and post-Soviet rock. He shows that the term first gained traction from around 2000 – which coincides with the rise of the radio station *Nashe Radio* promoting Soviet rock discussed below.

Grebenshchikov (Akvarium), Konstantin Kinchev (Alisa), and Iurii Shevchuk (DDT) currently perform in huge auditoriums.[88]

Picture 9: Viktor Tsoi's grave at the Bogoslovskoe cemetery (St. Petersburg). He remains popular even more than 20 years after his death. Picture taken in St. Petersburg in 2013.

Current popular culture also pays its tribute to the legends of *russkii rok*. Songs are covered by contemporary groups e.g. Zoopark's *Starye Rany* (Old scars) by Al-

---

88. Besides those already mentioned other singers and groups within or close to this style, according to the musicians I talked to, were Piknik, Chaif, Splin, Chizh, Auktsyon, Grazhdanskaia Oborona, and Aleksander Bashlachev.

isa (Alisa 2007b), Kino's *Mama anarkhiia* by Svoboda (Various Artists 2008b), or Grazhdanskaia Oborona's/Egor Letov's *Moia oborona* (My defense) by Vadim Kurylev (Kurylev 2003) and are also collected on regularly released tribute albums for groups considered *russkii rok*, e.g. for Kino (Various Artists 2000), for Akvarium's vocalist Grebenshchikov (Various Artists 2003c; Various Artists 2003d), and for Zoopark's vocalist Maik Naumenko (Various Artists 2005d).[89] Contemporary groups like Leningrad incorporate references to *russkii rok* bands, like the song *Gruppa Krovi* (Leningrad 2000) discussed above. Songs are also heard in movies, e.g. Akvarium's 1985 song 212-85-06 (Akvarium 2002b) in the 2006 movie *Piter FM* or the use of music from various 1980-*russkii rok* bands in the 2008 movie *Stiliagi* (Hipsters – which thematically plays in Post-Stalin Moscow of the 1950s...).

Finally, the radio station *Nashe Radio* also plays an important role: The station primarily focuses on Russian-language popular music. In an interview the general producer Mikhail Zotov, who together with the station's founder Mikhail Kozyrev developed the stations *format* (cf. Kozyrev and Barabanov 2007b, 48), defined the style as such:

"This station presents a huge reservoir of Russian music: on our waves one hears russkii rok from the 1980s, 1990s, pop-rok from the 1990s and the beginning of the 21ˢᵗ century, as well as some kind of element of metal and contemporary ethnic [music]."

(Zotov and Bogdanova 2007 – Russian: p. 322)

What is striking when listening to the station is the abundance of *russkii rok* – even the contemporary songs aired include many currently (still) active *russkii rok* bands. When I asked Elena Danilova (2006), the *Nashe Radio's* St. Petersburg office director, about the proportion she answered that the mix consisted of 60% older (1980s/90s – *russkii rok*) and 40% contemporary music. The program *Letopis'* (Chronicle), which specifically discusses older (rock) groups, plays an important role here: "'Chronicle' – it's a program about such famous albums of musicians who contributed to the music. It's aired once a week." (Danilova 2006 – Russian: p. 321) These "important recordings and musicians" are primarily focused on the Soviet rock-heritage such as Akvarium's album *Treugol'nik* (Triangle, released 1981 – Akvarium 2002a) and Alisa's album *Energiia* (Energy, released

---

[89]. Andrei Tropillo is frequently responsible for these (and similar) compilations, having released Various Artists (2003c, 2003d, 2005d).

1985 – Alisa 1986) and the early 1990s. In other words, mostly *russkii rok*. *Nashe Radio* can thus be said to contribute to a canonization of *russkii rok* legends by airing the music (being the only radio station heard nationwide doing so).

3.3.3.1 The musicians' perception of *russkii rok*

"Complete shit! Next question!"[90]
(Parygin 2006)

Spitfire and Leningrad's trumpet-player Roma Parygin's (2006) response "Complete shit!" when asked about *russkii rok* is symptomatic for the attitude some musicians in St. Petersburg present when asked about their musical preferences and touches on another discourse within the St. Petersburg scene: *russkii rok*.

Following in Roma's vein Vitia, Con Brio's guitarist, saw *russkii rok* as "primitive" and "horrible" (Kultashov 2006). A general consensus was that *russkii rok* is focused on the lyrics at the cost of the music as exemplified by Sasha's following quote:

"Because russkii rok – is more biased towards the lyrics, but pop-rock, that is biased towards music, pretension on music I would say. It is when, I think, brains don't suffice, then people say: 'And we play pop-rock.' When they can't write good lyrics."
(Rudenko 2006 – Russian: p. 327)

This lyric-centric approach to *russkii rok* is not only seen among musicians, but also in Russian research on Russian-language popular music which considers *russkii rok* lyrics as rock poetry (cf. the almost annually appearing anthology *Russkaia Rok-poeziia* – Russian rock-poetry – co-published by Iurii Domanskii). Vitia pointed out that the *russkii rok*-sound is also conserved in bands from the 1990s he considered *pop-rok* (e.g. Zemfira, Mumii Troll', and Brat'ia Grim – Kultashov 2006). As in the discussion above on underground vs. commercial, the term *pop-rok* is used to point out that the music has a more popular appeal while at the same time distancing it from *popsa*. Furthermore, the groups labeled *pop-rok* by Vitia and other musicians are aired on *Nashe Radio* – a further indication of the fluid boundaries between underground and commercial, rock and pop/*pop-rok*, as well as the higher exposure *russkii rok* has had in relation to more contemporary forms of rock.

Historically *russkii rok* has been linked to the so called *bardovskaia pesnia* (bard songs) which in turn traces its roots to songs from Soviet penal camps and the urban pre-revolutionary genres *gorodskoi romans* (city ballad) and *blatnaia*

---

90. *Polnoe govno! Sleduiushchii vopros!*

pesnia (underworld song) (Steinholt 2005, 103ff). Sasha Nevskii voiced a common opinion:

> "Well, roughly speaking, russkii rok is, in principle, songs where one could take an acoustic guitar and perform them with two chords. [...] With Russian [pagan] culture it has nothing in common, because all our Russian rockers – they are strongly attracted by the bard song. You take any group. Take DDT. If you remove all the musicians from there and leave Shevchuk with an acoustic guitar, that will be absolutely the same thing. Or Grebenshchikov. No, Grebenshchikov lately, in the last albums, he tries harder with the instruments, but again we were at his last concert. It was clear that he did not write the arrangements himself, that is, no concept of instrumentation, that is he only invites good musicians, who can improvise along with him. But in general his music sounds like a total salad because he somewhere has elements of blues, here elements of reggae, there also some kind, and to top it all the arrangements are a total salad. Hence it is sometimes better to listen to Grebenshchikov with an acoustic guitar and it, let's say, conserves some kind of style, his own. It is his playing with guitar rather than that strange instrumentation."
> (Vladimirov 2005 – Russian: p. 320)

The linking of *russkii rok* with the bard tradition (e.g. Bulat Okudzhava, Vladimir Vysotskii) stresses once again the primacy of the lyrics over the melody.[91] Nevskii's comment that the songs can be played on a guitar with two chords (thus being harmonically uninteresting) also reflects on Vitia's assertion that *russkii rok* is based on four chords (Kultashov 2006).[92] In addition to Shevchuk and Grebenshchikov, Bashlachev and Kinchev were frequently mentioned as bards. These are together with Naumenko (Zoopark), Letov (Grazhdanskaia Oborona), and Viktor Tsoi (Kino) arguably the most influential singer-songwriters of *russkii rok*.

Aleksandr Bashlachev (1960-1988) occupies a special position here – being an intermediary between the bard and rock tradition (cf. Troitsky 1987, 111).[93] Dis-

---

91. Commenting on Grebenshchikov's 2008 album *Loshad' Belaia* (White Horse – Akvarium 2008) and my criticism that Grebenshchikov was recycling his musical material from previous albums Andrei Ivanov replied that Grebenshchikov was always more of a poet than a musician and that the lyrics were – as always – current and to the point (pers. comm., 16.12.2008).
92. Akvarium's former bass-player Mikhail Feinshtein-Vasil'ev (2002) argues that the voice timbre and lyrics were what made Vladimir Vysotskii important for Russians, not his guitar playing which was grouped around the same 3 or 4 chords.
93. The recordings of his works consist primarily of him singing and accompanying himself on an acoustic guitar (with either 7 or 12 strings – it is at times hard to hear on the recordings) with simple chord progressions, where the guitar functions more as a rhythm instrument than as a harmonic foundation. His signature song *Vremia Kolokol'chikov* (Time of the Little Bells – Bashlachev 1999) consists of em and C alternating on the first beat of each new measure. The melodic line is a recitative primarily around B and C (following the chord progression). Cf. Troitsky (1987, 149) and Burlaka (2007a, 136) for a list of recordings.

covered and promoted by Artem Troitskii in 1984 he was active within the Leningrad and Moscow rock scene performing both solo and with musicians like Shevchuk and Kinchev until he committed suicide on February 17th, 1988. He has had a major impact on songs of his contemporaries, amongst others Kinchev (Alisa), Tsoi (Kino), and Dmitrii Reviakin (Kalinov Most) – an influence that has remained until today (Burlaka 2007a). A book on Soviet popular music carries the title of his song *Vremia Kolokol'chikov* (Time of the Little Bells – Smirnov 1994) and Sasha Rudenko listed him as a major influence during the interview – especially on the song *Kholodno Nam* (We are cold – not part of Svoboda's active repertoire, cf. p. 189ff). This influence is also manifested in mini-festivals in his honor such as a memorial concert for Bashlashev where Sasha accompanied himself on the guitar and performed *Kholodno Nam* (*Kamchatka*, 17.02.2006).

Touching on ideology, the St. Petersburg Times' music journalist Sergei Chernov criticized *russkii rok* for being primitive music with "messianic ideas" since the musicians involved see the music on the same level as Western rock:

"Russkii rok – that is the group DDT, the group Chizh i Kompaniia. Hard to formulate. As such a little messianic, which is more than music, which comes with some kind of religious ideas, or such primitive music and with some kind of mandatory touch of Russian folklore or Russian whatever. The group Chaif: Just all that [...], when the club TaMtAm opened, it had the rule that russkii rok should not be there at all. I found that russkii rok – that is the group Akvarium, the group Grazhdanskaia Oborona, and still another group. They are just different aspects of it. [...] The TaMtAm idea, I think, was purely such an international one, that there was no such provincialism there. Another idea of russkii rok is that they are not worse than Western groups and that it has its own idea which is sort of Russian and a lot of people, probably, they have a lot of fans, a lot of people, probably, think so, but it is not that interesting, I think."

(Chernov 2006a – Russian: p. 331)

A reason for the club *TaMtAm's* mythologization is that people from St. Petersburg claim it opened as a reaction to the bands associated with the LRK. Seva Gakkel modeled the club on US-indie clubs focusing on unknown bands who did not copy the canonized groups of his generation (Zaytseva 2006, 8). The bands originating and performing at *TaMtAm* (e.g. Markscheider Kunst, Leningrad, Tequilajazzz) orientated themselves stylistically away from the groups associated with the LRK and towards other styles like ska, rockabilly, punk, South American, and African styles.

This attitude remains until today. Answering a question about his role in *russkii rok's* fate, Leningrad's vocalist Sergei Shnurov answered: *"Mogil'shchika!"*

(grave digger – qtd. in Shergina 2009). I also encountered this negative view in Berlin where Yuriy Gurzhy dismissed *russkii rok*:
> "That, which was created in the USSR – badly recorded music with mostly pathetic and political lyrics. Today mostly uninteresting musically."
> (pers. comm., 24.04.2006 – German: p. 314)

Besides touching on the lyrical and musical qualities, this comment points to a common perception of the rock groups active in the 1980s as being against the system. The line of argument is that musicians criticized the government and thus helped bring down the Soviet Union. Two bands frequently mentioned are DDT and Televizor as pointed out by Sharapov:
> "Mid to late 80s there were a lot of rather political mainstream bands like DDT or Televizor. They had been promoting quote-unquote democratic values and society and they were like saying and singing stuff against communism and totalitarianism and bands like Grazhdanskaia Oborona as well which were more on the underground level, but still they were rather popular and still are."
> (Ivanov 2005)

This idea that many rock bands in the 1980s either actively battled the socialist regime or showed their resistance by placing themselves outside the general Soviet society is also expressed in previous research on Soviet rock. The probably most influential example is the sociologist Thomas Cushman who applies the term "counterculture" to the Leningrad/St. Petersburg scene. He defines "counterculture" as
> "a community of similarly situated social actors who share values, perceptions, beliefs, and cultural symbols which stand in opposition to the dominant, 'normal' culture of Soviet industrial society. 'Rock musical counterculture' refers to a group of individuals who share [...] a common commitment to the autonomous production and dissemination of rock music without overt or covert interference by 'outside' political or economic forces."
> (Cushman 1995, 8)

Influenced by subcultural theory Cushman isolates the rock community from general society. Recent research, however, dispels this myth. The popular music scholar Yngvar Steinholt (2005) analyses the LRK as a self-governing musical reservation and uncovers both the internal and external forces which position the different actors (musicians, curators, KGB etc.). The LRK itself was – just like the *VIAs* 15 years earlier – an attempt to gain control over amateur rock groups in Leningrad, thus the production and dissemination of rock music was very well also (indirectly) influenced by outside forces.

Going a step further, looking at Soviet society in general, the anthropologist Alexei Yurchak argues that

> "late socialism became marked by an explosion of various styles of living that were simultaneously inside and outside the system and can be characterized as 'being *vnye*.' [...] [B]eing *vnye* was not an exception to the dominant style of living in late socialism but, on the contrary, a central and widespread principle of living in that system. It created a major *deterritorialization* of late Soviet culture, which was not a form of opposition to the system. It was enabled by the Soviet state itself, without being determined by or even visible to it."
>
> (Yurchak 2006, 128)

In other words, people both were part of the Soviet system, taking part in official meetings and working (even the amateur rock musicians had day jobs like boiler room stokers or janitors) while at the same time living outside the system, doing what pleased them. They were living in what they believed was an eternal system which then unexpectedly collapsed – poignantly summarized in the title of Yurchak's book "Everything Was Forever, Until It Was No More".

This view also affects previous approaches to *russkii rok* as inherently political. The late publisher and lyricist for the Soviet group Nautilus Pompilius, Il'ia Kormil'tsev (2006a) claimed that there were no anti-Soviet songs before perestroika. Steinholt (2005) argues in a more nuanced way that since the LRK functioned as a self-governing musical reservation the first "political" songs like Televizor's *Tvoi papa – fashist* (Your dad's a fascist – Televizor 2001) could at the time of the song's recording be seen more in the light of an internal power struggle than as an explicit criticism of the government.

Returning to Sharapov's comment, Shevchuk (DDT) and Mikhail Borzykin (Televizor) are today the two most vocal and outspoken musicians from the 1980s, critically commenting on social issues and, especially Borzykin, criticizing the government. In regards to their activities in the 1980s this has to, however, be seen in a more nuanced way.

Contemporary musicians' reluctance (or outright hostility) towards *russkii rok* – which, with a general audience, remains immensely popular today – has several reasons: The possibility of playing and performing popular music in the 1970s and 80s was restricted. While the LRK offered an organization and a performance venue, most musicians were self-taught amateurs, which is reflected in the musical quality and the command of their instruments and criticized today. Furthermore, the technical equipment (both for live concerts as well as recording equipment) was not comparable to that of European and US-American groups of the time. That said, the musicians had a broad listening biography and knowledge of European and US-American popular music and made an important contribution to Soviet and post-Soviet popular music (Steinholt, pers. comm., 16.10.2008). This is important to keep in mind from today's perspective.

Another reason for this distancing from *russkii rok* is to promote one's own style as something different and new. A part of this is also a break with the older generation who, as Soviet rock heroes, get more media coverage on radio and tv, play in stadiums, and are thus seen in Andrei Burlaka's words, as "pop" (cf. quote on p. 122) – in other words "commercial". This break is also reflected in the role *TaMtAm* played and CD compilations like *Russkii Andegraund* (Various Artists 2006b) which focus on locally, but not nationally established contemporary groups. Here the discourse overlaps with the underground vs. commercial discussion mentioned above.

That said, I also encountered a general hostility among musicians towards Russian popular music and a preference for European and US-American popular music (e.g. Limp Bizkit, System of a Down, Jamiroquai). One example is Svoboda's drummer, Misha Nefedov (pers. comm. 13.04.2005) who said that he does not like Russian rock because Russian bands in general cannot make good music. This answer is particularly interesting, since he played with one of the legends of *russkii rok*, Alisa, for about 15 years.

While the former two discourses position the bands within the rock scene (in opposition to the "commercial other") the *russkii rok* discourse is an internal scene discourse which should be seen more as a way to position one's band in relation to the rock tradition (it is, however, also a discourse around commerciality since the remaining active *russkii rok* groups are quite successful). This is music with which the musicians are more familiar due to its stylistic closeness. As I will demonstrate, based on Svoboda's creative work (cf. p. 189ff), the *russkii rok* tradition remains an important influence on contemporary groups – from outright dismissing it as Leningrad does to (subtly) referring to *russkii rok*-songs as Svoboda does.

3.4 Concluding remarks

In the previous discussion the St. Petersburg scene has been approached as a geographically bounded entity (somewhat in line with a single sited field common to "traditional" ethnomusicology and older concepts of scene – e.g. Cohen 2001; Shank 1994). Here I have charted the scene from three sides. I first focused on the band's (specifically Svoboda's) network outlining a community of actors with (several) roles involved in the local musical life. These groups are united under the label *rock as a musical culture*. This was then linked to social hubs – physical venues where the scene is made visible. The third part focused on overarching shared perceptions (or tastes and values) which unite the people in the St. Petersburg scene and at the same time outline an audible boundary separating them from other scenes.[94]

Focusing on *production* (here understood as composing, performing, recording), the scene-approach combined the material conditions present in St. Petersburg with the daily workings of musicians as they cope with these conditions. This has provided a basis for discussing the discourses since they are in part influenced by these conditions and effectively also shape the music made in St. Petersburg. The aim has been to show both how musical life within the scene is similar to other places and at the same time to point out specific differences (linked to history, geography, and economics) which make the St. Petersburg scene unique. One point is the transition to a capitalist economy following the collapse of the Soviet Union – traces of which still can be felt today in the lack of performance venues and affordable practice rooms. On the positive side, this transition has made quality instruments and other equipment more readily available – which is also reflected in the city's amount of recording possibilities.

Another uniqueness is the city's history, especially its past as a center for Soviet rock music. St. Petersburg's reputation as a rock city has remained until today and indirectly comments on how the music is produced – both in terms of how it is

---

94. Disregarding the St. Petersburg-Moscow rivalry, this discussion has primarily focused on the local level. St Petersburg is, however, part of a translocal music network and thus a node in a world wide musical network. Another node within this network is Berlin and the fortnightly musical event *Russendisko*. The *Russendisko* offers some different perspectives when conceptualized through the scene theory especially its relationship to place: originally anchored in Berlin the event has become both translocal as well as to some extent virtual. These dynamics will be discussed in chapter 8.

composed (by a singer-songwriter or the band itself) and how it is played (by the band itself). This is in opposition to *popsa* which on the surface is widely perceived by St. Petersburg musicians to be composed by a producer who picked a good-looking person to record and perform the song accompanied by a mostly anonymous band. At the same time the rock-pop discourses show the complex negotiations regarding musical belonging and how groups are categorized since the boundaries are fuzzy, even overlapping and dependent on the perspective of the individual.

While music cannot refer to a specific place on a denotative level as discussed in the following chapter certain schools or common stylistic traits can emerge which then become synonymous for that specific place. This is primarily due to different bands (and producers) within a scene influencing each other – e.g. what has been promoted as the *Seattle* or *Nashville sound*. When discussing these sounds based on what record labels and the media promote, it is easy to forget that a scene incorporates a much wider range of musical styles. Here a production approach which focuses on the underlying networks, social hubs, and discourses is more inclusive since the point of departure is the location per se, not a predefined narrow set of musical criteria based on 1-2 bands or the roster of certain record labels. This focus also uncovers the fact that the musicians active are not a homogeneous group but include in St. Petersburg both conservatory trained musicians, mainly on the woodwind and brass instruments, as well as music school or even self taught musicians mainly playing rhythm-section instruments.

While the musicians' opinions are influenced not only by their observations and interactions with other musicians, but also by the media and other information sources, musicians and actors in St. Petersburg had nuanced views regarding the music in St. Petersburg. This collides with what might have been a more monolithic view if the focus had been on the marketing strategies of the record labels, a media reading of the groups, or a consumption reading of the scene.

Drawing on musical productions and musicians' statements, the following chapter picks up on St. Petersburg's local meaning by outlining how musicians anchor their creative work in the city.

4 The musical embedding of St. Petersburg

> Nina, my head hurts
> Oh, meat-pies! I must have eaten some-kind of shit
> Nina, my head hurts
> Oh fuck
> Nina, my head hurts
> Brush teeth
> They are stalking me
> Nina
> He, he, washing [his] eggs [balls]
> Nina (NOM 2002 – Russian: p. 302)

Starting with a synthetic xylophone continuously playing staccato eights over a d accompanied by a chromatic ostinato bass line (from b to d and back) a slightly nasally sounding man repeats *Nina, my head hurts* over and over again (the lyrics are shaped like an inner monologue). In the course of the song the man adds *Oh, meat-pies!*[95] *I must have eaten some-kind of shit*, claims he is being stalked, brushes his teeth, exclaims *Oh fuck* and ends the song washing his testicles. At first glance, this song does not seem to convey any feeling of place nor *signifyin'* (Gates 1988) on any specific popular music genre. While the language sung in (Russian) could be used as an indicator of location, the lack of dialects in a narrow sense which can pinpoint a speaker to a certain village or city in Russia makes it hard to give a location.

The song's video clip (NOM 2007) does not add any clarity, being very static and consisting of three main settings: Two men (one with a red made-up nose, the other with a green one) standing in front of a wall with one half painted yellow and the other half painted red. The next setting contains two half way opened doors with a man dressed in a huge fur hat looking out. The third setting is a dark sound stage with a small catwalk in the middle with what looks like a piece of broken glass protruding. Alternatively one or two men pose on the stage in different costumes. While the movements of the people are coordinated with the music (e.g the phrase *Nina, my head hurts* is said as a dialog between the two men in front of

---

95. Meat stuffed with mashed potatoes.

the colored wall) there is no overlap between the semantic meaning of the lyrics and the action in the clip.

In short, the clip is open to a wide range of interpretations due to the lack of a linear narrative both visually and on the level of lyrics (on the musical level the repetitious synthetic xylophone could be read as a metaphor for the headache hammering away). However, Andrei Kagadeev, NOM's bass-player and one of the vocalists, provided some information which placed the clip within a very local experience:

> "In the 1990 or 1991 [...] the first rap-singles [appeared and I] invented with my brother this kind of Russian stupid rap based on some words which we heard in our communal flat, where we lived all our childhood with our mad neighbor. [...] For us it was kind of parody to the whole rap. Rap was a quite energetic music with all this reciting and we made [it] very cool, very electronic with xylophone and with this drum machine. It was for us very funny."
>
> (Kagadeev 2004)

Andrei also pointed out that he is inspired by everyday situations in St. Petersburg, which is reflected in NOM's general creative work. These statements provide two hints which place the song musically within transcultural flows and at the same time link the lyrics to a (very) local experience: Despite all its absurdity, *Nina* reflects the daily lives of many inhabitants of St. Petersburg, living in a so called *kommunal'naia kvartira* or *kommunalka* (a communal housing system typical for the Soviet Union) with, at times, strange neighbors. At the same time, the song is an appropriation of (or *signifyin' on*) rap which by the early 1990s had become a globally accessible idiom. Through *de-* and *re-mediaization*, the members of NOM appropriated rap in their own specific way.

Describing NOM Andrei said that the main idea behind the group was to carry on the tradition of Russian absurd literature like Nikolai Gogol' and the St. Petersburg poets linked to the post-revolutionary avant-garde of the 1920s, namely Danil Kharms, Aleksandr Vvedenskii, and Nikolai Oleinikov (also referred to as the *OBeRIu*-group). This places the lyrics within a local literary tradition further anchoring the group to St. Petersburg.

As this example shows, *Nina* can be closely linked to St. Petersburg (or Leningrad depending on the perspective) and a very common way of living in Soviet and post-Soviet Russia. In other words, the song can function as a metaphor for life in a *kommunalka*. But this knowledge is not a given: A casual listening to the song does not necessarily uncover these elements nor does the song readily function as a rap parody. The clearest influence is probably the literary link based on what can be perceived as absurd lyrics – but only for a knowledgeable Russian-speaking audience.

On a local level, discourses around a specific sound like the *Liverpool Sound* help construct an identity in opposition to others (e.g. Manchester, London). However, as Sara Cohen (1997) demonstrates, there is not really a specific Liverpool sound, rather it is a construction used to show why musicians from Liverpool are special. This is similar to the discourses described in chapter 3 in relation to St. Petersburg. I want to round off that discussion by exploring if and how groups from St. Petersburg construct an explicit link between music and place in their creative work. My point of departure – which goes back to the identity discussion in chapter 1 – is that music does not carry an intrinsic meaning which can be decoded. It is the listener who creates this meaning discursively, at times with the help of the composer (if s/he explicitly communicates that) and/or a music critic if the listener accepts or understands the statements. This is because music from a semiotic perspective lacks a *denotative* level – specifically what Jakobson (1981) terms *referential* function. This means that unlike language, music as well as sounds cannot directly refer to something outside of music.[96]

Due to music's ability to be a vessel for several (arbitrary) identities it can, however, on a *connotative* level mediate a specific location[97] in a powerful way. Using the *Manchester sound* as an example, the urban studies scholar Giacomo Bottà argues that popular music has the

"ability to implement places in a credible authentic way, forming new modalities to conceive and perceive them [places]. This is the result of layering: popular music products and practices mediate places as *textscapes, soundscapes* and *landscapes.*"
(Bottà 2006b, 123)

I agree with Bottà's way of analyzing how a specific place (or locality) is mediated through a tri-partite model, examining the images used (*landscapes*), the lyrics and promotion material (*textscapes*), as well as drawing on local music traditions and sounds (*soundscapes*). Using music as a metaphor for place, however,

---

96. Music can establish an internal reference system through repetitions and variations, e.g. the so called *Sonatensatzform* (which is, however, also based on arbitrary conventions). While it, in combination with images/lyrics as in Wagner's use of *Leitmotive*, can establish a link to something outside a sonic system (the sword Nothung, the Ring, Fafner, Siegfried, Tarnhelm etc.) music cannot by itself refer to e.g. emotions, a house, city, or region.

97. With this I mean a location unrelated to where the music is heard by the listener (unless the two locations happen to be the same one).

carries the risk of placing an inherent meaning within music. While a musician's style of playing can be very local, based on the fact that his/her teacher is from the same place, a local teaching tradition etc., these elements are not normally linked to a certain location (and even when it is, as in Norwegian traditional music, the link to locality is first manifested through talking about the music).

As the example above has shown, some kind of reference has to be established to link music to place. This can be done discursively as Andrei's narration showed and/or through personal (visual) observations. In Born and Hesmondhalgh's words "musical meaning is intensely bound up with visual and narrative texts." (2000a, 11) One strategy often used when incorporating sounds from a specific locality is *pars pro toto* (or synecdoche) and metonymy (in other words, a syntagmatic combination): the opening phrase *Ostorozhno, dveri zakryvaiutsia!* (Be careful, the doors are closing) from Reggistan's song *Reggi, reggei* (Reggistan 1999, cf. p. 153ff) refers to the subway in St. Petersburg. It is a sound (or phrase) any hearing person who has used the subway in St. Petersburg would recognize and thus functions as a metonymy of St. Petersburg. Another example is the song *Moskva i Mariuana* (Moscow and Marihuana – Ackee Ma-Ma u.r.b. 2005, cf. p. 124) which opens to the church bells from the Spasskaia Tower in the Moscow Kremlin, heard and televised, among other times, in the Russian president's New Year speech at midnight. The distinct melody of the chime functions as a *pars pro toto* of the Moscow Kremlin and thus as a metonymy for Moscow (the song also being about Moscow). But both these metonymies only imply locality if the person listening has heard them before as a specific reference to St. Petersburg respectively Moscow.[98]

While it is thus hard to communicate place through music intrinsically, place can both be a very influencing factor in the production of music as well as it can be an important aspect of the band image. Here, as discussed in chapter 3, the local infrastructure can be an influencing factor, but also the city itself and how the artists perceive the city can influence the musicians' creative work. Bottà's distinction between *image, aural,* and *textual levels* (I prefer these terms) provide a good way to examine how those three levels can interact to anchor a group locally (or to examine which layers provide a local anchoring and which do not).

---

98. I do not specifically discuss metaphors here since the link between place and music is even more personal and arbitrary.

An example of how the promotional material (and thus textual and image level) dominates the anchoring, is the compilation *My iz Pitera* (We're from Piter – Various Artists 2003a), which sports a vague collage of photographs from St. Petersburg on the cover and thus implicitly links the 20 groups featured to St. Petersburg. The names of two groups point to St. Petersburg: While the group St. Petersburg Ska Jazz Review directly invokes the city in its name, the group Port(812) points to the city's telephone code (812) as well as the fact that St. Petersburg is a port. At first glance the CD's songs do not seem to convey St. Petersburg in any way. A closer look, however, reveals the statement *Pochustvuite nastoiashchii piterskii ROK!* (Feel real Piter ROCK!) on the booklet as well as the song *Popsa* by the group Brigadnyi podriad (cf. p. 118). This can be seen as a comment on the St. Petersburg/rock vs. Moscow/pop discourse thus providing a local anchoring.

Several musicians I talked to, such as Tania (Ackee Ma-Ma), expressed their personal love for the city. In Tania's case this also was reflected in her creative work. When asked why she chose *Urban* as the title of her first CD (Ackee Ma-Ma u.r.b. 2005) she answered:

> "Because with us it happened that our first album appeared, and all the songs were somehow connected with the city. I, in general, really love the city and even the song 'Sankt-Peterburg', although it's German, it's written about our city. Probably I am a fan of Piter."
>
> (Iatsenko 2006 – Russian: p. 332)

The visuals on the CD invoke a city which very well could be St. Petersburg (but with a reference to Moscow since the booklet's cover depicts a sign of the Moscow-based chain *Kofe Khauz* – Coffee House – in the background). The inside of the booklet shows the band walking down an alley whose architecture looks like St. Petersburg, and the inside of the jewel case depicts the entrance to a house which is run down – also a common sight in St. Petersburg (but also in other places in Russia). The CD opens with the song *St. Petersburg* (sung in German) and the tracks are interlaced with street sounds placing it in an urban context which could be St. Petersburg. The song *Moskva i Mariuana* is indirectly linked to St. Petersburg since the lyrics criticize Moscow. But besides these indirect hints and Tania's statement the visuals and sound could also refer to a different city since neither the rivalry with Moscow nor *Kofe Khauz* is limited to St. Petersburg.

Picture 10: Cover of Billy's Band's album *Parizhskie Sezony*.

Billy Novik (Billy's Band) also draws on images from St. Petersburg. The opening page of the band's website during my fieldwork depicted the door to an apartment with several door bells – probably because it functions as a *kommunalka* – which is a common sight in St. Petersburg (Billy's Band 2003a). The albums *Parizhskie Sezony* (Parisian seasons – Billy's Band 2003b) and *Otorvemsia Po-Piterski* (Let's celebrate in St. Petersburg style – Billy's Band 2005) both draw on images from the city – the former by depicting what seems to be the view from where the canal Moika flows into the canal Fontanka (with a view of the houses on the street *nab. reki Fontanki* – cf. Picture 10 and Picture 11). The latter's pictures (a broken window, a bench with flaking paint) could be from any (Russian) city, however by virtue of the disc's name, the thickness of the blurred drain pipe on the cover as well as Billy's city of origin, the evidence points to St. Petersburg. The lyrics contain references to the city including street names (e.g. *Sadovaia Ul.*, *Malaia Morskaia*), parts of St. Petersburg (e.g. Kupchino) and also the famous *White Nights*. Billy employed this as a conscious (marketing) strategy:

> "It seems to me that in a lot of my songs I have lines about some streets, these are real streets. There is for example the street Malaia Morskaia somewhere, somewhere a song about Kupchino. When you apply particular names, certain names in

the song, which exist in reality, then it, I think, makes the stories more realistic [...]. And in Piter I have this possibility, because I know. I imagine for example what the crossing between Nevskii and Malaia Morskaia is like. If I sing about that, those people who also understand, they will understand precisely what I am singing about."

(Novik 2005 – Russian: p. 326)

Here the geographical references are used as an authentication strategy – a way of making the songs more realistic and more accessible to the audience. Billy can employ this strategy since he is from the city himself and thus can convincingly communicate those places.

Picture 11: View from where the canal Moika flows into the canal Fontanka. Picture taken in St. Petersburg in 2011.

Most of the groups I talked to were, however, more ambivalent about the role the city played in their creative work and had to think for a long time before answering. The musicians in Iva Nova linked St. Petersburg to their group since they met in the city:

LenaZh: "We live in Petersburg. I was born in Petersburg, Lena [Novikova] came to study here [...] Katia also lived here, Inka lived far from Petersburg, moved to Piter to study, Nastia also came to study and to do music. So we live here, this is our city. That is the only reason for the connection to Piter."
David-Emil: "Do you use Piter in your music?"
LenaZh: "No, I don't think that there are elements of Piter." [laughs]
Katia: "We have Petersburg in our blood, it is hard for us to say which elements it has."
Inka: "But we haven't composed any concrete songs about Petersburg yet."
(Fedorova et al. 2005b – Russian: p. 323)

Here the city functions as a meeting place but has no direct influence on their music. In other words, being from St. Petersburg does not play a major role in the group's band image.

While some groups incorporate references to St. Petersburg (some easier to decode, some ambiguous, and some harder) this was not widespread and Iva Nova's answer above reflects a more common notion about groups not directly anchoring the city in their creative work.

As an emotional attachment, St. Petersburg played an important role for individual musicians (like Tania, Billy, and Efr – as seen in his statement on p. 33) and functioned as a general influence on the musicians' working conditions. Due to music's lack of a denotative level, this is not necessarily expressed in the product, but more in their talking *about* the music in general (as discussed in the previous chapter regarding infrastructure and discourses). This includes indirect links to St. Petersburg expressed in the *russkii rok*-tradition. Groups also by virtue of being from St. Petersburg anchor themselves in the city in their promotion and in statements during concerts.

This discussion has also placed St. Petersburg within transcultural music flows: The song *Nina* pointed out the interaction between a local experience and transcultural flows. This kind of cultural exchange plays an important role in appropriating what is perceived to be from a certain locality into a new setting and how it is ascribed a different meaning than that ascribed in the point of origin. Jamaican popular music, specifically ska and reggae provide a good example, since the styles not only show the complexities of how music flows, but also since the styles have, through de- and re-mediaization, become an important part of the St. Petersburg scene. While certain recognizable traits are associated with ska and reggae, the St. Petersburg re-mediaizations are embedded within its own network of meaning, which will be explored in the following chapters.

5   Reggae and ska in St. Petersburg

> In a difficult hour, in minutes of success
> In the circle of friends or just alone,
> In the cold winter, hot summer
> This motive will be with you:
>
> Reggie, Reggie, Reggei
>
> Everything can be easy, can be difficult
> People are like songs: their music is life
> Beauty and happiness, warmth and tenderness
> In each of you, in each of you,
> In each of us
>
> Reggie, Reggie, Reggei
> *Reggi, reggei* (Reggistan 1999 – Russian: p. 308)

In 1985 UB40 performed a three-day concert at the Leningrad sport arena *Iubileinyi* with the after-party at the LRK (Andrei Ivanov, pers. comm., 04.03.2009). Inspired by the concert Andrei Ivanov became interested in reggae and in 1990 joined the group·Streetboys as their vocalist. Andrei said that since there were no clubs to play in, they took to the streets, performing at the crossing *Nevskii prospekt*, the main street in the city center, and *Dumskaia Ulitsa* – hence the name – and at first playing covers of Bob Marley, Third World, Alpha Blondy, and Black Uhuru. Andrei added that by playing on the street they became acquainted with people from Holland and Germany who brought them new reggae records from abroad to study (Ivanov 2004). The band eventually became Reggistan and still remains active today playing a mix of covers and their own songs.[99] The line-up changed over the years – also including non-Russians: René (vocals, guitar from Burundi), Anzh Kombo (guitar, from Congo) and Emanio (vocals, from Jamaica). Several times in conversations with me Andrei stressed the importance of the "Africans" for both himself and the band's style. The song *Reggi, reggei* (Reggistan 1999 – the first two verses are in the quotation above) provides a good

---

99. According to Andrei Burlaka (2007b) they are the first band in St. Petersburg where reggae dominates the style.

example:[100] Andrei sings the first verse, René the second and Emanio sings what Andrei (pers.comm., 13.11.2008) calls the *ragga* part (toasting over the drum/percussion and bass). Not only are the timbres of the vocalists different, but also the diction (both René and Emanio have distinct accents when singing in Russian) – including Emanio toasting in English with a Jamaican (?) pronunciation (the transcription is in normalized English – I left the beginning in Russian marked by italics to point out the language shift):

> "*Vy gotovy? Ea. Vy gotovy? Ea. Smotri! Ia pridu, ia pridu, ia seichas pridu. Ia pridu, ia pridu – obiazatel'no pridu!*[101] We no give a damn about the color of our skin, one hit you with the rhythm in a dancehall style. Got to make your move because it fun feel a good and we are coming with the rhythm in a dancehall style. Roll you belly like we don't just care, forget about the propaganda – this for real. Sit upon the rhythm like we don't look scared, feel comfortable with the drum and the bass. He knows just where them [unclear] mmm, la-la-la-la-la. *Davai!*[102]"

(Reggistan 1999)

While promoting the *native other* can be understood as both an essentialization based on origin and skin color as well as an authentication strategy, it should be seen more as a form of cultural flow where these musicians, through their cultural background, brought new and important impulses to the groups' creative work.

This Streetboys/Reggistan example demonstrates how meetings within the *form of life* level (locals meeting migrants) influence the musical style of a group. Furthermore, it shows how the flow of humans and media are linked in disseminating and advancing a stylistic knowledge. This points to the fact that reggae and its older sibling ska, have become globally accessible styles – even cultural symbols – which at the same time retain an imaginary link to an idealized Jamaica (Rastafarianism, music, national symbols) where the music originated. This chapter focuses on these flows and their role by discussing ska and reggae in St. Petersburg.

---

100. Musically the song incorporates a keyboard playing chords on the upbeats, a second keyboard sounding like a hammond organ, playing chords, and a third one playing what sounds like short horn riffs. Besides a bass playing a two bar riff consisting of two licks (both starting on the 3 and ending on the 1) either electric drums or a drum kit (the bass drum accents all four beats and the snare plays right before the 2 / 4 and on the 2+ / 4+) make up the rhythm section. The harmonic progression is I – IV V – I / C – F G – C.
101. Are you ready? Yeah! Are you ready? Yeah! Look! I'm arriving, I'm arriving, I'm arriving now! I'm arriving, I'm arriving – definitively arriving!
102. Let's Go!

Picture 12: Reggistan. Andrei Ivanov and the keyboard layer Pavel Zelenin performing at the club *Purga* in St. Petersburg (22.09.2005).

While arguably two different styles catering to a different audience, I choose to discuss ska and reggae together since, on the production side, the musicians playing the music overlap. Furthermore, while musically related, the styles have been demedialized differently in St. Petersburg: while reggae roots itself in Jamaican and international reggae, ska has mainly been appropriated as ska-punk. This chapter shows – especially for ska-punk – that the local pioneers of the 1990s and not necessarily the original Jamaican ska and British ska-punk groups, are the main source of inspiration for contemporary musicians in St. Petersburg.

5.1 Style indicators of reggae and ska

Both *ska* and *reggae* are musical styles which emerged in Jamaica in the late 1950s and onward following a rise in national awareness and the country's independence in 1962. The styles themselves are a blend of different influences including local music (*mento*) and Afro-American music from the United States. The main *style indicator* – defined as "any musical structure or set of musical structures that are either constant for or regarded as typical of the 'home' musical style" (Tagg 1999, 28) – for both is the accented up-beats/backbeats.

Chang et al. (2005, 61) date the period when ska emerged and dominated Jamaican popular music from 1960 to mid 1966. The music journalist Stephen Davis offers the following musical characteristics for ska:

"Absorbing the instrumentation of the swing bands and the pulse of rhythm and blues, infused with bass-driven mento, Jamaican musicians developed a native rhythm called SKA. This used a 4/4 shuffle rhythm close to classic rhythm and blues, with an afterbeat originally played on piano, whose sound the term sought to approximate. In these ensembles, horns and reeds emphasize the guitar's chordal beat, and the trombone came to dominate solo sections"

(Davis n.d.)

Focusing more on the rhythmic interaction, King (2002, 22ff) points out that Jamaican ska is characterized by the use of a horn section, an upbeat tempo (110-130 bpm), staccato offbeats played on the guitar (aided by piano and horn section), which is contrasted with accents on the downbeat on the drums (which are rhythmically aided by a walking standup bass).

Today the rhythm, together with the use of a horn section playing (short) riffs, provides the main style indicators for the musical style *ska*.

In the music of the late 1960s, the rhythm slowed down, the horn section gradually faded away and the electric bass gained more prominence. This new style became known as *reggae* – whose era according to Chang et al (2005, 61) spans the period from 1969 to 1983:[103]

"A new regular two-chord guitar pattern provided persistent counterpoint to the bass and drum riddims. The chords of the guitar and keyboard were meshed so that their accents took on reggae's characteristic pulse-like metre."

(Davis n.d.)

Both the labour shortage in the United Kingdom in the 1950s and early 1960s (Hebdige 1987, 90) as well as poverty and anti-Rasta repression in Jamaica since the early 1960s (Manuel 1988, 78) resulted in migration from the West Indies which created Caribbean communities in the former colonizer, United Kingdom. These migrants brought and played ska and subsequently reggae, which not only became popular within the already established Caribbean emigrant communities, but also with white Mods, Rude Boys, Skinheads, and Punks (Barrow and Dalton 1997, 325ff; Webb 2007, 14) – in other words, the flow of humans and interaction on the form of life level. Besides the United Kingdom, the music spread to the United States early on.

But there was also a flow of phonograms enabled through, among others, the businessman and producer Chris Blackwell, one of the founders of *Island Records*. Blackwell started distributing records in the West Indian Ghettos of London in 1962 and had a record shop in Notting Hill/London (Hebdige 1987, 79,90ff; Webb 2007, 16). Hebdige (1987, 91f) argues that "Jamaican ska (and later reggae) was easily transported to Britain because, as we've seen, records have always been at least as important as live music in Jamaica." The music also developed further, with local musicians and Jamaican emigrants combining reggae and ska with punk and hard rock (Manuel 1988, 78).

Besides distributing and selling records in the West Indian communities Blackwell (and others) started to market reggae in the 1970s to a white European-American audience. This was done through a "careful tailoring of audio and visual texts to fit audience biases and record-label market preconceptions" (Alleyne 2000, 19) which included changes to the sound, instrumentation, lyrics, band image, and graphical layout (King 1998, 45ff). Marketed as rebel/protest music this

---

103. A third related style, rocksteady, bridged the ska with the reggae era.

form referred to as *international reggae* and first embodied in Bob Marley and the Wailer's style is often juxtaposed with Jamaican *roots reggae* of the late 1960s.

International reggae became a commercial success not only catapulting Jamaican bands to fame, but also influencing African, US-American and European musicians (cf. Alleyne 2000). In addition to the music and its artists, symbols of Jamaica (primarily the Jamaican tri-colore) and references to Rastafarianism have since become global commodities. While popularizing reggae and Rastafarian philosophy to a broad audience, the actors linked to the success of international reggae were also criticized for straying away from reggae and rastafarian core values.

5.2 *"We're not Rastamen, we're reggae-people"*: Reggae in St. Petersburg

"We're not Rastamen, we're reggae-people."[104]
(Iatsenko 2006)

The above mentioned cultural symbols were also present in St. Petersburg, especially at ska-punk and reggae concerts. These included visible elements linked to reggae (e.g. dreadlocks, garments in the Jamaican tri-color, pictures and silhouettes of marijuana leaves, and Bob Marley) as well as people smoking marijuana. Two reggae musicians I interviewed, the previously mentioned Andrei and Ackee Ma-Ma's vocalist Tania Iatsenko, also confirmed that reggae enjoyed some popularity in the city (Ivanov 2004; Iatsenko 2006). Drawing on his observation as a musician and former *art direktor* of the dedicated reggae club *Dzhambala* Andrei said

"I think that reggae has a varied contingent, first, because the music is going through some kind of second wave. Thus now this music is interesting for those who are 19-20 years old and simultaneously, I think, that there are people coming who are already 30-40 years old."

(Ivanov 2004 – Russian: p. 323)

The reason for this popularity was, in his opinion, the positive and calm aspects of reggae. This makes it attractive and easily accessible to a broad range of listeners who include both the last Soviet generation as well as young adults. Besides the inherent musical qualities (calm, energetic, positive) Andrei mentioned he also attributed the music's popularity to reggae's inherent struggle for the African rights proclaimed in the lyrics. Such struggles were, in his opinion, not

---

104. *My ne rastamany, my reggery.*

foreign to listeners in a post-Soviet Russian reality, where many Soviet complexes were still present.

That said, both Tania and Andrei lamented that the inhabitants of St. Petersburg barely knew what reggae was about – the common associations being dreadlocks and red, green, and gold berets, which had become stylish in St. Petersburg. Referring to these individuals Andrei added

"He knows very little about reggae. He knows – Bob Marley, that you have to smoke ganja [marijuana], and that's it, as a rule, and he doesn't know anything more. Thus I think that it is a superficial effect, fashion. I think that it is fashionable."

(Ivanov 2004 – Russian: p. 323)

This points to a reception of reggae which has been influenced by the marketing of international reggae (images of marijuana, the colors red, green, and gold, as well as Bob Marley as the central icon – cf. King 1998, 47f).[105] This superficiality (or use of clichés) was also at times seen at *Dzhambala*, where the waiters wore bandanas with marijuana leaves (the bandanas could be purchased at the club) and where an African waiter was employed.

Both Andrei and Tania also distanced themselves from Rastafarianism. Andrei is a practicing Buddhist and criticized Rastafarianism for being a young religious mix. He added that it would be quite hard to be a practicing Rastafarian in Russia. While Tania defined reggae as her life and realization – as the music where she found herself – she pointed out that the members of her group were not *rastamany* (Rastamen) also distancing herself from the religion. Instead both Andrei and Tania defined themselves as *reggery* (people who play reggae, reggae-people)[106] – Tania using *white reggery* – in other words stressing the musical, not the ideological aspect.[107]

Smoking marijuana is also frequently associated with Rastafarianism and reggae (as the case with *Dzhambala* above shows). The consumption as well as dealing was also common amongst musicians in St. Petersburg. While there are songs

---

105. This should also be seen within the context of how Andrei and Tania position themselves as insiders within the reggae community.
106. Analogous to *rokery* – rockers
107. On Reggistan's now defunct website, the group also distanced themselves from Rastafariansim: "One of the goals which ReggaeStan has given itself, is the popularisation of Reggae style music in Saint-Petersburg and in Russia. But the activity and philosophy of the group should not be connected with so called rastafarianism which has only African roots. Rhythm, lightness, melody are what ReggaeStan wants to bring to its listeners. The words of the songs – in Russian are on common human themes." (Reggistan n.d.)

which specifically deal with marijuana by the group Respublika Dzha, Markscheider Kunst (see below), Svoboda, and Ackee Ma-Ma, those songs do not necessarily reflect on the musician's consumption habits. Rather the lyrics reflect a commonly made linking of reggae and marijuana. In Svoboda's case, a song based on a reggae rhythm about smoking marijuana – *Ganzhubeilo*[108] – evoked different opinions between Svoboda's fans Denis and Anton: While Denis condemned the song as provocative, since drugs are bad, Anton commended Sasha for bringing up the topic, since in his eyes everybody smokes anyway, but nobody talked about it (Vashkevich and Lukanin 2006).[109]

When discussing the reggae played in St. Petersburg Andrei also pointed to one possible way of music's de-mediaization – by covering original artists:

"In our reggae culture people very often play music from 1978-80. Don't know why they do that. Maybe they don't have the material, they have not heard, you could say. Because we definitively have a big deficit: if you now go to any music store, in the best case they at once offer Bob Marley, UB40, or some kind of reggae compilation, as it is, from 1978-80. That is, accordingly, what people have heard, they also do."

(Ivanov 2004 – Russian: p. 323)

The recordings serve as a point of departure for the local bands, who adopt it to their local musical possibilities and abilities. Andrei went on to criticize a general musical conservatism in the local groups, since they, in his view, primarily imitated the international reggae of the 1970s, and people were not listening to newer material from the 1990s and 2000s. Experimenting with more contemporary forms of reggae and combining the music with the possibilities enabled through digitalization and computers was unusual he pointed out. This he attributed to the lack of newer material in shops and the peoples' lack of knowledge.

Tania had a similar observation stating that in Russia it is common to play roots reggae, defined by her as reggae in a 1970s style. She stressed that reggae had developed from the 1970s, so roots reggae had to be adopted to the 21st century. This was the reason why they played what she called *urban reggae* – a form of reggae with harder sounds than roots (or "original") reggae groups:

"As a starting point we take the reggae tradition, that is, you could say, reggae-drums, reggae-bass, but, let's say, the bass-guitar sounds tighter, the drums more di-

---

108. The song's tempo was slightly slower than the group's other songs, the guitar accented the offs and the horns imitated a Jamaican dub delay effect.
109. I never saw them use marijuana or other drugs, but on the other side, they had a huge consumption of alcohol which still remains the primary drug in Russia.

verse, our Raggamuffin sounds tougher. In general, the music sounds tougher due to the guitar which plays with a fuzzbox [distorted], but, I think, and due to that, that our performance, especially at concerts, is more emotional. That is, if you take Jamaican roots-reggae for example then you can relax to that music on the beach and it can be background music. I think that our music can be liked or not liked, but it will probably not be taken for background music."

(Iatsenko 2006 – Russian: p. 332)

While Tania (and others in St. Petersburg) frequently invoked the term *roots reggae* neither Andrei nor Tania distinguished between *roots* and *international reggae* nor did they comment on the shift started with Blackwell's promotion of Marley. While their criticism regarding the lack of knowledge in St. Petersburg is that other musicians only know what is referred to as *international reggae*, both Tania and Andrei's main complaint was that the music is outdated and should be adopted to a more contemporary sound, e.g. expressed in Tania's *urban reggae*.

Tania added that is was possible to add different styles to reggae:

"I think, first of all that reggae music is very wise, after all it comes from the roots, we cannot turn away from them [the roots], disregarding that it is urban-reggae and, thanks to its wisdom, to reggae jazz and some blues can be added, mix everything a little. That is, it can take up different styles because of its wisdom."

(Iatsenko 2006 – Russian: p. 332)

This can, for example, be heard in the song *Sensimil'ia* (Ackee Ma-Ma u.r.b. 2005) which includes a piano solo of arpeggiated scales drawing on jazz improvisational clichés (and reflects Tania's background as a jazz pianist).

Tania mentioned Dr. I-Bolit as an example of a musician from St. Petersburg who plays roots reggae.[110] One of the most visible reggae musicians in St. Petersburg, he is usually seen in a top hat colored in the Jamaican tri-colore[111] and frequently heard at local reggae festivals. His 2004 album *Go Rastaman Go* (Dr. I-Bolit & Tribal Roots 2004) pays tribute to reggae and Rastafarianism on several levels: Visually it incorporates the Jamaican tri-colore, lions, and two drawn musicians with dreadlocks. The lyrics employ Rastafarian code words like *Jah* (God), *Babylon* (Earth / modern society), *Rasta* (short for *Rastaman*) and includes a special thanks to Haile Selassie I. Musically most of the songs are in a laid back tempo with a pulsating guitar accenting the backbeats. While there are lyrics in Russian

---

110. Other groups mentioned were Respublika Dzha who had moved to Moscow and Dzha Divizhn based in Moscow (Iatsenko 2006).
111. In that image he also made a short visual guest appearance in the 2006 movie *Piter FM* directed by Oksana Bychkova.

and French (the CD features the Congolese vocalist Seraphim Selenge Makangila as a guest vocalist), the majority of the songs are in a stylized Jamaican English.[112]

Picture 13: Dr. I-Bolit (aka Andrei "Rastaman" Kunitsyn). Picture taken in St. Petersburg in 2013.

---

112. One of the times I meet Dr. I-Bolit at a concert (26.05.2005 at Ul. Lomanosova 5) he insisted on speaking English with me. His English was incoherent and with an imitated Jamaican accent.

The key motor of reggae in St. Petersburg is, however, Tania.[113] She frequently organizes reggae festivals (e.g. in honor of the Jamaican New Year or Bob Marley's birthday – cf. Picture 14)[114] hoping to create a local reggae community whose absence she laments (Iatsenko 2006). Besides Ackee Ma-Ma, Dr. I-Bolit, and Reggistan other dedicated reggae groups from St. Petersburg are DiaPositive and Bro Sound. Many more bands pay tribute to reggae by incorporating reggae style indicators, including Soviet rock groups like Chaif and Akvarium. Akvarium occupies a special role, since the group from the beginning of the 1980s to the present has repeatedly composed songs close to reggae – including a compilation of their reggae songs released in 2005 (Akvarium 2005).[115] Thus through the group's sheer impact on Soviet and post-Soviet popular music, Akvarium has also familiarized its listeners with reggae style indicators.

Another current example is Markscheider Kunst, founded in 1992 and today a veteran of the (post-Soviet) St. Petersburg music scene. Their style is influenced by musics from Central and Southern America (initially also African). One of these influences is also reggae which can be heard in their adoption of the *Rasta-poet* (Wadada n.d.) and Respublika Dzha's vocalist Zhak/Dzhakobo Montekki's poem *Den'gi* (Money) on their album *St. Petersburg – Kinshasa Tranzit* (Markscheider Kunst 2004).[116] Here Montekki sings the poem together with Dr. I-Bolit and Seraphim.[117]

---

113. While it might be tempting to argue that this breaks with the misogynic traits often linked to reggae and rastafarianism, Tania's role reflects more on her organizational skills and contacts (she also works as a freelance music journalist). A male reggae musician I talked to criticized Tania for not being a good reggae performer because she is a woman. Since misogynism was widely present within the male-dominated popular music community of St. Petersburg, the comment is not necessarily specific to reggae.

114. *Akimama Iamaiskii Novyi God* (Ackee Ma-Ma's Jamaican New Year – Red Club, 09.12.2004) featured DiaPositive, Reggistan, Ackee Ma-Ma, Dr. I-Bolit and Seraphim; *Den' Rozhdeniia Boba Marli* (Bob Marley's birthday – Red Club, 05.02.2006) featured Seraphim's Simba Vibration, Ackee Ma-Ma, Bro Sound, Svoboda, Pinches Tiranitos, Afrodisiac, Raggapop, and Andrei from Reggistan.

115. Cf. Steinholt (2005) for a discussion of Akvarium's 1982 song *Aristokrat*.

116. The album was recorded in 1996 and 1998, released 1999 and re-released in 2004.

117. Musically the song is in a medium tempo (about 120 bpm), sporting a pulsating hammond like organ (not listed on the liner notes) continuously playing a g on the 1+, 2+, 3+ and 4+ and together with the guitar alternatively playing a G and a F major triad on the backbeats (2 and 4). The lyrics primarily consist of phrases which are repeated with little or no variation, stressing that for a Rastaman both money and houses are marijuana – the refrain *Money – it was invented as a mean of deceit, For a Rastaman money is marijuana*

While it is very hard to point out why groups in St. Petersburg and Russia have appropriated reggae (going beyond a personal appreciation of the music) it is easy to see how the flow has reduced reggae for a large part of the population to a few recognizable key style indicators (here expanded to include non-musical aspects – marijuana, dreadlocks, the colors red-green-gold, Rastafarianism, and musically, an accent on the off-beats). This points to how musical styles are reduced and commodified as easily identifiable packages and flow between borders, and where the cultural context is to a great extent sidelined or reduced – something Alleyne (2000) labels *cultural dilution* when discussing Euro-American reggae inspired artists.

Picture 14: Flyer from *Den' Rozhdenia Boba Marli* (*Red Club*, 05.02.2006).

(*Den'gi – eto pridumannyi sposob obmana, dlia rastamana den'gi – marikhuana*) was often quoted to me in conversations. In other words, the song draws on several clichés linked to reggae lifestyle.

Talking about how reggae influenced global popular music Roger Wallis and Krister Malm apply the term *transculture* to reggae: "the transculture assimilated elements of reggae." (Wallis and Malm 1984, 303). In their eyes, transculture, or "transnational music culture is the result of a combination of features from several kinds of music" (Wallis and Malm 1984, 300). In other words, it is a globally accessible music library. Viewed from a music industry perspective, their model is based on an interaction between different local music cultures and the transculture. Here the local cultures both contribute and draw from the transculture:

"Through the transculturation process, music from the international music industry can interact with virtually all other music cultures and sub-cultures in the world, due to the worldwide penetration attained by music mass media"

(Wallis and Malm 1984, 301)

This model can, to some extent, be used to explain how the music is commodified and reduced to certain key stylistic traits or style indicators, however the processes of musical flow are more complex: While a powerful force in promoting music, the music industry's production is quite broad and not limited to a certain finite number of styles. Furthermore, the appropriation of popular music in new contexts is complex and determined by a number of factors influenced by the different frames mentioned above – for example state interaction, consumer demand, the language used, migration patterns, and the music that (other) musicians listen to. Furthermore, this model takes for granted that local musicians want to interact with the transculture, it does not address ideological differences present. These hurdles are also valid for "peripheral" musics becoming part of the transculture. In addition to its musical qualities reggae became "assimilated by the transculture" due to a number of factors both related to Jamaica's colonial and post-colonial history, migratory paths to England, an acceptance of the plight of third world countries in Europe and the United States (an aspect Andrei pointed out as important for St. Petersburg), language sung in (English) and Bob Marley's appeal both as a singer as well as a freedom fighter. These extramusical qualities have contributed to influencing the appropriation of reggae in others places. Related to this is what (new) meanings music takes on and if these are compatible with that of the music which inspired it. Besides reggae, other peripheral musics influencing the transculture are sparse (especially in languages other than English and Spanish).

The industry's reach should also be seen as limited – influenced amongst other things through a shift in the distribution of music. While Anglo-American popular music (which is what they primarily allude to) plays a role in influencing musicians around the world, so do other musics which do not belong to the transculture, but which also play an important role. These musics might not become known on a global level, but remain highly audible and influential on a regional level (e.g. Bollywood music or Russian *estrada*). In addition, the remaining major labels of the music industry are not necessarily the dominant player anymore: social networking sites like *facebook, last.fm,* and *youtube* as well as specialized record labels like *Eastblok Music* have emerged as important players. These changes enable musicians (as well as listeners) to find the most obscure music with a few clicks on the internet and raises the question that if a transculture exists, where are the boundaries? Does the transnational music industry still play a leading role in musical innovation? Or has the transculture been replaced by an eclectic mix?

I will return to some of these points when discussing the flow of post-Soviet music to the *Russendisko* in Germany in chapter 9. Another important aspect is the fact that not only foreigners or highly mobile people influence others within transcultural flows, but also locals active within the form of life level: Andrei introduced Tania to reggae (according to both of them), just as Prokhor introduced elements of ska to Svoboda's musical style (discussed below).

While there is a budding reggae community in St. Petersburg as the discussion above has shown, the boundaries to ska are quite fluid. The above mentioned festival for Bob Marley's birthday (cf. Picture 14) is but one example of reggae festivals where groups playing ska, such as Svoboda, have participated. Another example is the reggae compilation *Dzha do it* (Various Artists 2008b), which features both reggae groups (e.g. Ackee Ma-Ma, Reggistan, DiaPositive) and ska groups (e.g. Svoboda, Porto Franco, Batareia).

5.3 "And that word grooves": Ska in St. Petersburg

> I know a three letter word
> and that word grooves.
> The Hockey team from the Neva banks
> And the music which we play.
>
> S-K-A, Skaaaaa Let's go!
>
> The word ska [СКА] is similar to dick [хуй],
> Because it has the same amount of letters
> But in the word dick there is much less
> Of that Groooooovvveee
>
> S-K-A, Skaaaaa Let's go!
> *SKA* (Leningrad 2000 – Russian: p. 301)

Originating in St. Petersburg the band Leningrad (active since 1997) is currently among the most well-known ska-punk groups in Russia. Leningrad positions itself in relation to the average (male) Russian, who over-employs *mat* (swearing as the use of *khiu* – dick – in the epitaph points to) and Leningrad's vocalist Sergei "Shnur" Shnurov sings about sex, drugs, alcohol, and everyday problems from the perspective of a Russian (working class) male. The group's songs incorporate and mix influences from Russian and Soviet as well as Western popular culture. In the song *Ska* (Leningrad 2000) Shnur sings about how groovy ska is, accompanied by an aggressive rhythm and horn section playing in a ska-punk style[118] – a style which many groups in St. Petersburg (and Russia) are currently influenced by.

Leningrad is, however, not the first group to be influenced by ska in Russia.[119] According to Andrei Burlaka, ska appeared in Russia with the Beatles' song *Obla-*

---

118. The horn section plays a backing riff during the refrain and at the end the musicians take turns soloing (trumpet, trombone, tenor saxophone, and tuba). The bass plays mainly arpeggiated triads in quarter notes while a slight distorted electric guitar accents the offs of every beat playing chords. A keyboard continuously plays the chord's root note on the 1 and the remaining notes of the chord on the 2, 3, and 4. The high hat doubles the guitar's accents on the off beats while the snare accents the 2 and 4. The bass drum, which was hard for me to hear on the recording, seems to accent all the beats on the on-beat.
119. This part on ska in Russia is based on short phone interviews with Andrei Ivanov (St. Petersburg, 16.03.2006) and Andrei Burlaka (St. Petersburg, 17.03.2006) as well as e-mail correspondence with the music journalist Sergey Chernov (02.08.2006).

di oblada[120] and the first band to play ska in the Soviet Union was the Leningrad band Strannye Igry which debuted in 1982.[121]

While ska was not incorporated by many bands in the 1980s, the style experienced a boost of popularity in the 1990s when people were able to travel abroad and were more exposed to Western popular music. In St. Petersburg the group Dva Samoliota, which emerged in the late 1980s/early 1990s, was one of the first groups of this generation to include elements of ska. It was followed by Spitfire (founded late 1992), who combined ska with punk and contributed to popularizing the style. In Moscow, the group Distemper (founded 1989), also combining ska and punk, has been an important influence. Finally, the group Leningrad, through its success, is often credited with the popularity of ska in Russia:[122]

> "Well, I think that it always has been like that in the pop-world, [...] there are pioneers and copy-cats and once Leningrad was so big/famous [...] For many people it was a revelation, [...] a discovery, that such a musical direction existed and at that time Shnurov [Leningrad's vocalist], I think, had been telling [people] on his homepage about ska – what it is and such – and Spitfire as well, well the band, that always [has played] ska, he also advertised for them. [...] I think that many people simply found out about ska through Leningrad and then the idea to play just that, because it is currently well received."
>
> (Gurzhy 2005 – German: p. 312)

While the above mentioned groups have been influential, other popular and visible Soviet and Russian bands from the 1980s and 1990s like Markscheider Kunst and (to some extent) Akvarium have not only contributed to the awareness and spread of reggae, but also ska.

During my fieldwork, there were quite a few local bands such as JD & the Blenders, Froglegs, St. Petersburg Ska-Jazz Review, Batareia, Barocco Flash, Porto Franco, Svoboda, Beshenye Ogurtsy, and Banana Gang drawing on ska. "Drawing on ska" is intentionally used since the bands incorporate style indicators of ska and combine it with other indicators, primarily from punk. This was also mentioned by Andrei Burlaka, when he talked about how ska is recontextualized in St.

---

120. According to Everett (1999, 188) the song is written in a "clipped-backbeat Jamaican ska style popularized [...] by Desmond Dekker and the Aces". The Beatles were a major influence in the development of popular music in Russia.
121. The group, whose origin dates back to 1979, took the lyrics from French dadaists (e.g. Tristan Tzara and Raymond Queneau) published in Soviet poetry anthologies. Musically they were inspired by the groups Madness, Specials, and Bad Manners among others. In 1985 the band split into Igry and Avia and the musicians have remained an important local influence (Burlaka 2007d, Chernov, pers. comm., 02.08.2006).
122. The musicians from Spitfire have been a part of Leningrad since 2002.

Petersburg adding that nobody in Russia plays like the original ska artists.[123] These local groups tend to combine ska with punk – which was backed by Sergei Chernov's following comment:

> "In the 2000s ska in its ska-punk form is very popular in St. Petersburg and Moscow clubs (the Moscow-based bands Distemper and Skal'pel', for example, not to mention Spitfire), but not with the general public."
>
> (pers. comm., 02.08.2006)

Andrei Ivanov added that ska derived its popularity from punk, which was and still is popular. He explained that Russians like to drink and when they are drunk they like to move, jump (*skakat'*) and push/shove (*tolkat'*), which ska and punk encourage. Chernov had a similar comment when discussing the group Leningrad:

> "Probably it [Leningrad] has managed to blend ska and the Russian anarchic, drinking spirit and became sort of band for everybody, from rednecks to yuppies."
>
> (pers. comm., 02.08.2006)

Andrei Ivanov added that reggae is not so popular in Russia, because it is more profound, slower, and with a different energy. Andrei Burlaka noted that it is too cold to play "Southern music", such as ska, in Russia, and that this is why the groups play a mixture. Groups are also conscious of this, for example S.O.K. which advertises their music as *"Reggi narodov severa"* (Reggae of the Northern peoples – SOK n.d.). Finally, Alexander Kasparov, one of the directors of the record label *Eastblok Music*, commented on the popularity of ska like this:

> "I think for the Russians that is a good rhythm, good music, and has to do with the Russian rhythm, with Chastushka, or with all others... It's not too foreign for Russian ears this ska rhythm."
>
> (Kasparov and Siebert 2006 – German: p. 315)

Chastushki (Pl., Sg. *Chastushka*, from *chasto* – rapid) are a widespread vocal-instrumental genre which often have humorous (and obscene) lyrics. The musical accompaniment (traditionally balalaika and accordion) can have the chord root on the down beat and the triad on the upbeat which makes the upbeat sound accented – a possible explanation for Alex's link between ska and *chastushka*.

While these comments show a certain degree of essentialization of Russia and Russianness,[124] they also demonstrate how Russians place a claim on ska as having

---

123. Burlaka did not specify if he was referring to Jamaican or British groups (or both). Based on the groups that influenced Strannye Igry the groups were probably more strongly influenced by British groups.
124. The dichotomies like fast/slow, cold/warm, as well as North/South (here white/black could be added) also point to prevalent prejudices in terms of *self* and *other*. I will discuss ques-

inherent Russian elements. In other words, ska is not only seen as a foreign import, but something that can be traced to earlier Russian music styles and (essentialized) cultural traits – thus it is "Russian".

While the first generation of bands were influenced by British and Jamaican groups, subsequent generations are also influenced by the first generation. The demediaization of ska-punk through Spitfire, Distemper, and Leningrad has mainly produced groups playing within a similar style blending elements of ska and punk, which is quite different from the Jamaican ska it hails from (and similar to Andrei's criticism of local groups copying 1970s style reggae). Here local interaction between musicians plays an important role since most musicians learn from other local musicians either by face to face contact or at concerts and through media (form of life and market frame). While "older" groups (with older musicians) like Markscheider Kunst or Spitfire also know and listen to Jamaican and British ska (Markscheider Kunst also helped organize a concert with the Skatalites in St. Petersburg 2007 which was then cancelled), younger ones (those from the bands which appeared in the 2000s) had a more limited knowledge of the music. One example of such a "young" band which has Leningrad as one of its models is Svoboda.

Picture 15: Svoboda's business card.

5.3.1   *Ukra-Ska Pung I*: Svoboda and ska

Playing *Ukra-Ska-Pung*[125] (cf. Picture 15) Svoboda markets itself as a ska-punk band with Ukrainian elements. Some of the group's concerts have specifically focused on ska/reggae contexts. During my tenure, Svoboda regularly performed at

---

tions of representation in chapter 6 and chapter 10.
125. When asked why *Pung* and not *Punk* Sasha replied that Pung sounds "cooler" although the word in itself is meaningless (Aleksandr Rudenko, pers. comm., 21.06.2006).

the reggae-club *Dzhambala* as well as ska/reggae-specific festivals like *RaSKAlbas* (*Staryi Dom*, 01.04.2005 – cf. Picture 16) or the above mentioned reggae festival *Den' Rozhdenia Boba Marli* organized by Tania. There are also connections to other ska-bands – some amicable, some competitive (e.g. a former trombone-player plays with the ska-group Beshenye Ogurtsy).

One of Svoboda's influences is Leningrad. Discussing Leningrad and its influence on Svoboda Sasha said:

> "No less to make fun on the border of some kind of hysteria, some kind of craziness, some kind of mad buffoonery, that's what Leningrad is, that's in principle what I like in their work and also what I try to achieve in my own creative work. There should be some kind of dance, a sort of wild joy, not insanity as such. It should be, so I think, freedom as well, liberation from the problems, complexes that people have."
>
> (Rudenko 2006 – Russian: p. 327)

The freedom from complexes and the crazy cheerfulness in part refer to Leningrad's use of *stiob*, a very specific and subtle form of Russian irony, and their over-employing of *mat*, Russian curse words. Sasha has adopted their use of *Russian* curse words (and not *Ukrainian* as the band's Ukraine focus would suggest). Another important influence is Leningrad's role in promoting ska-punk in Russia. When discussing musical issues during rehearsals Sasha would sometimes hint at Leningrad, saying at one point while working out harmony parts for *Choboty* (Boots) that the arrangements have to be better than Leningrad's (pers. comm., 23.12.2005). Sasha added that people should say Svoboda sounds better than them.[126]

Not disregarding Leningrad as influential, Sasha also gathers inspiration from groups that he considers to be successful and who have a good stage presence. As an example, Sasha remarked at a concert with Distemper (*Port*, 31.03.2005) that the horns in Svoboda should be more active on stage – dancing like Distemper's horn-section. His complaint was that although he is active in acting out the songs on stage, Svoboda's horn section (and also rhythm section) was boring to look at, because we were static. This is linked to the band image – how the band is marketed and perceived by the audience – just like Sasha's Ukrainian heritage (cf. p. 181ff).

---

126. During my tenure we also covered three songs by Leningrad. This was, however, out of necessity since we played two gigs in Lodeinoe Pole (03.-04.02.2006) and the concert organizers requested those songs.

Musically, the songs remain mostly within a ska-punk idiom where style indicators from ska such as the accent of the up-beats/backbeats and the use of a horn section playing short riffs are taken and mixed with punk style indicators such as sustained (power) chords on the downbeat, straight beat, and I-IV-V progressions. These two idioms tend to alternate with the verse usually drawing on the ska rhythm and the refrain usually on the punk idiom.

Picture 16: Flyer from *RaSKAlbas* (*Staryi Dom*, 01.04.2005).

One example of this is Svoboda's cover of Kino's *Mama anarkhiia* (Mother anarchy, Kino 1986; Svoboda 2007 – cf. also p. 69): The verse is over a ska rhythm where the guitar together with the high hat accents the offs on all four beats of the measure while the bass shifts between the root and fifth in the triads on each beat. The snare accents the 2 and 4 and the bass drum the 1 and 3. The refrain answers with a hard rock/punk idiom where the heavily distorted guitar creates a sound wall and changes chords together with the bass on the downbeat of every measure. The high hat plays slightly shuffled fourth notes, accenting the on-beat while the snare continues to accent the 2 and 4. The bass drum plays a four measure riff, mainly accenting the 1 and 3, but accenting the 3+ in the second and fourth bar.

5 REGGAE AND SKA IN ST. PETERSBURG   173

Figure 3: Wave form excerpt of *Mama anarkhiia*. This excerpt marks the rhythmic and energetic difference between the ska and the hard rock/punk idiom (separated by the vertical line at 35.5s).

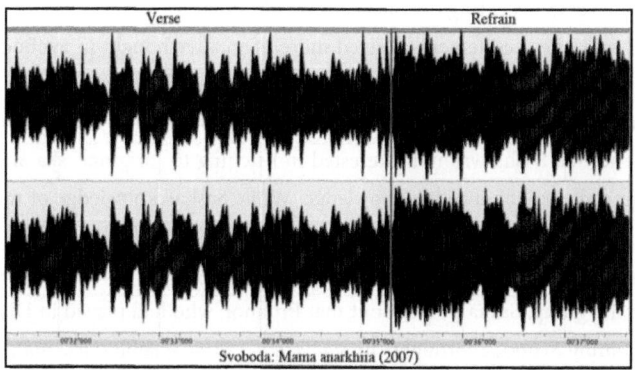

Svoboda: Mama anarkhiia (2007)

This can also be seen in the song's wave form (Figure 3): In the last three bars of the first verse (it spans the beginning of the wave form excerpt to 34,1s) two peaks are grouped together and then almost fade out (e.g. 32,5s-32,7s – the only exception being 32-32,2s where the guitar sustains the sixteenth note). The first peak in such a group is the bass on the down-beat while the second, mostly shorter peak, is the guitar playing a staccato sixteenth on the offbeat – thus marking the ska idiom. The punk idiom in the refrain is marked by a sound wall – the guitar playing on the down-beat and the chord remaining sustained represented in the wave form through the amplitude not decaying between beats.[127] The wave form also marks the energetic difference in the overall sound quite well – the ska idiom being quieter and more open than the punk idiom. This structure is also found in other songs like *Choboty*[128] and *Marusia*.[129]

---

127. In this excerpt the guitar starts a bar before the refrain with a glissando on the down beat (34,1s) before playing sustained chords on the following down-beats.
128. Rhythmically the song alternates between a ska-rhythm in the verse and the interludes where the guitar first plays on the backbeats (2 and 4) and then on the off-beats (1+, 2+, 3+, 4+) while the bass drum playing two eights on the 1 and 3 and the snare accents the 2 and 4 with the high hat accenting the off-beats. In the refrain the rhythm shifts to a rock rhythm with a distorted guitar first playing chords and parts of the triad with the rhythm ♩ . ♩ ♩ ♪ |♩. ♩ ♩ and in the second part playing sustained chords on the down beat while the drum accents the 1 and 3 on the bass drum and the backbeats on the snare while playing the off-beats on the hi-hat.
129. The rhythm section primarily alternates between a ska rhythm in the verse (with the guitar accenting the 1+, 2+, 3+ and 4+) and a hard rock/punk rhythm in the refrain (with the

In general, the horns either double the verse and refrain melody in the introduction, refrain, and solo or play a recurring riff – mainly in the refrain. While there were some riffs in the verse, the horns mostly did not play rhythmic backings in the verse, accenting the off-beats/ska-rhythm.

That said, the ska-elements arrived more as an afterthought in Svoboda's style, which, in the beginning, was closer to the *russkii rok* idiom (cf. p. 189ff). An acquaintance often pointed out to me that Sasha did not know anything about ska or reggae and that Sasha was not interested in listening to "original" ska and reggae artists in order to enhance his knowledge. While Sasha's knowledge of music and musical technique (especially regarding the horn section) was limited, he did compensate for this through the other musicians: Trying to persuade Prokhor not to leave the group, Sasha pointed out that Prokhor, who had played in DiaPositive before joining Svoboda, brought the *slabye doli* (weak syllables/accents), the style indicators linked to ska/reggae, to the group and thus was needed in the group. In this sense Sasha was right, Prokhor was (besides Sasha) the major musical force in the band both during rehearsals and as a second frontman during concerts. This is also a good example of Sasha's determination to create a good band by constantly striving (mostly successfully) to find good musicians and developing the band image among its predetermined lines.

5.4   Concluding remarks

This chapter has shown that the flow of humans and media are linked in disseminating and advancing a stylistic knowledge and in what ways the flows contribute to how certain style indicators are filtered and thus become representative. Here St. Petersburg can, within a global popular music network, be considered the periphery where style indicators belonging to ska and reggae are de-mediaized by local groups creating new forms of musical expression. These draw on both the style indicators as well as local influences such as Leningrad's use of curse words, (post-)Soviet references, and, in Svoboda's case, the use of Ukrainian elements playing on Russian-Ukrainian cultural ties as will be discussed in the following chapter. What remains central in this process is *human agency*. This has been im-

---

guitar playing sustained chords on the downbeat). The drum, however, plays the same rhythm in both sections with the bass drum on 1 and 3, snare on 2 and 4 while the hi-hat primarily plays the 1+, 2+, 3+ and 4+.

portant in both how reggae and ska flowed to Great Britain through (labour) migration from its (former) colonies and how tourists and traveling musicians brought the music to Russia. These flows also reflect Soviet educational ties with, for example, African countries, whose students came to Russia to get a higher education. While most returned, some, like Seraphim, remained in the country. In other words, the flows follow structured migration paths based on existing center-periphery relations.

But not only migrating musicians like Seraphim and Reggistan's René, Anzh Kombo, and Emanio play a role, I have also argued that certain local key actors like Andrei, Tania, and Leningrad's musicians play a central role within the form of life level. They provide inspiration and guidance for other local musicians, thus functioning as a *filter* between a foreign musical style and local musicians. While the images drawn upon remain recognizable as originating in Jamaican ska and reggae and retain an imaginary link to an idealized Jamaica (Rastafarianism, music, national symbols), this filtration of style indicators creates a local music tradition which not only draws on these globally accessible styles, but also on a local Russian tradition.

St. Petersburg is, however, only one node in the evolution of ska and reggae, which at least goes back to ska and reggae's de-mediaization in Great Britain and the United States, sparking the emergence of international reggae as well as ska-punk. What makes the local tradition interesting is not only the fact that the reggae and ska-punk groups overlap, both personnel- as well as performancewise, but also that the ska-punk tradition has become an audible symbol of Russian popular music at the *Russendisko* in Berlin. Here ska-punk-derived styles dominate the listening experience – creating the opposite impression to what one would perceive in St. Petersburg, where those styles make up a niche[130] – something I will return to in chapter 9. At the same time, the flow to Germany has inspired German-based bands to further develop the music.

This flow of music to Berlin, however, decontextualizes the St. Petersburg bands, where the local band identity is replaced by a new one linked to the *Russendisko-scene* and local discourses. Returning to Svoboda, the next chapter discusses those aspects of the band identity which the group uses to market itself

---

130. *Russkii rok* and other forms of rock music based on a rhythm section (1-2 guitars, bass, drums, and vocalist) remain the dominant (rock) style within the St. Petersburg scene.

within the St. Petersburg scene – the Ukrainian heritage – and which is partially lost through the transcultural flows.

6 Russian perceptions of Ukraine

> "It is no secret that Ukrainian sounds funny to the Russian ear. It is such a funny version of the Russian language. But in a good way funny."
>
> (Oleg Skrypka, qtd. in Chernin 2006, 515 – Russian: p. 329)

Despite Ukraine's post-colonial struggle mentioned in chapter 1

> "[t]he majority of Russians still see the Ukrainians as 'malorossy' [Little Russians], as a part of the Russian Nation and do not understand why the Ukrainians strive for their own language, their own culture and their own state."
>
> (Kappeler 2003, 53 – German: p. 315)

Kappeler (2003, 37) adds that during the 19th century Ukrainians were primarily looked upon as a picturesque variant of the Russian people who spoke Russian which had been un-purified by Polish influence – something the Ukrainian band Vopli Vidopliasova's (VV) vocalist Oleg Skrypka alludes to in the epitaph. This notion of cultural and ethnic unity was reflected on by many people I talked to in St. Petersburg. They referred to Ukrainians as a brother people and the country as a part of Russia. When I asked Vitia (Con Brio) about his attitude towards Ukraine he answered:

> "But they were at one time part of Russia. I think that because they separated from us, they didn't become another, from us differing country. I think they remained a part of us, but don't want to admit that."
>
> (Kultashov 2006 – Russian: p. 325)

This attitude that Ukraine is inherently a part of Russia is not limited to informal conversations within the form of life frame, but is also demonstrated in the Russian music station *Nashe Radio's* music policy (cf. p. 211) as well as in the lyrics to Oleg Gazmanov's 2005 song *Sdelan v SSSR* (Made in the USSR – cf. p. 219).

This view of Ukraine as a part of Russia did not make the Orange Revolution too popular in Russia, especially in the media coverage. The negative coverage of Ukraine continued during the gas-crisis winter 2005/06. Most people I talked to were of the opinion that Ukrainians themselves were to blame for the problems they experienced after the revolution (e.g. rising gas prices, inflation). While stressing the historical unity with Russia, one person argued that Ukraine is dependent on Russia since they do not have any natural resources of their own (Igor, pers. comm., 15.02.2006). Another person said that while Russia did not need Ukraine,

Ukraine was dependent on Russia (Tania, pers. comm., 27.01.20006). Also regarding music I heard complaints:

> "And before this stupid election in Ukraine, [...] three times we played in Kiev in the Ukraine [last year]. And I was very satisfied, it was very good for me, it was quite developing, so it's quite [a] pity that they are now, I think, [...] going backwards with all [these] problems since they have good clubs and good this sub-culture in Ukraine. And it was I think supported by even some money, because they had some independent music festivals also, which is quite rare for and impossible for Russia for instance."
>
> (Kagadeev 2004)

For Andrei Kagadeev (NOM) Ukraine was seen as a model since its government apparently supported popular music – and the Orange revolution brought, in his view, the demise of those conditions.

That said, people differentiated between politics and normal people/music as the Svoboda-fan Denis pointed out:

> "There is some kind of hostility towards Ukraine, that they submit to American influence, but when you are at concerts – the atmosphere is a little different, it is – not a national disagreement. That, what he [Sasha] sings in Ukrainian, the listener likes – just let him sing, no questions."
>
> (Vashkevich and Lukanin 2006 – Russian: p. 319)

In response to such comments in Russia, the popular Ukrainian group Okean El'zy's lead singer said both on *Nashe Radio* and during a packed concert the same evening (*BKZ Oktiabr'skii*, 31.01.2006), that listeners could learn more about Ukraine by attending their concerts than by watching Russian TV.

As mentioned, one aspect of post-colonial studies focuses on representation. Discussing exoticism in 19th century music, the musicologist Carl Dahlhaus (1980, 252) argues that not the exoticism's origin, but the function it fulfills in Western art music is important. Around the same time Edward Said (1994, 71f) raises a similar point when discussing the use of Orientalisms:

> "[W]e need not look for correspondence between the language used to depict the Orient and the Orient itself, not so much because the language is inaccurate but because it is not even trying to be accurate. What it is trying to do [...] is at one and the same time to characterize the Orient as alien and to incorporate it schematically on a theatrical stage whose audience, manager, and actors are for Europe, and only for Europe."

Here Said highlights questions of representation, especially representations of the colonized *Other*. The term *Other* is used here since this representation does not – as Said's quote points out – *reflect on* the colonized's own self and resulting identities, but is an artificial collective identity *created by* the colonizers. Used as a domestification tool this identity is based on the colonizer's perception of the colonized and thus in opposition to the colonizer's own self – a strategy Said labels *orientalizing*.[131] In other words, the representation is instrumentalized as a tool to define and control the Others while at the same time establishing a normative self of the Europeans.[132]

Returning to the post-Soviet sphere, by drawing on discourses portraying Ukrainians as a picturesque variant of Russians, but who are slightly stupid and dirty (cf. p. 204, Fn. 175), or, by defining Georgia's president Mikhail Saakashvili as a tie-eating lunatic (as circulated in Russian media after the Russian-Georgian war 2008), the defined are domesticated and rendered powerless by virtue of definition (the description acting as a *pars pro toto* for the countries' inhabitants). At the same time the definers (Russians) are rendered superior by virtue of being the opposite (smart, urban, cultivated, literate, sane, rational). The fact that these representations do not reflect the reality is not of interest for the colonizer since the aim is to control the colonized and garner support at home.

As a group based in St. Petersburg who plays for a local audience, Svoboda operates within a rich semiotic field. The group's music draws on conventions ("codes recognizable to a sizable audience" – McClary 2000, 151) from popular music including a regular form (verse-refrain structure), harmonic progressions, and instruments used in popular music. In other words, they draw on a "shared cultural memory, available for citation in the production of new meanings" (McClary 2000, 42). This shared cultural memory is also context dependent. While the conventions mentioned have a more global appeal, Svoboda also draws on a more limited shared cultural memory – or more precisely a collective Soviet and Russian memory – by drawing on stereotypes of Ukraine and the *russkii rok*-tradition. The Ukrainian aspect plays a special role here since it is embodied in

---

131. Approaching the term from a feminist and post-colonial critique Born and Hesmondhalgh (2000a, 47, Fn. 1) argue that the term *other* "denote[s] those groups of people that white Western heterosexual men have usually defined themselves against, and whose selfhood they have tended to deny."
132. This form of representation emerges with changes in travel writing through European ventures to America, Asia, and Africa starting from the 15th and 16th century. Ania Loomba points out that these writings mark "a new way in thinking about, indeed producing, these two categories of people [Europeans and non-Europeans] as binary opposites." (Loomba 2005, 53) She goes on saying "[t]he definition of civilisation and barbarism rests on the production of an irreconcilable difference between 'black' and 'white', self and other." (Loomba 2005, 53)

Sasha's personal identity, adding an element of perceived authenticity when performing in St. Petersburg. At the same time it draws a recognizable boundary between Ukraine and St. Petersburg. The following discussion will continue to focus on Svoboda's band image and how the group draws on traditional music and stereotypical images of Ukraine – thus participating to some extent in the above mentioned discourse.

While some songs do have references to traditional material, much material used by Svoboda cannot be traced to a melodic, rhythmic, and harmonic origin within traditional music. The use of or talk about traditional music is rather a way to deviate from the norm, to characterize the music as special (and to assert a form of national identity) – thus the references fulfill a function (as in Said's point). Within a Russian context these references and the discourses around the group can still be recognized by the audiences.

The Ukrainian vocalist Ruslana has a similar approach to appropriating traditional material by drawing on the music and images of a Ukrainian ethnic minority, the Hutsuls – described in the second half of this chapter They, however, protested against their depiction as a backward, rural group.

Once the music reaches an international audience, however, any degree of faithfulness to the origin loses its importance since the potential audience lacks the knowledge to recognize them anyway. More important is the function those references fulfill making the music sound *different* from "traditional" rock/pop. Here questions of how bands are promoted in Germany and how this relates to the target group are important – especially the use of clichés. This is in line with Said's previous quote since by promoting the music to a German audience the main focus is promoting the music as alien.

A parallel can be found here between Berlin and St. Petersburg with St. Petersburg's inhabitants referring to the Ukrainians as slightly backwards and a picturesque variant of the Russians, while Berlin's inhabitants exoticize the Russians and Ukrainians, building on the clichés of the wild and savage East (vodka, bears in the street etc.). I will return to this in chapter 10.

6.1 Ukra-Ska Pung II: Svoboda and Ukraine

While discussing the groups' style Sasha said

"Okean El'zy write serious songs in Ukrainian language, because they live in L'vov. I like them a lot [sarcastic laughter]. Among our things, merry, energetic music such as 'Hey, Hey, Bratan!' [Bro] is closer to Vopli Vidoplasova."

(Rudenko 2006 – Russian: p. 328)

While both Okean El'zy and VV (Vopli Vidopliasova) sing in Ukrainian (and both supported the Orange Revolution), Okean El'zy plays a straightforward generic rock/pop and has, to some extent, a boy group image in contrast to VV, which humorously draws on elements from Ukrainian folklore,[133] combining it with a rock idiom. Both groups tour and are well known in Russia. Positioning Svoboda between those two Ukrainian bands, Sasha places his band closer to VV, and he has, on several occasions, mentioned that he is inspired by VV. This drawing on (perceived) Ukrainian folklore (and Ukraine in general) is furthermore reflected in the self-proclaimed style *ukra-ska-pung*.[134]

Drawing on his Ukrainian background Sasha contributes to marking the group as Ukrainian during concerts with announcements such as "We just arrived from Ukraine", "The next song is a Ukrainian folksong" etc. and by sometimes addressing the audience in Ukrainian. The band also appropriates Ukrainian historic material: A concert scheduled for October 26th, 2007 was advertised in memory of the Ukrainian anarcho-communist Nestor Makhno (cf. Picture 17):

"Soon Svoboda's concerts timed to the birthday of the legendary freedom fighter Father Makhno will be held. Especially, since the leader of the group is native to the same place. The first concert – 26th of October in Roks club, where you will see the theater show 'Makhnograd': gorilka [vodka], champagne, Ukrainian songs, slem[?], and a lot of fog."

(Svoboda 2008 – Russian: p. 329)

---

133. I employ the term *folklore* here since it is equivalent to the Russian term *fol'klor* which besides *narodnaia muzyka* (folk music) was the predominant term used in Russia when discussing Svoboda. Furthermore, Svoboda taps into the folklore tradition based on stylized traditional music, not contemporary traditional music.

134. On Svoboda's website they also refer directly to the Hutsuls, an ethnic minority from Southwestern Ukraine that also serve as inspiration for Ruslana: "Music – it is freedom, and Svoboda's music – that is a mixture of ska, reggae, folk, melodic Hutsul-tunes and explosive punk" (Svoboda n.d. – Russian: p. 329). While Sasha also mentioned the Hutsuls as an influencing element during the interview, none of the songs we played during my tenure are based on Hutsul themes or show any other obvious Hutsul musical traits.

Not only does the advertising text link the concert to Ukraine, but also the flyer where the word *anarkhiia* (anarchy) is written in Ukrainian (*анархія*), not Russian (*анархия*).

Picture 17: Flyer from Svoboda's Nestor Makhno-concert (*Roks Club*, 26.10.2007).

This notion of difference is also perceived and received by the audience, which primarily consists of people living in St. Petersburg predominantly from the age range late teens to mid 30s.[135] Sasha is referred to as *khokhol* (topknot/tuft of hair), slang for a Ukrainian, by the group's fans. While Sasha (Rudenko 2006) sees the word as context sensitive, having both positive and negative connotations, this colloquialism commonly used in St. Petersburg seems to have mainly negative associations.[136] The fans also seem to think that some of Svoboda's songs are actually

---

135. However, the concert in honor of Makhno was criticized by an anarchist from Moscow, for merely using Makhno as a ploy. He complained that the organizers and Svoboda had no idea about Makhno and his ideas (Shvedov 2007).
136. After a concert by the Berlin-based band Apparatschik at the Viennese *Ost Klub* (13.07.2007) I was in the backstage area and witnessed how a member of the security, who said he was from the former Soviet Union (though he refused to say exactly where) almost got into a fight with the Ukrainian bass balalaika-player because the guard insisted on calling him *khokhol*. Instead, the balalaika-player insisted on being addressed only by his

traditional Ukrainian songs. While some songs draw on Ukrainian folklore, are sung in Ukrainian or employ specific Ukrainian words, these are stereotypical markers of Ukraine. This use reflects how Svoboda markets itself as something different or even exotic through the use of Ukrainian elements – something Andrei Burlaka reflected on:

> "There as well, so to say, is a new topic – such Ukra-pop [...] Of course the Ukrainian language doesn't play such an important role there because, understandably, it's, well, cool. And so the music really touches something there. There are similar playing [groups] from Piter, but [it] is [...] an added exotic, such a folkloric [one]."
> (Burlaka 2005 – Russian: p. 318)

Andrei Ivanov (pers. comm., 18.12.2005) picked up on the fact that singing in Ukrainian is a marketing ploy, a marker of difference (fulfills a function). He said that it was stylish (*modno*) to sing in Ukrainian, and that if Svoboda only sang in Russian it would be a copy of Leningrad. This marketing edge is also reflected in how Sasha described the band:

> "Punk, ska with elements of grunge [...] With Ukrainian lyrics, Ukrainian and Russian. More not pure Ukrainian, but a Ukrainian-Russian mixture [*surzhik*], so it's understandable in Russia, Ukraine, and Belarus. And mostly happy songs, serious songs are in Russian."
> (Rudenko 2006 – Russian: p. 328)

In other words, Sasha sees his language choice, a mixture of Russian and Ukrainian (*surzhik*), as deliberate so the audience can more easily understand the lyrics – also evident in the following discussion of Svoboda's songs. Ukraine is thus employed as a homogenous *Other*, not drawing on a specific local tradition. The exotic elements Andrei Burlaka refers to are primarily based on Russian clichés of Ukrainian folk music/lore – something Sasha also acknowledges himself:

> "And that in the other songs [there] is also more stylization from Ukrainian folklore [...] I simply love the Ukrainian folk song – that's also me, you see, I think that this on some level springs from nostalgia, when I lived over in Moscow from 1995."
> (Rudenko 2006 – Russian: p. 328)

---

real name. Another example of the negative use I encountered in a Russian language textbook (aimed at foreigners) released in 2008. The book uses the word in three out of four examples of comparative constructions in Russian grammar: *khitryi kak khokhol* (sly as a Ukrainian), *khoziastvennyi kak khokhol* (economical as a Ukrainian) and *upriami kak khokhol* (stubborn as a Ukrainian) (Starovoitova 2008, 69). Not only are they highly pejorative stereotypes but, instead of using the neutral word *Ukrainets* (Ukrainian), the choice of a colloquial one by the author is marked, adding further to the inherent derogation.

Not only does Sasha point out that the folklore stylization is employed as a marker for Ukraine, it is also linked to his own background through a longing for (or an idea of) home – his nostalgia. This stylisation can primarily be seen in the songs *Mama Anarkhiia, Choboty, Marusia,* and *La-la* to be discussed next.

6.1.1 *"As folklore as it gets"*: Svoboda and Ukrainian coloring

I have briefly discussed how Svoboda establishes a Ukrainian identity on the discursive level. The following discussion shifts the focus to the level of the songs and how this identity is supported by the choice of material.[137]

The main way of asserting Svoboda's Ukrainian identity is through language use as seen in the previously discussed cover of *Mama anarkhiia* (Various Artists 2008b). Here Kino's narrative is maintained but sung in Ukrainian. Sasha does not speak Ukrainian, but, as mentioned, *surzhik*.[138] The anthropologist Laada Bilaniuk (2005, 17) gives the following short definition:

"In Ukraine the blending of features of Russian and Ukrainian merited its own label, 'surzhyk', originally a term for a low-grade mixture of wheat and rye flour [...] The forces that led to language mixing in Ukraine began under Russian tsarist rule and continued under the Soviets. Such language mixing was typical of peasants who came to the city and used their native Ukrainian linguistic forms while trying to speak the more prestigious urban Russian, a language they did not know well."

She argues further that the definition of *surzhik* is mainly ideological since it "can refer to a high degree of code-switching by bilinguals or to a linguistic code in which the elements of the two languages are inextricably fused." (Bilaniuk 2005, 105)

Bianiuk (2005, 135ff) lists five linguistic features common for *surzhik*'s deviation from standard language, four of which are central in Sasha's case:[139] semantics, lexicon, morphology, and non-standard forms on the phonetic and phonological level.

---

137. This will be done by primarily focusing on the songs *Mama anarkhiia* (Various Artists 2008b), *Marusia* (Various Artists 2008c), *Choboty* (Svoboda 2005), and *La-La* (Svoboda 2007). The complete lyrics as well as Kino's version of *Mama anarkhiia* can be found in Appendix B. I would like to thank the Slavic studies scholars Tamara Lönngren and Martin Paulsen both for pointing out some of the following aspects to me and for their help transcribing the songs' lyrics. This section would not have been possible without their assistance!
138. Cf. Yekelchyk (2010) for a discussion of the Ukrainian singer Verka Serdiuchka and her use of *surzhik*.
139. The fifth feature, syntax, does not seem to play a major role.

For some Ukrainian listeners, Sasha's pronunciation of the word "fire" in *Choboty* sounds distinctly Russian – /ognia/ and not /vohniu/ – though, in fact, his is a mixture of Russian and Ukrainian since he does not apply vowel reduction. On other occasions, he applies phonetic features found in standard Russian. For example, while the (r) symbol is identical, the pronunciation is very different – primarily /g/ in Russian and /h/ in Ukrainian This also occurs with the words "leather" and "city": /bugaia/, /gorod/ and not /buhaia/ respectively /horod/. In other places in the song *Choboty* he pronounces the "г" as /h/, e.g. /hodyna/ (times) and /pohody/ (weather).

Another phonetic feature Sasha mixes are the vowels "и" (Ukrainian – IPA: /ı/) and "ы" (Russian – IPA: /ɨ/) – both transcribed /y/. According to Bilaniuk (2005, 136), "[t]he Ukrainian 'и' is a high-mid front unrounded vowel [...], whereas the Russian 'ы' is a high close central unrounded vowel". This can be heard in the pronunciation of *zlye* (evil) where the /y/ is pronounced as a "ы" (злые – *Choboty*).

The song *La-la* also offers a mix of Ukrainian and Russian where Sasha combines the pronunciation of the Ukrainian *pryviz* (brought) with the Russian *privioz*. The resulting word is pronounced /pry-vioz/ where the first half is pronounced Ukrainian with a hard /r/ and the second half (after the hyphen) Russian.

Another audible element of *surzhik* related to Sasha's pronunciation is the use of Russian phonological rules, e.g. vowel reduction. While vowel reduction, especially the merger of /o/ towards schwa (/a/) when following an accentuated syllable, is quite common in many Russian regions including Moscow and St. Petersburg, vowel reduction is mostly absent in Ukrainian. The Russian technical term for the reduction /o/ towards schwa when referring to different dialects within a single language is *akan'e*, the lack of it *okan'e*.[140]

A lack of reduction is predominant – even when Sasha uses Russian words e.g. *ohorchiv* (in Russian the pronunciation with *akan'e* would be /agarchiv/). Vowel reduction can, however, be heard several places like in *Marusia* where Sasha consequently pronounces the word *iahodi* (berries) as it would be pronounced in Russian, /iagady/. Two things happen here: the /o/ is reduced to /a/ and the /h/ is

---

140. Vowel reduction is not limited to /o/, but can also include a merger of /e/ to /i/. This can be heard in *La-La* and the word *mekhanik* (mechanic) which Sasha pronunces /mikhanik/.

pronounced as /g/. Reduction can also be heard in /maskal'/ (Muscovite, instead of /moskal'/ – *Mama anarkhiia*), /razmaliuvali/ (colored, instead of /rozmaliuvali/ – *Mama anarkhiia*) and /Nevskamu/ (Nevskii, instead of /Nevskomu/ – *Choboty*). Interestingly enough here Sasha does not reduce the preposition *po* to /pa/ so the phrase is half-reduced: /po Nevskamu/ (on Nevskii, the reason is probably that *po* here is stressed by itself followed by a short pause and not contracted with *Nevskomu*, in other words not pronounced /panevskamu/).

Another instance of *surzhik* is the *lexical deviation* found in Sasha's use of Russian words. These are amongst others *ogorchiv* (offend, pronounced /ohorchiv/ instead of *rozgnivav* – *Marusia*), *odit* (dressed, instead of *vdiagnuty* – *Choboty*), *babla* (money – *Choboty*), *veter* (wind, instead of *viter* – *Choboty*), *v khariu* (in the muzzle, face – *Choboty*), *krutye* (cool – *Choboty*), *bedlam* (mess – *La-La*) and *klas* (class, cool – *La-La*).

Related to the lexical deviation is the *semantic* one. The Russian word *gorod* (city) has a different meaning than the Ukrainiàn *horod* (kitchen-garden, market-garden). In *Choboty's* lyrics the word clearly signifies "city" thus in the Russian meaning. In Ukrainian the word *misto* would instead be used for "city" or "town" while the syntactically similar Russian word *mesto* means "place".[141]

On the level of *morphology*, he at times uses Russian endings, specifically in the 3. person plural present tense: *My i graiem* (we also play, instead of *graiemo* – *Choboty*), *my tantsiuiem* (we dance, instead of *tantsiuiemo* – *Choboty*), *my hartsiuem* (we prance, instead of *hartsiuemo* – *Choboty*) and *my vam pokazhym* (we show you, instead of *pokazhymo* – *La-La*).

Returning to the lexical level, Svoboda's Othering of the music is not limited to language as sound, but also to the choice of words. In *Mama anarkhiia* Sasha has swapped key nouns with Ukrainian cliché terms frequently applied by Russians:

- *domoi* (home[wards]) is replaced by *do khaty* (to the [peasant] hut – the Russian equivalent of *khata* is *izba*).
- *Papa – stakan portveina* (Dad's a glass of port) is replaced by *Bat'ko stakan horilky* (Father is a glass of [pepper]vodka).[142]

---

141. Many Russian words have an "e" or "o" where Ukrainian words have an "i", e.g. the Russian words *mesto*, *sok* (juice), *veter*, and *kot* (cat) become *misto*, *sik*, *viter*, and *kit* in Ukrainian. One way Russian speakers make fun of Ukrainians is through replacing a written "o" and "e" in Russian words with an "i" and pronouncing it /i/.

142. According to Vasmer (1996) *Bat'ko* is the first diminutive of *batia* (father), in Ukrainian:

- *Soldat* (soldier) is replaced by *moskal'* (Muscovite). In Ukraine and Belarus *moskal'* can signify a Russian or (originally) a soldier (Gramota n.d.). It should be noted that during my tenure with the band, Sasha only used *soldat*, so adopting Ukrainian elements like *moskal'* can be seen as a continuous process.[143]

The words *khata* and *horilka* point to an important inspirational source for Sasha when constructing his idea of a Ukrainian identity: influences from Ukrainian folklore.[144] When I asked about *Marusia* and *Choboty* Sasha said

> "which are closer to folklore, yes – or that very same La-La – it is like that from the words. [...] And 'Selo moie puste, nenache vymerlo' [my village is empty, as if it's died out] that also has some kind of Ukrainian folklore to it, because folklore most of all is in the Ukrainian villages. It is those khaty [peasant houses], mazanky [clay-walled huts], [...] salo [pork fat], horilka [vodka] – well, I try not to use those kinds of clichés, 'salo', 'horilka' because it is the main cliché [...] Yes, you can say that also La-La relates to that [folklore]."
>
> (Rudenko 2006 – Russian: p. 328)

Sasha draws on elements and cliché-phrases from Ukrainian folklore which he associates with villages and (peasant) weddings. While distancing himself from clichés here he still incorporates them both in the lyrics (*horilka* and *khata* both appear in *Mama anarkhiia*) as well as in his stage show props (vodka bottles, traditional clothing etc.).

That Sasha announces some of the songs as Ukrainian folk songs has the effect that some fans actually believe they are – *Choboty* being a case in point (cf. Yekelchyk 2010 for a short mention of *choboty* and *surzhik*). When I asked Sasha, he said that *Choboty* is a stylization of Ukrainian folk songs – at least on the level of lyrics:

> "Choboty, of course, is as folklore as it gets. There is even an identical song. This year we were in Ukraine and went to the shops to buy these Ukrainian wedding songs, yeah. And I've been told earlier that there is such a song 'Choboty' – I simply heard such a phrase 'Boots made of bull-leather, are not afraid of the cold nor noth-

---

bat'o. The second diminutive, *batiushka*, has replaced *bat'ko* in modern Russian, whereas the archaism is still observed in titulars for certain leaders of the South-West, e.g. Ukrainian anarchist *Bat'ko Makhno* or the President of Belarus, *Bat'ko Lukashenko*. Whereas port wine has become a symbol of 1980s Leningrad rock, *horilka* is the Ukrainian word for vodka. In Russia *horilka* can also mean vodka with red chili peppers (and honey), usually marketed as a Ukrainian speciality.

143. In a newer version of *Mama anarkhiia*, *Moskal'* had been replaced with *Makhno*, the Ukrainian anarchist (*Russkii rok* with Zhenia Gliuk, *Radio Roks*, 05.11.2008).

144. This is his use and definition of Ukrainian folklore. Since I discuss the perception in Russia the accuracy of his statements in regard to what is considered Ukrainian folklore in Ukraine is not relevant here.

ing.' Well, I decided to write such a song. And afterwards I was told: 'But such a song does exist, and it's a folk song.' Fomich always told me. [...] we look for choboty, put it on, we listened – now, well, there's only 'Boots, boots made of bull-leather, are not afraid of the cold nor nothing. Boots, boots you're mine, you cause trouble, you're mine' [should be 'me'] That's also from somewhere in Ukrainian folklore – there're also many songs of the sort because Ukrainian wedding songs were also collected from the county folklore.'

(Rudenko 2006 – Russian: p. 328)

In other words, the refrain is inspired by a phrase taken from Ukrainian folk poetry. The song itself starts with the vocalist singing about his/her experience of moving to the capital – Moscow – and how the boots save him from the cold – paralleling Sasha's biography.

According to the Slavist Tamara Lönngren (pers. comm., 15.10.2008) *choboty* were very important in Ukrainian village life. The use of bull-leather stresses their value by emphasizing their durability reflected in *choboty* being passed down through the generations. Furthermore, the topic of boots (*choboty*) is also prevalent in Russian folklore, e.g. the song *Valenki* (felt boots), a well known Russian folk song (*russkaia narodnaia pesnia*). Sasha draws on this familiarity when he sometimes during concerts jokingly replaces *choboty* with *valenki* or announces the song as *Valenki*.

Returning to the language issue, the above quote also demonstrates Sasha's trouble speaking Ukrainian, with an instance of incorrect grammar: Sasha quotes the song he heard on the record as *"Choboty, choboty z buhaia, Ne boiatsia kholoda nichoho. Choboty, choboty, vy moi, Narobyly klopotu vy moi"*.[145] The last *vy moi* (you're mine) should be *meni* (me) – in other words not *You caused trouble, you're mine* but *You caused me trouble*. While this could be a slip of tongue, it is a quite odd one since the second *vy moi* does not make logical sense.

In regards to the use of Ukrainian folklore, *Marusia* plays a special role in *Svoboda's* repertoire being the only song to melodically recognizably draw on Ukrainian folklore:

"Or Marusia. That is 'Marusia one, two three, guelder-rose', that is even – 'Unharness, boys', that's all but the most Ukrainian folk song, which would have been sung a very long time ago and which has been sung to this very day at dinner tables, at weddings, everywhere. That's what Ukrainian color is."

(Rudenko 2006 – Russian: p. 329)

---

145. Boots, boots made of bull-leather, are not afraid of the cold nor nothing. Boots, boots you're mine, you cause trouble, you're mine

The song is a cover of the well known Cossack/Ukrainian folk(lore) song *Marusia* (also known as *Rozpriahaite, khloptsi, konei* – Unharness, boys) and was the first Svoboda song to be officially released – included on the compilation *Ukraine do Amerika* (Various Artists 2008c).[146] *Marusia* has, however, been adopted to the group's style: Besides being shortened to four verses, Svoboda's version, recorded in 2005, is not dialogic and lacks a harmonization of the verse and refrain, two aspects that can be heard in several folklore versions of the song. Sasha's vocal timbre tends either towards chest voice or screaming. While his use of chest voice is close to that of the male soloist singers in folklore ensembles, such as *Kubanskii Kazachii Khor* (Various Artists 2004d), it differs from the pressed (nasal) timbre used by the female singers of Russian and Ukrainian folklore (including the folklore ensembles). The screaming is a tribute to the punk/rock idiom. The only harmonization of the melody is in the horn section, where at the second four bar period of the refrain the trumpet parallels the trombone voice a third up. There is a ritardando in the seventh bar of the last verse and the refrain starts freely (more or less in half time) accelerating towards the end. This kind of ritardando and accelerando seems to be taken from folklore recordings (e.g. Suzirya 2000). Here Sasha also imitates the folklore recordings by using his chest voice and adding a little vibrato when starting on the refrain.

In other words, the contribution to Ukrainian identity – what Sasha refers to as coloring (*kolorit*) – is provided by the song itself. This song also taps into a shared (Soviet) cultural memory since the audience recognizes the well-known melody and lyrics (including the language – Ukrainian) having been, amongst others, part of the well-known *estrada*-singer Iosif Kobzon's repertoire: It is perceived as something different. While the song is associated with Ukrainian and/or Cossack folklore, it takes on a stronger Ukrainian identity within Svoboda's context, where it is promoted as a Ukrainian folk song (*narodnaia pesnia*) during concerts.

6.1.2 Svoboda's *russkii rok* legacy

As I have shown in the previous section the Ukrainian identity dominates the group. However, Svoboda's music is also shaped by the *russkii rok* legacy discussed

---

146. A newer version taken from the debut album (Svoboda 2009b) was included on the soundtrack (Various Artists 2012b) for the movie *Russendisko* (directed by Oliver Ziegenbalg and released in 2012).

in chapter 3. While Sasha does not define Svoboda's style as *russkii rok*, he does place ideological elements he sees in *russkii rok* – good poetry (*poeziia*), freedom (*svoboda*) and rebellion (*buntarstvo*) – as influencing elements in the group's creative work. Talking about the group he added that he originally never thought he would sing Ukrainian songs. He wanted to play serious songs like Aleksandr Bashlachev (cf. p. 137) who Sasha places in the *russkii rok* lineage based on the poetic quality of his lyrics (Rudenko 2006). Bashlachev influence can be seen in the following incident:

While I was interviewing Sasha (09.01.2006), we were interrupted by some of his friends. They asked Sasha to sing and he complied. Taking an acoustic guitar, he sang three songs: The first and the third song where by Bashlachev, while the second one was one of Sasha's songs titled *Kholodno nam* (We are cold). Sasha added that that song was more in the tradition of *russkii rok* than Svoboda's other songs. A couple of days later Sasha brought a recording of Svoboda from 2003 playing *Kholodno nam*. While not an active part of Svoboda's current repertoire, it was a part of the original repertoire. Sasha referred to this song as an example of *russkii rok* and added that it now is intended for a different project whose attributes are "serious" and "acoustic". I later heard Sasha perform this song accompanying himself on an acoustic guitar at a memorial to Aleksandr Bashlachev titled *Den' pamiati Aleksandra Bashlacheva* (Memorial Day to Aleksandr Bashlachev – Kamchatka, 17.02.2006).

The recording Sasha gave me features the band without a horn section. The rhythm is a rock rhythm, the drums playing a shuffled 6/8 beat,[147] and featuring an acoustic guitar with steel strings as well as a distorted electric guitar. The voice starts off calmly, accompanied by the acoustic guitar playing arpeggiated chords. The song gradually builds up towards the end with the vocals pressed (almost screaming) and both the drums and the distorted electric guitar becoming more prominent in the soundscape. The lyrics (cf. p. 307) are poetical, using metaphors, and are not as straight forward as Svoboda's other lyrics (this matches a comment Sasha made that his serious songs are in Russian).

Kholodno nam is not Svoboda's only song incorporating the *russkii rok* legacy: *Mama anarkhiia* taps right into it by being a well-known Soviet *russkii rok*-an-

---

147. Snare accenting the four while at times the high hat continuously playing the eights. The bass drum is too unclear to be heard (or simply overpowered by the bass).

them. While adhering closely to Kino's (1986) original, Svoboda's version (Various Artists 2008b) has been adopted to the group's style. Most notably this is done through the addition of a horn section (trumpet, trombone), a slightly faster tempo and a different key. As discussed above (cf. p. 170ff) the rhythm and sound alternates between the verse and refrain.[148]

Another song inspired by Kino is *Dengi* (Money) where both the gestus and timbre of the opening guitar riff are influenced by *Spokoinaia noch'* (Good night – Kino 1988). Sasha (Rudenko 2006) also pointed out that *La-La* is influenced by the Russian (punk) group Grazhdanskaia Oborona's *Vse idet po planu's* (Everything is going as planned – Grazhdanskaia Oborona 1988) bass line.[149]

Vitia, Svoboda's first guitarist who played a major role in forming the repertoire pointed out that the group's style had developed:

"The style probably changed a little. From *russkii rok* it changed to something like punk. Then it went over to ska-punk with horns there, in places even reggae is present"

(Kultashov 2006 – Russian: p. 326)

Those changes continued with Prokhor, who prior to joining Svoboda had played in other ska/reggae bands (cf. p. 174). Thus the *russkii rok*-legacy is now not part of the official narrative of Svoboda instead being replaced by ska and ska-punk. However, the influences are still there, especially through the musical references mentioned above. Furthermore, Sasha's choice of using Russian for what he calls "serious" songs (e.g. *Dengi*) indirectly implies a nod of respect to *russkii rok's* preoccupation with the lyrics.

---

148. More subtile changes are in the form where an interlude in Kino's version is left out and the song starts with trombone and trumpet playing the verse and refrain (both during the intro and solo the trumpet and trombone primarily follow the melody sung by the singer). Furthermore, Svoboda adds three extra bars to the refrain.
149. While it might have been the case in the beginning, the current bass line in *La-La* is c#5 A5 – E5 B5 (i5 VI5 – III5 VII5) while *Vse idet po planu's* is A5 F5 – C5 E (i5 VI5 – III5 V) thus ending on the V, not VII (although the VII could be seen as a V with the root missing).

6.1.3 Svoboda's multifaceted band identity

> "It's understandable just like that. I hear a song and understand, this is from here, this is from there. That is Sex Pistols, that is the group Kino. It is in general not bad. He [Sasha] has a certain concert magic, that is good."
>
> (Burlaka 2005 – Russian: p. 318)

What makes Svoboda interesting is how the music reflects on both a more global popular music style drawing on conventions from popular music[150] and at the same time draws on a more regional or local set of references – as demonstrated by Andrei Burlaka's quote. These include references to groups and composers like Nirvana, The Offspring, Sex Pistols, and Beethoven.[151] The band also draws on a shared cultural history – the Soviet Union and Russian Empire – which gives the group a specific national and regional meaning. This both refers to Soviet, Russian, and Ukrainian bands (Kino, Leningrad, Grazhdanskaia Oborona, VV) as well as Ukrainian stereotypes (stereotypes can be seen as a very fixed set of cultural codes). This shows that the band's identity is multifaceted (and fluid) including various referents.

The Ukrainian stereotypes contribute to the Ukrainian part of the band image, which has been the focus here. This Ukrainian identity is primarily expressed through the lyrics in Sasha's deliberate *surzhik*. The band also uses key words linked to Ukrainian peasant life which Sasha strongly associates with folklore. Only one song (*Marusia*) is an actual cover of a traditional song which is both considered Ukrainian and/or (depending on how the cultural and political boarders are drawn) Cossack. Here the question of the exact origin of the music, which often is central within discussions of traditional music (e.g. Norwegian traditional music), is virtually unimportant and can be read (or heard) differently depending on the cultural background of the listener. In St. Petersburg it is mostly perceived

---

150. The songs follow a regular, mostly 8 bar period, have a verse-refrain structure and some songs are based around I-IV-V chord progressions (e.g. *Mama anarkhiia* and *Super Para*). This makes the songs recognizable for a popular music audience who can place the songs within a set of conventions. One a more specific level, Svoboda, through the use of *style indicators* (Tagg 1999, 28), makes the songs recognizable within the idioms of ska and punk.
151. While *Dengi* is also influenced by Nirvana's *Come As You Are* (Nirvana 1991), the song *La-La*'s opening riff bears a strong resemblance to Nirvana's *Smells like Teen Spirit* (Nirvana 1991) as well as The Offspring's *Self Esteem* (The Offspring 1994)). *Super Para* draws on both Beethoven's melodization from *An die Freude* (4th movement of his 9th Symphony) as well as the bass riff from Sex Pistol's *Anarchy in the U.K.* (Sex Pistols 1993).

as a (generic) Ukrainian influence which fulfills the requirements to be considered an exotic *Other* by the fans.

The process of building and maintaining a Ukrainian identity is, in the daily practice, however, fluid and produces different representations depending on the context: Some songs (*Pogoda, Mama anarkhiia*) exist in both Russian and Ukrainian language versions. Depending on the situation, Sasha can focus on singing songs only with Ukrainian lyrics (e.g. the festivals *RaSKAlbas 2 – Staryi Dom*, 01.04.2005 – and *Okna otkroi!* – 02.07.2005). On the other hand, he can also focus on singing predominantly Russian lyrics.[152] Most of the time, however, there is a balance biased towards Ukrainian lyrics.

This can also be seen and heard in the band line up where a *baian*, an instrument prominent in Russian and Ukrainian folklore, was added in 2007/2008. Visually Sasha, who is very lively on stage – dancing and acting to the songs – also uses stage props like his jacket, a mug of beer (for the song *Pogoda* about drinking beer), a cigarette (for the song *Ganzhubeilo* which is about smoking/not smoking marihuana), or random objects on the stage. Here Sasha's training as an actor is an influence. After I left, the use of stage props has focused more on the Ukrainian identity with a Ukrainian style leather jacket and hat, leather boots (*choboty*), *vyshivanka* (an embroidered shirt widely used in Ukraine), a vodka bottle, and, during a concert on the old or Orthodox New Year (according to the Julian calendar, 13.01.2008), even two elderly female singers of traditional music in traditional clothing. After the Makhno concert mentioned above, Sasha acquired a hat similar to Makhno's and a huge skull and cross bone flag which also seems to be linked to Makhno.

Another element which underlines the constructedness of this identity is, as discussed, Sasha's poor command of the Ukrainian language, hence his use of *surzhik* (touching semantics, lexicon, morphology, and non-standard forms on the phonetic and phonological level). This was not only repeatedly pointed out to me by musicians I talked to in St. Petersburg and Berlin, but I also experienced

---

152. An extreme example was during a private New Year's party for a company (*korporativnaia vecherinka*) we were hired to play at *Dzhambala* (29.12.2005). Here Sasha even sang *Mama anarkhiia* in Russian. The party's motto was "Jamaican New Year" so the ska-identity was thus more important. Another reason was probably due to the fact that the audience consisted of people not normally present at our concerts, and for whom our Ukrainian identity was not important.

this personally while working on Svoboda's webpage: Sasha had to ask his partner for help when creating the content for the Ukrainian language pages of the site. This is, however, not really significant, since Svoboda's target group is primarily St. Petersburg's inhabitants and thus Russian speakers. *Surzhik* also makes the lyrics easier to understand as seen in the following answer to my question if it is hard to understand Sasha when he sings in Ukrainian:

> Denis: "No..."
> Anton: "...the idea is understandable..."
> Denis: "...but some lines fly away due to the fact that you don't know the language and they fly away with the whole sense, as for example, he removed the microphone and the word flew away: you can't get the whole line of what he sang about. There, it goes, goes, goes: half the words – it is just to swap the letters and everything he sings about is understandable. [Cf. p. 186, Fn. 141] And now the microphone flew away to the side, he lost one word, and already that whole connection of words from the Ukrainian language, already it is impossible to link it to Russian."
> Anton: "Without one word..."
> Denis: "...it is already harder to grasp."
> Anton: "For me it makes absolutely no difference whether he sings in Ukrainian or Russian. The only thing is, as Denis already said, that some phrases fly away, if he only sings in Ukrainian. I adore Tsoi's song Mama anarkhiia. I adore it in the Russian variant as well as – I won't say 'khokliatskii' [adj. of *khokhol*] – in its Ukrainian variant."
>
> (Vashkevich and Lukanin 2006 – Russian: p. 319)

Here Sasha's signaling of a Ukrainian *Other* (which is perceived by the fans) is more important than an accurate command of the Ukrainian language or music.

6.2 Excursion: Ukrainian popular music and Ukrainian nationalism

> "I think the orientation towards Russia and the Russian influence is dangerous. It is only about oil, that is all. A big bear with a Balalaika, Bullshit! We think that the only path for Ukraine goes Westwards, in order to be integrated with Europe."
>
> (Oleksandr Yarmola, qtd. in Arte 2008 – German: p. 316)

Russia's pressure on Ukraine, mentioned above, as well as portrayals like Svoboda's provoke strong emotional replies from Ukraine, like the statement above made by the group Haydamaky's singer Oleksandr Yarmola during an interview.

The following section shifts to a Ukrainian perspective and focuses on how the Ukrainian singer Ruslana Lyzhychko (probably most prominently known for her winning the *Eurovision Song Contest* 2004) asserts a sovereign Ukraine (distancing the country from Russia) both through anchoring her creative work in

6 RUSSIAN PERCEPTIONS OF UKRAINE   195

Ukraine as well as in the way she builds her band image and promotes herself.[153] While she, just like Svoboda, draws on traditional music and folklore, her strategy and implementation differs: She represents material from within what she considers her cultural territory and within the boundaries of her nation-state which today is sovereign from Russia. My discussion here is – in contrast to that of Svoboda – primarily based on a media reading of Ruslana's image as well as an analysis of her song *Kolomyika* (Ruslana 2003) as used in the eponymous video clip (Ruslana 2006a). This analysis is concerned with how the music video is locally anchored. As mentioned in chapter 4, this strategy can be examined on three levels, *lyrics*, *textual*, and *aural*.[154]

6.2.1   Ruslana's *Kolomyika*

The video to Ruslana's *Kolomyika* describes how an urban casting crew comes to a remote Hutsul village. The villagers dressed in traditional clothes promote themselves and their local traditions in a slightly country bumpkinish manner before finally resisting the casting crew.[155]

Figure 4: Beginning of the first verse of Ruslana's *Kolomyika*. The verse melody is based on these two phrases.

Oi, ku-va-la zo-zu-le-chka   tai ka-za-la ku-ku.   Ne-e py-tai me-ne da-re-mno   a be-ry za ru-ku.

On the textual level the song's lyrics (see p. 309) are placed firmly within a (West)Ukrainian context through the use of Ukrainian as the language and the title *Kolomyika* which is a dance, instrumental, and a vocal music genre from the Carpathian mountains (Hrytsa n.d., Olha Kolomyyets, pers. comm., 24.09.2007).[156] The verse follows the metric structure of a *kolomyika* being

---

153. I choose Ruslana since she is both well known within Ukraine as well as abroad – including Western Europe.
154. This section is a shortened version of Wickström (2008) which also includes a second case, Haydamaky's *Kokhannia* (Haydamaky 2007), left out here due to space constraints.
155. According to a sub-page on Ruslana's website (Ruslana n.d.) the clip directed by Eugen Mitrofanov (Ruslana 2006a) was shot in 2003 in the Carpathians mountains and in the Lvov museum *Shevchenkivs'kyi hai*.
156. Gemba (2007, 144) also notes that it can be a Ukrainian variant of the Russian *chastushka*.

(4+4+6)+(4+4+6) where two lines are one unit (Shumady and Vasylenko 1969, 423, Olha Kolomyyets, pers. comm., 24.09.2007):

Oi, ku-va-la | zo-zu-le-chka | tai ka-za-la ku-ku.
Ne py-tai me- | ne da-re-mno | a be-ry za ru-ku.[157]

This is also reflected in the rhythm sung which can be either 12 eight notes and two quarter notes or 13 eight notes and one dotted quarter note (Shumady and Vasylenko 1969, 423) – see Figure 4, first two bars.

The lyrics were written by Oleksandr Ksenofontov, Ruslana's co-producer and husband (Gemba 2007, 139). They are about unfulfilled or lost love and do not relate directly to the clip. Despite this discrepancy, the narration's form is used in the dramaturgy: While Ruslana sings the verse and refrain, the following interjection (which comes twice) is sung by some village men (in a call-and-response pattern with trumpets answering):

Oi, kuvala zozulechka
Oi, kuvala ta i spivala
Zbudyla moie serdechko[158]

Thus the narrative works on two levels: the content of the lyrics (which can only be understood by listeners who speak Ukrainian) and the unrelated story of the video clip (which can be understood without the lyrics) using the lyrics as a dramaturgical effect.

On the level of images, the clip is anchored through the depiction of different instruments linked to traditional music (accordion/*harmoniia*, *baraban*, trumpet, trombone, fiddle, *tsymbaly*, *sopilka* – the accordion/*harmoniia* and *baraban* are however not heard),[159] the clothes worn (e.g. *vyshivanka*),[160] tapestries, the food, and the rural setting. Since *kolomyikas* are also a dance genre, the dancing in the clip could be a form of anchoring. The dancing is, however, not in the center of

---

157. "Oi, the little cuckoo cried and said ku-ku. / Don't ask me in vain, but take [me] by the hand". According to Tamara Lönngren the correct diminutive should be *zozulen'ka*, a diminutive on *chka* as in *zozulechka* is more common in Russian (pers. comm., 15.10.2008) – in other words, a form of *surzhik*.
158. "Oi, the cuckoo cried / Oi, it cried and sung / It excited my heart". As with *zozulechka* the correct diminutive should be *serden'ko*.
159. *Harmoniia* is a free reed button accordion, *tsymbaly* is a trapezoidal hammered zither, the *baraban* a drum while the *sopilka* is a woodwind instrument similar to a flute (Noll 2000, 811, 816).
160. According to Ruslana's webpage "[a]uthentic costumes were used during the shooting of mass scenes" and "[e]ach hucul [sic] traditional costume appearing in the video is at least 100 years old." (Ruslana n.d.)

the clip and while the clip draws on elements which could be from traditional dances (incorporating chain dances, couples, and individual dancers), the style looks too choreographed.

On the aural level, melodic and rhythmic fragments in Ruslana's song seem to be based on traditional music and draw on elements from *kolomyikas* (the liner notes state that the music is composed by Ruslana and Ksenofontov, using motives from Hutsul *kolomyikas*). As already discussed regarding the lyrics, the metric system (4+4+6) and the rhythm sung in the verse is a trait of the genre. The trumpet/trombone/*tsymbaly*[161]/*sopilka* riffs as well as the vocals are based on a scale with a lowered third and an augmented fourth (see Figure 4 and Figure 5). According to Hrytsa (n.d.), this together with a sharpened seventh (missing here) is a characteristic mode of Hutsul music. Noll (2000, 809) points out that the augmented fourth is commonly heard in traditional music from the Carpathians. Furthermore, the timbre of the instruments (brassy trumpets, *tsymbaly*, *sopilka*, *baraban*) evokes, in contrast to the electric guitar and bass, a traditional association. These traditional instruments are featured throughout the song, thus providing a constant reminder.[162]

Figure 5: The trumpet and tsymbaly part (intro) in Ruslana's *Kolomyika*.

Finally, while Ruslana's vocal timbre fits into a popular – not traditional – music idiom (her voice, however, sounds strained), her singing style draws heavily on ornaments – both mordents and portamentos (sliding into the tone) – which places the style not necessarily within a Hutsul, but a South-East European/Turkish/Orientalist idiom. This is especially audible in the first four bars, where she

---

161. *Tsymbaly* is not mentioned in the CD-liner notes, however it can be heard on the recording.
162. The instruments appear primarily as a response. While the trumpet and trombone are usually heard without vocals, the *sopilka* parallels the vocals (mainly in the verse and refrain). The *soplika* and *tsymbaly* also appear without vocals together as a response to the trumpet and trombone (but not in the end of the last refrain).

sings rhythmically freely in half time (see Figure 6, the melodic skeleton is the same as in the verse – see Figure 4).

Within her other musical work Ruslana also incorporates elements from traditional music/Hutsul music. Her CD *Diki Tantsi* (Ruslana 2003) states that it is a *Hutsul'skyi Proekt* (Hutsul project) and the tracks also include *floyara* (a flute-like woodwind instrument) and *trembita* (alpine horns used by the Hutsuls) besides the traditional instruments mentioned above. While the music is credited to Ruslana,[163] the songs *Ples, Arkan, Kolomyika, Hutsulka,* and *Oi, zagrai my, muzychen'ky* are, according to the liner notes, based on motives from Hutsul dances/melodies.

Figure 6: Sonogram of the first bars of Ruslana's *Kolomyika*. The darker line starting at about 200 Hz and spanning between 200 and 500 Hz is Ruslana's voice. The jaggedness of the line indicates the use of vibrato and ornaments, while the vertical leaps indicate portamentos (e.g., at 2 s and 8 s).

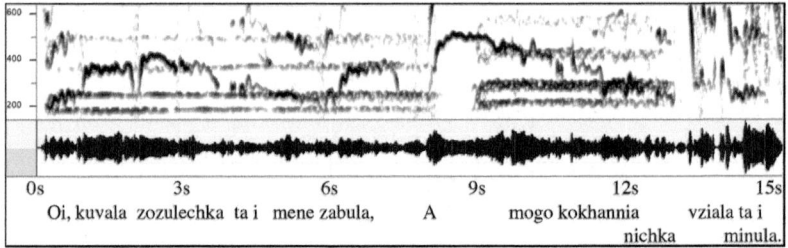

The CD-booklet itself primarily depicts Ruslana showing a lot of skin. One of the costumes seems to be based on traditional (folklore) patterns. There are also images taken from Ruslana's clip *Znaiu ia* with the artist standing on the top of a mountain holding a tambourine, driving through a lake in a jeep, and giving a rock concert. A group of people (Hutsuls) can also be seen chain-dancing in traditional costumes in a village.

These elements play a role as markers in the identity construction that places Ruslana in Ukraine and links her closely to the Hutsuls. One important aspect mentioned in the discussion of representation above is the fact that it is not possible (or even necessary) to verify Ruslana's claim that the music she uses is of Hutsul origin (hence my use of *traditional music* in the discussion). The material

---

163. Except for *Kolomyika* which is credited to both Ruslana and Ksenofontov.

6 RUSSIAN PERCEPTIONS OF UKRAINE   199

functions to localize Ruslana's music in a way consistent with the discourse of her band, thus the question of its authenticity is secondary in the promotion of her music. I will return to this aspect below.

Besides signifying Ukraine, these markers also serve as style indicators for world music within the world music discourse. Discussing musical strategies in Finnish contemporary folk music, the ethnomusicologist Juniper Hill labels similar markers: "[d]isembodied sonic markers of participation in the world music scene" (Hill 2007, 69). She adds that

> "[the] use of these 'exotic' accompaniment instruments [frame drum, djembe, didjeridu] serves less as a reference to particular cultures in Africa and Oceania and more as trendy markers of globality signifying participation in a contemporary 'world music' scene."
>
> (Hill 2007, 71)

In other words, it is a form of authentication strategy.

Obviously, this kind of incorporation of style indicators associated with Ukrainian traditional music is not limited to Ruslana. Other bands promoted outside Ukraine use similar material and strategies as well (e.g. Haydamaky, Mad Heads XL, VV, and Perkalaba).[164]

6.2.2 *"Preserving the cultural heritage"*: Band identity construction based on traditional music, history, and politics

The incorporation of local sources is, however, not restricted to audio-visual and performative levels, but also touches on the manner in which Ruslana (as also other bands) portrays herself and is perceived. Talking about Ruslana and her creative process, Alexander Kasparov, one of the directors of Eastblok Music, said the following:

> "[Ruslana] regularly makes these folkloristic expeditions to the Carpathians. And she explores that, goes with the whole team and finds new beats, new musical structures. She always comes back with a lot of musical luggage and is always very satisfied and [she] told me, that [this] is very influential."
>
> (Kasparov and Siebert 2006 - German: p. 315)

This focus on traditional Ukrainian music is also described on the English version of Ruslana's web page:[165]

---

164. I am aware of the fact that this only represents a small selection of Ukrainian bands and that other internationally active Ukrainian bands like Okean El'zy do not incorporate traditional elements. Okean El'zy, however, predominantly tours Russia unlike the other bands which primarily target countries west and north of Ukraine – Said's European theatrical stage (Said 1994, 71f).
165. The content on the Ukrainian pages appears identical to the English content.

"For her Wild Dances Project Ruslana conducted expeditions to the Carpathian mountains discovering rhythms, dances and costumes of the ancient culture of the mountains which were on the brink to being forgotten and integrated them into a modern show, thus preserving the cultural heritage."

(Ruslana n.d.)

These quotes stress and romanticize the influence of regional traditional Ukrainian material on the music played by Ruslana. This "culture of the mountains" specifically refers to the *Hutsuls* – thus framing the music within ethnic categories.

Ruslana cites *cultural heritage* as an important motivation in her creative work. Combined with the reference to ethnic musics, this is part of the authentication strategy aimed at the world music market outside the Ukraine. Here Ruslana focuses on one area (*Hutsuls*/Carpathian mountains) with her *drive-ethno-dance* (Ruslana n.d.). Together with singing in Ukrainian (which clearly stakes her position in the Ukrainian language debate) she touches on the discourses around Ukrainian national identity.

This brings us to the *Orange Revolution* of 2004. Ruslana[166] (as well as the groups Haydamaky, Okean El'zy, and VV) supported the Orange Revolution and the rhetoric used on her web page should also be read in this light:[167]

"Ruslana actively supported the democratic processes in Ukraine in winter 2004/2005 and in [...] spring 2006 she was elected Member of Ukrainian Parliament. The main issues she intends to push in politics are cultural issues, the Euro-integration of Ukraine and youth politics."

(Ruslana n.d.)

Here Ruslana states her support for a democratic Ukraine. This support is also referred to in her creative work: Ruslana's clip *Dance With The Wolves* (Ruslana 2006b) shows Ruslana dressed in an orange sweater, participating in the revolution. In addition, she was featured on the compilation *Pomaranchevi pisni* (Or-

---

166. According to Klid (2007, 122) Ruslana tried to remain neutral during most of the campaign and thus also performed for the Ianukovych camp. She officially endorsed Iushchenko on November 17th, 2004, four days before the rigged run-off vote on November 21st, 2004, which ignited the protests.
167. It is hard to determine when the texts quoted were written and posted on her websites. A WHOIS-domain search at www.domainwhitepages.com on December 3rd, 2007 does not reveal when www.ruslana.com.ua was created. In the internet archive Wayback Machine (Wayback Machine n.d.), which has archived the internet since 1996, the first pages for www.ruslana.com.ua appeared by June 14th, 2001 (however Ruslana's current flash-based version appeared around or before September 28th, 2002). Since Ruslana's page is flash-based, it is not possible to track changes in the content using the Wayback Machine.

ange songs – Various Artists 2004a).[168] Due to space limitations I will not discuss this clip here (cf. Helbig 2006 and Klid 2007 for a discussion on the role of popular music in the 2004 election campaign and during the Orange Revolution).

As mentioned in my short historical overview of Ukraine in chapter 1, language politics were an important issue of the revolution. The Orange block and the groups performing distinguished themselves by using Ukrainian. This appropriation of the Ukrainian language within Ukrainian popular music goes back to the Soviet Period. Bahry (1994, 251f) lists VV as the first group of the fourth wave of Ukrainian rock to sing in Ukrainian.[169] The first music festival which required all songs to be in Ukrainian was the *Chervona Ruta Festival* in 1989 (in Chernivtsi, West Ukraine). As Bahry (1994, 250) writes:

"The Chervona Ruta Festival and the subsequent concerts were united not so much by genre of music, because they included a potpourri of various styles, but rather by the theme of Ukrainian language and Ukrainian national revival."

The *Rock Sich festival* in Kiev 2005 organized by VV's singer Oleg Skrypka should thus not only be seen in the light of the Orange Revolution, but also in this lineage. It was only open to bands singing in Ukrainian (Khinkulova 2006)[170] – but not necessarily limited to groups from Ukraine: Svoboda performed at the festival September 7th, 2008. This opposition to Russian influences might also explain why Ruslana as of October 2013 only has given concerts in Moscow and Kazan'.[171]

6.2.3 *"Ethnic sounds of the mountain people":* Ruslana's Ukrainian anchoring and questions of representation

Ruslana's strategy can be framed within Stokes' (1997b, 6) discussion on ethnicities being constructed through boundaries of opposition mentioned above. In ad-

---

168. The album *Pomaranchevi pisni* was reissued by Eastblok Music in Germany (under license from Comp Music) as *Ukraina – Songs of the Orange Revolution* (Various Artists 2005e). The clip *Dance With The Wolves* is included on the reissued compilation as a bonus video track.
169. She adds, however, that VV also purposely sang in Russian in protest to being pressured by the newly founded *Ukrainian Popular Movement for Restructuring (Rukh)* to sing in Ukrainian only.
170. Unlike the musically inclusive *Chervona Ruta Festival*, the *Rock Sich festival* also sported another dichotomy, rock vs. pop, where pop was excluded by the organizers – without defining what pop was. However, there could also be a link between music perceived as pop and singing in Russian: two BBC articles (Fawkes 2004; Khinkulova 2006) report that Russian language pop enjoys a huge popularity in Ukraine.
171. The concert list on (Ruslana n.d.) went back to 2004 and the list on the current website (Ruslana 2008) goes back to 2007.

dition to using Ukrainian as a singing language and supporting the Orange Revolution Ruslana erects boundaries as a Ukrainian by labeling her material "ethnic" and placing it within certain regions (thus drawing on perceived Ukrainian traditions and internal *Others* like the Hutsuls). The singer, as discussed above, anchors herself in one place. The national level is, however, also present in her narrative and activities: she places her music within a Ukrainian (historical) context, performs in Ukraine (as well as abroad) and is politically engaged. These choices have different reasons, one of which is marketing – especially marketing abroad. As already mentioned, combining popular music with local or ethnic musics (or hybrid musics) within the world music market functions as an authentication strategy. In this case the music is marketed as "ethnic sounds of the mountain people of the Hutsuls with modern rock, pop and dance elements" (Ruslana n.d.) where a dichotomy is created between the "modern" musical styles and the ethnic (whose synonym here is "ancient"/"traditional"). Eastblock music's promotion of Haydamaky's first album released abroad titled *Ukraine calling* (Haydamaky 2006)[172] provides a similar example:

> "Haydamaky manage to build bridges and combine Ukrainian roots, which spring in the mysterious Carpathian Mountains, and Western production standards."
> (Eastblok Music n.d.)

Here, the national level is literally rooted in the Carpathian Mountains, promoting the music as something natural, exotic, and Ukrainian. The national boundaries are loosened a little by the reference to "build bridges". However, the bridges referred to are Western production standards, which again place Haydamaky in the naturalized savage category: only by the aid of Western technology (in other words, civilization's progress) is that music made accessible to a broader market. This orientialization strategy is supported by images of Haydamaky's vocalist on the CD with his chest bare, as well as Ruslana displaying a lot of skin and her use of leather clothes – creating an image of savage (or at least "closer" to nature) Ukrainians (cf. p. 277 for a similar marketing example by the Vienna based *Ost Klub* when promoting the band Russkaja).

---

172. Actually re-released in a new packaging is more accurate, since besides the bonus track the songs are identical to the album *Perverziia* released in Ukraine (Haidamaky 2005). On another level the album's title could also be a reference to The Clash's *London calling* (Clash 1979).

While there are strong marketing demands behind these choices,[173] I would argue against a reduction of Ruslana's identity to pure economic interests. Being politically active and supporting a revolution which could have ended violently – while being a great marketing ploy – would be a quite extreme form of marketing opportunism and could also have hampered her future career. Furthermore, Ruslana has been active both as a Ukrainian parliamentarian (2006-2007) and in trying to improve the conditions for children suffering from the aftermath of Chernobyl. In addition to being related to marketing, her strategy should thus also be seen as political.

Since Ruslana places what she calls "ethnic elements" within a wider Ukrainian context, a more useful concept to understand her identity is a post-colonial lens. David Chioni Moore (2001, 118) argues that

"one result of extended subjugation is compensatory behavior by the subject peoples. One manifestation of this behavior is an exaggerated desire for authentic sources, generally a mythic set of heroic, purer ancestors who once controlled a greater zone than the people now possess."

In other words, this entails building an identity based on perceived cultural elements from a pre-colonial era which is considered purer. Through this lens Ruslana appropriates what she perceives as authentic sources, which are found in the traditional music influences. Haydamaky also embodies this desire in their name which refers to the 18th century Haydamaky partisan movement.

Ruslana's appropriation and representation of the Hutsuls, where she recycles national stereotypes which reaffirm that the Hutsuls are backward and still adhere to their "ancient" traditions – thus being "pure" or "unspoiled" by modernity is similar to Svoboda's strategy mentioned above. She does this on her website by distancing the Hutsuls from a contemporary urban setting, and by placing them back in time and relocating them in space – exoticising them:

"Here, high in the mountains, where the people live in different time and dimension, has [sic] Ruslana found the source of inspiration for her new 'Hutsulian project'. That's where you find true Ukrainian exotics!"

(Ruslana n.d.)

This can also be seen in the portrayal of the Hutsuls in the clip mentioned earlier. They wear their traditional costumes and perform songs in a country bumpkinish way at the end of the music video. On a sign in the video advertising the

---

173. Another marketing strategy (and attempt to tap into the world music market) is Ruslana's use of Peter Gabriel's *Real World Studio* (UK) to master her album. The album itself was recorded in *Luxen Studio* (Ukraine).

casting the word *kasting* is replaced with *vybori* also belittling the Hutsuls by implying that they do not understand Anglo-American borrowings/modern Ukrainian (*kasting*) and instead need a Ukrainian synonym (*vybori*). Furthermore, above that casting sign there is another small posting belittling the Hutsuls saying *Korova – drug liudyny!* (The cow – friend of the people!).

This representation of the *Other* by Ruslana leaves out the reality that the Hutsuls are equally a part of the 21th century. Their resentment of Ruslana's portrayal led them to lobby the regional parliament of the Ivano-Frankivs'ka oblast' against being labeled savage (*diki*).[174]

6.3 Concluding remarks

As just discussed, both Ruslana's and Svoboda's (Sasha's) representations are from the dominant position, exploiting a backward *Other*. Similar to Ruslana's portrayal of the Hutsuls in Ukraine, Ukrainians were, during the Tsarist and Soviet times, regarded as uncultured peasants: "Despite urbanization and industrialization, Ukrainians are considered a people of uncultivated peasants, as 'chochly'" (Kappeler 2003, 54 - German: p. 315). This portrayal can be seen in 19th century literature, such as Gogol's *Evenings on a Farm near Dikanka* (Gogol 1985, 3-206), in Soviet movies (Bilaniuk 2005, 115), and is reflected in jokes about Ukrainians told in Russia (Shmeleva and Shmelev 2002).[175]

Thus, Svoboda constructs an identity of Ukraine by creating an exotic *Other*, built on existing (Russian) clichés of Ukraine – in other words, reproducing (colonial) stereotypes. This is linked to marketing the group in St. Petersburg for a local audience: Sasha himself has become a Russian citizen and had no plans of returning to Ukraine during my stay. He is trying to distinguish Svoboda from other groups in St. Petersburg by building on an entity with a common history and

---

174. Cf. Sonevytsky (2006) for a discussion of Ruslana's appropriation of Hutsul material and the linked politics of auto-exoticism and resistance, and Gemba (2007) for an analysis on how Ruslana constructs a tri-part image based on a regional myth, ethnic anchoring, and a stylized female figure.
175. According to Shmeleva and Shmelev (2002, 61f) Ukrainians are portrayed in jokes as stupid, greedy, sloppy/unclean, and as people who only eat lard while making fun of Russians by speaking a "broken Russian" (in other words, Ukrainian – cf. Skrypka's quote, p. 177). Sasha alluded to the lard when talking about Ukrainian humor with the following joke: *"Tikha Ukrainskaia noch', no salo nado perepriatat'!"* (Silent Ukrainian night, but the lard has to be rehidden! – Rudenko 2006)

shared past, but which has become distanced from its former colonizer. As discussed in the beginning of this chapter, Ukraine is perceived by many Russians as a part of Russia and Russia – especially the political elite – has a keen interest (both historical as well as strategically) that Ukraine remains within the Russian sphere of interest.

When looking at their use within their respective home countries there is also a major difference between Svoboda's appropriation of traditional Ukrainian material and Ruslana's: Sasha's project based in Russia is not one of a post-colonial desire for nation building/nationalism, but of creating an exotic *Other*, built on existing clichés of Ukraine, in other words reproducing the colonial stereotypes, which are employed as a marketing strategy. Thus, he is using material from a different national (and sovereign) entity while Ruslana is representing material from within what she considers her cultural territory and within the boundaries of "her" nation-state – a post-colonial desire for sovereign nation building. While Ruslana's use also raises questions of ethics in representation, she is performing *her* heritage, as a Ukrainian friend pointed out to me in response to my critique of Ruslana's appropriation.[176] While some (the Hutsuls) object to this kind of representation, others take pride in this music as an assertion of their participation in a sovereign Ukraine. As I argue elsewhere (Wickström 2008) the group Haydamaky also represents material from within what the group's members considers their cultural territory and within the boundaries of "their" nation-state. Both Ruslana and Haydamaky use their creative work to distance themselves from what they perceive is a Russian hegemony. Thus the question of representation differs in Russia and Ukraine. This, however, changes once the music arrives at the *Russendisko* in Berlin and will be discussed in chapter 10.

This and the previous chapter have also focused on the elements Svoboda draws on to make up a band image which the listeners can recognize and – if it appeals to them – appropriate. Those elements do not necessarily have to be the Ukrainian elements, they can also refer to ska-punk or other aspects. What is, however, important here, is that a common reference frame – a shared under-

---

176. She argued that Ruslana is from Lvov which is perceived as the capital of Western Ukraine – the only place in the Ukraine where "ethnic" Ukrainian symbols remain – and thus Ruslana can use Hutsul and other "ethnic" elements (Nataliya Chumak, pers. comm., 13.01.2009).

standing of the codes – exists, making it possible to interpret this semiotic field partially due to a shared (popular) cultural heritage from the Soviet Union.

This band image can provide the listener with *one* possible interpretation of the band's identities. Being essentially a collective identity, the promoted band identity is both based on the musicians' shared identities as well as a more specific mediated band identity, which can, as in Svoboda's case, be based on a member's personal identity (this is similar to a personal identity in the sense that the identity is but one representation of the band's habits). These habits are also reflected in the band's musical style which draws on the members' musical background – such as incorporating references to (post-)Soviet, Jamaican, and Anglo-American popular music based on the musicians' listening biographies. The band image is constructed both on the discursive level (band promotion, utterances during concerts etc.) as well as on the creative level (songs, albums, music videos, performances etc.).

Leaving the local level, the next chapter focuses on how popular music is used in promoting Russian national identities by focusing on four established bands whose roots can be traced to the 1980s. Besides providing more context for the post-colonial perspective, this also shows how *russkii rok* and its musicians are in part becoming co-opted by the government. It also is an example of Hannerz's frame *state* – especially how the government tries to appropriate *russkii rok* for their means.

7 Popular music and ideas of the Russian nation

> "When visited this week, the popular arty indie bar Fidel boasted a sign on its door saying 'No Entrance for George W. Bush, Condoleezza Rice and Mikhail Saakashvili,' the name of the U.S. Secretary of State spelt with five typos. The name of Ukraine's president Viktor Yushchenko was added in handwriting."
>
> (Chernov 2008b)

Fidel is a music bar located in the center of St. Petersburg and a popular hangout for both musicians and fans. Even though the comment barring Bush, Rice, Saakashvili, and Iushchenko came in reaction to the short Georgian-Russian war in 2008, such political statements were (while mostly not that extreme) common when talking to people in St. Petersburg and also expressed in musicians' creative work. Although seemingly putting Russia on a path towards a booming economic recovery based on a surge in oil and gas prices during his first tenures, President Vladimir Putin at the same time stoked national sentiments reminding the citizens of the Russian Federation (and the world) that Russia remains a superpower. The result was not only a positive patriotism, but also a (borderline) chauvinistic nationalism. Besides relations to the Baltic states, which have been problematic since the 1990s, two new thorns appeared with the 2003 *Rose Revolution* in Georgia headed by Mikhail Saakashvili and the 2004 *Orange Revolution* in Ukraine headed by Viktor Iushchenko and Iuliia Tymoshenko – with popular music playing a supporting role in both revolutions. This – especially in the relationship to Georgia – has been combined with a xenophobic stance towards migrant workers from primarily the Caucasus region (racist stickers targeting migrants from the Caucasus region and Central-Asia as well as Jews were commonly visible on the subway and in other public places). A first culmination occurred in 2006, a year which was witness to two large scale anti-migrant events: The arrest of four alleged Russian spies in Georgia resulted in an en-masse deportation of Georgian migrant workers on charges of not having valid papers. The second event was an anti-migrant pogrom following the death of two Russians in an interethnic pub brawl in Kondopoga (Karelia, North-East of St. Petersburg). Furthermore, the eastward expansion of NATO – with former members of the Warsaw Pact joining the alliance – has also created much concern and anger – especially towards the United States – on the governmental level, which trickled down to the people I talked to.

While the previous discussion touched on a Russian view of Ukraine, the following discussion focuses on how music is used to construct and maintain identities on a national level. I approach this by examining how (popular) music is appropriated and employed in constructing a *DiKoIdentität* in Russia, especially in the utterances and creative work of Boris Grebenshchikov (Akvarium), Konstantin Kinchev (Alisa), Oleg Gazmanov, and the group Piligrim. This is in form a national identity, but one which in content is on a continuum between ethnic and supra-national. Two songs I discuss in the following exemplifies this: *Slava Rossii*, (Hail Russia) by the group Piligrim, evokes a national identity which tends towards an ethnic concept (Slavs), while Gazmanov's *Sdelan v SSSR* (Made in the USSR) tends more towards a regional supra-national identity based on the Soviet Union.

In order to discuss this, a short overview of Russian history and national identities is necessary. As mentioned in chapter 1, I see *national identities* as a collective discursive construct which is in constant evolution (*DiKoIdentität*) – however, the ideas that make up these identities are quite persistent, giving them an air of primordialism. When discussing national identities in relation to Russia, it is important to distinguish between *state* and *nation*. While the former is based on certain autonomous institutions in possession of a power and a taxation monopoly, the latter is based on a form of (imagined) community. The Russian empire can be looked at as a state, however, the concept of a nation emerged only in the 19th century with the rise of nationalism. That said, even up to the First World War it is questionable if the Russian empire can be referred to as a nation-state, which Anthony Smith (2003, 32) defines as a state which draws its legitimacy from principles of nationalism, and whose members possess a certain degree of national unity and integration but not necessarily cultural homogeneity.

7.1   *Russkii* vs. *Rossiskii*: Russian national identities

When Russian nationalists, fascists, and neonazis go around chanting *Rossia dlia Russkikh* (*Russia for Russians* – cf. Picture 18) the commonly used English translation for *russkii* (*Russian*) is ambiguous: the English word *Russian* denotes both *russkii* (ethnic Russian) as well as *rossiskii* (citizen of the Russian Federation). Severnye Vrata's vocalist Sasha Nevskii touched on this difference when describing his bands musical style:

> Sasha: "Our specialty is pagan music and in it we use folklore melodies. In some songs on some albums to a large extent, in some to a lesser extent."
> David-Emil: "And that is Russian [*rossiiskii*] folklore?"
> Sasha: "Yes, but not rossiiskii." [laughs] "Russia [*Rossiia*] and Russians [*Russkie*] – those are different things."
> David-Emil: "What is the difference?"
> Sasha: "Rossiia – that's a state in which a lot of different people [ethnicities] live, but Russkie are in principle, they are in general Rusy – that is the name which we did not give ourselves. That is we had Slavs: Drevliane, Poliane, Krivichi. Velikorossy, Malorossy, Belorossy. And the Byzantine called everybody Rusy."
> (Vladimirov 2005 – Russian: p. 321)

Sasha's quote quite aptly describes one of the cores of Russian nationalism today which in general can be seen as a continuum between two poles:

One pole of Russian national identity is based on a shared ethnic and cultural background of the *Velikorossy*, *Malorossy*, and *Belorossy* (roughly equivalent to ethnic Russians, ethnic Ukrainians, and ethnic Belarusians) – which Sasha included as Rusy. These three ethnic groups are commonly referred to as East Slavs and their languages are grouped within East Slavic languages. This identity traces its roots back to the "origin" of present-day Russia, the *Kievan Rus'* and *Muscovite Russia*. The Kievan Rus' is believed to have come into existence in the late 9th and early 10th century along a trade and plundering route linking the Baltic sea with the Black sea where the Varangians (of Nordic descent) ruled over people living in the area and quite rapidly assimilated (the people living there are eventually referred to as East Slavs and the rulers as the Riurik dynasty). In 988 Prince Vladimir embraced Byzantine Christianity, thus introducing and establishing the religion within the region (Kappeler 2005). This early link between religion and the Kievan Rus' has become an important component of this *ethno-cultural approach* (and explains in part the mighty revitalization of the Russian-Orthodox religion after the fall of the Soviet Union). It is also reflected in Kappeler's (2005, 9f) question if the defining criteria for (a Russian) ethnicity should be the language or if maybe the orthodox religion, which would also include Ukraine and Belarus, would be a better approach.

Picture 18: Graffiti *Rossia dlia Russkikh* (Russia for Russians). Note the use of SS-Runes for both *Rossia* and *Russkikh* and the celtic cross which has been adopted by the white power movement in the "o" of *Rossia*. Picture taken in Taganrog in 2004.

The Kievan Rus' developed into a loose conglomeration of principalities with Kiev as its original center and at times main force. Following the Mongolian invasion (1237–1240), the principality of Moscow slowly emerged as the new power center (hence *Muscovite Russia*). The beginning of Russia as a *poly-ethnic empire* – the other pole – is often dated to 1552 and Tsar Ivan IV's (also known as Ivan the Terrible) conquering of the Khanate of Kazan.[177] This approach analyzes Russia as an empire arguing that the Russian Empire, the Soviet Union, and the Russian Federation were and still are poly-ethnic entities with Moscow/the Russian Soviet Federative Socialist Republic as the dominant power. This approach both underlines a cultural unity in a shared language of the empire (Russian) and a common supra-cultural heritage (e.g. literature and music).[178]

---

177. While agreeing that there are good reasons for dating the emergence of a poly-ethnic empire with the conquering of Kazan, Kappeler (1992, 19ff) argues that this covers up the fact that the subjects of the Kievan Rus' were also poly-ethnic.
178. The Russian empire maintained this poly-ethnic approach long into the 18th century, the top priority being to maintain social and political stability in the empire. Attempts of a stronger social-cultural integration emerged from 1830 onwards under Tsar Nikolai I and picked up speed from 1863 with the rule of Tsar Aleksandr II. These efforts were, however, both in time and scope not equally enacted among the different subjects. The goal was not to assimilate all the subordinates and while influenced by nationalism not to create a unit-

Fast forwarding to today, these two poles also explain the Russian Federation's current attempt to guard its sphere of influence in the *Blizhnee zarubezh'e* (Near Abroad – a term used in Russia for the former Soviet republics), which makes a post-colonial perspective productive. Both from the perspective of a a supra-national poly-ethnic state (e.g. preserving Russia's influence among the sovereign Georgia and break-away regions like the Chechen Republic, South Ossetia, Transnistria, and Abkhazia) as well as an ethno-cultural preservation (the East Slavs which includes the sovereign countries Ukraine and Belarus), Russia can be seen as a form of empire not only trying to maintain its influence in the former colonies but also highlights the dependence between the colonizer and colonized.

7.2 *Nashe Radio*: Made in Russia?

> "The most complete collection of Rock 'n' Roll and all that is fashionable in our music today. Our music! Our radio! Made in Russia!"
> (Jingle on *Nashe Radio* St. Petersburg during 2005 and 2006 – Russian: p. 332)

The previously mentioned radio station *Nashe Radio* (cf. p. 135) provides a good example of how the issues of national identity interact in every day life.[179] Their jingles often end with *Nashe Radio, sdelanno v Rossii* (Nashe Radio, made in Russia) implying a national limitation to the music (in other words, music from Russia). While they contribute to a canonization of *russkii rok*, their geographical focus is not limited to the current borders of the Russian Federation: they also air bands from the "near abroad": Ukraine (VV, Okean El'zi), Moldova (Zdob si Zdub) and Belarus (Liapis Trubetskoi). When I asked about that, Elena Danilova (2006), the St. Petersburg station director, replied that in the Soviet Union it used

---

ed nation-state (Kappeler 1992).
179. Starting broadcasting in December 1998, *Nashe Radio* was the first project of the *LogoVAZ News Corporation* founded by Boris Berezovsky and Rupert Murdoch with Mikhail Kozyrev as the general producer (until February 2005). Besides *Nashe Radio*, the *LogoVAZ News Corporation* also included the station *Radio Ul'tra* (started broadcasting November 2000), and the record company *Real Records* (founded in 1999) (Yarotsky 2002). Their roster contains groups from Russia, Ukraine, and Belarus covering both rock and pop (Real Records n.d.). Most of their rock musicians are also heavily featured on *Nashe Radio*. Today *Nashe Radio* is part of the holding *News Media Radio Group* which also includes the radio stations *Best FM* and *Ul'tra* (both limited to Moscow).

to all be the same, in other words, her thinking was in terms of a multi-ethnic entity. At the same time the thinking reflects an ethno-cultural approach, since the countries in question are primarily Ukraine and Belarus – the East Slavs.

Nashe Radio's all inclusive approach to music made in Russia is also shared by the Russian record label *Misteriia Zvuka*[180] as well as in books on "Russian" popular music (e.g. Chernin 2006) and how record stores in St. Petersburg categorize Belorussian and Ukrainian groups.

This form of inclusive nationalism is thus not limited to *Nashe Radio*. What, however, makes the station so interesting is that they are more or less the only Russian-wide radio station focused on Russian-language rock music – broadcast by satellite to a network of local *Nashe Radio* franchise stations throughout Russia. Furthermore, the Moscow station's programming can be heard internationally over a live stream (Nashe.ru n.d.).

Besides its national reach, another important aspect of *Nashe Radio* is its target group – in Elena Danilova's words both the "young" (born after 1987) who "fell in love with the music not long ago", and those who "grew up with the music" (born between 1967 and 1981) (Danilova 2006). This was backed by statistics received from Danilova for St. Petersburg as well as *TNS Gallup AdFact's Radio Index* (Taylor Nelson Sofres n.d.).[181]

Its national reach as well as its target group also made the station an important reference point for the bands I was involved in (not necessarily a positive one as the discussion in chapter 3 regarding *pop-rock* shows). Many of my acquaintances

---

180. On their web-page they lump Ukrainian bands they promote (VV, Okean El'zi) in the category *russkii rok*: "'Russkii rok' also includes such album projects of the company 'Misteriia Pablishing' like 'Vopli Vidopliasova', 'Okean El'zi', Chizh, Zapreshchionnye barabanshchiki, Va-Bank", Ariia, Sergei Shnurov." (Misteriia Zvuka n.d. – Russian: p. 333)
181. While the Radio Index for the whole population is public, the detailed ratings by focus groups are not. Danilova was so friendly to provide me with detailed statistics for the period May-July 2006: In St. Petersburg *Nashe Radio* had a daily reach of 5,2% (place 16 out of 30) for the period May-July 2006 and 5.7% (14 out of 29) for the period September-November 2007. Its Average Quarter-Hour (AQH) share was for that period 2006 3,4% (place 16 out of 30) and 2007 3,29 (place 14 out of 29) for the total population of St. Petersburg, however 6,89% (4th place out of 22 stations polled) for the target group 18-45 and an income for one in 2006. According to other statistics provided by Danilova the station's main listening group are young people between 25 and 39 (34%) followed by 12-19 (27%), 40+ (21%) and 20-24 (18%). The gender is biased towards a male audience (61% vs. 39% female listeners).

listened to the station (and Sasha even incorporated some of the jingles in announcements during our concerts).

Thus due to its (inter)national reach and a target group including the last Soviet generation, the station plays an important role shaping not only a "Russian" rock discourse (rock here used in a broad sense) but also creating a feeling of community by defining the music as *nash* (ours), creating an imagined imperial Russian rock community including the now sovereign descendants of the Kievan Rus'.

7.3 Popular music and the ruling elite

This link between popular music and nationalism is not limited to *Nashe Radio*'s music policy, it is also established by musicians: Boris Grebenshchikov (Akvarium) and Konstantin Kinchev (Alisa), two musicians within the *russkii rok*-tradition often featured on *Nashe Radio*, provide good examples of this connection. They, however, create different alliances: while there is a link between representatives of the government and Grebenshchikov, Kinchev's connection is more to representatives of the Russian-Orthodox church.[182]

7.3.1 Boris Grebenshchikov and the government

Both Russian-Orthodox baptised and a practicing Buddhist,[183] Grebenshchikov tries to maintain an apolitical image, however he subtly supported Putin's policies in a 2007 interview. To the newspaper *Izvestiia* (News) he said: "[N]ow I see how, towards the end of his eight-year period, Russia has begun to improve little by little" (*I vot seichas ia vizhu, kak k kontsu ego vos'miletnego sroka Rossiia nachinaet chut'-chut' vypravliat'sia* – Grebenshchikov, qtd. in Loriia 2007). He defines "his" a

---

182. This and the following section on nostalgia are a reworked excerpt from Wickström and Steinholt (2009).
183. He is parodied for his flirtation with different religions in a video by the St. Petersburg artist collective *KOLKhUi* of which NOM's Andrei Kagadeev is a member (Akvarium and NOM 2008). Using the song *Bespechnyi russkii brodiaga* (Carefree Russian Tramp) from the eponymous album (Akvarium 2006) the parody depicts a Grebenshchikov look-a-like walking through the city playing the guitar and drinking with two Buddhists, a Muslim, a Jewish klezmer fiddler, a Russian-Orthodox priest, a Catholic monk, and a FSB-agent (where he subscribes a cooperation commitment – a hint to his meetings with Surkov discussed below and to rumors that he collaborated with the KGB in the Soviet Union).

little later in the interview as "the line chosen by our government" (*liniiu, kotoruiu nashe pravitel'stvo vedet*). Here, the word "government" clearly alludes to Putin and Putin's tenure.

Grebenshchikov has also been in official contact with the government: In 2003 Putin signed a decree awarding Grebenshchikov the order *Za zaslugi pered Otechestvom – IV stepeni* (Of Service To The Fatherland – 4th Class) for his contribution to music, which was presented by St. Petersburg's governor Valentina Matvienko. In 2005 he, together with other musicians (Sergei Shnurov, Vyacheslav Butusov, Zemfira Ragazanova, the group Bi-2 as well as the managers of Chaif and Splin), secretly met with the then deputy head of the presidential administration and one of Putin's main ideologues, Vladislav Surkov. On the official agenda was the absence of rock music on Russian television, copyright piracy in Russia, and an initiative to launch a national organization to promote Russian rock music. Sergei Chernov, however, interprets the meeting as a precaution against a Russian color revolution, similar to the one in Ukraine 2004, which was supported by local musicians.[184]

In the wake of the meeting, on May 22nd, 2005, Grebenshchikov began hosting *Aerostat*, a weekly music program on the state-owned *Radio Rossii* (Radio Russia – Radio Rossii 2007), while Ramazanova performed at Lake Selinger at the 2005 summer camp of *Nashi* (Ours), the ruling-party *Edinaia Rossiia's* (United Russia) youth organization. The following year's event featured Butusov (Nautilus Pompilius/Iu-Piter), Uma2rman, Bi-2, Korol' i Shut, Multfilmy, and Kukryniksy (Chernov 2006c).

There is no proof that these events have any connection with the Surkov-meeting. They, however, still represent an interesting coincidence within a broader tendency of an officialisation of *russkii rok*. While it can be argued that *Nashi* is a youth organization and its use of rock is in line with the musical taste of its members, rock (and popular music in general) is also frequently directly instrumentalized by the government to mark various celebrations and to enhance its appeal with the younger electorate.[185] *Ia vybiraiu Rossiiu – Rossiia – vpered!* (I vote for

---

184. Cf. Bratersky (2006), Chernov (2005b, 2006b, 2006c, 2007), Kormil'tsev (2006b) and Staff Writer (2005a) for more information.
185. Both the musicologist Ruth Dockwray (2005) in her work on rock anthems, as well as Philip Tagg (2007) in his analysis of the musical celebration of the Queen's 2002 golden jubilee have pointed to a similar appropriation of popular music for official representations

Russia – Russia – ahead!), the 2008 celebration of the presidental elections on Moscow's Red Square March 2nd (the election day), is but one example of this development. Among the bands performing were Splin, Chaif, Nochnye Snaipery, and Bi-2 – groups that also regularly receive airplay on *Nashe Radio*. The highlight of the event was when Vladimir Putin as well as the at-that-point-assumed newly elected Dmitrii Medvedev interrupted the group Liube's performance at the celebration to thank the voters for their confidence in them.[186]

This demonstrates both how the official attitude towards rock music, with the elite deeming the music suitable for official representation, as well as how the rock musicians' (especially those who emerged in the 1980s) attitude towards the elite has changed. This re-conforming and canonization of *russkii rok* also reinforces the ambivalence towards the genre amongst the (younger) musicians and music scene as discussed in chapter 3. Even some voices from within its own ranks are turning to dissent, violently ridiculing the collaboration of the *russkii rok*-giants, thereby facing a very real risk of losing airplay and invitations to perform. The group Televizor with its vocalist Mikhail Borzykin is probably the most prominent example of a former LRK-group openly criticizing the current government musically, in interviews, as well as participating in the *Dissenters March* and being harassed because of its actions.

While the above section has described some of the links between artists aired on *Nashe Radio* and the government, there are also links between some of the musicians and the church.

---

in the UK.
186. Putin at the same time issued a stern declaration to Western observers that the election was democratic and fair. The video can be seen at the Russian president's website (Putin and Medvedev 2008).

7.3.2 *Rock 'n' Roll Cross*: Kinchev and the Church

> Denis: "From the last albums many don't understand those lyrics, because Konstantin Evgen'evich [Kinchev] hit himself with religion and he writes lyrics on the basis of that Russian orthodoxy. He might be totally into it all, but for the fans..."
> Anton: "...some songs are incomprehensible."
> Denis: "For the young, they understand him from his old songs, albums, which were released earlier, when the lyrics were written about, their idea was that everything is forbidden, but we still play and sing."
> Anton: "And now: Russian orthodoxy, religion."
> (Vashkevich and Lukanin 2006 – Russian: p. 319)

A heavily promoted song on *Nashe Radio* during 2005-2006 was Alisa's *Rock-n-Roll Krest* (Rock 'n' Roll Cross) from the 2005 album *Izgoi* (Social outcast – Alisa 2005). The lyrics (here the final verse and chorus) describe how the protagonist finds religious salvation after years of a life full of vice:

> When sunset covers shadow
> And stars lure the day with dreams
> I will stand closer to the fire under the face of Heavenly Power
> And we shall live, and begin to sing
> In salty sweat, destroying death
> Behold – Again, the Rock 'n' Roll cross is flaming at the center of the light.
>
> Where the blue distances spilled over their edges,
> I beheld how the glow flowed over grass and dew,
> And my wagon moved on from my nesting place into the night,
> Since then along the roads the Rock 'n' Roll cross has been flaming.
> (translated by Yngvar Steinholt – Russian: p. 297)

The quoted passage is distinguished musically from the rest of the song (in a guitar driven hard rock idiom) by the inclusion of a (mainly) female, angelic-sounding choir singing on vowels. The video clip (Alisa 2007a) subtly draws on religious symbols: Kinchev makes the devil's horn sign during the first chorus, before forming his hand in an allusion to the sign of the cross in the manner of the *starovery* (old believers). In the following interlude he strikes the pose of crucifixion – a frequent Kinchev-pose at live concerts. The medieval motifs in Kinchev's lyrics and his frequent use of archaisms usually contain references to Russian history and tradition, and to the orthodox faith, which have replaced his earlier fascination for a pre-Christian Rus' (Yngvar Steinholt, pers. comm.).

Kinchev's is a telling example of the revival of the Russian-Orthodox faith since the 1988 church millennium. According to the Russian music journalist Denis Stupnikov, Alisa's 2003 album *Seichas pozdnee, chem ty dumaesh'* (It's later now than you think – Alisa 2003) became Alisa's "first album, fully and wholly consistent with the spirit of canonical Russian-Orthodoxy" *(stavshii pervym al'bomom, tselikom i polnost'iu vyderzhannym v dukhe kanonicheskogo Pravoslaviia.* – Stupnikov 2006).[187] Kinchev's religious zeal is not lost on his fans as Anton and Denis' comments above show. It also is expressed in fan memorabilia, which includes banners reading *Alisa – My Pravolsavnye* (We are Orthodox)[188] and the Russian-Orthodox cross.

On April 6th, 2006, Kinchev, Iurii Shevchuk (DDT) and other rock musicians met with then Metropolitan (now Patriarch) Kirill, chairman of the Department for External Church Relations, and other members of the Moscow Patriarchate. The Patriarchate's website states that Kinchev and Shevchuk, who were both baptised in the Russian-Orthodox faith,[189] explained how their work differs from other popular music artists and how their lyrics are suitable to provoke thought in the listeners (here the *russkii rok*-legacy shines through by focusing on the lyrical message). Other issues discussed during the meeting included the possibility of orthodox sermons at rock concerts and rock music's potential for missionary work.[190]

In his songs and utterances Kinchev blends this Russian-Orthodox spirit with a heavy dose of Russian patriotism – like his vision of Russia's united political and religious power expressed in a 2007 interview:

"In general I see future Russia in a symphony of power: In all decisions the secular power is supposed to receive the clergy's blessing, the president has to walk hand in hand with the patriarch, then also the power will be strengthened. In general, Putin currently holds a good position."

(Kinchev, qtd. in Shugailo 2007 – Russian: p. 325)

---

187. *Nashe Radio's* former director, Mikhail Kozyrev, notes a shift in Kinchev's lyrics coinciding with the work on that album – the lyrics reminding Kozyrev of patriotic Soviet poetry *(agitbrigada)* (Kozyrev and Barabanov 2007a, 28f).
188. *Pravoslavnye* is also a song on Alisa's album *Solntsevorot* (Solstice – Alisa 2000).
189. Or in the words of Andrei Kagadeev: "And in their ranks, you'll also find those who drank themselves to Russian-Orthodox Christianity." (Kopeikin et al. 2001) Both Kinchev and Shevchuck have a history of alcohol and (in Kinchev's case) drug abuse.
190. According to Stupnikov they also touched on the pop-rock discourse: Kinchev declared *Fabrika Zvezd* (cf. p. 127) real Satanism and Shevchuk encouraged the Metropolitan to ask Putin for more rock on TV.

Nebo Slavian (The Heaven of the Slavs – Alisa 2003) is a good example of Kinchev's patriotic vein: The song starts with a heavily distorted guitar rhythm accompanied by a straight 4/4 beat on the drum. Above that the keyboard plays a simple melody in e-minor sounding like a very synthetic double reed instrument.[191] The video (Alisa 2008) shifts between the band playing in both a studio and a forest clearing and is intermixed with a pastiche of movie clips starting with Sergei Eisenstein's *Aleksandr Nevskii*, footage from a movie about the Napoleonic war, the Second World War, and finally from a contemporary battleship of the Russian Navy[192] – the unifying visual theme being how Russia and its predecessors successfully suppressed foreign invasions. This is aptly demonstrated in the clip's opening quote *If somebody invades us with a sword, from the sword he will also perish. On that stands and will stand the Russian soil!* (Russian: p. 298, in this instance taken from the movie *Aleksandr Nevskii*) and the refrain which at the end of the song is heard to the sound of marching soldiers seen piling up confiscated flags from Nazi-Germany:

> We are whetted by the seeds of the horde
> We are subdued by the basurman yoke
> But in our veins boils
> The heaven of the Slavs
> And from the Peipus shore
> To the ice of Kolyma
> All this is our soil!
> All this is us!
>
> (translated by Yngvar Steinholt – Russian: p. 298)

Here there are references to oppression by the Mongols ([Golden] Horde, Basurman yoke) whom the Slavs ultimately succeeded in beating. The term Slavs implies not only Russia, but also Ukraine and Belarus. This is mirrored in Kinchev's statement expressing the idea of returning to the *Kievan Rus'* made during a press conference in Kiev 2008: "I am for a great, Holy Rus with Kiev as its capital. The capital has to be here, and the country has to be called 'Rus'" (Kinchev, qtd. in Riabov and Lubenskii 2008 – Russian: p. 325). This provocative statement should additionally be seen in the light of Kinchev's contempt of the

---

191. This might be an attempt at trying to imitate a shawm since Kinchev's songs tend to orientate themselves towards medieval times.
192. One of the CDs sponsors is the Press Service of the Russian Navy.

7 POPULAR MUSIC AND IDEAS OF THE RUSSIAN NATION   219

Orange Revolution and Iushchenko-government which is also reflected in his creative work such as the 2008-song *Vlast'* (Power – Alisa 2008).

In other words, Kinchev's creative work at least during the last decade fuses a strong patriotism (if not nationalism) based on the medieval conception of the *Rus'* with a religious dimension – in other words, drawing on an ethnic (and Slavophile inspired) conception of a Russian national identity.

7.4 Nationalism and nostalgia

While it is easy to describe many current developments in Russia as examples of new forms of chauvinist nationalism based on Russia's post-colonial situation – as Kinchev's statements clearly show – I think that the issues are more complex and nurtured by multiple factors besides a recurring national pride. Such issues include the need for a continuous experience of common history, the dominating role of Russia within the Soviet Union, a reaction to the chaotic post-Soviet realities of the 1990s, and the new economic achievements – all factors which have contributed to a new wave of *nostalgia*. I emphasize "nostalgia" apart from nationalism, especially apart from its chauvinist forms. At the same time it is also a part of nationalism in the form of a search for a golden past which can provide the path to the future. The main idea here is to give more nuances to the debate.

With the following two cases I want to broaden the perspective in terms of popular music by including a singer considered *popsa* (Oleg Gazmanov) and a group playing heavy metal (Piligrim). Gazmanov presents a poly-ethnic approach including states of the former Soviet Union while Piligrim's approach remains within the boundaries of today's Russian Federation – on a lyrical level poly-ethnic, however visually strongly emphasizing a mono-ethnic Russian-Orthodox heritage (similar to Alisa's).

7.4.1 Gazmanov's *Sdelan v SSSR*

One highly popular song which can easily be read (if not misread) as blunt Great-Russian nationalism is Oleg Gazmanov's *Sdelan v SSSR* from 2005 (Gazmanov 2005). It begins with the following words (Russian: p. 299):

Ukraine and the Crimea, Belarus and Moldova
That is my country
Sakhalin and Kamchatka, the Ural mountains

That is my country
The Krasnoiarsk Territory, Siberia, and the Volga Region,
Kazakhstan and the Caucasus, and the Baltic States as well.

Obviously, the country that spans from Ukraine and the Baltic states to Kamchatka and Sakhalin disintegrated in 1991, and many of the area's inhabitants will violently oppose being called citizens of Gazmanov's country. The following discussion will take a closer look at the accompanying music video which can be found on Gazmanov's homepage (Gazmanov n.d.):

The lyrics, accompanied by a singalong melody, a medium tempo and a rhythmic structure with clear accents, describe the protagonist's pride in his home country. The lyrics are organised around the listing of names. First come geographical names, then famous people, organisations, institutions, industry products, and events (e.g. Lenin, Stalin, Gagarin, Pushkin, torpedoes, KGB). These chains each contribute to defining the endeared nation, as summarised in each final verse line: *That/This is my country*. The refrain proceeds to make the already obvious explicit: *I was born in the Soviet Union, I was made in the USSR*.

The guitar introduction melodically alludes to a (national) anthem and is backed by keyboard, bass, and a drum groove, which accents the cymbals and high-hat – in a manner alluding to official pomp. The first part of the song evokes the feeling of a live stadium concert, the middle part moves towards a rap recitative, and the refrain has vocal overlays of a mass audience singing along with Gazmanov. This stadium feeling is enhanced by adding reverb to signify a vast space, by keeping the accompaniment slightly uncoordinated to imitate a live performance, and a cheering crowd joining in the refrain and the verse response lines. The participation is encouraged by the rhythm section's beat, where the snare clearly accents the two and four for clapping hands, and structurally both after the introduction and the first refrain, where only the drum's basic groove is played.[193] Simultaneously, in the video the band encouragingly clap their hands.

While the musical features stress the participatory aspect of the song – creating a communal experience – the images stress the central message of the lyrics – being a proud Soviet-Russian citizen. This is reflected in the band's outfits, which include printed shirts and scarves advertising *Rossiia* and *SSSR*, Soviet army sym-

---

193. The basic drum groove during the verse is a two bar riff, with the bass drum hitting the 1, 2+, and 3 in the first and the 1, 2+, and 3+ in the second bar, the snare accents 2 and 4, while the high hat stresses all the beats.

bols, hammer and sickle, as well as the Russian Federation's coat of arms – the double-headed eagle. The theme colors are the national red, white, and blue and audience members are shown waving Russian flags. Gazmanov's outfit also embodies a post-Soviet reality and, arguably, a pre-Revolutionary Russia. He wears a barely noticeable Russian-Orthodox cross next to a dog tag, thus uniting the Pre-Soviet, Soviet, and post-Soviet in one continuous entity.

Body movements support the lyrics: *It is my country*, which is repeated in all the verses, is accompanied by a hand movement or clapping. In the first chorus, during Gazmanov's repetition of the line *I was made in the USSR*, the keyboard-player points to the letters *SSSR* on his shirt in sync with the lyrics. Finally, the highly energetic performance of the song is reflected in the video's accelerating clip-rate, showing the enthusing audience being brought to a boil.

Nostalgia for the Soviet era appears to be strongest in the Russian Federation and ethnic Russians within the post-Soviet space. Seen in the light of the historical Russian hegemony of the USSR, and of recent, more vulgar forms of great-Russian national chauvinism, the song's merging of the USSR and the Russian Federation may easily be taken as an example of the latter. Still, positive national pride and patriotism, a celebration of common history and achievements, and love for the motherland is not necessarily incompatible with a longing for peaceful poly-ethnic unity. The desire for a peaceful community is expressed in the recitative's two final lines, where Gazmanov questions how the other former Soviet republics can get along without Russia:

The borders are choking us, can't go without a visa,
How do you get along without us, please let us know, friends!

which is followed by a bar of musical silence while the crowd keeps cheering and the echo of the phrase fades out.

This jibe at the visa regimes between former Soviet republics points back to a perceived golden era of harmonic Soviet co-existence under Russian supervision, where cultural contacts were close and popular singers of various republics made up the Soviet *estrada*. The previous discussion on how Ukraine is viewed in Russia is a good example of the frustration Gazmanov alludes to since Ukraine – especially the eastern part – has historically been close to Russia (hence also Kinchev's idea of *re*-forming the Holy Rus with Kiev as its capital). The timing of the song's release in 2005 is also important since it follows the color revolutions in Georgia and Ukraine as well as the implementation of a visa regime to the Baltic States and Georgia – in other words, an intensification of the post-Soviet (post-colonial) division between Russia and some former Soviet republics.

These events also reflect that on the other side of the borders former Soviet republics, especially the Baltic States, Ukraine, and Georgia, do not necessarily subscribe to such a rosy view of what they perceive as the colonial past. Seeing a possibility to distance themselves from Russian and Soviet hegemony, many are de-russifying national history and limiting the role of Russian as an official language. This in turn has angered the Russian government, thus intensifying the rift.

7.4.2 Piligrim's *Slava Rossii*

Like Alisa, Piligrim's *Slava Rossii* (Piligrim 2007) plays on present day Russia and its Russian-Orthodox heritage. The lyrics hail Russia and its might, peaking in the refrain (Russian: p. 302):

> Hail Russia! The great power!
> Hail Russia, hail the people

The verses, however, stress an inclusive poly-ethnic, if categorical nationalism:

> And Tatars and Russians and Buriats and Jews,
> And Chechens and Chukcha and Bashkirs and Karels.
> All the people of Russia will be forever united.

Still, as in Gazmanov's song, an implied ethnic Russian hegemony serves as the glue of the Federation. Piligrim's song also starts from a geographical definition of Russia's territory (*From the Baltic Sea to the Kurile chain*) and features the Federation's coat of arms (*Our double headed eagle, open your wings*). The reference to religion is, however, more subtle: *The sun gilds the churches' domes*.

The accompanying video clip for *Slava Rossii* (Gruppa Piligrim n.d.) interplects two plot lines: it opens to a burning religious icon, a pillaged village, a desolate battlefield with scavenging crows, and a young girl dressed in white hiding in the woods. It then shifts to a sci-fi portal which opens to a stage where Piligrim's musicians perform. This is musically accompanied by the sound of fire, crows, and a synthesizer playing a choral-like melody. The drums offer an anacrusis with the bass, electric guitar, and synthesizer setting in on the downbeat to images of arriving mounted knights. The medieval plot continues with the approaching knights rebuilding the village, images which are displayed on stage in the cross-clipped live concert scenes. Again, audience participation is highlighted with images of fans cheering and joining the singer in the chorus.

Thus the clip combines heavy metal (leather, phallic electric guitars, metal, chrome) and medieval imagery (knights, icons, wooden huts, and churches) with concert footage, that is in contrast to the previous images in the clip by featuring a young stylish audience and a futuristic stage set.

While Gazmanov's stressing of his heritage downplays religion, Piligrim's clip appears to openly promote the Russian-Orthodox heritage of Russia, thus suggesting a pseudo-missionary agenda not found in the lyrics. This ranges from the opening image of the burning icon of the Holy Mary and the infant Jesus (which alludes to the Mongol invasion, the civil war, and Soviet anti-religious campaigns), the iconic image of Christ's face on the knight's banner, a strong, axe-swinging carpenter with a clearly visible cross around his neck, and his creation – a resurrected wooden church. There appears to be little room for Gazmanov's secular nostalgia for the Soviet Union in Piligrim's images of a post-heretic national-religious resurrection.

Piligrim's vocalist Andrei Kovalev, who happens to be a member of the Moscow city parliament for *Edinaia Rossia*, has also been involved in organizing festivals glorifying Russia, e.g. *Slava Rossii, Slava Moskve* (Hail Russia, Hail Moscow), which in 2006 he co-sponsored with the ruling party. The festival ended with all the participants performing *Slava Rossii* together.[194]

While Gazmanov is quite popular in Russia, I should add that most people I talked to (as well as comments on *youtube* and *rutube*) did not have a high opinion of Piligrim mainly based on its musical qualities (especially the vocalist's). Sergei Chernov summarizes those remarks quite aptly when writing about a free concert in St. Petersburg: "It makes sense because Piligrim's music is so horrible that it is very unlikely that anybody would pay to listen to it." (Chernov 2008a) I decided to include the clip since it has attracted attention – even being under heavy rotation on the music channels when it came out (Andrei Ivanov, pers. comm., 29.12.2007) – and people were aware of the band when I asked. Furthermore, it provides a good example of conflicting views of Russia's national identities.

---

194. The clip can be found on their website (Gruppa Piligrim n.d.).

7.4.3 Nostalgia

It appears that two types of nostalgic nationalism are represented in the cases: one with and one without the Soviet past. The former, represented by Gazmanov's song, is fully compatible with the government-induced positive patriotism and Putin's reclaiming of an indiscriminate historical pride, while making sure to include references to Russian-Orthodox Christianity and to portray himself as a Russian-Orthodox beliver. The latter (Piligrim) revels in the segments of the Orthodox Church, whose patriotism for obvious historical reasons is virtually incompatible with the Soviet,[195] hence Piligrim's omission of explicit Soviet references and their focus on medieval Russia (this to some extent also applies to Alisa).

The previous discussion of Alisa, Gazmanov, and Piligrim can be framed as different aspects of nationalism rooted in a common heritage (with or without the Soviet dimension), however, the picture could be more nuanced. While there is little point in denying that questions of nationalism play an obvious role here, it would also be fruitful to study these songs within the framework of nostalgia.

In her discussion of nostalgia and post-communist Russia, the Slavic Studies scholar Svetlana Boym (2001, 57ff) outlines a shift between the perestroika years and the early 2000s, marked by the beginning of Putin's presidency and the Kursk accident in 2000. She argues that perestroika brought with it a focus on historical memory, combined with a de-ideologisation of the Soviet myth. This was linked to a *reflective nostalgia* which called the absolute truth propagated by the Soviet elite into question and focused on the process of longing in itself, rather than what Boym labels the "homecoming", "the return to a home that no longer exists or has never existed" (Boym 2001, xiii).

This nostalgia gradually shifts during the 1990s to what Boym terms *restorative nostalgia*, which stresses the homecoming, the transhistorical construction of a lost home. It focuses on truth and tradition – creating a national memory based on a single plot of national identity – and protects the absolute truth (Boym 2001,

---

195. The Russian-Orthodox Church is still torn between its history as having been violently persecuted and as having been infiltrated by the security-apparatus during the Soviet era. Simultaneously, post-war KGB infiltration still binds influential parts of the Church to the present security apparatus of the FSB, while other forces within it still oppose these connections. The latter are far more prone to remember the militant atheism and heretic campaigns of the 20th century and would be virtually immune to officially approved nostalgia for the Soviet past (Yngvar Steinholt, pers. comm., 15.01.2009).

xviii). The Putin-tenure has strongly focused on restorative nostalgia, e.g. by characterizing the Soviet Union's collapse as the biggest geopolitical disaster of the 20th century (Putin 2005); by the visions of a unique brand of democracy based on Russian values (here the influence of the Slavophiles can be seen); by the showing of military muscle (the restoration of strategic bomber patrols, the war with Georgia); by re-vitalising Russian foreign policy, and by restoring Russia's image as one among several world superpowers. This *restorative nostalgia* combines a distinct Russian flavor with a global language of communication and distribution:

"Commercial mass-produced nostalgia put new technology and distribution to retro use. Russian nostalgia was made not only for domestic but also for tourist consumption, and thus has to be easily digestible and convertible."

(Boym 2001, 67)

What makes the Russian restorative nostalgia of a glocal type so compelling is its pastiche of Pre-revolutionary and Soviet images represented by the previous examples. The music-video montages blend elements of common history with the local, yet draw on different aspects of a shared cultural memory of contemporary Russia, including aspired official national identity. Gazmanov reflects the desire of a common heritage based on a shared imperial past, mainly the Soviet past, but pre-revolutionary national figures are included and serve to underline Russia's leading role. Alisa and Piligrim draw on a glorified Russian (medieval) past and the Russian-Orthodox heritage, while remaining ambivalent towards, or avoiding altogether, the Soviet era – similar to the Slavophile's search for the pre-Petrine roots of Russia. The desire for a lost home is also reflected in the growing number of people actively calling themselves Russian-Orthodox and participating in religious activities.[196]

7.5 Concluding remarks

Even though I use the term *construction*, the previous discussion has also demonstrated how resilient specific identities can be – they cannot be changed from one moment to another. Both Sasha's Ukrainian accent when speaking Russian as well as Kinchev's transition to a Russian-orthodox inspired rock music are here cases in point. While the former retains his mark of otherness even after living in Russia

---

196. In some sense Alisa, Piligrim, and Oleg Gazmanov also embody a continuity from the Soviet time, Kinchev and Gazmanov both started their careers in the mid 1980s and the history of Piligrim, re-founded in 2004, goes back to the 1970s.

for more than 10 years, the latter's transition from an enfant terrible within the LRK to a devote believer has almost spanned two decades (and for which Kinchev by some is still ridiculed).

In addition, band images tend to be a theoretical (or ideal) construction promoted by the band, but which exist in relationship to a number of competing identities ascribed by the fans. These together contribute to the overall image of the band as perceived by the listeners and others and can be colored by other factors like performance, reviews, as well as by other listeners' comments. This is, as shown, because identities are not only dependent on a person's habits, but also shaped in communication with others and, more broadly, by society and its prevalent discourses.

While music does not have an inherent meaning and thus cannot refer to a specific place on a *denotative* level it can, on a *connotative* level, both reinforce a message anchored in the performance (lyrics, images) or prevalent discourses as well as refer to a specific place. This referentiality can both be instrumentalized by the state for its purposes as well as by musicians incorporating national ideologies in their creative work as in the case with Alisa, Piligrim, and Gazmanov. These musicians, as well as Grebenshchikov, have been Soviet socialized and survived the post-Soviet turmoil professionally. Despite their differing ideologies they share a nostalgia for an earlier stable period and through their respective popularity their ideologies are also influential among their fans. While arguably a post-Soviet band generationwise, Svoboda taps into a similar nostalgia by both drawing on *russkii rok*-elements and, more importantly, on Russian cliches of Ukraine, which both appeals to its listeners, but also influences the listeners' perception of history and geography.

What makes this chapter's approach appealing to music from the post-Soviet space are the overlapping and competing discourses which stem from the Soviet legacy colliding with a post-Soviet Russia. Here Russia's heritage as an empire also shines through in the post-Soviet post-colonial reality, which is not limited to the examples discussed but is also reflected in other parts of popular music. One example is *estrada*, whose currently active musicians, for the most part, were born and started their careers in the Soviet Union. Amongst those performing in Russia today are not only Russian natives but also singers born in Belarus (Boris Moiseev), Ukraine (Sofia Rotaru, Verka Serdiuchka), Georgia (Valerii Meladze) and Bulgaria (Filipp Kirkorov) to mention a few.

The Russian *Eurovision Song Contest* entry in 2009 also reflects this legacy of a poly-ethnic Soviet Union colliding with current post-colonial geopolitical realities: the Ukrainian singer Anastasiia Prikhod'ko performed *Mamo* (Mom), a song written and produced by Konstantin Meladze (Valerii Meladze's brother), a Georgian born Ukrainian citizen living and working in Russia and with lyrics in both Ukrainian and Russian. The choice of this song sparked a huge (media) controversy. While some (including the Liberal Democratic Party) decried the choice as unsuitable (foreign national singing a song in a foreign language) others (including the tv-station broadcasting the contest) saw the song as a message of Soviet unity (Oliphant 2009). This shows how prevalent these discourses around (national) identities are within Russian popular music and society, as well as how the state, to some extent, wields its power. State controlled media provides space for performances of the previously mentioned musicians while at the same time excluding younger groups. While the *russkii rok* groups are not omnipresent, they have made inroads – especially in relation to the groups I encountered during my fieldwork.

Another post-Soviet reality is the mass emigration to countries like the United States, Israel, and Germany following the Soviet Union's collapse. These migrants retain ties back to their country of origin not only linguistically but also culturally – allowing for the transcultural flow of cultural products to countries outside the former Soviet Union. One example is the *Russendisko* in Berlin – the focus of the following chapters.

8 The *Russendisko*-scene

> "The Russendisko is a sound-system, in other words a DJ-collective with two people – those being me and Wladimir. [...] We play music which we like. [...] That is music from the former Republics of the Soviet Union. [The songs] are primarily sung in Russian, sometimes in Ukrainian or [...] Belarusian."
>
> (Gurzhy 2005 – German: p. 312)

Run by two post-Soviet emigrants, the musician Yuriy Gurzhy (from Khar'kov/Ukraine) and the author Wladimir Kaminer (from Moscow/Russia), the *Russendisko*[197] was born in 1999 after Olga Kaminer, Kaminer's wife, suggested that Yuriy and he should organize a party with Russian music for their friends.[198] Eventually the event was hosted at the then newly (re)opened *Tanzwirtschaft Kaffe Burger*,[199] a club in Berlin-Mitte (Kaffee Burger n.d.), and gained in popularity – especially after Kaminer's highly popular debut book *Russendisko* was published in 2000 (Kaminer 2000).[200]

The interior, kept in the style of an East German bar (including a stylized East German menu on the wall), is a reminder that the club is situated in former East-Berlin. Providing a post-Soviet and Russian flair, vodka is served and Soviet cartoons as well as movies are shown muted on TVs above the dance floor. For the die-hard fans there are also music compilations and fashion accessories (t-shirts and underwear). In 2004 the DJs founded the label *Russendisko Records* and in

---

197. *Russendisko* in its normal meaning refers to a disco for emigrants from the post-Soviet countries. Through the activities of Yuriy and Kaminer it has, however, become a synonym for their event and the music they play.
198. Parts of this and the following chapter has previously been published in Wickström (2007).
199. The venue has with minor interruptions and name changes been a pub/cafe since it was built in 1890.
200. The book was made into a movie in 2012 (directed by Oliver Ziegenbalg) and included a soundtrack with bands featured at the *Russendisko* – including Svoboda's *Marusia* (Various Artists 2012b).

December 2006 Kaminer co-opened his own club, *Club Rodina*.[201] The event was staged at both clubs until Kaminer left *Club Rodina* in May 2007.

At the *Russendisko* Yuriy and Kaminer play music linked to the former Soviet Union. This includes both groups from the countries of the Commonwealth of Independent States (CIS – predominantly Russia, Ukraine, and Belarus) as well as from a post-Soviet emigrant community touching mainly Germany and USA.

As in St. Petersburg the underlying social relations provide a space for social communication between the participants, the DJs, musicians whose music is played, and the organizers – and thus the scene. This network of actors is dynamic with shifting roles: e.g. Yuriy and Kaminer play double roles as DJs and organizers (Yuriy even plays a third role as a musician). In addition, the featured musicians as well as other actors within the scene also function as guest DJs.

The boundaries are not only blurry regarding the roles of the actors within the scene, but also delimiting one scene from other scenes. Yuriy is involved in the band Rot Front, which has some songs in Russian which have been included in the *Russendisko* compilations (Various Artists 2003b, 2004c, 2005c, 2008c, 2012b, 2013). The band also regularly performs at *Kaffee Burger*. While the band's two leading figures, Yuriy and Simon Wahorn, apparently met at the *Russendisko*, Wahorn is Hungarian and the band consists of both Germans and emigrant musicians from Hungary and the former Soviet Union. Linking Rot Front to emigrant music in Berlin (and thus touching another potential scene), Yuriy said that the group is a typical cross-over band from Berlin: "I would not necessarily call Rot Front a Russian band, because [...] it is a result of a unique Russian-Hungarian connection" (Gurzhy 2005 – German: p. 312). In other words, Rot Front is situated on the boundary to the *Russendisko* (and also other) scene(s). Other bands' relationships are even more complex and span several scenes.

Both *Kaffee Burger* and *Club Rodina* (while it existed) host other events and the *Russendisko* is not confined to these two social hubs. Unlike the St. Petersburg scene which is geographically delimitated the *Russendisko* is a translocal concept

---

201. *Rodina* is Russian for motherland which Kaminer (2006) translates to German as *Heimat* (Home, lit. native land, land of birth). His choice of wording is deliberately ambiguous since nationalism which *Heimat* indirectly alludes to still is a tricky subject in post-Nazi Germany. Cf. Rutten (2007) for a detailed discussion of Kaminer's (mis)use of German and further references as well as Morley and Robins (1990) and Peck (1992) for a discussion of the term *Heimat*.

tied to an event, not a locality per se. As mentioned in previous chapters, the concept of scene has been broadened from originally being a geographical delimitation of musical practice to include genres of cultural production and loosely defined social activities. This makes the concept of scene a useful tool when describing a genre of cultural production, anchored locally originally, but sustained through transcultural flows to other localities: the *Russendisko* phenomenon is neither limited to the two DJs nor locally to Berlin. During my stint in Berlin I also visited an event advertised as "Barbaric lounge with DJ Nata (Novosibirsk) (Propeller Barbie Dance: Ska, Ragga, Gypsie, Polka, Electro, Turbo, Folk, and more from Russia)" (Kulturportal Russland n.d. – German: p. 332) at *Mudd club*, also located in Berlin-Mitte. Not only did the resident DJs play music from the *Russendisko* compilations and Russian bands, they also included music from the Balkans such as the music of Goran Bregovic. Similar events have been appearing across Europe and Israel both through Kaminer and Yuriy's tours with the *Russendisko* concept and locals starting similar projects like Armin Siebert, one of the co-founders of *Eastblok Music*, the *Russophobie-Party-Kollektiv* in Nürnberg (Russophobie n.d.), DJ Schum/Iura Kharlamov with the *Russenparty/Russendiskothek* in Halle (Schum n.d.) and the *Russian Style Discoteka* at the Postgarage in Graz (Postgarage n.d.).

Inspired by Bennett's (2004, 223) trichotomy (cf. p. 47), I focus on the *Russendisko*-scene, which is primarily based in Berlin (thus *local*). However, the DJ's both travel and host the *Russendisko* in other localities and *Russendisko*-imitations have appeared, making the scene *translocal*. Finally, the *Russendisko* is also *virtual* (podcasts, myspace-profile, radio show, website). Hence the *Russendisko*-scene is situated in a continuum between the local, translocal, and virtual.

Thus, even though the original event is located in Berlin, there is a translocal musical community involved with this music on the production side, which can be grasped through the scene-concept. While this community is connected through the actors and provides social hubs – primarily clubs which host the event – producing a sense of community within the conditions of metropolitan music life – there are also differences in how the scene is structured compared to a locally bounded scene like St. Petersburg. The main one is that the *Russendisko*-scene is more strictly organized around a specific musical style (cf. p. 257ff). While there are discursive scene boundaries present, an important scene boundary is grouped around the target group, the German majority population. A closer reading of the *Russendisko*'s emergence provides some more context here. Thus this discussion shows how the concept of scene can be employed for something that is not geographically bounded to one locality.

8.1 Boundaries

While the *Russendisko-scene* is positioned in the above mentioned continuum there is (at least in this case) a main social hub, the original event at *Kaffee Burger*. The farther away the analysis moves from that, the more fluid the boundaries get and the harder it gets to determine what is within and what is outside the scene. This especially applies to the exploration of events inspired by, or similar to, the *Russendisko* and of bands involved in the *Russendisko*. While the boundaries are intentionally kept fluid to avoid strict categorizations, I would, for the moment, like to concentrate on the original event at *Kaffee Burger*, thus some form of delimitation is needed. This can be done through Lundberg, Malm, and Ronström's concept of *arenas* (cf. p. 102).

The *stage* here designates the performance area (*Kaffee Burger*) while *backstage* is where the performance is prepared (selection of which music to play – similar to the role of the *art direktor* in St. Petersburg). *Offstage* covers what is not in focus within the arena (musics outside the DJs' criteria like "pop" music or Soviet groups, groups ignored and/or condemned by society). However, music forms from the offstage can emerge if certain conditions in society change or if the form adopts to dominant norms (Lundberg et al. 2003, 53ff). This is the case with the *Russendisko* itself, where a strong post-Soviet emigrant community in Berlin (see the following chapter) connected with Wladimir Kaminer's popularity as an author positively changed the conditions of acceptance for popular music linked to the former Soviet Union outside the emigrant communities – and thus influenced the auditorium.

8.1.1 Auditorium: German speaking audience

"We started this mainly to present this music to other people, the Russians know what this is about."

(Gurzhy 2005 – German: p. 312)

A closer look at the *Russendisko*'s auditorium reveals that the target group differs from other events of the post-Soviet emigrant community by primarily catering to a non-emigrant audience – something which Yuriy alludes to in the opening quote. He added that the Russians mainly remain among other Russians.[202] When asking different regulars about the *Russendisko* I was told that around 15-20% of the participants were Russians. In addition, I also observed that since I started frequenting the event in spring 2004, the number of tourists and people speaking neither German nor Russian as their primary language has risen considerably.

Further indications that the target group is not Russian speakers are the *Russendisko* DJs' past radio shows and podcasts on *radiomultikulti* as well as their CD *Radio Russendisko* which contains short stories intertwined with music packaged as a radio show: these are all in German. This targeting of a German speaking audience can also be seen in the DJs' conscious exotization and play on Soviet and Russian clichés normally employed by Germans (as discussed in chapter 10).

Hannerz (1996, 136f) provides a sequential model within what he labels world cities, which examines how the *form of life* level interacts with the *market* level and thus creates new types of meaningful forms. This framework sheds some light on the evolution of the *Russendisko* and can be seen as a more detailed version of how music goes from offstage to onstage.[203]

In Berlin the presence of a large post-Soviet emigrant community in the 1990s allowed for the exchange of ideas. Yuriy pointed out that when he became acquainted with Kaminer they would exchange tapes and listen to and discuss post-Soviet popular music (Gurzhy 2005). This kind of communication about music happens on the form of life level and is quite common among musicians. Hannerz (1996, 136) argues that in the first phase of his model, meaning and meaningful forms flow fairly freely within what he calls sub-cultural community – here the post-Soviet community in Berlin, a community large and cohesive enough to offer both moral and other non-material support to its members.

As mentioned above, Kaminer's wife suggested that they stage a dance party for friends. This coincided with an offer to organize a party with Russian music from the organizers of *Cafe Zapata*, the cafe in the Berlin art house *Tacheles*. They staged the event, which despite both technical problems and their inexperience as

---

202. Used here as a synonym for people from the post-Soviet area.
203. There are also other factors which have shaped the development of the *Russendisko* such as the general history of discotheques and club culture which I have not had the resources to focus on within the frame of this book.

DJs, was a success. As a consequence they were invited to host the event regularly in the then emerging *Kaffee Burger*. According to Hannerz's model, this can be seen as the beginning of the second stage where:

> "a higher degree of division of cultural labor is introduced within the community. Apparently the latter has also reached another kind of critical mass here, where it is profitable enough to commoditize subculturally distinctive items for consumption by community members, as an alternative to the free flow of the form-of-life framework."
>
> (Hannerz 1996, 136f)

Here, the meaningful forms – the music – move into the market frame, becoming a commodity and also enter the public arena. This is also the stage where media, stores specialized in products from Russia, as well as groups performing for emigrants belong – these are, however, still focused on the emigrant community.

Through both staging the event regularly and through Kaminer's success as an author, the event evolved into a cultural commodity. As a cultural commodity, the event is also more visible – becoming a part of the wider cultural market place – the third stage of Hannerz's model – and creating a scene. This in turn allowed for others to copy or develop the idea further with similar events, but also through specializing in marketing the music (*Russendisko Records*, *Eastblok Music*) and post-Soviet groups performing for a non-emigrant market.[204] Yuriy's comment that "the Russians know what the *Russendisko* is about" also reflects on the event as a cultural commodity: The post-Soviet migrants speak Russian and have their own networks as well as stores where they can access the post-Soviet popular music they want to hear and are not dependent on somebody's idiosyncratic music taste. Most of the German majority population, however, does not speak Russian nor know where to start, thus the cultural market offers them a way to become familiar with (a part of) this music.

Placing the *Russendisko* within this larger context we can trace the event's target group and thus also uncover some of the *Russendisko*-scene's boundaries. This not only uncovers a cultural marketplace for the music (and thus the reach of the scene) exploited by other events and companies, like the following discussion of

---

204. Hannerz points out that the stages of the model can also coincide with each other and in this case the first and second stage overlap – e.g. that groups from the former Soviet Union also performed for the emigrants before the *Russendisko* became popular.

Eastblok Music, but also places the music played at the event in contrast to music of the post-Soviet migrant community living in Germany.

8.1.1.1 *Eastblok Music*

> "We come more, of course, from the world music and the alternative corner, because that is how you have to start. It is simply a Russendisko-audience and it is a world music-audience. That is, for a start, our base target group."
>
> (Armin in Kasparov and Siebert 2005 – German: p. 315)

With its office right next to *Kaffe Burger*, the record label *Eastblok Music* is another institution in Berlin with the specific goal to promote Eastern European music in Western Europe, and which primarily targets non-emigrants. Run by Armin Siebert (Germany) and Alexander "Alex" Kasparov (Russia/Armenia), both formerly employed at EMI's Eastern European division and both with a background in music management, journalism, and media, the label was founded on November 1st, 2004. Inspired by the *Russendisko*'s success in opening up Eastern European music to a new audience, they saw the potential for releasing Eastern European groups in Western Europe. This they have been doing with critical acclaim. Rooted within the world music market, they received the *WOMEX (World Music Expo) Top Label Award 2006* mainly due to the success of the album *Ukraine Calling* (Haydamaky 2006) and the compilation *Café Sputnik* (Various Artists 2005b) (Gift Music n.d; World Music Central 2006).

Armin and Alex (2005) identified four target groups linked to the *Russendisko* and their label: People involved with Eastern Europe through studies, visits etc, a few Eastern Europeans, young people who, in Armin's words, are fed up with Anglo-American mass music and are looking for an individual alternative, and, finally, people between 30 and 50 who are looking for interesting new musics. This listener typification reflects their focus on the world music market which markets itself in part as an alternative to the (perceived) dominant Anglo-American music market.

Since the *Russendisko* DJs also have their own record-label, *Russendisko Records*, I asked Armin if the market was big enough for two such labels. He replied that there was enough music for both labels and added that the labels focused on different kinds of music. *Eastblok Music* does not only focus on music from the former Soviet Union, but on Eastern Europe in a broader sense (Kasparov and Siebert 2005).

This is reflected in their catalogue which includes compilations of Ukrainian popular music linked to the Orange Revolution (Various Artists 2005e), electronic music (Various Artists 2005b) and popular music (Various Artists 2012a) from Russia, Ukraine, and Belarus, and music from the Balkans (Various Artists 2005a, 2006a, 2008a) as well as albums of Russian (Leningrad 2006; La Minor 2009; Markscheider Kunst 2010), Ukrainian (Haydamaky 2006, 2008), Belorussian (Lyapis Trubetskoy 2010), and other Eastern European groups (e.g. Little Cow 2007; Shukar Collective 2007; Shazalakazoo 2011). In 2012 they released their first album of a Berlin-based group, SkaZka Orchestra's second album *Kalamburage* (SkaZka Orchestra 2012 – the musicians' roots are, however, from the former Soviet Union and most of the lyrics are in Russian). Their online shop (Eastblok Music n.d.) also distributes Eastern European groups not released by them, as well as T-shirts and other merchandise. In contrast, the releases by *Russendisko Records* limit themselves to the groups played at the *Russendisko*, in other words groups from a post-Soviet sphere, primarily living in Russia, Ukraine, and Belorus, as well as emigrants from those countries living primarily in Germany and the United States.

In addition to releasing albums, *Eastblok Music* organizes music events, mainly promoting the bands they release. Both owners work as DJs in local clubs (including guest dj-ing at the *Russendisko*) and Armin moderates the fortnightly radio show *Nightflight* on *Radio Fritz* where he plays Eastern European popular music.

Thus, *Eastblok Music*'s existence can partly be credited to the success as well as being a part of the *Russendisko*-scene – including similar target groups. There are also musical similarities between the music played at the *Russendisko* and the music *Eastblok Music* releases (cf. p. 260ff). This is in part reflected in overlapping groups, especially Leningrad, Lia Minor (Russia), and Haydamaky (Ukraine). Finally, as mentioned, both Armin and Alex participate in the *Russendisko*-scene through (guest) dj-ing.

At the same time *Eastblok Music* extends (or even goes beyond) the boundaries of the scene by covering Eastern Europe in general – specifically focusing on the Balkans. This includes a broader range of musical styles than the *Russendisko*.

8.1.1.2 Radio Schum

Another entity promoting popular music from the former Soviet Union was the monthly radio show *Schum* (Noise) on Radio Corax (Halle) from 2002 until 2007. Run by DJ Schum (aka Yury Harlamov), the show was bilingual with DJ Schum primarily speaking Russian and his German-speaking co-presenters Peter Kirschnick and Katja Eismann making a rough translation into German. The show presented mainly contemporary popular music from the post-Soviet space as well as groups based in Germany with ties to the post-Soviet emigrant community (cf. the quote on p. 56). While overlapping with the music played at the *Russendisko*, the show presented a much broader selection, including music released by *Eastblok Music*. As Yury wrote in an e-mail message to the Russian Popular Music list hosted by Yahoogroups:

"We have an internal restriction – we do not play pop, estrada, and so called 'shanson', that is blatniak. Very little rock-popsa. Some hip-hop and electronic music. All other styles, played, so to say, 'by hand' are present. We play Russian, Ukrainian, Belarusian, if we find, Moldavian, and sometimes Eastern-Jewish music."

(Harlamov 2005 – Russian: p. 314)

What they have in common with the *Russendisko* and *Eastblok Music* is the exclusion of the Russian genres pop, *estrada*, and *shanson*. The focus on "handmade" music, in other words a critique of so called electronic and computer music, was also stressed by Yuriy Gurzhy (2005) as well as Matthias Angerer (2007), the director of the Viennese club *Ost Klub*, as important. This is similar to the focus on how music is produced within the St. Petersburg scene.

DJ Schum and his co-hosts described the groups played, where they come from, and explained some typical elements related to those groups. This combined with the bilinguality points toward a target group of both speakers of Russian and of German.

Furthermore, DJ Schum also djs the monthly *alternative russen-diskothek* (alternative Russian-discotheque) at the club *Hühnermanhattan* in Halle. Thus while not located in Berlin, the activities of DJ Schum are also part of the translocal *Russendisko*-scene. As with *Eastblok Music*, the music overlaps with that played at the *Russendisko*, but is at the same time stylistically much broader.

These three examples, *Russendisko*, *Eastblok Music*, and *Radio Schum*, as well as other events not mentioned, make up the scene's social hubs connected through a social network of actors where the djs travel around Germany and/or draw on material from other actors within the scene (e.g. DJ Schum has presented new releases from *Eastblok Music* on the show). These events and entities share a common target group which is to a large extent made up of non-Russian speakers. Distinguishing here between the regular audience at the Berlin event and a general audience, this target group is part of the auditorium of an extended translocal (to some extent even imagined) *Russendisko*-scene.

8.1.2 Boundary: Russian speaking audience

The above mentioned extended *Russendisko-scene* does, however, not necessarily cater to a Russophone audience. The heterogenous group of post-Soviet emigrants are not only divided by their reasons for emigrating (discussed in the following chapter) but also by taste.[205]

Alex points to the group's heterogeneity when he mentioned that the three groups, ethnic Germans, Jews, and (what he termed) "alternative" Russians had different conceptions of how to party in Berlin: The "alternatives" frequent the *Russendisko* and similar clubs such as *Club SSSR* and *Mudd Club* and mix with Germans. The ethnic Germans primarily went to discos organized by promoters playing Russian pop-music in clubs like *A-lounge* reflecting similar nightlife events in Russia.[206] The Jews, who sometimes also visit the events of the ethnic Germans, primarily frequent clubs in Charlottenburg like *90 Grad*. Alex also pointed out that the clubs frequented by both the ethnic Germans as well as the Jews were *pafosnyi* (bombastic – Kasparov and Siebert 2006). Together with Armin Alex pointed out that the local discotheques and youth clubs catering to ethnic Germans and Jews focus on Russian-language popular music like Russian pop/*estrada* and house – thus contrasting with the music played at the *Russendisko* (Kasparov and Siebert 2005). While I do not have first hand observations from Berlin, the description of the events frequented by the "non-alternatives" reflect venues and behavioral patterns in St. Petersburg.

---

205. This has not been the focus of my research, so my account is primarily based on second hand observations. Future research should focus on this area to get a better understanding of the music habits of the post-Soviet migrant community and how these aid in both creating a (non-)emigrant identity and in the process of integration.
206. The similarity traits he mentioned were Russian pop music, fights, tight security, and vodka. In a newspaper interview Yuriy Gurzhy referred to these places by saying: "The emigre population often requires trendier clubs with a lot of gold. ... We [Russendisko] don't conform to Russian tastes." (Gurzhy, qtd. in Chernov 2003)

Making these events appealing to an *émigré* audience, they also combine music with Soviet/post-Soviet popular culture like the *Diskoteka Stolichnaia* (Discotheque of the Capital, 08.03.2008) which included two Berlin teams of the *Klub Veselykh i Nakhodchivykh* (Club of the Merry and Resourceful), originally a Soviet humor show dating back to 1961, which is still running and where teams compete against each other. This, at the same time, excludes a German-speaking audience, who lacks the necessary references.

This diverse taste in music can also be seen in *Pi-Rok (π-Rock)*, a (now defunct) Germany-wide organization founded in 2001 targeting a Russophone audience.[207] Based around the website www.pi-rock.de, they provided a platform for promoting Russian-language popular music in Germany. The music hosted on the organization's website ranged from what is perceived as *pop* to *rock* reflecting current trends in popular music. Besides the language the music did not really differ from popular music produced by their non-migrant peers. In addition, the organization arranges festivals named *Solianka* (a Russian vegetable-meat soup), consisting primarily of groups based in Germany, but also hosting guests from the former Soviet Union.[208] The organization was weak in Berlin, however there were some bands registered with them which I contacted during my fieldwork in 2009.

While it is hard to generalize about their musical style, there are some interesting observations to be made. Most bands are made up of amateurs. Besides the language (primarily sung in Russian), the music does not seem to differ from popular music produced by their non-migrant peers. If one listens closely, however, there are some interesting observations to be made, which link the music to the musicians' former country of origin.

8.1.2.1 Crossing

One example is the group *Crossing*, based in Berlin. Founded in 2004 the group consists of ethnic Germans from Russia and Kazakhstan who, at the time of the interview, were between 25 and 40 years old. The name is an allusion to them be-

---

207. Both Israel and the USA, which also have large Russian speaking immigrant populations, have similar organizations called respectively *Russkii Andegraund v Izraile* (The Russian Underground in Israel) and *Russkii Rok-klub v Amerike* (The Russian Rock Club of America). Note that the word *Russian* is used as a homogenizer just like *die Russen* in German.
208. There is a recording studio, *Pi-Rok Records*, associated with the organization. Furthermore, *Pi-Rok* have released the compilation *Pi-Rock Zona V.01* (Pi-Rock Zone – Various Artists n.d.).

ing at the crossing of two cultures – that of their origin and Germany. When I interviewed them in 2009 they rehearsed in a youth/women's club – located in a residential area in Marzahn – a borough in the eastern part of Berlin where a lot of ethnic Germans were settled.

Their 2007 album *Chast' Zhizni* (Part of Life – Crossing 2007) and 2009 album *Ia ne Gagarin* (I'm not Gagarin – Crossing 2009) consists of guitar driven songs within a rock idiom and with Russian lyrics. When I played the album to some friends in St. Petersburg after the fieldwork, the first response was "This sounds like Makarevich, that sounds like Chaif, Splin, Chizh etc." In other words, Crossing's music was compared with (post-)Soviet singers and groups from the 1980s and 1990s. This is both based on the language, vocal timbre, harmonization, and intonation as well as the guitar riffs, groove, and the overall sound.

I made similar observations with the other bands I talked to during that fieldwork stint: the music played by the bands sounded like well known Soviet and post-Soviet bands – clearly presenting a musical link between Berlin and the musicians' country of origin.

This was also acknowledged in the interviews – the musicians were very upfront in pointing out what music they listened to and what musical influences were important. Here Soviet and post-Soviet music was part of their listening biography. This is not that surprising considering that the musicians were born in the former Soviet Union before emigrating, spoke Russian, and some still had family in their country of origin. Furthermore, the bands they mentioned were active while they lived in the Soviet Union, Russia, respectively Kazakhstan. At the same time this music does not reflect the local popular music from e.g. Kazakhstan but a regional Soviet / post-Soviet popular music from the centers St. Petersburg and Moscow.

What was interesting, however, was the selection of music they listened to – especially compared to the musicians I interviewed in St. Petersburg. As discussed in chapter 3, musicians within the rock-idiom in St. Petersburg have strong opinions regarding what is considered *russkii rok*. They draw a line between their music and both *russkii rok* and *popsa*.

The groups I talked to in Berlin, however, had a much more relaxed relationship to both *russkii rok*-groups and *popsa*-bands. In addition to the groups considered to be *russkii rok* (Chaif, Kino, Splin, and Chizh), Crossing's definition of *russkii rok* included Smyslovye Galliutsinatsii, Liube, and Bi2 – bands that would not have been included in that category in St. Petersburg (Baburin et al. 2009). Instead those three groups were placed in a continuum spanning from pop-rock to *popsa*. Another example was given by Anton Gornung (2009), the Berlin-based singer of the metal-band Affekt. The band is inspired by the Soviet/Russian metal band Aria and by its former singer Valerii Kipelov. During the interview Anton mentioned that he also liked the compositions of Konstantin Meladze (cf. p. 227). Meladze, both a producer and composer, is clearly linked to *popsa* and no musician within the rock idiom I talked to in St. Petersburg would have admitted to liking Meladze.

While the discourses are in part used by St. Petersburg-based bands to position themselves in the market, the Berlin-based bands do not have this need: They are primarily amateur bands playing within the emigrant community and do not have to regularly compete for venues to perform in. Instead the groups collaborate, sharing rehearsal rooms and performing together at club festivals. Thus the music feeds on memories of their past and functions more as a reminder of where the musicians came from and the music they listened to before emigrating.

At the same time the musicians also listen and play contemporary popular music from the post-Soviet sphere. One example was Crossing playing the riff to Okean El'zy's (*Lukava*) *Kishka* (Sly cat – Okean El'zy 2003) during a break while I heard them rehearse in Berlin on December 7th, 2009. This can also be heard when listening to *Radio Russkij Berlin* (Radio Russian Berlin) a Berlin-based Russian language radio station.[209] Aimed at the emigrants, the music played on the station primarily consists of *popsa* but it also includes *russkii rok* and contemporary groups within the rock-idiom like Nautilus Pompilius, Vopli Vidopliasova, and Markscheider Kunst as well as borderline cases like Liube and Mashina Vremeni. This is a format that does not exist within the playlists of local St. Petersburg radio stations. As the website puts it:

> Radio Russkii Berlin – that is new and old hits from Russia. [...] The radio station strives to support its listeners in maintaining their cultural roots while at the same time creating a link between German and Russian cultures.
>
> (FM n.d. - Russian: p. 333)

---

209. The radio station belongs to the media group *RusMedia* founded 1996 which, among others, also publishes the newspapers *Russkaja Germanija*, *Russkij Berlin*, and *Rheinskaja Gazeta*.

Another important fact linked to radio is that by living away from the centers of post-Soviet popular music, the emigrants are also limited in their exposure to new music. One way of keeping up to date is by radio, however the selection aired is filtered by the station's format thus limiting the exposure to other musics. Similarly, most Soviet and post-Soviet bands touring Germany are bands from the 1980s and 1990s as well as well-known bands of the 2000s. Those are mostly bands that the emigrants listened to before leaving, those played on *Radio Russkij Berlin*, or promoted through the *Russendisko* (cf. chapter 9). While the internet theoretically provides a useful tool for finding new music, it still poses the challenge of information overload making it difficult to uncover new influences.

In other words, the music played by these emigrants reflects a listening biography influenced by the time they lived in their country of origin and Soviet and post-Soviet bands from the centers, not local or regional popular music from e.g. Kazakhstan. Living in Germany and infrequently returning to their country of origin, they are not so much affected by local discourses in the former Soviet Union. Thus, the Berlin-based bands tend to have a broader acceptance of Soviet and post-Soviet popular music than their St. Petersburg based peers.

As already mentioned, Yuriy Gurzhy's comment above regarding Russians who know what the music played at the *Russendisko* is about, reflects on the ability of the post-Soviet emigrants to find the music on their own – something this discussion has also shown. Another reason they do not necessarily frequent the *Russendisko* is that their music taste, just like that of their non-post-Soviet peers, is very diverse. As I will discuss in the next chapter, the post-Soviet emigrant community in Germany is not homogenous hence it is difficult to speak of *one* diaspora as well as a smiliar music taste (what, however, remains to be seen is how the first generation of post-Soviet emigrants born in Germany develops and what music these people will draw on).

While the *Russendisko* has an added exotic element (cf. chapter 10) which appeals to a German speaking non-emigrant crowd this does not necessarily apply to the majority of Russophones. They tend more towards shared (popular) cultural symbols such as the above mentioned *Klub Veselykh i Nakhodchivykh*, which they recognize from when they grew up in the former Soviet Union or from visits to the post-Soviet republics, as well as tours of bands from the 1980s and 1990.

[210]The Russophone audience is thus another part of the *Russendisko*-scene's boundaries.

8.2 Concluding remarks

> "We were also the first place in Berlin [...] where the Russians and Germans communicated with each other in a relaxed way. [...] I am still proud that quite many Russian-German couples found each other there [at the *Russendisko*]."
>
> (Gurzhy 2005 – German: p. 313)

As I have discussed above, the *Russendisko* can be conceptualized as part of a scene centered around a musical event. Here, the relationship to locality is looser than with the St. Petersburg scene, since both the event is hosted in different places in Germany and there are other, similar events and activities. Instead, the scene is grouped around certain musical characteristics and an imagined origin of the music. This is due to having one original event to trace the scene back to as well as having two DJs who filter the music played through their personal taste.

The emigrant community living in Germany is a heterogenous group, whose diverse cultural/musical activities are, however, overshadowed by the attention the *Russendisko* gets. This disproportionate attention is in part because the event specifically targets non-Russian speakers – the majority population – through its promotion, as discussed in chapter 10. Thus, while the *Russendisko* might function as a meeting point between a (small) group of Russian speaking emigrants and "Germans" as Yuriy claims, the different target groups that I outlined do not make it an integration event *per se*.

Compared to other countries with large post-Soviet emigrant communities (Israel, United States, Great Britain), this success also makes the *Russendisko* quite unique as an event. At the same time, the *Russendisko*-scene's translocality also means that the scene's consumers are more heterogenous – while the regulars in one locality know each other, regulars taking part in similar events in e.g. Halle probably do not know regulars attending the *Russendisko* in Berlin.

Despite the geographical disparity there are also some shared values within the scene. When discussing post-Soviet popular music with the actors in Germany, St.

---

210. During 2013 and 2014 *russkii rok* bands such as DDT and Iu-Piter (Vyacheslav Butusov) as well as newer bands such as Okean El'zy, Dekabr', Splin, Chizh i Co, and Piknik have toured Germany playing primarily for a Russian-speaking audience.

Petersburg's reputation as a rock city was intensified and idealized. Here a disdain for electronic/computer based music was present and the stress was on "hand made music" – music performed by "real" musicians on "real" instruments – which was, for them, embodied in rock, not pop. In other words, they were making a distinction based, amongst other things, on the (perceived) production style. Since St. Petersburg has historically been the center of Soviet rock, this underlying perception remained on a discursive level (but was not necessarily reflected in the groups selected).

Musically, however, a change occurs which can be traced to the production side: While DJs (re-)produce music in the sense that they provide a musical experience based on their skills of creating a DJ-set, adding sound effects and to an extent changing the music, make them more *secondary producers* since their raw material is primarily music produced by somebody else. By limiting this raw material to a specific geographic entity and ideological choices, the *Russendisko* is also a good example of how a local sound can emerge through filtering processes – and which theoretically could be marketed as a specific "sound", as discussed in the following chapter. At the same time this filtering also acts as a boundary setting, the *Russendisko* musically apart from other events within the migrant community.

In other words, the *Russendisko* as a trans-local scene also builds upon shared values which influence what music is played. While the musical boundaries are fluid and dependent on the event's DJ, there still is a core based both on ideology ("hand-made") and specific stylistic traits creating similar events across Germany and Austria. The scene concept thus not only includes local music production but enables a focus on translocal events as part of *one* scene.

While I have demonstrated that the *Russendisko*-scene is connected to St. Petersburg, the question remains how and why the music flowed to Berlin. The *Russendisko* is not a poster boy for the disjunctures of global flows but builds upon a market created through post-Soviet migration to Germany and specifically to Berlin. This includes both St. Petersburg musicians moving to and groups frequently performing in Berlin as well as the *Russendisko* and other DJs heavily drawing on groups from St. Petersburg, among others places, at their event. In other words, there are strong ties between St. Petersburg and Berlin which have enabled the flow of music. These ties will be examined from the perspective of transcultural flows of media and people in the following chapter and shed light on musical processes and cultural influences present both in St. Petersburg and in Berlin.

9 The post-Soviet emigrant community in Germany

> Oioioi – the Russians are coming
> Na zdorov'e [To your health] – And they are already here![211]
> *Die Russen Kommen* (EAV 1997)

EAV's *Die Russen Kommen* (EAV 1997) parodies clichés associated with the "Russians" moving to Germany and Austria in the 1990s – the last of four waves of Soviet emigration in the 20th century. While the last wave coincided with the collapse of the Soviet Union the first big wave of emigration to Germany was triggered by the Soviet Union's birth, the Russian revolution. Here political opponents fled the civil war and applied for asylum in Germany, with Berlin becoming the center of Russian migration and culture during the 1920s (Schlögel 1994; Darieva 2004, 41, 100ff). The first wave of emigration also provided an audience base for the *Russian folklore lineage* on which the *Russendisko* in parts builds upon and parodies (cf. chapter 10).[212]

Emigration was, however, tightly controlled and only open to members of certain ethnic and religious groups. While ethnic Germans after the Second World War, for historical and political reasons, settled in Germany, Jews primarily went to Israel and the United States. After the collapse of the Soviet Union, emigration became easier and Germany emerged as the most important receiving country. Due to this significant impact my focus is on this last wave of emigration.[213]

Roughly speaking the groups differ in aspects of ethnicity, religion, and geographic distribution in their home country and can be categorized as follows (cf. Dietz 2000; Wickström 2009a):[214]

---

211. *Oioioi – die Russen kommen! Na zdorov'e – Und schon sind sie da!*
212. The second wave was due to the displacement of Soviet civilians and soldiers after the Second World War while the third came in the 1970s and consisted primarily of Soviet Jews and dissidents. The fourth wave started in the late 1980s including Jews and ethnic Germans and in the 1990s also Russians and other groups who emigrated due to economic difficulties and hope of a better life abroad (Lohr 2004).
213. While there are some migrants from the earlier waves, these do not play a significant role in the cultural activities I explore here. Both in Great Britain (Darieva 2004, 139) and the United States (Laitin 2004, 19) there is a gap between the Soviet and post-Soviet migrants, something which would be worth exploring further for the German context.
214. Due to a legistlationary shift in Germany regarding immigration which substantially tightened the rules for post-Soviet immigration the statistics presented here are only until

- *Ethnic Germans*, who predominantly belong to a Protestant denomination. Besides Russia they mainly come from Kazakhstan, Kirgistan, and other central Asian states. In German they are referred to as *Spätaussiedler, Russlanddeutsche*, and *Wolgadeutsche*. Their return is guaranteed in the *German constitution* as well as in the *Federal Expellees Act* and with their repatriation certificate these immigrants receive the German citizenship. In the period 1991 to 2005 1 931 083 ethnic Germans moved to Germany (Kiss and Lederer 2006, 65).[215]
- *Jews*, who primarily come from the urban centers in the European part of the former USSR. They were accepted through the *Quota Refugee Act*, originally established in 1980 to admit refugees from South-East Asia as humanitarian refugees (e.g. Vietnamese Boat People). They can apply for citizenship once they become eligible (normally after 8 years of residence in Germany). By December 31st, 2005, 205 645 Jews from the former Soviet Union had emigrated.[216]
- *Ethnic Russians* (*ethnic Ukrainians* etc.), who are primarily (Russian-)Orthodox or atheists. These consist of asylum seekers, professionals, students, and marriage migrants. About 185 931 Russian, 130 674 Ukrainian, and 18 037 Belorussian citizens, to name a few post-Soviet nationalities, were residing in Germany in 2005 (Statistisches Bundesamt 2006). The problem with these numbers is that they include Jewish emigrants who retain their original citizenship until they are eligible to apply for German citizenship.

Thus, based on these numbers and a conservative estimation, there are at least 2.6 Million Russian-speaking immigrants in Germany at the moment – making them at least the second largest group of immigrants residing in Germany.[217] Of

---

2006.
215. While I could not find any definite numbers for 2006 13 288 ethnic Germans moved to Germany from the former Soviet Union in the period 2007-2009 (Bundesverwaltungsamt 2009, 2008, 2007). Compared to the previous years this shows a significant stagnation in post-Soviet emigration.
216. The numbers are based on Kiss and Lederer (2006, 68) which covers 1993 through 2005. This number also includes 8 535 Jews who immigrated to Germany before November 10, 1991 – before the procedures of the *Quota Refugee Act* were adopted (Federal Ministry of the Interior 2005, 58). Starting January 1st, 2005 the *Quota Refugee Act* has been replaced with the *Immigration Act*.
217. There were 7.256 Million registered foreign citizens residing in Germany in 2006 (in 2011 there were 7.370 Million). This is about 8,81% of the total population of 82.315 Million (in 2011: 81.831 Million – Statistisches Bundesamt 2012). The largest immigrant group by nationality are Turkish (1 688 370 in 2008) followed by Italian citizens (523 162 in 2008) (Kiss and Lederer 2009). Taking naturalized immigrants neglected in this statistic into

those at least 70 000 (but more probably around 200 000) are currently living in Berlin.[218]

This chapter will first return to the term *diaspora* and its applicability for this community before discussing the flow of music from the post-Soviet sphere to the *Russendisko*. Here I will focus on how the music is filtered around certain style indicators and thus is creating a recognizable *Russendisko*-sound.

9.1 The post-Soviet emigrant community in Germany – a diaspora?

On an abstract level it is possible to define this group of emigrants as a diaspora. This is implied by the group's common denominator *Russen*, which remains in everyday use and public perception, arguing that they have the same origin, that they are embedded in a transnational network, and that they (mostly) speak the same language. That said, both the mentioned demographics as well as comments made by people I interviewed, support a more fragmented group.[219]

Darieva (2004, 127f) touches on this fragmentation regarding the preferred settlement areas in Berlin. While she emphasizes that the migrants settle in all the districts, preferred areas are Charlottenburg, Wilmersdorf, and Schöneberg, which are upper middle class districts in the former West. A part of the ethnic Germans (coming mainly from Siberia and Kazakhstan) have settled in the outer boroughs Marzahn, Hohenschönhausen, and Lichtenberg, which is partially due to federal state settlement policy. Located in Berlin's former Eastern section, these

---

consideration the numbers point out that if the post-Soviet immigrants are considered a (supra)nationality they numerically make up at least the second largest group of immigrants in Germany and compete with Turkish immigrants for first place.

218. As of December 31st, 2008 there were 25 099 (up from 24 206 on 30.06.2006) citizens of Russia, Belarus, and Ukraine residing in Berlin (Berlin.de – Der Beauftragte für Integration und Migration 2008 based on material from the Statistisches Landesamt Berlin). Between 1993-2004 about 42 000 ethnic Germans from the former Soviet Union moved to Berlin (this is a rough estimate based on Ohliger and Raiser 2005, 21), so a conservative approximation is that at least 70 000 Russophone migrants are currently living in Berlin. In reality this number is probably higher – estimations range from 120 000 to 300 000 (Armin and Alex, pers. comm., 11.10.2005; Russkaia Germaniia 2008; Wieck 2008).

219. Solomon (2008, 79) makes a similar argument regarding the heterogeneity of migrants from Turkey living in Germany: "The broad category 'Turks in Germany' or 'the Turkish diaspora in Germany' thus masks an [sic] huge internal diversity in this group, which can include ethnic Turks who are Sunni Muslims or Alevis as well as people who self-identify as Kurds, Circassians or Laz".

are considered problem areas with higher concentrations of anti-semitism and racism. This corresponds to Armin and Alex's observations, which added a third category, "the alternatives", settled around Prenzlauer Berg and Mitte (Kasparov and Siebert 2005 – both Kaminer and Yuriy lived in Prenzlauer Berg while I was conducting fieldwork).[220] This separation has also been pointed out by the migration researcher Barbara Dietz:

> "the Jewish immigrants first of all integrate into Jewish communities in Germany [...], whereas ethnic Germans increasingly integrate into ethnic German minority enclaves"
>
> (Dietz 2000, 649)

While at first glance this segregation seems logical based on the emigrants' ethnic backgrounds, Darieva (2004, 77ff) argues that the segregation is primarily state-imposed by the host country. By imposing the ethnic categories *ethnic German* and *Jewish*, which are linked to different expectations and institutions (Jewish community, organizations for ethnic Germans) and were officially almost void of meaning in the Soviet Union,[221] the state imposes an artificial split, which Darieva labels *re-tribalisation*. While this is certainly part of the reason, I also suspect that this is based on class differences, since Jewish migrants (primarily from urban centers in the Western part of the former Soviet Union) tend to have a higher education than ethnic Germans, who tend to come from the peripheries (cf. Dietz 2000, 642f).

Another element complicating the use of diaspora is the fact that the emigrants' identities are not straightforward. The categories mentioned above are partially derived from historical circumstances, but also from German bureaucracy. Personal identities of the emigrants are more complex, in part due to intermarriage in the Soviet Union[222] and in part due to a common, a-religious Soviet socialization. While the migrants' identities were not always straightforward in the Soviet Union, the German categorization of the emigrants does not necessarily

---

220. Bottà (2006a, 6) argues that, in part due to housing politics in the GDR, Prenzlauer Berg emerged as a preferred area of settlement for the "creative class" coming from West Germany and Eastern Europe.
221. But not in consequence which can be seen in deportations/mandatory resettlements of ethnic Germans and a latent festering anti-semitism during the Soviet Union.
222. When in the Soviet Union intermarriages between two "nationalities" produced children, the child could choose his/her nationality listed in the passport at the age of 16, e.g. "A child of a Jewish father and non-Jewish mother could put down 'Jew.'" (Gorenberg 2008) – even tough the child according to the *halakha* (Jewish law) is not Jewish.

represent their own perceived identity either. When discussing groups of a population it is important to differentiate between the individuals' official identity and their personal identities. This allows for overlapping identities.[223]

One example of how these different identities overlap is Yuriy. While a large part of the music he djs together with Kaminer comes from the territory of the former Soviet Union, Yuriy stressed, when discussing the music played at the *Russendisko*, that he makes an effort to incorporate music by *emigrants* from the former Soviet Republics (cf. his quote on p. 257). This concept validates an important issue raised by Solomon (2006, 9f), when he stresses that in diasporas, the homeland is just another node in a complex transnational network. While Yuriy maintains the former Soviet Union as a reference point, he, at the same time, participates in a transnational network of former Soviet inhabitants – a post-Soviet emigrant identity.

Gurzhy also participates in another transnational network, the Jewish (ur-)diaspora, which overlaps with parts of the post-Soviet network. His project Shtetl Superstars Soundsystem & Shtetl Mafia, run together with the musician Lemez Lovas focuses, according to the project's *myspace* page, on "Funky Jewish Sounds" (Shtetl Superstars Orchestra n.d.) – in other words, music with links to the Jewish experience. The associated compilation *Shtetl Superstars* (Various Artists 2006c) includes different genres and languages from mainly Europe, North America, and the Middle East. The common reference is any form of Jewishness, both religious and cultural (e.g. lyrics in Yiddish, klezmer, the Jewish hymn *Adon Olam*, excerpts from *kiddush*, immigration experience, Ghetto life, Nazi extermination) mixed with style indicators from hip hop/rap, ska, klezmer, reggae, rock, and surf. On the CD Yuriy, who is Jewish, performs with the group Amsterdam Klezmer Band. These two projects show two identities, a post-Soviet and a Jewish one – however,

---

223. The political scientist David Laitin (2004) filters out the Jews when he examines the identity politics of the Russian Jewish diaspora in Brooklyn (New York). His reasoning is based on the diasporic group electing a primary (collective) identity which can further their position within their host society. He argues that the Jewish identity is worth more in the United States and compares those findings with Israel where the Russian identity is chosen, because it helps the emigrants advance there. While his study shows what strategies emigrant communities use to advance themselves, I think that reducing emigrants' identities to primary and secondary identities de-complex their cultural heritage and interlinking multiple identities. This excludes possible interconnections with other post-Soviet communities on the cultural level (music, literature etc.).

his self is more complex. When I posed the question what he feels like he answered:

> "Oh, that is really complicated. [...] So my mother is Jewish and my father has Russian, Ukrainian, Polish, and Greek blood [...] And my mother tongue is Russian, even though I come from Ukraine and I live in Berlin [...] Well, I have this luxury to reinvent myself all the time. [...] The Jewish element is very important and I think much about it [...] The Russian language is also very important for me, since I grew up with it. [...] That is really, that is very hard, that is always different and I think that that is also ok [...] So today I am a Russian, tomorrow I am a Jew, the day after tomorrow a Ukrainian [...] Well the people also don't exactly know [...] what to expect from me, as a nationality, I think that is very exciting, that brings you continuously to new adventures."
>
> (Gurzhy 2005 – German: p. 313)

This statement demonstrates the identity-complexities quite well: a band image/professional identity is based on a representation of *one* habit which depends on the situation. A person's subjectivity is made up of several habits which are more complex than just a reduction to binaries of Jewish/Russophone and a dominant identity. It also shows that Gurzhy is very conscious about the different habits he can draw on to promote his projects and how to use the identities strategically. The answer, furthermore, reflects how he positions himself due to the extensive media coverage he gets from his projects. In other words: the statement is a representation of what he thinks is important for me as an ethnomusicologist to hear. It is also probably influenced by a general awareness of multiple identities in the Berlin discourse, where *multiculturalism* is a commonly used label. Finally, belonging to the first emigrant generation, he still has strong emotional ties to his home country, something which must also be considered.

The differentiation between an individual's state-given official identity and his/her personal identities is also highlighted by Ong respectively Turino: While Ong labels this "the split between state-imposed identity and personal identity caused by political upheavals, migration, and changing global markets" (Ong 1999, 2), Turino writes

> "while one's legal status (passport, required military service, taxes) places one objectively within a given state, being part of a diaspora or nation requires a subjective recognition and acceptance; one has to 'join up', that is, identify with that social formation."
>
> (Turino 2004, 5)

Turino goes on to argue that

"[l]ike nations, diasporic formations are not objective entities but are constructed identity units, based on signs and discourses of similarity and unity."
(Turino 2004, 5)

In order for a diaspora to exist, a diasporic consciousness – a form of imagined community (Anderson 1991) – is needed. This is a crucial question, since it is one of the factors that distinguish an immigrant/transmigrant community from a diaspora. However, as Solomon points out, this "joining up" is not necessarily a conscious choice implied by Turino, but maybe "the emergent, aggregate result of a number of separate individual consumption choices" (Solomon 2006, 6) e.g. listening to Russian popular music.[224]

My aim is neither to argue that the post-Soviet community in Berlin is a sustainable diaspora, nor that it is not. Further research and a broader temporal perspective (including the second and third generation – cf. Butler 2001, 192; Turino 2004, 6) to see if a historical continuity exists within the community (cf. Tölölyan 1996, 29) is needed to see how the post-Soviet community in Berlin will develop. The purpose of this discussion has been to uncover some of the complexities surrounding the post-Soviet community in Berlin, and to highlight the fact that the term diaspora also glosses over differences within a group which is perceived from the outside as a diaspora. This is also the reason I have chosen to use the term *(post-Soviet) emigrant community* when referring to emigrants from the former Soviet Union living in Berlin.[225]

Returning to the transcultural flows, the emigrants, especially the first generation, brought their cultural heritage and language with them – maintaining ties to their country of origin. This can be seen in stores selling (imported) Russian products (from food, alcohol, and household products to souvenirs) as well as in Russian language print and online publications like the weekly newspapers *Russkii Berlin* (Russian Berlin) and *Berlinskaya Gazeta* (The Berlin Newspaper, their transcription), the monthly magazine *Izium* (Raisin), and the website 007-Berlin

---

224. Tölölyan touches on a similar concept with a fluid model where the emigrants shift between being ethnic and a part of the diaspora: "Ideally, it would be preferable to speak of individuals and communities who behave as ethnics in some spheres of life, as diasporans in others and, most importantly, who shift from one to the other: mobility is an internal as well as an external characteristic of the contemporary ethnodiaspora." (Tölölyan 1996, 18)

225. *Russian language community* could be another appropriate term. Darieva (2004, 262ff) concludes her book arguing that the language Russian becomes a super-ethnic collective identity category free from the state-imposed ethnic markers used to mobilize readers of Russian language media.

(007-berlin.de n.d.). Besides the previously mentioned Russian language FM-radio station *Radio Russkij Berlin* there are Russian language shows on other radio and tv stations including on the now defunct *radiomultikulti*.

Not only do these forms of media demonstrate that emigrants retain a link to the home country/point of origin, but it also shows that there is a viable market for post-Soviet products – including cultural products in the new home as discussed in the previous chapter. This also enables Russian groups and performers to tour Berlin and Germany.

9.2 "Who are these guys from Svoboda?": The flow of music to Berlin

> Efr: "You see, it turns out that we have to travel a lot in order to work. When did we play the last concert in Piter? [...] In Moloko in the middle of April, and our next concert will only be on June 2nd [...] It is if you want to earn at least some more or less decent money for the concerts, then you have to do it that way. We still have to travel somewhere" [...]
> David-Emil: "So you play more in Berlin than here?"
> Efr: "In Berlin quite a lot more."
>
> (Efremenko 2005 – Russian: p. 322)

As Markscheider Kunst's vocalist Efr pointed out, the band travels often in order to earn money – even playing more often in Berlin than at home (at least that year). Since traveling to Europe is expensive, the group plays several concerts in different cities – not only catering to the market of emigrants but also broadening their visibility. This has been aided by the success of the *Russendisko* which is, as mentioned, closely linked to Wladimir Kaminer's success as an author of emigrant literature and other events drawing from the *Russendisko's* popularity. In his books which are originally written in German, Kaminer also touches on post-Soviet popular music, thereby increasing the music's visibility outside the post-Soviet migrant community which in terms of the arena-model went from *offstage* to *onstage* (Lundberg et al. 2003).

Berlin can also look back at a tradition of Russian and Soviet history. As already mentioned Berlin was a center of Russian culture outside Russia in the 1920s. The link to the Soviet Union continued after World War II, with the presence of Soviet soldiers in East-Berlin and the German Democratic Republic's close ties to the Soviet Union for geopolitical reasons.

9 THE POST-SOVIET EMIGRANT COMMUNITY IN GERMANY 255

Finally, Berlin's role as a multicultural city should also be considered as a catalyst. Besides its history and low cost of living in the 1990s/early 2000s, one of the aspects that has made Berlin probably the most exciting multinational and vibrant European capital today, is its openness to events that bring people of different origins together, thus facilitating cultural exchanges. *Karneval der Kulturen* (The Carnival of Cultures) and *Fête de la Musique* (The Celebration of Music) are probably the best known, but *radiomultikulti* and other events and institutions also contributed to these exchanges.

Markscheider Kunst is a good example of a band that draws on mixed crowds. Efr stressed that they do not want to play for emigrants. He mentioned this when discussing their first tour of the United States in 2005:

"For us it isn't interesting to go and play for emigrants. That is we, of course, would like to, in our calculations, function for a local audience. But now we went and played lets say within the line of the Russian Rock Club of America and everything was very, it was better than we expected."

(Efremenko 2005 – Russian: p. 322)

While they play for a mixed (in other words, non-emigrant) audience in Germany, their first mini-tour of the United States (which seems to have been through the *Russian Rock Club of America*) primarily attracted emigrants – who still make up an important primary market for many bands (especially ones not within the *Russendisko* style such as Akvarium).[226]

Due to emigration from the former Soviet Union, Berlin and Germany have become an attractive market for established and known groups from Russia and Ukraine to tour in – groups like the St. Petersburg bands Markscheider Kunst, Leningrad, Lia Minor, Iva Nova, Akvarium, and Dobranoch' can frequently be heard in Berlin (and Germany). Touring bands – a good example of how music flows aided by people – are only one way music travels and is introduced to a (potentially new) audience. In Berlin *Eastblok Music*, which specializes in releasing groups from Eastern Europe in Germany (and Europe), as well as stores like the Polish owned *Pigasus – polish poster gallery* (located right next to *Kaffee Burger*)

---

226. This can also be seen through who the *Russian Rock Club of America* invites. The target group is Russian speaking emigrants (Yaroshevskiy 2007) and many groups who have performed within their activities have been around since the 1980s and early 90s e.g. DDT, Akvarium, Raznye Liudi, Chizh & Co, Iu-Piter (Russian Rock Club of America n.d.). In other words, groups who the last Soviet generation have grown up listening to and who are not necessarily played at the *Russendisko*. Cf. also footnote 210 (p. 243) for bands touring in Germany for a Russian speaking audience.

which import and sell Russian (and other Eastern European) music, focus more strongly on the flow of media. While human agency is still involved (people traveling to Eastern Europe or negotiating with distributors and groups in Eastern Europe), the main product is a recorded medium. Finally, the internet also provides access to mediated music, especially from Russia, where much music can be found within the torrent networks as well as on the *ru-net* (the Russian-speaking part of the internet).

When asked how they acquire the music played at the *Russendisko*, Yuriy summed up these forms of flow quite well:

> Yuriy: There are always people who commute back and forth and we order it [music] because we try to maintain an overview of new stuff. Furthermore, we have gotten to know the musicians quite well since we had personal contact with them when we prepared [...] the Russendisko CDs and they always send us something. [...] So, we have personal contact and our sources. It is actually not that hard at the moment and you can also find a lot as MP3s in the internet.
> David-Emil: And do you also travel to Russia?
> Yuriy: Very rarely, *very* [stressed] rarely. Wladimir was just back for the first time in several years. I was also in Ukraine, right. But that is more of an exception, since, well, no big desire and no time.
>
> (Gurzhy 2005 – German: p. 313)

As the above quote shows both the flow of people traveling between the former Soviet Union and Berlin as well as media play an important role. Furthermore, they have established contact with the musicians who also send/transmit their music either personally when on tour or through intermediaries. This network works so well that they rarely have to go back to Russia or Ukraine to acquire new music. Both Armin and Alex from *Eastblok Music* also pointed to networks and contacts who send them music, however they stressed traveling to Eastern Europe and buying recordings locally as an important element for them in acquiring new music (which makes sense since they cover a wider musical area than the *Russendisko* DJs). That said, they were not worried about finding new music, the pool to draw from was quite extensive (Kasparov and Siebert 2005).

In other words, the *Russendisko* itself has emerged as a node within the music network and is a place of exchange – visitors come up and talk to the DJs and give them music/demos, thus also placing the flow of music on the form of life level in direct interaction.

One example is how Svoboda flowed to Berlin with my help, which started with the following phrase: "Who are these guys from Svoboda? Are there more

MP3s to listen to?" (*Wer sind diese Jungs von Svoboda? Gibts da mehr mp3s zu hören?* – Yuriy Gurzhy, pers. comm., 12.08.2005)

Preparing my fieldwork in Berlin in August 2005 I had written to Yuriy and Kaminer. Yuriy answered within 30 minutes and asked about *Svoboda*.[227] I told him I was the group's trumpet-player and I could bring him a copy of *Svoboda*'s demo CD when I arrived. He replied that he really liked the music. Then, during the next e-mail exchange he wrote:

> "We would be happy to have Svoboda's Demo, Marusia is currently our big favorite :) What is the band currently doing?"
>
> (Yuriy Gurzhy, pers. comm., 23.09.2005 – German: p. 312)

As it turned out *Marusia* (at the time available on the group's website) was already being played at the *Russendisko*. Once I got to Berlin I interviewed Yuriy and gave him the demo CD. When I subsequently visited the *Russendisko* (08.10.2005) they played (at least) two of the songs (*Marusia* and *Choboty*) and Yuriy said that they had also played another song (*Pogoda*) on their monthly radio show *Russendisko Club mit Wladimir Kaminer und Yuriy Gurzhy* (*Russendisko Club with Wladimir Kaminer and Yuriy Gurzhy*) on *radiomultikulti*.[228] Thus *Svoboda* was recontextualized within an emigrant music event in Germany. A closer look at the music played at the event can cast some light on the selection processes present.

9.3 The *Russendisko*'s music

> "Geographically it is the 15 former republics [of the Soviet Union] or people who come from these republics, because I also try to pay attention to so called emigrant music"
>
> (Gurzhy 2005 – German: p. 313)

In order to examine the music played at the *Russendisko* it is necessary to situate the stage which provides the platform for the groups (Lundberg et al. 2003). As Yuriy's opening quote hints, the music played is selected geographically based on musicians from the former Soviet Republics, also if they live outside that geo-

---

227. I had not mentioned this in the correspondence. I suppose Yuriy had checked my home page and under "news" seen the link to Svoboda's website.
228. The playlist for October 8th 2005 lists the song as "Svoboda" by the group Svoboda released as a Demo (radiomultikulti n.d. with a playlist search for October 8th 2005).

graphic area. The emphasis on emigrant music (music created geographically outside the states of the former Soviet Union), was stressed by Yuriy and is supported by a cursory look at the released compilations and the music played at the event. The music is selected by the two DJs who thus function as *gate keepers*, both *backstage* (as *bouncers* selecting which groups to admit) and on *stage*, deciding what is included on stage and in playlists and what not. During the interview Yuriy was not too keen on defining the musical style:

> "What is very important: [...] the music here is context free, so to say. [...] Our taste is... Well, it is about good or bad music and not the music currently played or not played on the radio. [...] We don't draw on charts or similar things or what [...] currently is in or not in or out."
>
> (Gurzhy 2005 – German: p. 313)

While the music has been moved from a post-Soviet context, it is far from context free. Even though the listeners might not know the music they have certain expectations when going to an event advertised as *Russendisko* staged at *Kaffee Burger*. Within this context the music is ascribed a different meaning (influenced by the *Russendisko* DJs, German stereotypes of Russia, and what I label the *Russian folklore lineage* – discussed in the following chapter) from that ascribed by listeners in St. Petersburg.

Yuriy added that the best way to know what music they play was to look at who is included on the *Russendisko* compilations. Three of the previously discussed groups, Markscheider Kunst (Various Artists 2003b, 2004c, 2004b), Leningrad (Various Artists 2003b, 2004b) and Svoboda (Various Artists 2008c) are represented on the compilations and are often heard at the event. On a musical level, what these three groups have in common is that they all have a horn section and are inspired by ska (as well as reggae among other styles). Using the common characteristics of these three groups as a point of departure, can a *style indicator* be identified for the music played at the *Russendisko*? Asked again about the music played Yuriy replied:

> "Musically [...] I'm not too comfortable with musical styles. It's possible to say that it's somewhere between ska, reggae, folk, and, don't know, Balkan. [...] Exactly in our cross-over times it's hard, because the band playing ska today, will play hip-hop tomorrow."
>
> (Gurzhy 2005 – German: p. 314)

These styles overlap with the traits Alex mentioned when talking about the *Russendisko*'s music: that the main style is ska-punk and rock, and that the music should be danceable. Armin added that they also play some klezmer-inspired music, but that the music is mostly rock and pop, and not what is called electronic music nor other music styles (Kasparov and Siebert 2005).

If we compare Svoboda's *Marusia* with Leningrad's *SKA* (cf. p. 173/p. 188 respectively p. 167), there are some similarities: the use of horns (Svoboda: trumpet, trombone; Leningrad: trumpet, trombone, tuba, tenor saxophone, baritone saxophone), that play both melody and backings. Another similarity is heard in the guitar, which accents the off-beats supported by either the snare (Svoboda) or high hat (Leningrad). This rhythmic accompaniment is, as discussed in chapter 5, also known from the styles reggae and ska (but accents on the off-beats do not necessarily only refer to those two styles).

These *style indicators* are also present when listening to the compilations released[229] as well as heard at the *Russendisko*. Elements perceived as "folk" music from, amongst other places, Ukraine, Russia, and Moldavia as in *Marusia* are frequently incorporated (other indicators include the use of minor modes and the style of harmony singing). Another striking element at the *Russendisko* are songs that draw on music from the Balkans (use of horns, embellishing the melodies with for example trills, brassy timbre). Finally, the use of Russian and related Slavic languages affect the timbre of the vocalists. These elements are *Russendisko's* predominant *style indicators*.

However, this does not imply that the songs played belong to one homogenous style. The songs come from an eclectic mix of different groups covering different (sub)styles (e.g. rock, ska-punk, salsa, mambo, klezmer, folk rock, *blatnaia pesnia*) yet not always with the mentioned style indicators. Although playing with a horn section (trumpet, trombone, tenor saxophone) Markscheider Kunst's music is more influenced by mambo, salsa, and other Latin American rhythms. Furthermore, the DJs incorporate German popular music with links to Russia such as Boney M.'s *Rasputin* (Boney M. 1978) and Dschinghis Khan's *Moskau* and *Dschinghis Khan* (both Dschinghis Khan 1979), whose style indicators place them within popular music from the 1970/80s, especially Disco. This also includes old Soviet Songs (or covers) like VIA Volga-Volga's cover of *Moi adres – Sovetskii*

---

229. Especially for the groups Distemper, Leningrad, St. Petersburg Ska-Jazz Review, Rot Front, 5'Nizza, Svoboda, Haydamaky, Spitfire, Lyapis Trubeckoy, Skalariak, Male Factors, and Markscheider Kunst. The spelling reflects the transcription of the groups on the CDs. As of December 2013 the compilations were Various Artists (2003b, 2004c, 2004b, 2005c, 2008c, 2013).

Soiuz (My address is the Soviet Union – VIA Volga-Volga 2008) originally performed by the Soviet VIA Samotsvety around 1973 based on Vladimir Kharitonov's eponymous poem from 1971.[230]

The songs played also depend on the DJ. When a member of the Amsterdam Klezmer Band guest-dj-ed (22.07.2006), the style indicators of the music he used brought associations with klezmer music (acoustic, minor scales, embellishments on the melodies) and Russian groups playing in the style of Dobranoch'.

Other music not frequently played and not featured on the compilations but very present in Russia are groups which emerged and were popular during the Soviet period (*russkii rok*), such as Akvarium, DDT, and Alisa. Some of these groups which are still active today, such as Akvarium, occasionally tour Germany. Music styles also excluded include what in Russia is referred to as *estrada* (e.g. Alla Pugacheva, Filip Kirkorov) and the slightly overlapping *popsa* (e.g. VIA Gra, t.A.T.u., and the singer Zhanna Friske) which Yuriy referred to as "pop" (Gurzhy 2005).

To sum up, through filtering processes (personal taste, "disco-suitability") a consolidation of certain markers has emerged making the music played at the *Russendisko* a group of recognizable styles.

9.3.1 "Russian popular music" – a new sound?

Through the *Russendisko*'s focus on a non-emigrant audience, the participants are not necessarily exposed to other Russian popular music. They are mainly acquainted with the music played at the *Russendisko*. As mentioned above, the DJs select music based on their taste, which seems to encompass certain style indicators. *Eastblok Music*'s Armin and Alex said the music at the *Russendisko* contained

---

230. Samotsvety's version is grouped around drums, bass, and vocals where the drums imitate the sound of a train by playing sixteenth notes on what sounds like a closed high-hat. Different instruments and instrument groups (strings, saxophones, guitar) play fills at various times (which changes after each verse and refrain) – reminiscent of what in Western art music is called a *through-composed song*. Volga-Volga's versions fits more within the *Russendisko* characteristics mentioned above – especially in the refrain with the guitar and high-hat accenting the 1+, 2+, 3+, and 4+. The song is also more "coherent" in the instrumentation featuring a horn section (trumpet, saxophone, and maybe a trombone) consistently playing riffs assisted by an accordeon/baian. Unlike Samotsvety, the guitar is used as a rhythm, not melody instrument and is thus part of the rhythm section. Finally, the consistent sixteenth notes played on the high-hat reminiscent of a train is only present for 8 bars in the intro. Samotsvety's song is also alluded to in the refrain of Leningrad's *www* (Leningrad 2002).

typical Russian elements. This referred to a specific Russian rhythm, melody, language, melancholy, and passion (Kasparov and Siebert 2005). Furthermore, when I asked about the traits of Russian music in Russia, Armin noted the following:

"Yes, otherwise much local coloring and that I think is something special in a worldwide comparison, I mean for me there is something very special Russian, just out of my feeling and if somebody could position that [on the market], just like Latino music managed to accomplish in the last 20 years, then I see a chance that Russian music will become a synonym for a certain sound and that would be good."
(Kasparov and Siebert 2005 – German: p. 315)

In other words, they see a possibility of creating a genre of Russian (or post-Soviet) popular music based on the criteria mentioned above within the *Russendisko* context. This is an interesting marketing move since it replicates and builds on the style indicators which characterize the *Russendisko* as well as taking advantage of a lack of competing events promoting different post-Soviet popular music to a non-emigrant audience. These style indicators are not only referred to on a discursive level, but are also reflected musically in four of *Eastblok Music's* released albums (Haydamaky 2006, 2008; Leningrad 2006; La Minor 2009). In addition, elements of this style can also, to some extent, be heard in the *BalkanBeats* compilations (Various Artists 2005a, 2006a, 2008a) and the album by the Hungarian group Little Cow (2007). Thus, the style indicators mentioned by Armin and Alex could equally signify a broader Eastern European genre (as Yuriy's reference to "Balkan" in the quote on p. 258 also hints at).

The *Russendisko* and *Eastblok Music* play an important role in filtering what groups are played in Germany, thus creating a recognizable sound for the *Russendisko's* and other events' participants. A specific "Russian" sound still remains a distant goal and reducing *Eastblok Music's* releases to music within these style indicators would simplify their catalogue: both the compilations *Ukraina – Songs of the Orange Revolution* (Various Artists 2005e) and *café sputnik – electronic exotica from russia* (Various Artists 2005b) touch other musical styles and genres as well. *Ukraina – Songs of the Orange Revolution* also reflects a different marketing strategy by drawing on a then current event, the *Orange Revolution* in 2004. But Armin's words point to a development in Germany and Austria: There seems to be a consolidation of specific style indicators which is referred to as *Balkan* – something I will return to in the following chapter – which also includes the style indicators mentioned here. Instead of a specific nationality (Russian) this is regionally applied where Russia, while historically not a part of the Balkans, is included.

9.4 Asymmetries in the flow

One of the differences between Hannerz's concept of transcultural flows and Appadurai's concept of global flows within his system of scapes is how the flows are structured: While Hannerz retains a sense of center – periphery relations ("I doubt, however, that we are at a point when it has become entirely impossible to tell centers and peripheries apart" – Hannerz 2000, 6), Appadurai argues that these flows are increasingly following non-isomorphic paths and that the different flows (or scapes) are in disjuncture with each other – making the flows unpredictable (Appadurai 1996) – a position the ethnomusicologist Mark Slobin (1993) also adopts.

While at first glance there is a sense of un-structuredness to these flows (e.g. the popularity of post-Soviet popular music in Berlin) a closer look reveals that we are dealing with a network of center and periphery relationships, where the relationship between these two points is marked by social power, material resources, and prestige (Hannerz 1996, 67). Hannerz refers to meanings and meaningful forms emerging within the continuum center-periphery as creole culture, being "a combination of diversity, interconnectedness, and innovation" (Hannerz 1996, 67).[231]

Hannerz's model seems more precise – at least here – since it also enables us to look at different existing paths of circulation: Russia is embedded within different subnetworks of center and peripheries e.g. Germany or the United States. Looking at Russia from the perspective of cultural production it is a center within the former Soviet Republics with Russian-language popular music being available in the former republics. However in Europe it belongs to the periphery, where there is a stronger flow of Western European and US-American cultural products to Russia than from Russia to Western Europe (the main exception being the Russian faux lesbian group t.A.T.u.).

---

231. Another, probably more often applied, term with a similar meaning within popular music studies and ethnomusicology is *hybridity* (cf. p. 63).

At the same time the three countries are also embedded within the same global network with its center and peripheries relations. This can be seen in the flow of reggae and ska from a (colonial) periphery, Jamaica, to the former colonial center, Great Britain, with its large community of Jamaican migrants, and the United States. From these two centers the music then flowed to places like the Soviet Union which can be considered the periphery here and from there to Germany.

This also leads to looking at the flows as not a free for all, but as asymmetrical. For the flow of humans, one important group is international migrants. As I have previously discussed, both St. Petersburg and Berlin are attractive for migrants, albeit different ones. While St. Petersburg (and Moscow) are centers in a post-Soviet reality, mainly attractive to migrants from the former Soviet Republics and Chinese citizens, Berlin (and Germany) have, due to liberal immigration laws for ethnic Germans/Russians of German descent (*Spätaussiedler*) and Jews from the former Soviet Union, become very attractive to citizens of the former Soviet Union – making the two Russian metropolises part of the periphery.

This also relates to how post-Soviet music flows *to* Germany while at the same time music produced by post-Soviet emigrants living in Germany does not necessarily flow back to e.g. Russia. Most of the people I talked to in Berlin mentioned that neither emigrant music nor the *Russendisko* would be especially interesting for an audience in Russia. There have been some emigrant bands that performed in St. Petersburg/Moscow (e.g. Gogol Bordello and Red Elvises – both based in the United States), but such occurrences are rare. This music is the link to the emigrant's origin and thus more interesting within the post-Soviet emigrant community. Finally, the DJs in Germany also act as filters (gate keepers) since they select the music presented to a wider audience. These factors make Berlin a musical periphery in comparison to St. Petersburg/Moscow in terms of post-Soviet migrant music.[232] At the same time, Germany is a center regarding other forms of popular music produced in Germany and groups from Germany which flow to Russia (e.g. Rammstein).

The financial flows are also asymmetric. Being played at the *Russendisko* and similar events is a chance for Russian groups to heighten their visibility, tour

---

232. Slobin (1993, 18) raises a similar point when discussing how music links diasporic communities: He argues that Polish polka bands in the American diaspora have different local styles, some which dominate others. These stylistic differences have, however, no influence on Polish polka bands in the homeland.

abroad, make their music known to a non-emigrant audience, and, hopefully, earn more money than they could in Russia. As mentioned above Markscheider Kunst plays more concerts in Germany than in Russia. As discussed, there is a lack of clubs in St. Petersburg which fit the band's requirements. Another reason for this is the financial limitations in Russia – the country is big and it is even for established St. Petersburg bands discussed in chapter 3, such as Markscheider Kunst, too expensive to tour there without a sponsor. Finally, their visibility and thus popularity outside of the centers St. Petersburg and Moscow, is limited, which also limits the ability to perform without a sponsor to cover eventual losses. On the other hand, it is economically viable to rent a bus and tour Germany and Europe two to four times a year, as Markscheider Kunst and other bands do. This enables them to secure financial stability enabling them to pursue their creative work, which they would not necessarily achieve as musicians in Russia due to the financial and infrastructural limitations already mentioned.[233]

The possibility to tour, however, only exists for groups with the necessary financial means and contacts. For example, while Sasha dreams of playing abroad, Svoboda does not have these possibilities. Besides the fact that some of the band members lack *zagranpasporty* (foreign passports), the initial costs are too high to risk going on tour. Furthermore, the lack of contacts in Europe to organize the tour further limits their (and other groups') possibilities. Recording and distributing music while earning money from the distribution is not very likely either:

"Given the problems of piracy, however, and the related unwillingness of many Russians to actually pay for anything, record labels, regions, and radio stations have invested little time or money in funding CD production. Concerts guarantee (most of the time) cash in hand; discs do not."

(MacFadyen 2008)

As the quote from the Slavist David MacFadyen's blog on Russian popular music argues and my own observations also show, recordings in Russia tend to be used to promote bands, not necessarily to earn money, partially due to rampant

---

233. Guilbault (2001) touches on similar issues when discussing transnational Caribbean musicians: They lead transnational lives and are internationally successful, which lead the inhabitants of their home society to believe that the musician's local needs are satisfied. This is not the case and thus the transnational way of life is reinforced, because the musicians cannot support themselves in their home country. Furthermore, she points out that "Caribbean superstars, as transnationals, are dependent upon Caribbean diasporic populations and organisations for their living" (Guilbault 2001, 189).

pirating.[234] Ironically, Armin from *Eastblok Music* stressed the difficulties in releasing material from Eastern Europe in Germany:

"The list of stuff we could publish is huge. That is not the problem. It is much harder to sort out the rights, to organize everything legally and also to figure out [...] what could work [in the market] here."

(Kasparov and Siebert 2005 – German: p. 315)

While the major record labels have license and distribution deals with local Russian and Ukrainian labels (e.g. EMI's licensee was *Comp Music Ltd.* in Ukraine and *Gala Records* in Russia), the Russian labels are not necessarily distributed outside the post-Soviet territory – one of the reasons for *Eastblok Music* to establish itself – but at the same time showing how the flow of music is limited.

These asymmetries regarding distribution are to some extent being leveled due to technological advances: On the production side, technology that enables remediaization is becoming more easily accessible and more affordable especially regarding home studios as well as computers with (pirated) sound studio software (at least in the big cities). Furthermore, while physical distribution of local groups in Russia remains limited, virtual distribution has become easier through the use of MP3-files and online music portals such as http://music.lib.ru and online communities such as *rutube, youtube, myspace, facebook,* and *vkontakte* – at least in order to raise a group's visibility (financially, piracy remains a major problem).

Finally, besides a heightened visibility at the *Russendisko* and similar events, the groups are not financially compensated for being played there (unless they are featured on one of the compilations).[235] They do, however, benefit from some organizational help from the actors in Germany (organizing concerts, promo-

---

234. Cf. Schuepp (2008) for a similar argument regarding Turkmenistan. According to statistics tracking the estimated losses due to copyright piracy for records and music provided by the International Intellectual Property Alliance (IIPA) the level of piracy peaked in 2005 with an estimated 67% of the market being pirated (and a claimed loss of 475.9 Mio USD). In 2007 58% of the market belonged to pirated recordings (with a claimed loss of 313 Mio USD). The complete numbers from 2001 to 2007 are (in Mio USD and % of market): 285.0 – 64% (2001), 371.9 – 66% (2002), 405 – 64% (2003), 411.9 – 66% (2004), 475.9 – 67% (2005), 423.0 – 65% (2006), 313.0 58% (2007). The statistics are taken from the IIPA's annual Special 301 Recommendations, which only provide numbers up to 2007 – the situation has, however, not improved according to the 2014 report (International Intellectual Property Alliance n.d.). These statistics should also be read with caution since the IIPA lobbies on behalf of the music industry.
235. Svoboda received a one time payment of 250 Euros in addition to some copies of the CD for being featured on the sampler *Ukraine do Amerika* (Ukraine to America – Various Artists 2008c).

tion), who also profit from the *Russendisko* as one of their income sources. The audience profits as well, since they have access to new and potentially unfamiliar music otherwise closed to them.

9.5 Concluding remarks

The aim of this as well as chapter 5 has been to complicate the notions of cultural flows. While Appadurai's (1996) scapes-model provides a good point of departure for examining cultural phenomena, Hannerz's approach offers a more nuanced view since the latter introduces aspects of power and access within his four frames. Another point is that while there are instances of non-isomorphic paths with different flows/scapes in disjuncture to each other, many processes celebrated as global and non-predictable draw on existing/older center-periphery relations which are also linked to questions of power and access. This has been demonstrated here with post-Soviet emigration to Germany, where Germany's history as well as targeted simplified immigration policies play a role in attracting specific groups (ethnic Germans and Jews). In other words, these cultural flows follow certain paths of migration which in some way or another are predetermined and have historical and social reasons, The German government's role in attracting post-Soviet migrants also demonstrates that the nation-state has not lost its importance – a point better reflected in Hannerz's than in Appadurai's model.

What makes the discussion tricky is that center-periphery relations are relational depending on the perspective (which makes Appadurai's non-isomorphic paths an attractive, but misleading alternative): The emergence of Berlin as a center for post-Soviet popular music fits with the city's reputation as a center for the creative arts due to low costs of living in part due to a wide availability of cheap housing. Within this line of thinking the emergence of the *Russendisko* can be explained as a result of several coincidences where the city has functioned as a catalyzer.

While the event fits Berlin's creative image as one of Europe's avant-garde and "hip" cities, it is, when looking from the perspective of the emigrant community (who listen to other musics and frequent other events – cf. chapter 8), actually part of a periphery in terms of post-Soviet popular music. Here the main centers are St. Petersburg and Moscow. This center-periphery relationship is also seen in the primarily one-way flow of post-Soviet popular music from the former Soviet Union to Germany aimed at the migrant market. While the popularity of the music played at the *Russendisko* will probably fade over time, the ties the emigrant community has to the former Soviet Union will remain – including their ties to popular music. It remains, however, to be seen if the community over time will consolidate itself as a diaspora or if the emigrants will slowly assimilate. Thus, within a German and European context Berlin today remains a regional center of post-Soviet popular music.

The flow of music also points to one of the differences between the developments in St. Petersburg and Berlin. In St. Petersburg this has primarily been through music people have heard through media (determined through what has been broadcast on radio/tv or stored and thus transported to St. Petersburg on recordings), live concerts (which, however, presupposes an audience to make a tour profitable), and musicians who, through touring Europe and the United States, have come in contact with other music and musicians. This has influenced local bands who have been inspired by the music. In Berlin these elements are also present, especially with the large emigrant community, who provide a base audience for concerts. The agency of the *Russendisko*-DJs and the *Eastblok Music* owners, however, have played an important role in promoting the music to a *new audience* thus enabling its popularity (as has Kaminer's success as an author).

A central component of their agency is filtering the music where a narrow selection of Russian (and post-Soviet) popular music is played based on specific criteria. A similar argument could be made regarding ska and reggae in St. Petersburg, based around the key local actors. The second generation groups like Svoboda exemplify one way such a filtration can develop a new local tradition over time.

This process of reducing musical diversity is similar to that of musical revivals where certain stylistic traits and key performers are elevated through the revival and thus become part of the discourse around the music (cf. Livingston 1999; Wickström 2003). Another parallel specific for Berlin is that the music has been made available to a new social group that attribute new meanings to the music.

While the discussion here has focused on how music has been transported over time and space between locations, I have not focused in detail on what (new) meanings arise when the music that was "grabbed out of the torrent" (Diehl 2002,

11) is performed within its new locality. While the *form* of the music remains similar, the *content* ascribed by the new groups playing the music as well as their audience shifts – in part colored by more specific local and regional discourses. This will be examined in the following chapter based on the reception of Russian folklore in Germany.

10 Post-Soviet popular music in Germany

As I have discussed above, Russian popular music is not limited to the post-Soviet sphere but has become a part of transcultural flows to Europe, Israel, and the United States. While the previous discussions have been limited to describing the phenomenon itself and associated filtering practices, this discussion will focus on the musical shift of meaning accompanying recontextualization in a new location, specifically Berlin and Germany/Austria. While the conventions from popular music can be interpreted by listeners in Germany, more local and regional codes such as the groups' positioning used within the Russian market and references to Soviet popular culture are lost. Instead another group of collective memories sets in, drawing on German stereotypes of Russia and Ukraine as well as on broader stereotypes of *the East*. The bands become labeled *Russian* as implied by the term *Russendisko*, and thus *exotica from Russia* – for Berlin listeners.

While Svoboda already uses Ukraine to promote itself as a recognizable *Other* in St. Petersburg, the form of exotization changes into a Pan-Russian/-Slavic one at the *Russendisko*. This also applies to groups like Markscheider Kunst, who shift from a perceived Latin-American-African identity (based on their style and former singer Seraphim) to a Russian-Latin-American one. Leningrad is perceived as a group of everyday working-class male Russians (smoking, drinking, cursing) in Russia – as something the listeners there can identify with (a Russian male collective identity) – and remain Russian. However they lose the specific Russian details and become exotically Russian based on origin rather than content. Thus listeners in Berlin who do not speak Russian or know Russia find other ways to identify with the groups since they cannot identify with the groups based on shared (Russian) local experiences, references, and command of language.

In the following, I will first place the *Russendisko* within a German and Western European reception history of Russian folklore (what I label the *Russian folklore lineage*[236]), then focus on how the *Russendisko* creates an exotic identity for its German listeners. I conclude the chapter by placing this development within the

---

236. I use this term since it is based on a stylized perception of Russian traditional music.

broader frame of *BalkanBeats* – which also enjoyed popularity in Germany and Austria during the 2000s.

10.1 *Kasatchok Superstar*: The European Russian folklore lineage

As the musicologist Marina Frolova-Walker (2007) argues, one version of *Russian national character* to emerge in the 19th century and to be exported abroad focused on an exotic and orientalist style. It emerged from the musical lineage Glinka – *Kuckha* (the group of St. Petersburg based composers centered around Mili Balakirev) and was promoted by the impresario Diagilev at the turn of the 20th century in Paris.[237]

Russian literature, however, produced a different notion of *Russian national character*: Inspired by Herder and emerging Romantic nationalism, writers following Pushkin (e.g. Gogol, Dostoevskii, Chekhov) explore aspects of what becomes known as the *Russian soul* – an abstract concept associated with melancholy and tragedy. This has also often become associated with Russian folklore, as the following excerpt from a 1957-*Don Cossack Choir's* playbill shows: "Melancholic music from the wide Russian home, simple folk songs, delicate lullabies, ballads" (*Melancholische Musik der weiten russischen Heimat, schlichte Volksgesänge, zarte Wiegenlieder, Balladen* – qtd. in Kucher 2007, 67).

There has been a European reception history of imagined Russian folklore which is closely linked to the Russian revolution and resulting emigration. This tradition differs musically from the Russian art music promoted by Diagilev by focusing on Russian folksongs/folklore, Cossack songs, military marches, and religious choral music, as well as by playing on the *Russian soul*. The probably first successful group in this lineage was Serge Jaroff and his *Don Cossack Choir*, founded in 1921 in Turkey with exiled Cossack officers who had fought with the

---

237. The musicologist Richard Taruskin points out that the musical trope *nega*, which emerged in the Glinka-*Kuchka* tradition as a sign for the East and *Other* in Russia, became a metaphor for Russia for a French audience through Diagilev's promotion of Russian music (Taruskin 1997, 182). The Russian art music promoted by Diagilev (which was a selection and not a broad cross section of Russian art music in general) was in Paris seen as exotic and colorful by its European audience. This also removed the music played from its Russian context where e.g. the *Kuchka* distanced themselves from the urbanized *protiazhnaia pesnia* (drawn-out song) of Glinka and their contemporaries. Instead they tried to find a more "authentic" and "uncontaminated" layer of traditional music by returning to the villages to collect music (Frolova-Walker 2007).

White army. This (and the music they sang) appealed to Russian emigrants who made up a considerable base of their audience. Living in Germany until the Second World War and then in the United States, the group not only extensively toured Europe and North America, but also South America, Australia, and New Zealand with enormous success. They also released several recordings and were featured both in German as well as in Hollywood movies. The ensemble's period of activity ended in 1979 (Kucher 2007).

Other Central- and Western-European-based Cossack choirs emerged from 1924 onward. In 1928 the Soviet Union had a similar male choir and dance ensemble linked to the Red Army (Kucher 2007, 66). This lineage also included instrumental groups like Evgeni Pavlovski's Balalaika orchestra,[238] ethnic Germans expelled after the Second World War like the singer Alexandra, or pseudo-Russians like the German singer Ivan Rebroff (aka Hans-Rolf Rippert).

Not only limited to male choral music and associated folklore dance groups, this lineage evidently influenced popular music: The song *Casatschok* which refers to a Cossack folk dance in 2/4 (Lehmann 2008) provides a good example of (popular) music production in the 1960s and of how this music spread to other European countries and local languages: The Bulgarian singer Boris Rubaschkin made an arrangement in 1967 which by 1969 had been licensed and covered in Denmark, Sweden, France, Spain, and Germany (coverinfo.de n.d.).

Images of Russia and Russian folklore also had an impact on the disco styles of the 1970s – especially the choreography and costumes. Remains of this can be heard at the *Russendisko* today: Boney M's *Rasputin* (1978), Dschinghis Khan's *Moskau* and *Dschinghis Khan* (both 1979) are regularly played at the event. The Austrian group EAV's *Die Russen kommen* (EAV 1997) also draws on this lineage by imitating the male Cossack choirs as well as a balalaika and by singing with a fake Russian accent (including Russian words like *na zdorov'e* and *russkii [sic] mafia*).

Musically this tradition is kept alive today both through visiting choirs such as the numerous *Don Cossack Choir*-copies (cf. Picture 19) and the Red Army choir, as well as through German and Austrian groups. While some of the musicians have ties to the Russian community, they simultaneously draw on the persisting

---

238. Based in Copenhagen, the orchestra is still active.

folklore lineage. Two of them are Apparatschik and Russkaja which are regularly played at the *Russendisko*.

Picture 19: *Bolschoi Don Kosaken* concert poster. Picture taken in Berlin in 2009.

10.1.1 Apparatschik

"Descendants of these emigrants formed a band in the West that loudly but sensitively draws attention to the unique musical culture of Machorka Tabakistan: Apparatschik"

(Apparatschik 1994)

Hailing from the (fictive) island *Machorka Tabakistan* situated between Russia and Alaska on the 180° longitude, the group Apparatschik plays *Volxmusik*.[239] Using Russian sounding names like Oljeg Marosow/Matrosov, Desto Trotzki, and Ivan Matrosov,[240] the musicians blend Russian folklore with a rock idiom, continuing the Russian folklore lineage. These references to Russian folklore include *balalaikas* (a *prima* and a *bass balalaika*) and a *baian*. Furthermore, they perform in Soviet uniforms, traditional shirts like *vyshivankas* and *tel'niashkas* (blue and white striped shirts worn by Russian sailors) and during concerts use Russian phrases between songs, creating an audiovisual connection to what they claim is *Machorka Tabakistan* – an allusion to Russia.

The band's leader is the German Olaf Opitz (aka Oljeg Marosow/Matrosov). Olaf, who speaks some Russian, studied guitar at the popular music department of the conservatory in Dresden. He started playing what he called Russian music around 1987/88 and founded Apparatschik around 1988/89. Its shifting line-up consists of both Germans and post-Soviet emigrants.[241] Based in Berlin, they primarily tour Germany, Austria, and Switzerland. Currently about 80% of Apparatschik's songs are based on Russian folksongs (his term)[242] which are then adapted while 15-20% are self-composed songs (Opitz 2006).[243]

---

239. A reference to *Volksmusik* – Folkmusic.
240. *Moroz* is Russian for frost and *matros* is Russian for sailor. The suffix *-ov* is commonly used in Russian surnames. *Trotzki* is a reference to the Russian/Soviet revolutionary Lev Davidovich Trotskii, born Lev Davidovich Bronshtein, who was hounded and finally murdered with an ice pick by Stalin's agents in Mexico. Together with *desto* it in German also takes on the meaning more defiant (*desto* meaning more, bigger and *Trotzki* being a russification of *Trotz* – defiant). *Ivan* is one of the default names used for male Russians when referred to by foreigners.
241. When I heard them perform in Vienna (13.07.2007), the *balalaika*-player was from Ukraine and the *baian*-player from Belorus. The drummer was German.
242. These include (their titles) *Valenki, Katia, Poliushko, Marusia,* and *Kalinka – Kalinka,* which is one of the best known Russian folk songs, is included in a live version on the second *Ost Klub* compilation (Various Artists 2007c).
243. Olaf added that he originally did not want to write his own songs. This step was taken due to the rising popularity of Russian traditional music and bad experience with people copying his concept and arrangements. By writing his own songs he has more control over

Picture 20: Apparatschik. The band performing at *Ost Klub* in Vienna (13.07.2007).

---

the use of his material through copyright protection (while arrangements offer some protection, traditional music itself is in the public domain thus not covered by copyright).

Drawing on German clichés of Russia and Russian folklore, Apparatschik offers a new twist to how Russian folklore is performed and seems to be quite successful with that. This has also inspired other bands, who copy the approach (such as the Berlin-based bands Cosmonautix and Bloody Kalinka which I will not discuss here).

10.1.2 Russkaja

While Apparatschik still remains close to the folklore roots, the Vienna-based group Russkaja provides a good example of the general idiom heard at the *Russendisko* (cf. p. 257ff) while at the same time using the folklore elements as an additional kitsch factor. Their 2008 debut album *Kasatchok Superstar* (Russkaja 2008) includes a DVD with clips from different live performances, one being the Viennese *Donauinselfest* on June 24th, 2007:

After seeing the band jamming on the stage, the drummer makes a short announcement in Austrian with a fake Russian accent,[244] followed by a break which ends on an e-minor chord with the e used as a pedal tone. Slowly entering the stage, the vocalist Georgij Makazaria sings the opening refrain to *The Volga Boatmen's song*, a traditional Russian song, twice. Instead of going down a fourth the second time he sings the refrain, he ends the last word (*raz* – one) a fifth up – in other words, an octave higher. The word is sustained and extended to a scream, transitioning the song to Russkaja's *Barabany* (Drums). While the band vamps over the opening riff to *Barabany*, the vocalist Georgij Makazaria screams "Let's go guys, ignite [unclear] the group Russkaja" (*Davai rebiata, zazhigaem [unclear] gruppa Russkaja*).

Not only the choice of material is important here, but also the performance style: Russkaja's vocalist clearly adheres to the style of Ivan Rebroff (and the cliché of deep-Russian operatic basses like Fedor Shaliapin), using full chest voice and starting in the low-range when singing the traditional tune.[245] His posture is calm as he stands almost motionless with outstretched arms. The shift to the song *Barabany* is both audible (through the scream) and visual with the vocalist breaking

---

244. Earlier on the DVD the drummer is heard speaking accent-free Austrian.
245. During a talk in Vienna in April 2008 one of the comments I got was that Georgij Makazaria looked a little like Ivan Rebroff – both have a beard, are well built (but not heavy) and have the same facial form.

his static pose, ripping his arms over his head and then dancing. *Barabany* fits well into the *Russendisko*-idiom by using a horn section over a ska-punk beat.

Picture 21: Russkaja's *Kasatchok Superstar* promotion sticker. Picture taken in Vienna in 2008.

The name of the album, *Kasatchok Superstar*, as well as the graphical layout clearly allude to this lineage. The album cover depicts the group's members each crouched down on one leg with the other leg kicked out while their arms are folded and kept perpendicular to their chest (stereotypically referred to as *Cossackdance*). The other side of the digipack (and stickers which were visible all over Vienna during my visit in April 2008 – cf. Picture 21 and the bottom part of Picture 22) depicts a silhouette of a dancer with the same pose.

Both Russkaja and Apparatschik thus help maintain stereotypes of Russians as an exocticized *Other*. This is not limited to the musical level, but includes the use of outfits which are clearly recognizable as "Russian" (either traditional clothes or navy/red army uniforms and accessories) as well as through speaking German with a Russian accent/syntax.

10.1.3 Irrational East: Russians as an exocticized *Other*

The promotion used is also an important factor in maintaining stereotypes of Russians, as demonstrated by this advertisement for a Russkaja concert at the Viennese *Ost Klub* November 4th, 2005:

"It is like a hurricane which, coming from the East at top speed, is racing towards one and grips one. Without mercy. Nobody other than the group RUSSKAJA is behind this 'nature phenomenon'. A mind-blowing ensemble with seven mind-blowing musicians from Russia and Austria who strike up to play like a storm, carries one away, and ecstatically gets the audience to dance. Because ska is interpreted by RUSSKAJA in such a forceful Russian manner one thinks that one is strapped to a vodkafilled sputnik-rocket and with that breaks the sound barrier. And because vodka at RUSSKAJA's concerts is also poured at top speed the audience can – at the latest at the encore – speak Russian fluidly and knows what it is like to dance pogo on the Red Square."

(OST * Klub n.d. – German: p. 333)

This announcement from *Ost Klub*'s website links what is portrayed as an emotional, hence savage, irrational, and feminized group from the East (in other words, a potentially dangerous *Other*) with such seductive powers that it even brings a "rational" Austrian audience to ecstasy. This irrationality is created by references to nature (nature phenomenon, play up like a storm, hurricane) which are linked to a vague East. Later this is identified as Russia through vodka, a sputnik-rocket [sic], and the Red square in Moscow. The Russianess is so profound that even Russkaja's interpretation of ska drips with Russianess (whatever that means). The announcement is, however, inclusive since it says that everybody can become Russian (including becoming fluent in Russian) by consuming enormous quantities of vodka. Through the concert the listeners can even experience a visit to Moscow. In other words, by becoming intoxicated the audience also has a chance of becoming irrational (another possible explanation is that Austrians are so artificial and uptight that they need alcohol to become "normal"/natural).

Clearly being a marketing ploy, the promotion should be read with some ironical distance. The clichés which are drawn upon (naturalizing the East, emotional/irrational Russians, alcohol as a tool for irrationality) reflect, however, on those present in Germany and Austria – especially the link to vodka. These are also recycled at the *Russendisko* and are not targeted at emigrants from the former Soviet Union, but at Germans and Austrians.

10.2 *"False Russians"*: The stereotyped strike back

> "The location *Russendisko* can/should more be seen as an exotic playground similar to the salsa-disco, provided by the 'good culture Russian' in the Western metropole."
> (Darieva 2004, 109 – German: p. 311)

What makes the *Russendisko* interesting is its play on stereotypes through the use of Russian and Soviet kitsch elements: Vodka is served at the bar, TV-screens above the dance floor show Soviet cartoons and movies, and the promotion posters used for the event are slightly altered (propaganda) posters from Soviet and Tsarist Russia. At *Kafe Burger* the preserved East German interior also contributes to this, turning the location into an *exotic playground,* as Darieva points out in the above quote.[246]

Traces of these Russian stereotypes can be found in the music played at the event as well as their CD releases – most directly on the compilation CD *Radio Russendisko* (Various Artists 2005c). The CD includes a cover of Boney M's *Rasputin* played by Berlin-based Dr. Bajan (Nikolai Fomin, he is also the vocalist

---

246. There is an ongoing mini debate about the *Russendisko* being part of the broader *Ostalgie*-phenomenon, a nostalgia for the former GDR. While the Soviet Union and the GDR shared cultural references (cartoons, movies, art styles etc.) and the *Russendisko's* romanticizing of Soviet propaganda imagery, the location, and its interior enables such an interpretation, the event clearly does not play on images from the GDR and a longing for that past. I agree with Bottà who writes: "An insight into Kaminer's work shows its actual distance from this phenomenon [Ostalgie], which is bound to a post-reunification desire for Heimat, solidarity, and tradition. Ostalgie is not sufficient to explain Kaminer's efforts or the 'Russian mania' as a whole, as its above-mentioned intercultural dimension is far from the idealisation of a German monocultural past." (Bottà 2006a, 7)

in Bloody Kalinka) as well as Alexandra's *Schwarze Balalaika* (Black Balalaika, originally from 1968) and Apparatschik's *Kürbis* (Pumpkin, based on traditional lyrics, but with their own melody).

The CD also picks up on these stereotypes and the Russian folklore lineage by playing with "false identities", the theme of the CD (which, produced in the form of a radio show, mixes songs with Wladimir Kaminer's short stories). The following quote targeting Apparatschik is a good example of this:

"For me the band Apparatschik is, by the way, a good example of successful integration: Well, they are the best, the best false Russians I have ever met. Very authentic!"
(Various Artists 2005c, Tr. 12 – German: p. 314)

Another example is one of the stories on the CD. Inspired by the movie *Men in Black II* and the double identities of aliens living in human beings (e.g. Michael Jackson and Elvis Presley) Kaminer makes fun of Ivan Rebroff. He specifically targets Rebroff's record *Frühling in der Taiga* (Spring on the Taiga) whose cover is compared to the movie *Antichrist II* (probably *The Omen II*). After describing Rebroff's physical appearance (including eyes which emit a glowing madness – *glühender Wahnsinn*) Kaminer comes to the conclusion that Rebroff is an alien personifying the Russian soul. This Russian soul Rebroff discovered inside himself as a child on a farm (here Kaminer seems to be referring to Superman). Other stories discuss (and make fun of) Boney M and Alexandra.

The discussion of fake identities also refers directly to debates in the 1990s and early 2000s regarding integration and stereotypes surrounding the ethnic Germans and Jews who settled in Germany. The state-imposed categories *ethnic German* and *Jew* as well as the ascribed German meaning linked to those categories, did not necessarily reflect the emigrants' identities and left little room for multiple or hyphenated identities. Based on a media analysis of major Russian-language newspapers in Berlin, Darieva (2004, 89ff) argues that the inconsistency between the official categories and the emigrants' own identities (and lack of integration/appropriation of the official values) contributed to a public debate which questioned the migrants' (imposed) ethnic identity. The concerning identity component was reduced and the migrants were lumped into the category *Russians*. In other words, since the emigrants did not live up to the expectations of the host country, their ethnic category was questioned (e.g. false Jews). This fits with another circulating stereotype of Russians as organized criminals.

This stereotype slowly shifted towards the end of the 1990s, being replaced by the *Kulturrusse* (culture Russian), partly in reference to the civil war émigrés of the 1920s and their cultural contribution to the city.[247] Through his success as an author, Kaminer almost embodies this romanticized notion of a culture Russian.[248] Despite his heavy Russian accent Kaminer also promotes an image of German over-identification, including owning a *Schrebergarten* (an allotment garden) and having expressed the desire to run for major of Berlin. The term at the same time creates a notion of the non-culture Russian who, if is not cultured, is probably savage...

One interesting aspect of Kaminer and Yuriy, is that they do not let themselves be passively labeled, but actively play with these stereotypes, throwing them back at the Germans and ridiculing them. By picking up the topic of fake (or false) Russians, Kaminer uncovers several forms of false Russians – in this case Germans.

In her article, Ellen Rutten (2007, cf. also Wanner 2005), primarily based on a literary analysis of the event and the booklets included with the compilations, argues that the *Russendisko* plays with German stereotypes of the "wild Russian", both on a textual as well as a symbolic level. The event thus parodies the German clichés of Russians, not the organizers or the event themselves. Besides the description of the event in their promotion and Kaminer's books, this "wild Russian" stereotype can also be found in the frequently played song *Moskau* (Dschinghis Khan 1979). The lyrics portray Russians as heavy vodka drinkers who throw their (empty) glass against the wall – a persistent (German) cliché of Russian alcohol consumption.

This form of promotion also affects the target group of the event. Discussing the use of Soviet and Russian symbols in Germany, Alex argued that the emigrants were not too interested but that the symbols were interesting for a German audience (cf. also Chernov 2003; Bottà 2006a; Rutten 2007 and chapter 8 regarding the target group):

---

247. Darieva (2004, 103) argues that this stereotype is also linked to the German model of multiculturalism where immigrants are seen as a cultural enrichment.
248. He has also become the most prominent example of successful integration – however not within the official category "jewish".

Alex: You can forget the Russians, Russians have no desire for these old things. You have big [unclear] for the Germans, the Russians want everything to be new, fancy – mostly, not all – but, it does not mean that much for Russians.
Armin: I'm not quite sure. Older Russians, I do think that they have a little nostalgia. Well, especially those who now don't have so much money. [...]
Alex: [...] For him [a Russian] it does not matter, for the Germans it is exotic, interesting.

(Kasparov and Siebert 2006) – German: p. 316

Bringing the discussion back to questions of representation, Rutten argues that the *Russendisko* caters to a non-emigrant audience through its conscious play on stereotypes and by reaffirming the (non-emigrant) self in opposition to the *Other*: "The Russendisko does not appeal to a 'We'-feeling, but to stereotypical perceptions of 'them', 'the Russians', 'the Others', 'the Foreigners.'" (Rutten 2007, 119 – German: p. 316)

10.3 The bigger picture: *Ost Klub* and *Balkanisierung*

These "Russians" are lumped together with other "foreigners" East (and South) of Germany, as e.g. demonstrated in the box-set titled *Beginner's Guide to Eastern Europe* (Various Artists 2007a), which contains three CDs respectively titled *Balkan Club, Balkan Brass & Gypsy Greats*, and *Eastern Bloc Rock & Fusion*. The cover of *Balkan Club*, however, depicts the St. Petersburg church *Spas-na-Krovi*. In other words, the geographical tag given to the CD (*Balkan*) does not correspond to the visual information given and no Russian/post-Soviet groups are featured on that CD.

This coupling of Balkan and Russia is, however, not unexpected. Besides post-Soviet popular music *Eastblok Music* has released three compilations of what they call *BalkanBeats* (Various Artists 2005a, 2006a, 2008a) and looking at the promotional material of post-Soviet emigrant bands based in Germany (e.g. SkaZka Orchestra, Rot Front) as well as clubs focused on those groups (e.g. *KGB Bar* in Freiburg, *Ost klub* in Vienna) the label *Balkan* alone or in combination (e.g. *Balkan Speed party, Balkan Klezmer Fusion, Balkan Gypsy Beats, Klezmer/Russian Folk/Balkan/Rock 'n' Roll*, and *Balkanisierungsparty* – Balkanization-party, cf. Picture 22) is quite often applied to post-Soviet groups.

Musically, as discussed in chapter 9, the groups also draw on elements from what is labeled Balkan music: fast playing horn sections with a brassy/rough timbre, scales which start with a minor second followed by an augmented second as well as klezmer (cf. also Yuriy's quote on p. 258).

Picture 22: Flyer from a *Balkanisierungsparty* featuring SkaZka Orchestra (*Supamolli*, 15.02.2008).

The above mentioned processes of exotization regarding Russians seems to be part of a larger process, including the Balkan states and Eastern Europe.[249] Within (German) popular music a general shift appears to be happening – away from an Arabian and Turkish-based orientalism to a romantic notion of the East (as in Eastern Europe). Musically this seems to be linked with a transition away from complex asymmetric rhythms or polyrhythms to symmetric rhythms with a clear indication of the beats.[250]

Closely linked to that is the music of one of Europe's internal (and heavily discriminated) Others, the Sinti and Roma, as well as music from Europe's South-East – as the following comment by *Ost Klub's* owner Matthias Angerer demon-

---

249. A prominent place where this conflation can be detected is the annual *Eurovision song contest* and the complaints in recent years from Western European countries that Eastern European groups are dominating.
250. This hypothesis is not based on a thorough examination of the music, just a hunch based on my own observations and feedback I have received when presenting this material (here I especially would like to thank Eva Fock and Anca Giurchescu for their comments). More research is needed here.

strates. Answering my question what the words "Russian" and "Balkan" mean for him in relation to music, he stressed much *passion* when playing, *virtuosity*, and the *instrumentation* (violin, accordion, horns). Furthermore, he said

> "I noticed [this] especially with the Gypsy-musicians: there you just notice that they so to say, sucked it [music] in with the breast milk [...] There the infant already, so to say, learns to play an instrument from the grandfather and that one notices in the playing. On the one hand one notices that they didn't study at any music-conservatory [...] Instead they just play with heart-blood, that many probably classically-trained musicians lack. They might be technically better, but never so... For me music just has much to do with passion and heart and if somebody really just gives everything and plays music, then there will always be more spirit transmitted than when somebody diligently plays the piece dryly."
>
> (Angerer 2007 – German: p. 311)

As in my critique above of Russkaja's concert promotion (probably written/ signed off by Angerer), Matthias Angerer naturalizes the Sinti and Roma musicians by stressing their *natural* way of learning (through breast feeding, by ear, in the family) in opposition to an *artificial* way linked to the conservatories. His description also draws on clichés linked to Sinti and Roma in popular music at weddings, in restaurants, and on the streets, where emotions are highly valued in contrast to the more reserved domains of Western art and church music.

This kind of rhetoric is not limited to Angerer and *Ost Klub* (and is made from a positive, multicultural stance, not a racist monocultural one). It also shows that the music played at the *Russendisko* and what is referred to as *BalkanBeats* not only seems to be on the same continuum, where boundaries overlap but in some places have become part of a conflation of Balkan and Russia. Here the label *Balkan* or (the more generic) *East* has been applied – as the name *Ost Klub* (East Klub) hints at:

> "The name of the place is, so to say, also its program, in other words, Eastern-European music or just Russian or music from the Balkans, but also further. The musical axis is for us, so to say, Vienna – Vladivostok [...] The East is wide and hence I think it also won't become musically boring too fast."
>
> (Angerer 2007 – German: p. 311)

While this conflation to the "wide East" can be looked upon as just another cultural trend which record labels, clubs, and musicians in Berlin as well as in Germany and Austria capitalize on, its underlying political message is troubling since it helps create a two-tiered Europe, which can be interpreted as a way to keep Russia (as well as Turkey, another country split between Europe and Asia) out. This is in part also seen by how both the European Union as well as NATO deals with Russia. It reflects an ethno- and religion-centric (as well as deeply egoistic) perspective of Western Europe which is more fitting of 19th century colonial powers than of the 21st century multicultural societies they in reality are.

10.4 Concluding remarks

As this final chapter has shown, the meanings discussed throughout this book are not fixed, but depend on the interpretation of the listener (whose opinion is also influenced by the promoted band image). This explains varying perceptions due to transcultural flows: Different audiences perceive music differently and embed bands in different local discourses – the *Russian folklore lineage* and the *Russendisko* provide a different reference frame to understand post-Soviet groups than what is present in a local St. Petersburg discourse by embedding them within specific German discourses. While Alisa, Gazmanov, and Piligrim draw on recognizable discourses when promoting their ideas of Russian national identities these would not necessarily be clear to a German audience.

This also demonstrates that transcultural flows do not necessarily contribute to a homogenization of world cultures since the meanings that emerge in the *form of life* and *market* frame reflect on specific local circumstances which are influenced by social networks, social hubs, and (discursive) scene boundaries, among other things. Here the focus on (musical) production plays a role since each location has its set of material conditions which also affect the creative work of the groups. Furthermore, taking migration patterns into account is important when looking at global flows since migrants and their offspring remain a major force in the circulation of cultural products. While the internet and social networking sites might change this, there are still barriers (language, different tonal and reference systems etc.) that limit circulation within a new audience group. This also means that a context sensitive approach to identities is essential in order to understand how they work in a given context. Thus an ethnographic approach – in this case as a participant-observing musician – provides an important tool when examining cultural production and circulation in social relationships.

Concluding words and outlook

A major motivation in choosing St. Petersburg as the main site of my research was that it allowed me to examine how music developed in a rapidly changing society. This development especially struck me in how much the city visually changed just between my first visit in 2002 and subsequent visit in 2004. Demonstrating Russia's economic recovery following the 1998 crisis as well as preparations for the city's 300th anniversary in 2003, these changes were in part aided by an increase in disposable income and availability of consumer loans to buy computers, televisions etc. This could literally be seen both in peoples' apartments as well as in the fact that huge shopping malls appeared throughout the city.

While these changes also affected the musicians, the music scene itself remained to some extent stable during that period. This is something the theoretical concept scene has helped show through its focus on different aspects of *music production*. While the most notable changes in St. Petersburg were clubs opening and closing, the *art direktors* responsible for the booking and who know the musicians did not change. Another reason for this stability is the fact that the actors in the scene were (and still are) not predominantly young teens, but encompass a wide age range including a large portion of middle age men – some of whom have been active since the 1980s. This especially applied to the more successful groups, but even in the "young" groups like Svoboda and Con Brio the youngest musicians were in their 20s. This supports Hesmondhalgh's (2005) argument that the commonly made link rock/pop and youth culture is not valid anymore.

Another point this book has made is that rock music in St. Petersburg today cannot be seen as a phenomenon outside of or in opposition to the general society as e.g. Cushman (1995) claims for Soviet rock. As the identity discussion has shown the groups not only reflect on scene internal discourses, but also participate in general societal discourses. Some of these discourses continue older discourses – especially regarding the general attitude towards the former Soviet republics which are still seen as a Russian sphere of influence. Post-colonial theory has provided a productive approach in pointing to Russia's desires by specifically focusing on relations to Ukraine through the perspective of Svoboda. Related to this are questions of representation – both trying to control one's own outward representation and how the *Other* is represented. These questions play an increasingly important role in a media-influenced society, in particular when relationships are tainted by conflicts and competing interests. Furthermore, marketing questions also play a role. By drawing on stereotypical representations known to the audience the cultural products can attract listeners. This is as much valid for St. Petersburg and Russia as it is for Berlin as I demonstrated with the *Russendisko* and related events.

At the same time the application of the theory here has demonstrated that a context sensitive approach is essential to understanding contemporary cultural processes. The *Russendisko* is thus not a coincidence of globalization, but provides a good example of transcultural flows which have been shaped by previous processes, in this case migration patterns which in part go back to the 18th century.

Reflecting on my fieldwork and writing these concluding words from a 2013 perspective – seven years after leaving Russia – the conclusion's opening statement remains valid: St. Petersburg as well as Russia both remain rapidly changing societies – both positively (as the increase in living standards for the majority of the population until 2008 has shown) as well as negatively (rising xenophobia, effects of the economic crisis). I experienced this shift personally during my visit to St. Petersburg in October 2008, which coincided with the economic crisis' ripples entering Russia. There was a feeling of insecurity that had become more prominent amongst those I talked to – especially since the effects of the crisis could be felt personally. The fewest I spoke with blamed the government for the crisis, but people were uneasy about what the future would bring and especially about how the government would handle the crisis. I was also asked about how the crisis was discussed in foreign media, hinting at a distrust for what the Russian media was disseminating. Andrei Ivanov was especially worried since he had just started to work as an *art direktor* in a new club. Due to his age (born 1960) he was concerned about how he would support himself if people started to save money and stopped going to concerts (while still working at the club he got a second job as a bank janitor in March 2009). This insecurity shifted to a more nationalist attitude among my musician friends during my last visit to St. Petersburg in August 2013 and included an unreflected Anti-Americanism, which was clearly fueled by the media (documentaries on TV about how America was responsible for atrocities in Syria, how Russian children adopted by Americans were mistreated etc.). The strategy employed by the media is to show how Russia is superior to other countries by focusing on the problems other countries have.

While I do not believe in Western fear mongering regarding Russia's future,[251] Russia faces several challenges where the problems musicians have to deal with (which I outlined in chapter 3) as well as that of the general working population are not granted high priority. These problems can also result in dramatic shifts in the next years. One of the Russian government's fears is that musicians could become part of a protest movement just like in the Orange revolution, where several music groups actively took part. This is one of the reasons government officials like Vladislav Surkov are courting *russkii rok*-musicians like Boris Grebenshchikov.

At the same time there are some constants that have remained since my departure both on a material level (musical infrastructure, the musicians' economic situation, active groups) as well as on a discursive level (*russkii rok*, underground vs. commercial, ideas of national identities and nostalgia as discussed above) and also a political level (while Medvedev's rhetoric was mostly milder than Putin's, his policies remained mostly a continuation of that of his predecessor's and successor's).

For future research this book's theoretical level can be a guide: The three overarching concepts (scenes, transcultural flows, identities) have served well as a framework for tackling popular music in St. Petersburg by both focusing on production at the local level and at the same time examining how different localities are connected. The use of identities as a point of departure for examining musicians and bands enabled me to incorporate the results from the scene perspective and at the same time look at how the identities shift through transcultural flows. It also allowed me to focus on nationalism, post-colonial theory, and diaspora from an identity perspective.

While this strategy answered many questions, this book also leaves questions unanswered and suggests new ones: In the wake of the recent economic downturn

---

251. This is especially aimed at doomsday predictions like the Eurasia Group's report "Fat Tails in an Uncertain World" (Eurasia Group 2009) which reeks of Western *Schadenfreude* over Russia's problems.

it would be interesting to examine its impact on the St. Petersburg scene in more detail. Within the scene there have been several changes – especially regarding the clubs – but at the same time many bands I examined are still active. However, they have also changed: I was surprised to find some St. Petersburg groups (including Banana Gang, a ska-group Svoboda often performed with and who had prior to that not distinguished itself as government critical) featured on a compilation (Various Artists 2007b) released by people close to the opposition group *Drugaia Rossiia* (Other Russia). Most of the songs on those compilations are (highly) critical of the current government. At the same time Svoboda recorded a NATO-critical song (Svoboda 2009b). Here an interesting approach would be to see how the economic climate has influenced the band images – including their attitude towards the government, nationalism, and xenophobia as well as how the government deals with the groups both promoting those they support and silencing those that take on a more problematic stance. This is not limited to direct government intervention but also includes clubs' booking policies, record labels etc. – in other words, the production side on a local level. At the same time a closer look at the audience is necessary to understand the relational aspect of these band identities and what meanings they create on the receiving side of the communication process.

Within the German emigrant community a stronger focus on the emigrants' music targeted at a Russophone audience would provide interesting material in examining their integration process and – in extension – providing more empirical material to re-examine the community as a diaspora – especially since many musicians today are either born in Germany or have spent a large part of their childhood there (in contrast to those I describe who came to Germany as young adults). Here it would also be interesting to examine what cultural resources they draw on and what role transcultural flows from Russia as well as the *Russendisko*-scene play in their lives. This would lead to a more nuanced theorization of personal identities. When examining the flows between Russia and Germany the discussion should be broadened to explore what impact the bands touring in Europe have on the local music production in St. Petersburg – this includes not only stylistic impacts, but also if the attitudes have changed regarding playing venues, salaries, ideas etc.

As I briefly discussed, the music played at the *Russendisko* also taps into a broader European popular music context, especially what is labeled Balkan music and *BalkanBeats*. Within the context of the yearly *Eurovision Song Contest* (ESC) Eastern European popular music has even been labeled a threat by West-European musicians (e.g. Neumann 2007). While the ESC should be examined critically and not be granted too much political and cultural weight, it would be interesting to compare entries based on their musical characteristics as well as the role the contest plays in Eastern Europe and the former Soviet republics. Here I am especially thinking about the ESC as a stage for post-colonial struggles as recent contributions from Ukraine, Georgia, and arguably Russia's 2009-contribution have shown. But also a wider, European perspective is important, because – as Solomon (2007) demonstrates with Turkey's 2003 contribution – the contest is also used to demonstrate a geographical and political affiliation with Europe.

While essentially being about popular music in St. Petersburg and Berlin this book's intention was to show how the local music production is embedded within local, national, and also European discourses. While Russia, due to its geographical position, both sees itself and is seen as a country which both is anchored in Europe as well as Asia, it remains an important part of Europe. Not disregarding the fact that its policies have to be addressed critically, a better understanding of Russia's history and culture is essential to enable us to live together in peace and stability.

Appendix A. Short biographies of people interviewed

The following section includes short biographies of the people I interviewed for the book. The biographies are based on the information provided by the people themselves, hence in some instances the names used are their stage names. This also explains why in some cases the date and place of birth are missing. The information regarding the groups they play in reflects the information at the time of my fieldwork so some musicians may currently play in different groups.

A.1 Matthias Angerer

born 1966, owner of the club *Ost-Klub*. Interview conducted in Austrian on July 13th, 2007 in Vienna.

A.2 Andrei Burlaka / Андрей Бурлака

born 1955 in Krasnoiarsk (Russia), music journalist and producer. Interview conducted in Russian on March 22nd, 2005 in St. Petersburg.

A.3 Sergei Chernov / Сергей Чернов

born 1960 in Leningrad, (music) journalist. Interview conducted in Russian on July 3rd, 2006 in St. Petersburg.

A.4 Elena Danilova / Елена Данилова

general director of *Nashe Radio* St. Petersburg. Interview conducted in Russian on June 21st, 2006 in St. Petersburg.

A.5 Sergei Efremenko / Сергей Ефременко

born 1972 in Leningrad, guitarist, vocalist, and lyricist in Markscheider Kunst. Interview conducted in Russian on May 25th and 26th, 2005 in St. Petersburg.

A.6 Evgenii Fedrov / Евгений Федров

born 1965 in Leningrad, bass-player and lyricist in the groups Tequilajazzz and Optimystica orchestra. Interview conducted in Russian on February 8th, 2006 in St. Petersburg.

A.7 Nikolai Fomin / Николай Фомин

born 1961 in Leningrad, *baian*-player in the group Dr. Bajan. Interview conducted in Russian on October 9th, 2005 in Berlin.

A.8 Yuriy Gurzhy

born 1975 in Khar'kov (Ukraine), guitarist and vocalist in the group Rot Front and DJ at the *Russendisko*. Interview conducted in German on October 5th, 2005 in Berlin.

A.9 Victor Harder

born 1969 in Ivanovka (Kyrgyzstan), accordion-player and vocalist in the group Cosmonautix. Interview conducted in German on July 24th, 2006 in Berlin.

A.10 Tat'iana Iatsenko / Татьяна Яценко

keyboard-player, vocalist, and lyricist in the group Ackee Ma-Ma U.R.B. Interview conducted in Russian on January 11th, 2006 in St. Petersburg.

A.11 Iva Nova / Ива Нова

Ekaterina Fedorova / Екатерина Федорова, born 1976 in Leningrad, Iva Nova's drummer.
Inka Lishenkevich / Инка Лишенкевич, Iva Nova's guitarist.
Elena Novikova / Елена Новикова, born 1975 in the Murmansk region (Russia), Iva Nova's bass-player.
Anastasia Postnikova / Анастася Постникова, Iva Nova's vocalist.
Elena Zhornik / Елена Жорник, Iva Nova's *baian*-player.

Interview conducted in Russian on March 12th and 28th, 2005 in St. Petersburg.

A.12   Andrei Ivanov / Андрей Иванов

born 1960 in Leningrad, vocalist in the group Reggistan. Interview conducted in Russian on December 20th, 2004 in St. Petersburg.

A.13   Dmitrii Ivanov / Димитрий Иванов

born 1978 in Leningrad, journalist and vocalist in the group Svinokop. Interview conducted in English on September 25th, 2005 in St. Petersburg.

A.14   Andrei Kagadeev / Андрей Кагадеев

born 1961 in Leningrad, bass-guitarist and lyricist in the group NOM, member of the artist collective *KOLKhUi*. Interview conducted in English on December 6th, 2004 in St. Petersburg.

A.15   Alexander Kasparov

co-director of the record label *Eastblok Music*. Interview conducted in German on October 11th, 2005 and July 19th, 2006 in Berlin.

A.16   Dmitrii Khramtsov / Дмитрий Храмцов

born 1973 in Leningrad, violinist in and leader of the group Dobranoch'. Interview conducted in Russian on April 18th, 2005 in St. Petersburg.

A.17   Evgenii Kiselev / Евгений Киселев

born 1977 in Moscow, *art direktor* at S-club. Interview conducted in Russian on January 30th, 2006 in St. Petersburg.

A.18   Elena Kolganova / Елена Колганова

born 1978, manager. Interview conducted in Russian on February 18th, 2006 in St. Petersburg.

A.19   Nikolai Kopeikin / Николай Копейкин

born in Tomsk (Russia), visual artist and associated with the group NOM, member of the artist collective *KOLKhUi*. Interview conducted in Russian on June 2nd, 2005 in St. Petersburg.

A.20   Viktor Kultashov / Виктор Култашов

born 1984 in Leningrad, guitarist and lyricist in the group Con Brio. Interview conducted in Russian on February 12th, 2006 in St. Petersburg.

A.21   Svetlana Loseva / Светлана Лосева

born in Leningrad, photographer, former manager of the groups NOM, Nol', and Nochnye Snaipery as well as former PR-director at the record label *Grand Records*. Interview conducted in Russian on September 6th, 2005 in St. Petersburg.

A.22   Anton Lukanin / Антон Луканин

born 1980 in Leningrad, works as a storeman. Interview conducted in Russian on January 30th, 2006 in St. Petersburg.

A.23   Billy Novik / Билли Новик

born 1975 in Leningrad, vocalist, standup-bass-player and lyricist in the group Billy's Band. Interview conducted in Russian on March 24th, 2005 in St. Petersburg.

A.24   Olaf Opitz

born 1965, *balalaika*-player and lyricist in the group Apparatschik. Interview conducted in German on July 21st, 2006 in Berlin.

A.25   Roman Parygin / Роман Парыгин

born 1979, trumpet-player and vocalist in the group Spitfire, trumpet-player in the groups Leningrad, St. Petersburg Ska-Jazz Review, and Optimystica orchestra. Interview conducted in Russian on June 23rd, 2006 in St. Petersburg.

A.26   Aleksandr Rudenko / Александр Руденко

born 1972 in Zhdanov (now Mariupol' – Ukraine), vocalist and lyricist in the group Svoboda. Interview conducted in Russian on January 9th and 15th, 2006 in St. Petersburg.

A.27   Armin Siebert

born 1973 in Parchim (German Democratic Republic), co-director of the record label *Eastblok Music*. Interview conducted in German on October 11th, 2005 and July 19th, 2006 in Berlin.

A.28   Andrei Tropillo / Андрей Тропилло

born 1951 in Leningrad, sound engineer, record producer, and label director of *AnTrop*. Interview conducted in Russian on May 23rd, 2005 in St. Petersburg.

A.29   Denis Vashkevich / Денис Вашкевич

born 1980 in Leningrad, works as a driver. Interview conducted in Russian on January 30th, 2006 in St. Petersburg.

A.30 Aleksandr "Nevskii" Vladimirov / Александр "Невский" Владимиров

born in Leningrad, guitarist, vocalist, and lyricist in the group Severnye Vrata. Interview conducted in Russian on December 22nd, 2005 in St. Petersburg.

A.31 Mikhail Yaroshevskiy

born 1969 in Khar'kov (Ukraine), one of the founders of the *Russian Rock Club of America*. Interview conducted in English on August 3rd, 2007 in New York.

Appendix B. Selected lyrics

B.1 Алиса: Rock-n-Roll Крест / Alisa: Rock-n-Roll Krest

(Alisa 2005 – cf. p. 216)
Оскал и дым, разгул и чад,
Обычный вечер городских волчат.
За тупиком тупики, и только тени врагов.
Я тоже жил наперекор,
Сам за себя рубил отказ в отпор,
На сотни судеб легли следы моих сапогов.

За годом год – угара муть
На бездорожье замыкала путь,
Я даже не замечал, что рою хляби болот.
В моей душе шаманил мрак,
Но, слава Богу, мне открылось как
Пороки под жернова, ведут слепцов в отмолот.

Там, где синяя даль разлилась по края,
Я увидел, как травы росой напоила заря,
И мой табор двинулся в ночь от насиженных мест,
С тех пор по дорогам пылит R-n-R-крест.

Топтать, не греть, любить, не мять,
Дарить от сердца, по душе терять,
Разгулы прожитых лет и тут кричи – не кричи,
Смотреть вокруг и видеть луч
За черной гарью, за бетоном туч,
И сдюжить, не пережечь огонь в огарок свечи.

Когда закат накроет тень,
А звезды снами заморочат день,
Я встану ближе к огню под лики Силы Небес.
И будем жить, и станем петь,
В соленый пот, пережигая смерть.
Смотри – нас снова в центр луча вплетает R-n-R-крест.

B.2   Алиса: Небо славян / Alisa: Nebo slavian

(Alisa 2003 – cf. p. 218)
Звездопад, да рокот зарниц.
Грозы седлают коней,
Но над землей тихо льется покой
Монастырей.
А поверх седых облаков
Синь соколиная высь.
Здесь, под покровом небес
Мы родились.

След оленя лижет мороз,
Гонит добычу весь день,
Но стужу держит в узде
Дым деревень.
Намела сугробов пурга
Дочь белозубой зимы.
Здесь, в окоеме снегов
Выросли мы.

Нас точит семя орды,
Нас гнет ярмо басурман,
Но в наших венах кипит
Небо славян.
И от Чудских берегов
До ледяной Колымы.
Все это наша земля!
Все это мы!

За бугром куют топоры,
Буйные головы сечь,
Но инородцам кольчугой звенит
Русская речь.
И от перелеска до звезд
Высится Белая рать.
Здесь, на родной стороне
Нам помирать.

Displayed at the beginning of the video clip (Alisa 2008 – Translation: p. 218):

"Если кто с мечом к нам войдет, от меча и погибнет.
На том стоит и стоять будет Русская Земля!"

B.3 Олег Газманов: Сделан в СССР / Oleg Gazmanov: Sdelan v SSSR

(Gazmanov 2005 – cf. p. 219)
Украина и Крым, Беларусь и Молдова –
Это моя страна.
Сахалин и Камчатка, Уральские горы –
Это моя страна.
Красноярский край, Сибирь и Поволжье,
Казахстан и Кавказ, и Прибалтика тоже..

Я рожден в Советском Союзе,
Сделан я в СССР

Рюрики, Романовы, Ленин и Сталин –
Это моя страна.
Пушкин, Есенин, Высоцкий, Гагарин –
Это моя страна.
Разоренные церкви и новые храмы,
Красная площадь и стройка на БАМе.

Олимпийское золото, старты, победы –
Это моя страна.
Жуков, Суворов, комбайны, торпеды –
Это моя страна.
Олигархи и нищие, мощь и разруха,
КГБ, МВД и большая наука

Глинка, Толстой, Достоевский, Чайковский,
Врубель, Шаляпин, Шагал, Айвазовский
Нефть и алмазы, золото, газ,
Флот, ВДВ, ВВС и спецназ.

Водка, икра, Эрмитаж и ракеты,
Самые красивые женщины планеты,
Шахматы, опера, лучший балет,
Скажите, где есть то, чего у нас нет?!

Даже Европа объединилась в союз,
Вместе наши предки сражались в бою.
Вместе выиграна Вторая мировая война,
Вместе мы – самая большая страна.

Душат границы, без визы нельзя,
Как вам без нас, отзовитесь, друзья

Я рожден в Советском Союзе,
Сделан я в СССР

B.4 Кино: Мама Анархия / Kino: Mama Anarkhiia

(Kino 1986 – cf. p. 184)
Солдат шел по улице домой
И увидел этих ребят.
"Кто ваша мама, ребята?"
Спросил у ребят солдат.

Мама – Анархия,
Папа – стакан портвейна.

Все они в кожаных куртках,
Все небольшого роста,
Хотел солдат пройти мимо,
Но это было непросто.

Мама – Анархия,
Папа – стакан портвейна.

Довольно веселую шутку
Сыграли с солдатом ребята:
Раскрасили красным и синим,
Заставляли ругаться матом.

Мама – Анархия,
Папа – стакан портвейна.

B.5 Ленинград: СКА / Leningrad: SKA

(Leningrad 2000 – cf. p. 167)
Я знаю одно слово из трех букв,
а в этом слове заложен грув
Хоккейная команда, с берегов Невы
И музыка, которую играем мы

С – К – А, Скаааа. Давай!

Слово СКА похоже на хуй, потому что
такое же количество букв
Но в слове хуй, гораздо меньше
Этот самый ГРРУУВВВ

С – К – А, Скаааа. Давай!

B.6 Markscheider Kunst: Красиво слева / Markscheider Kunst: Krasivo sleva

(Markscheider Kunst 2001 – cf. p. 33)
Красиво слева,
Красиво справа.
Сегодня Бундес,
Вчера Варшава.
Куда еще заведет лукавый?

На Невском холод,
В порту облава.
На Невском холод,
На Невском холод.

Сегодня вторник,
Вчера суббота.
Сниму квартиру,
Найду работу.
Устрою все, о чем ты мечтала.

Зима уходит.
Начнем сначала.

Зима уходит,
Зима уходит.

Мне 30 лет!
Все это время
Я был уверен,
Что мы в системе.
Рожденный жить и умереть обязан.

Иначе старость,
Беда маразм.
Иначе старость,
Иначе старость.

B.7 НОМ: Нина / NOM: Nina

(NOM 2002 – cf. p. 145)
Нина, голова болит (6x)
О, зразы! Я бы съел какую-нибудь заразу (4x)
Нина, голова болит (8x)
Уй-блядь
Нина, голова болит (6x)
Зубы почистить (2x)
Меня преследуют (2x)
Нина
Хе, хе, яйца моет

B.8 Пилигрим: Слава России! / Piligrim: Slava Rossii!

(Piligrim 2007 – cf. p. 222)
Мы с тобой родились в великой России
Все мы верим, что будет Россия сильной!
От Балтийского моря до Курильской гряды.
В мире нету прекрасней и краше страны.

Над огромной Россией, над великой страной
Наш двуглавый орел, свои крылья раскрой.
Над Россией моей солнце светит всегда,
Золотятся под солнцем церквей купола.

Слава России!
Великой державе!
Слава России,
Народу слава!

Бились насмерть с врагом наши деды, отцы,
Мы должны сделать все, чтоб сбылись их мечты
Мир свободы и счастья построим трудом.
И одною огромной семьей заживем.

И татарин и русский и бурят и еврей,
И чеченец и чукча и башкир и карел.
Все народы России будут вместе всегда,
Пусть горит над Россией надежды звезда.

B.9   Svoбoдa: Ла-Ла / Svoboda: La-la

(Svoboda 2007, Transcribed by Tamara Lönngren – cf. p. 184)
Село моє пусте,
Неначе вимерло.
А я купив квиток,
А я піду у кіно.
А я побачу кайф,
А я побачу хвільм
А я побачу секс,
Та не побаче він!!

Ла-ла...
Come on
Ла-ла....

На вулиці мороз,
і в мене ніс відпав
Михaнік фільм пры-вёз (cf. p. 185)
Михaнік фільм достав
Уже усі прийшли,
а він ще не відкрив
Ми винахід знайшли

В нас до танців порив

Ла-ла...
Come on
Ла-ла....
В нас до танців порив

Але зненацька в нас
ліхтар у клубі згас
Щоб не робить бедлам,
Пішли ми по домам.
Таке у нас село,
Ви приїздіть до нас
Вам буде весело
Ми вам покажим клас
Ми вам покажим клас
В нас таньці є і хлів
А ще кажіть про нас
Ви друзям всім своїм.

Ла-ла...
Come on
Ла-ла....
Ви друзям всім своїм.

B.10 Svoбoдa: Мама анархія / Svoboda: Mama anarkhiia

(Various Artists 2008b, Transcribed by Martin Paulsen – cf. p. 184)

Москаль йшов по вулиці до хати
І побачів ціх ребят
Хто ваша мама ребята
Спітав москаль у ребят

Мама анархія
Батько стакан горілки

Усі вони у шкіряних куртках
Усі вони великого росту
Хотів москаль піти мімо

Але це було не просто

Мама анархія
Батько стакан горилкі

Дуже веселую жарту
сигралі с москалом ребята
Розмалювалі червоне-блакитним
Заставлялі ругатіся матом

Мама анархія
Батько стакан горилкі

Мама анархія
Папа стакан портвейна

B.11 Svoбoда: Маруся / Svoboda: Marusia

(Various Artists 2008c, Transcribed by Tamara Lönngren – cf. p. 184)

Розпрягайте, хлопці, коней
Та лягайте спочивать,
А я піду в сад зелений,
В сад криниченьку копать.

Маруся,
Раз, два, три, калина
Чорнявая дівчина
В саду ягоди рвала.

Копав, копав криниченьку
У вішневому садку
Вийде вийде дівчинонька
Рано-вранці по воду.

Маруся, [...]

Знаю, знаю, дівчинонька,
Чим я тебе огорчив
Що я вчора ізвечора

Кращщу тебе полюбив.

Маруся, [...]

Вона ростом невеличка,
Ще й літами молода,
Руса коса до пояса,
В косі стрічка золота

Маруся, [...]

B.12   **Svoбoдa: Чоботи / Svoboda: Choboty**

(Svoboda 2005, Transcribed by Yevgeniya Z. Amis & Tamara Lönngren –cf. p. 184)
Я приїхав з України у столичні города
Та пришла лиха година: наступили
холода
Мати гроші на ісході, я одіт не до погоди
От такі от хлопоти – треба нові чоботи

Чоботи, чоботи з бугая
Не бояться холода і огня
Чоботи, чоботи з бугая
Не бояться холода
В чоботах, чоботах з бугая
Не боюсь ні холода, ні огня
Чоботи, чоботи з бугая
Дуже гарні чоботи

Ой не хочу працювати,
Рано вранці йти із хати
Я люблю пісні складати,
Я люблю пісні співати
Ми і граєм, ми танцюєм
У рок-групі ми гарцюєм
Аби я бабла скопив
Та пішов собі купив

Чоботи, чоботи з бугая [...]

Я гуляю по Арбату
Та буцаю сніжну вату.
І по Невскаму гуляю
Ветер в харю я пехтярю
І нехай морози злые,
І нехай завірюха
В мене чоботи крутые,
І в теплі нога

Чоботи, чоботи з бугая [...]

B.13   Svoбoдa: Холодно нам / Svoboda: Kholodno nam

(cf. p. 189)
Серой стеной вьюга встала,
Солью глаза замела.
Небо и землю смешала,
Спрятала искры тепла.
Ветер срывает крыши,
Но нет обратно пути.
Ты падаешь в снег,
Еле дышишь,
Но надо, но надо идти.

Холодно нам, снег следы заметает.
Ну а душа без любви замерзает.
Холод сжимает сердца,
Гонит нас с мест.
Мы все же идем до конца,
Ведь выход есть.

В небо непросто добраться,
Заледенели крыла.
Чтобы в земле не остаться,
Нужен огонь и слова.
Ждут уже темные бездны,
Чтоб побыстрее сожрать.
И кажется все бесполезным,

Но надо, но надо взлетать.

Холодно нам [...]

Но к солнцу вырвется кто-то,
Сгорит и вернется, чтоб жить.
Огненная его нота
Снег хоть чуть-чуть растворит.
Но лед очень медленно тает.
Не хочет никто умирать.
А времени жить не хватает,
Но надо, но надо пылать.

Холодно нам [...]

B.14   Реггистан: Регги, реггей / Reggistan: Reggi, reggei

(Reggistan 1999 – cf. p. 153)
В трудный час, в минуты успеха,
В кругу друзей или просто один.
Холодной зимой, жарким летом,
Этот мотив будет с тобой.

Регги, регги, реггей.

Все может быть просто, может быть сложно.
Люди как песни: их музыка – жизнь.
Красота и радость, теплота и нежность,
В каждом из вас, в каждом из вас,
в каждом из нас!

Регги, регги, реггей.

Дорогу! Мы к вам пришли!
Это станция "Регги, Регги, Регги"!
Переход на Dubwise
Быть или не быть? Вот в чем вопрос!

Нет кай [unclear] есть времени

Это сейчас или никогда

Смотрите на меня, я обязательно приду!
Вы готовы? Ea.
Смотри!
Я приду, я приду, я сейчас приду,
Я приду, я приду – обязательно приду!

We no give a damn about the color of our skin, one hit you with the rhythm in a dancehall style. Got to make your move because it fun feel a good and we are coming with the rhythm in a dancehall style. Roll you belly like we don't just care, forget about the propaganda – this for real. Sit upon the rhythm like we don't look scared, feel comfortable with the drum and the bass. He knows just where them [unclear] mmm, la-la-la-la-la. Давай!

Давай! Вставай!
Регги, регги, реггей

B.15 Руслана: Коломийка / Ruslana: Kolomyika

(Ruslana 2003 – see p. 195)
Ой, кувала зозулечка та й мене забула,
А мого кохання нічка взяла та й минула.
Гей-гей!

Ой, кувала зозулечка та й казала ку-ку!
Не питай мене даремно, а бери за руку.
Не питай мя, легінечку, чом така сумна я.
Ой, кувала зозулечка,
Покухала-заблукала,
Ге-е-ей, серце моє.

Закохаєшся, шиді риді дана,
Не сховаєшся – я твоя кохана.
Не питай мене, шиді риді дана.
Чи любов мине, шиді риді! Гей! Гей!

Ой, кувала зозулечка.
Ой, кувала та й співала.

Збудила моє сердечко.

Ой, кувала зозулечка та й кувати буде.
Гей! Кохала легінечка, повік не забуду.
А як зійшов місяць ясний, сонця не чекала.
Покохала, заблукала.
Нам кохання було мало,
Ге-е-ей, серце моє.

Закохаєшся, шиді риді дана,
Не сховаєшся – я твоя кохана.
Не питай мене, шиді риді дана.
Чи любов мине, шиді риді! Гей! Гей!

Ой, кувала зозулечка.
Ой, кувала та й співала.
Нам кохання було мало.

Ой, кувала зозулечка, правду говорила
Нам на біду кохання є,
А як сонце вітер збудить, понесе на крилах,
Збудиться серце моє.

Закохаєшся, шиді риді дана,
Не сховаєшся – я твоя кохана.
Не питай мене, шиді риді дана.
Чи любов мине, шиді риді! Гей! Гей!

Ой, кувала зозулечка.
Збудила моє сердечко.
Ой, кувала та й співала.
Нам кохання було мало,
Гей! Гей!

Appendix C. Quotes in their original language

The quotes from interviews have been transcribed verbatim and the language (grammar, syntax) has not been corrected.

C.1 Matthias Angerer

(Angerer 2007)

"Vor allem bei den Gypsy-musikern festgestellt: da merkst einfach, dass die es sozusagen schon mit der Muttermilch eingesaugt haben [...] Da lernt es das Kleinkind sozusagen vom Grossvater schon ein Instrument spielen und das merkt man auch beim Spiel. Man merkt einerseits, dass sie nicht auf irgendein Musikkonservatorium gegangen sind [...] Sondern die spielen es einfach mit einem Herzblut, das viele wahrscheinlich klassisch-ausgebildete Musiker gar nicht haben. Die sind vielleicht technisch mitunter besser, aber nie so.... Musik hat für mich sehr viel eben mit Leidenschaft und mit Herz zu tun und wenn jemand wirklich eben sein Volles gibt und Musik spielt, dann wird da immer mehr Spirit rüberkommen als wenn es einer brav ein Stück [...] trocken runterspielt." (Translation: p. 283)

"[D]er Name des Lokals ist so zusagen auch Programm, also osteuropäische Musik oder eben russische oder Musik aus dem Balkan, aber auch weiter. Die musikalische Achse für uns ist sozusagen Wien – Vladivostok [...] Der Osten ist weit und insofern wird's musikalisch, glaub ich, auch nicht fad so schnell." (Translation: p. 283)

C.2 Tsypylma Darieva

(Darieva 2004, 109)

"Der Ort *Russendisko* kann vielmehr als ein exotischer Spielplatz ähnlich dem der Salsa-Disko bezeichnet werden, der von 'guten Kulturrussen' in der westlichen Metropole angeboten wird." (Translation: p. 278)

C.3 Yuriy Gurzhy

(pers. comm., 23.09.2005)
"Auf Svobodas Demo würden wir uns freuen, Marusya ist zur Zeit unser großer Favorit :) Was macht die Band zur Zeit?" (Translation: p. 257)

(Gurzhy 2005)
"Für mich ist Szene ein Begriff, wo es viele Leute sind, die irgendwie ähnlich denken, ähnliche Vorstellung in Musik haben und immer wieder austauschen. Also in Petersburg [...] da siehst du irgendwie 10 Bands. Wenn du genauer hinschaust, da sind irgendwie so 20 Musiker, die in 10 Bands spielen." (Translation: p. 88)

"Das ist wieder so jetzt ein Klische, aber für mich ist das Underground [...] was nicht Mainstream ist. [...] Aber in der letzten Zeit [...] wie im typischen Fall von Leningrad, sehen wir mal wie Underground praktisch den Weg ins Mainstream findet, aber trotzdem irgendwie noch Underground bleibt." (Translation: p. 116)

"Na, ich glaube es ist halt in der Pop-welt immer so gewesen, [...] es gibt Pioniere und es gibt Nachmacher und sobald Leningrad so gross war [...] Für viele war das 'ne Offenbarung, [...] 'ne Entdeckung, dass es überhaupt so 'ne Musikrichtung gibt und Shnurov damals hat auch, glaub ich, auf seine Webseite immer so von Ska erzählt, was das ist und so und Spitfire noch dazu, also die Band, die immerschon immer Ska, so der hat auch für die damals heftig beworben. [...] [I]ch glaube, dass durch Leningrad sind viele Leute einfach auf Ska gekommen und dann auf die Idee, eben das zu spielen, weil es im Moment gut ankommt." (Translation: p. 168)

"Die Russendisko ist ein Soundsystem, also ein DJ-Kollektiv mit zwei Leuten – das sind ich und Wladimir. [...] Wir legen die Musik auf, die wir gut finden. [...] Das ist die Musik aus den ehemaligen Republiken der Sowjet Union. Es wird hauptsächlich auf russisch, mal auf ukrainisch gesungen oder [...] weissrussisch." (Translation: p. 229)

"Rot Front würde ich nicht als unbedingt russische Band bezeichnen, weil es [...] ein Ergebnis eines einzigartigen russisch-ungarischen Connections ist." (Translation: p. 230)

"Wir haben eigentlich das angefangen, weil wir wollten diese Musik den andere Leuten präsentieren, die Russen wissen worum es geht." (Translation: p. 232)

"Wir waren auch der erste Ort in Berlin [...] wo die Russen und Deutschen locker miteinander [...] kommuniziert haben. [...] Ich bin immer noch stolz darauf, dass es ziemlich viele russisch-deutschen Pärchen da den Weg zueinander gefunden haben." (Translation: p. 243)

"Oh, das ist ganz kompliziert. [...] So meine Mutter ist Jüdin und mein Vater hat russisches, ukrainisches, polnisches und griechisches Blut in sich [...] Und meine Muttersprache ist Russisch, obwohl ich aus der Ukraine komme und ich lebe in Berlin, [...] also ich hab diesen Luxus mich immer neu zu erfinden [...] Das jüdische Element ist für mich schon sehr wichtig und ich denke halt viel darüber nach [...] Die Russische Sprache ist für mich auch total wichtig, weil ich damit grossgeworden bin [...] Das ist schon, das ist sehr schwierig, das ist immer anders und das finde ich auch ok so [...] Also heute bin ich Russe, morgen bin ich Jude, übermorgen ein Ukrainer [...] Also die Leute wissen auch nicht genau [...] was sie unter mir so vorstellen sollen, so von Nationalität, das find ich sehr, sehr spannend, das bringt dich zu immer neuen Abenteuern." (Translation: p. 252)

"Es gibt immer wieder die Leute, die hin und her pendeln und wir bestellen es halt, weil wir versuchen zu überwachen, was da so neues gibt. Ausserdem kennen wir mittlerweile schon die Musiker sehr gut weil wir haben mit denen persönlich zu tun gehabt als wir [...] die Russendisko CDs vorbereitet haben und die schicken uns immer was. [...] Also, wir haben persönlichen Kontakt und haben unsere Quellen auch. Es ist eigentlich im Moment gar nicht so schwierig und als MP3s im Internet kannst du ja auch viel finden."

David-Emil: "Und fahrt ihr auch nach Russland?"

Yuriy: "Sehr selten, *sehr* [stressed] selten. Wladimir war jetzt zum ersten mal seit paar Jahren. Ich war auch in der Ukraine, genau. Aber das ist eher Ausnahme, weil also kein grossen Wunsch und keine Zeit dafür." (Translation: p. 256)

"Geographisch sind das also die 15 ehemaligen Republiken oder die Leute, die aus diesen Republiken kommen, weil ich auch [...] versuche halt mehr Aufmerksamkeit [...] zu so genannten Emigranten-musik [...] zu gewinnen." (Translation: p. 257)

"Was sehr wichtig ist: [...] Hier ist [...] diese Musik so kontextfrei so zu sagen. [...] Unsren Geschmack ist... Also es geht um guter oder schlechte Musik und nicht die Musik, die im Moment im Radio gespielt wird oder nicht. [...] Wir nehmen keinen Bezug auf Hitparaden oder so, oder das, was [...] im Moment so in ist oder nicht in oder out." (Translation: p. 258)

"Musikalisch [...] fühl ich mich nicht so wohl mit so Richtungsbezeichnung. Man könnte schon sagen dass es zwischen Ska, Reggae, Folk und, weiss ich nicht, Balkan ist. [...] Genau in unseren Cross-over-zeit ist es sehr schwierig, weil die Band, die heute Ska gespielt hat, wird morgen Hip-hop machen." (Translation: p. 258)

(pers. comm., 24.04.2006)

"das, was in der UdSSR entstanden ist – die schlecht aufgenommene Musik mit meist pathetischen und politischen Texten. Heute musikalisch eher uninteressant." (copy of e-mail, his orthography) (Translation: p. 139)

C.4 Yury Harlamov

(Harlamov 2005)

"У нас есть внутренние ограничения – мы не ставим поп, эстраду и так называемый 'шансон', то есть блатняк. Очень мало рокапопса. Немного хип-хопа и электронной музыки. Все остальные стили, играемые, так сказать, 'вручную' есть. Мы ставим русскую, украинскую, белорусскую, если найдем молдавскую и иногда восточно-европейскую музыку." (Translation: p. 237)

(Schum n.d.)

"Schum ist eine Radiosendung über 'Russische' Musik [...]. 'Russisch' in Anführungszeichen, weil für die meisten Deutschen (und häufig für die Russen selbst) alle russischsprachigen 'die Russen' sind. Und also legen wir auch die ukrainische, moldauische, weissrussische, jüdische Musik auf und fassen sie unter dem Namen 'Russisch' zusammen." (Translation: p. 56)

C.5 Wladimir Kaminer

(Various Artists 2005c, Tr. 12)

"Die Band Apparatschik ist übrigens ein Beispiel gelungene Integration für mich: Also, das sind die besten, die besten falschen Russen, die mir jemals begegnet sind. Sehr authentisch!" (Translation: p. 279)

APPENDIX C. QUOTES IN THEIR ORIGINAL LANGUAGE   315

C.6   Andreas Kappeler

(Kappeler 2003, 54)

"Trotz Urbanisierung und Industrialisierung gelten die Ukrainer noch immer als unkultiviertes Bauernvolk, als 'chochly'." (Translation: p. 204)

(Kappeler 2003, 53)

"Die Mehrheit der Russen sieht die Ukrainer noch immer als 'malorossy', als Teil der russischen Nation, und begreift nicht, weshalb die Ukrainer eine eigene Sprache, eine eigene Kultur und einen eigenen Staat anstreben." (Translation: p. 177)

C.7   Alexander Kasparov & Armin Siebert

(Kasparov and Siebert 2005)

Armin: "Wir kommen eher, natürlich, erstmal aus der World music- und aus der Alternative-ecke, weil so musst du anfangen. Es ist halt Russendisko-publikum und es ist World music-publikum. Das ist erstmal unsere Basis von Zielgruppe." (Translation: p. 235)

Armin: "Ja, ansonsten viel Eigenkolorit und das find ich ist was Besonderes im weltweiten Vergleich, also es gibt was ganz eigen Russisches für mich so vom Gefühl her und wenn man das entsprechend halt positionieren kann, so wie auch Latinomusik das in letzten 20 Jahren geschafft hat, dann sehe ich 'ne Chance, dass da russische Musik quasi auch ein Synonym wird für'n bestimmten Klang und das wär gut." (Translation: p. 261)

Armin: "Die Liste mit Sachen, die wir veröffentlichen könnten ist riesig. Das ist nicht das Problem. Es ist viel schwieriger [...] mit den Rechten das zu klären, das alles zu organisieren legal und entsprechend sich zu überlegen, [...] was funktionieren könnte hier, nicht was nur dort Klasse ist, sondern was auch hier funktionieren könnte auf'm Markt." (Translation: p. 265)

(Kasparov and Siebert 2006)

Alex: "Ich glaube, für die Russen, das ist eine guter Rhythmus, gute Musik, und hat etwas zu tun mit die russische Rhythmus, mit Chastushchka oder mit alle andere... Das ist nicht so fremd für die russische Ohre, diese Ska-rhythmus." (Translation: p. 169)

Alex: "[Ruslana] regelmässig macht diese folklorische Expeditionen nach Karpathen, regelmässig. Und sie recherchiert das, sie geht mit dem ganzen Team und sie findet die neuen Beats, die neue musikalische Strukturen. Sie kommt immer zurück mit grossen, musikalische Gepäck und ist immer sehr zufrieden und hat mir gesagt, das macht grosse Einflüsse." (Translation: p. 199)

Alex: "Die Russen kannst du vergessen, Russen haben keine Lust für diese alte Sachen. Das hast du grosse [unclear] für die Deutschen, die Russen möchten alles neues, schick – meistens, nicht alle – aber, das bedeutet nicht so viel für die Russen"

Armin: "Ich bin mir nicht ganz sicher. Ältere Russen, ich denk schon, dass sie ein bisschen Nostalgie haben. Also, gerade so bei welchen, die jetzt nicht unbedingt ganz viel Geld haben. [...]"

Alex: "[...] Für ihn das egal, für die Deutschen das Exotisch." (Translation: p. 281)

C.8 Ellen Rutten

(Rutten 2007, 119)

"Die Russendisko appelliert nicht an ein 'Wir'-Gefühl, sondern an stereotype Vorstellungen über 'sie', 'die Russen', 'die Anderen', 'die Fremden.'" (Translation: p. 281)

C.9 Oleksandr Yarmola

(Arte 2008)

"Ich halte die Hinwendung zu Russland und den russischen Einfluss für gefährlich. Es geht nur um Öl, das ist alles. Ein großer Bär mit Balalaika, Bullshit! Wir denken, dass der einzige Weg für die Ukraine nach Westen geht, um in Europa integriert zu werden." (Translation: p. 194)

C.10 Андрей Бурлака

(Burlaka 2005)

"Сейчас мало. [...] Первый клуб открылся летом 91 года, осенью открылось еще несколько клубов, в большей степени [...] Rock-n-Roll-ные и до, действительно, середины 90-ых в Питере [...] было там порядка 15 где-то там, куда можно было пойти. Некоторые работали там 3-4 раза неделю, некоторые работали раз-два в неделю там, кто чаще, кто реже. Пика все это достигло к 97 году, но в 97 году закрылись практически все ведущие клубы. Потом [...] как бы начались новые экономические отношения. [...]: хозяева помещений хотели больших и легких денег сразу. Поэтому в течение вот буквально там полугода закрылись 6 ведущих клубов: Орландина, с ней рядом Перевал, [...] Арт клиника, TaMtAm, 10 клуб, Wild Side, [...]. Но появился Молоко как раз там за год [до] этого и Грибоедов." (Translation: p. 103)

"Большинство музыкантов работают где-то еще. В Петербурге заработать очень трудно, потому что город сам по себе довольно бедный. Соотвественно, публика не может много денег оставлять в клубах. То есть если музыкант клуб поднимает цену, значит уменьшается количество публики, то есть денег больше не становится. [...] Соответственно, значит и музыканты не могут много получать денег." (Translation: p. 106)

"Раньше было при каждом, так сказать, микрорайоне городском так называемый ЖЭК. Да, это – организация, которая следила за тем, чтобы там водопровод там, да свет. Ну, так называемый ЖЭК – жилищно-эксплуатационная контора. То есть вот такое маленькое, как бы что ли представительство власти. При каждом был маленький красный уголок, вот такой культурный центр. Там, как правило, была какая-то аппаратура, и там репетировали группы. Таких клубов было, наверное, несколько сотен: сотни три или четыре в городе. То есть не в каждом, но вот во времена 70-ых, там да вот скажем там, по числу групп. Ну очень много репетировало в этих маленьких красных уголках, в ЖЭКах. А сейчас этого нет. Все закрыто." (Translation: p. 110)

"В принципе это – рок, но это понятно. Да, это – уже популярное искусство, это – уже массовое искусство. [...] поэтому просто у нас в России есть такое понятие как 'попса', то есть, это – такое низкоклассное Variety, поэтому есть некое дистанцирование, а так, в целом, по большому счету есть [unclear] люди, которые играют на стадионах. Это, в общем-то, уже поп-музыка. То есть, это не значит, что плохо, это понятно? Просто это – уже массовое искусство. То есть нельзя предполагать, что 10 000 людей, которые пришли на концерт ДДТ в спортивно-концертный комплекс, что они все понимают о чем поет Шевчук, что они все разделяют его духовные убеждения, искания. Просто это уже становится фигурой некой уже публичной, модой. Тоже самое можно сказать и о Гребенщикове." (Translation: p. 122)

"Эстрада? Поп-музыка, ты имеешь ввиду? Есть хорошая поп-музыка, есть плохая поп-музыка, везде есть хорошее и плохое. В рок-музыке даже слабая группа, она пытается что-то сказать, пытается что-то сделать. В эстраде, как мы только что говорили, там это – просто конвейер." (Translation: p. 122)

"Питер по-прежнему остается, я так понимаю, что для всей страны, для России или вообще для всего постсоветского пространства, неким оплотом культуры, потому что Москва со всей этой современной 'Фабрикой звезд', говоря в более общем смысле, понятно, что это. Все-таки у думающих людей это не может вызывать симпатии, а в России все-таки всегда достаточно много было людей думающих. Поэтому Питер по-прежнему остается таким городом надежды, от которого люди еще ждут чего-то настоящего. […] То есть, всегда были Москва – это коммерция, Петербург – это духовность." (Translation: p. 127)

"Вот тоже новая, так сказать, тема – такой укра-поп […] Украинский язык там, конечно, не играет такой важной роли, потому что, понятно, ну прикол. А так музыка достаточно там укладывается в какие-то… [Есть питерские] похожие играющие, но дополнительная экзотика, такая фольклорная." (Translation: p. 183)

"И так понятно. Я слушаю песню и понимаю, что это – отсюда, это – оттуда. Это – 'Sex Pistols', это – группа 'Кино'. Это вообщем неплохо. У него есть некая магия концертная, это – хорошо." (Translation: p. 192)

C.11   Денис Вашкевич and Антон Луканин

(Vashkevich and Lukanin 2006)

Антон: "[Денис] дал мне послушать вот эти три песни, и мне они запали в душу, особенно 'Отстой'. Ну почему-то отстойная песня, но очень веселая, потому что я в этой песне узнаю себя. Чуть ли не каждое утро. [laughs]" (Translation: p. 97)

Денис: "Пятница – последний день рабочий и по Нашему радио [...] объявляют [...] 'Клуб Молоко: Бригадный Подряд'. [...] Позвонил в то время еще будущей жене: 'Пойдем?' – 'Ну, пойдем'. И первой выступала Svoбода" (Translation: p. 98)

Денис: "Есть какая-то неприязнь к Украине, там то, что они творят под воздействием Америки, но когда на концерте, ты – это немного другая атмосфера, это – не национальная рознь. То, что он поет на украинском, нравится человеку – пусть поет, да не вопрос." (Translation: p. 178)

Денис: "Нет..."

Антон: "...по смыслу понятно..."

Денис: "...но некоторые строчки вылетают из-за того, что ты не знаешь языка, и они вылетают с тем смыслом, что, например, микрофон он убрал и одно слово вылетело и все: целую строчку ты уже не можешь понять, о чем он спел. Там, идет, идет, идет: половина же слов – это просто буквы поменять и будет все понятно, о чем поет. А так микрофон отлетел в сторону, одно слово потерял, и уже эта связка слов украинского языка, ее уже нельзя перекинуть на русский язык."

Антон: "Без одного слова"

Денис: "уже тяжелее будет это все осмыслить."

Антон: "Для меня абсолютно разницы нет на украинском он будет петь или на русском. Единственное, Денис уже говорил, что вылетают некоторые фразы, если постоянно на украинском. Я обожаю песню цоевскую 'Мама анархия'. Я ее и обожаю, как в русском варианте, так и – не буду говорить в хохляцком – в украинском варианте." (Translation: p. 194)

Денис: "Из последних альбомов многие не понимают этих текстов, потому что Константин Евгеньевич ударился в религию, и он пишет тексты на почве вот этого православия. Он в это во все, может быть, вникает, но для фанатов..."

Anton: "...некоторые песни не понятны."

Денис: "Для молодых, они воспринимают его по старым песням, альбомам, которые раньше выходили, когда тексты были написаны о том, смысл их был в том, что все запрещено, но мы играем и поем."

Антон: "А сейчас – православие, религия."(Translation: p. 216)

C.12 Александр Невский Владимиров

(Vladimirov 2005)

"У нас где-то на концерты приходят там от 300 до 600 человек [...]. Вот поэтому, собственно говоря, вот нам всегда было сложно в этом плане, потому что не очень много мест подходило. Ну и кроме этого, надо еще тоже учитывать то, что наша аудитория – это не самые состоятельные люди. Поэтому они не пойдут на концерт там, который будет проходить в каком-то очень дорогом месте." (Translation: p. 107)

"В европейском понимании продюсер – это человек, который отвечает за качество звучания альбома и выполняет необходимые требования, чтобы сделать это все в нужном звучании, в нужном формате, и пытается добиться этого, соответственно, от студии, от музыкантов. То в российском понимании продюсер – это некий такой 'папа', который вообще в принципе все вопросы решает. [...] То есть, они берут там каких-нибудь мальчиков, которые поют песни популярные, ну а делают они это плохо. Ну, в чем проблема? Главное, что есть какая-то харизма, а тут же можно нанять им музыкантов, которые за них все сыграют, вокал их на компьютере подредактировать как следует, снять клип дорогой, и все нормально." (Translation: p. 123)

"Ну, грубо выражаясь, русский рок – это – в принципе, песни, которые можно взять акустическую гитару и исполнить на 2 аккордах. [...] С русской культурой это, как раз, ничего общего не имеет, потому что все наши русские рокеры – они, скорее, тяготеют к бардовской песне. Ты возьми любую группу. Возьми ДДТ. Если убрать оттуда всех музыкантов и оставить Шевчука с акустической гитарой, это то же самое будет абсолютно. Или

Гребенщиков. Не, Гребенщиков в последнее время, последние какие-то альбомы, он более старательно к инструменталу подходит. Но опять же мы были на последнем его концерте: видно, что он же сам не пишет аранжировку, то есть нет концепции инструментала, то есть он просто приглашает хороших музыкантов, которые ему сходу могут наимпровизировать. Но вообщем его музыка слушается полным салатом, потому что у него где-то то элементы блюза, здесь уже элементы регги, там еще что-то, а с точки зрения аранжировки это – салат полный. Поэтому иногда даже Гребенщикова проще послушать под акустическую гитару и это, скажем, по крайней мере сохраняет какой-то стиль, его собственный. Именно его игра под гитару, нежели этот странный инструментал." (Translation: p. 137)

Саша: "Наша особенность в том, что у нас – языческая музыка, и в ней фольклорные мелодии используются. В некоторых песнях в некоторых альбомах в большей степени, в некоторых в меньшей степени."

David-Emil: "И это российский фольклор?"

Саша: "Да, ну не российский." [laughs] "Россия и русские – это разные вещи."

David-Emil: "Какая разница?"

Саша: "Россия – это государство, в котором много различных народов живет, а русские, в принципе, это вообще, русы – это имя, которое нам дали не мы сами. То есть у нас были славяне: древляне, поляне, кривичи. Великороссы, малороссы, белороссы. А русами называли всех византийцы." (Translation: p. 209)

C.13 Елена Данилова

(Danilova 2006)

"Летопись – это программа о таких знаменитых альбомах музыкантов, которые, которые внесли вклад в музыку. Она идет раз в неделю." (Translation: p. 135)

C.14 Сергей Ефременко

(Efremenko 2005)

"'На Невском холод, в порту облава' – это относит нас к дому, то есть это, скорее всего, – сравнительный элемент. Конечно, оно к Питеру относится, естественно, я писал бы все о Питере. Наверное, все эти все песни о Питере и о жителях Питера." (Translation: p. 33)

"Нет, есть приезжие ребята, конечно. В данном составе у нас приезжих – это [...] гитарист, второй Володя [...] ди-джеем был, приехал, родился на Урале, здесь живет уже, по-моему, лет 20, в Питере. Или наш трубач, Саня [...]. Он родился в Кирове и приехал сюда учиться в Институт Культуры на трубача, попал к нам в группу. Он года 4-5 живет здесь в Питере. [...] Серафим Макангила был из Конго. А Вадя Ягман, который играл у нас на трубе, – гражданин Израиля." (Translation: p. 54)

Ефр: "Видишь, это получается, что нам приходится много ездить, чтобы работать. Когда играли последний концерт в Питере? [...] В Молоке в середине апреля, а следующий у нас концерт будет только 2-ого июля [...] Это, если ты хочешь получать хоть какие-то деньги более менее приличные за концерты, нужно так делать. Нам приходится еще куда-то ездить [...]."

David-Emil: "Тогда вы больше играете в Берлине, чем здесь?"

Ефр: "В Берлине гораздо больше." (Translation: p. 254)

"Нам не интересно ездить и играть, скажем, для эмигрантов. То есть мы бы хотели, конечно, в расчете на местную публику функционировать. Но сейчас вот мы съездили и сыграли, скажем так, по линии русского рок-клуба в Америке и [...] все было очень, это было лучше, чем мы ожидали." (Translation: p. 255)

C.15 Михаил Зотов

(Zotov and Bogdanova 2007)

"Эта станция представляет огромный пласт русской музыки: на нашей волне звучит и русский рок 1980-х, 1990-х годов, и поп-рок 1990-х годов и начала XXI века, и какой-то элемент 'металла' и современной этники." (Translation: p. 135)

C.16 Елена Зыкова

(Electronic chat, 16.09.2005)
"a mne arktika nravitsya, pravda ne sam klub, a to chto tam igrayet – sam klub popsoviy kakoy-to, tam po nocham discoteki delayut)))) oni sovmeschaut 2 vida deyatel'nosty – vidimo prosto metal-klub derzhat' zdes' eto ne vygodno" (copy of chat transcription, her transliteration and orthography) (Translation: p. 118).

C.17 Андрей Иванов

(Ivanov 2004)
"Да, есть проблемы играть в Санкт-Петербурге в том плане, что, к сожалению, здесь не так много клубов, их мало. Не секрет, что Санкт-Петербург, – к сожалению, город, в котором не так много финансов, [...] хотя это действительно обидно то, что очень много музыкантов, хороших музыкантов, хороших групп, ездят работать в Москву, потому что в Москве как раз очень много клубов, в Москве, в принципе, платят хорошие гонорары, на которые музыканты уже могут принципиально как-то жить." (Translation: p. 128)

"Я думаю, что это – очень разный контингент, потому что, во-первых, музыка регги переживает сейчас некую вторую волну. Поэтому сейчас этой музыкой интересуются ребята, которым 19-20 лет и также, я думаю, что есть люди, которые приходят, которым уже 30-40 лет." (Translation: p. 158)

"Он о регги очень мало знает. Он знает там: Боб Марли, что надо курить ганджа и все, как правило, и больше он ничего не знает. Поэтому я думаю, что это – внешний эффект, мода. Я думаю, что это модно." (Translation: p. 159)

"В нашей регги-культуре очень часто люди играют музыку образца 78-80 годов. Не знаю почему они это делают. Может быть, у них просто нет материала, они не слышали, допустим. Потому что у нас, действительно, очень большой дефицит: если сейчас прийти в какой-нибудь музыкальный магазин, в лучшем случае, сразу предложат Боба Марли, UB40 или какой-нибудь сборник регги, как раз именно 78-80 года. То есть, соответственно, что люди слышали, так и сделали." (Translation: p. 160)

C.18 Ива Нова

(Fedorova et al. 2005b)

ЛенаЖ: "Мы живем в Петербурге, я родилась в Петербурге, Лена сюда приехала учиться, Катя тоже здесь жила, Инка жила далеко от Петербурга: переехала в Питер учиться, Настя тоже приехала учиться и музыкой заниматься. То есть мы живем здесь, это – наш город. То есть Питер только поэтому связан."

David-Emil: "Используете ли вы Питер в своей музыке?"

ЛенаЖ: "Нет, я не думаю, что есть какие-то элементы Питера." [laughs]

Катя: "У нас в крови Петербург, нам сложно сказать какие у него элементы."

Инка: "Но пока конкретных песен про Петербург мы еще не сочинили." (Translation: p. 152)

(Fedorova et al. 2005a)

Катя: "Ну клубов мало, да, в Питере, а групп много. Петербург музыкальный город вообще – гораздо больше, чем в Москве групп, хотя Москва больше. Но при этом большая очередь в клуб – концерт надо очень заранее делать – за 3 месяца там, за 2 месяца, потому что очень много коллективов, а клубов нет." (Translation: p. 105)

ЛенаН: "Проблема – это то, что мало клубов, не знаю, и мало денег и все, в России, то есть, что концерты в России – это основная проблема. Что на инструменты вечно денег не хватает и на жизнь там тем более."

Катя: "И поэтому многие музыканты работают, и музыка становится как хобби" [...]

ЛенаН: "А как клубов в Питере мало, то есть платят мало, в Москве там, ну так себе как бы. То есть нас спасают только вот европейские концерты, где ты сможешь, ну, подзаработать." (Translation: p. 105)

ЛенаН: "А вообще это – очень большая проблема. [...] У нас сейчас пока это – не проблема, на данный момент."

Катя: "Мы очень долго ездили."

ЛенаН: "Это всегда переезды постоянные, это вот. Вообще для музыкантов в Питере это – проблема, да." (Translation: p. 110)

Катя: "Это те люди, которые чаще, наверное, работают больше в кабаках. [...] Многие петербургские коллективы, которые часто играют в Москве, не все живут в Питере, потому что они не могут настолько часто играть, чтобы там жить. А часто выступают те, кто обычно работает в баре или кабаках."
ЛенаН: "Которые каждый день..."
Катя: "Да, это – работа. У нас – несколько другая. Это – разница музыканта того, который играет просто в баре каждый раз, ну там каждый вечер, как на работу он туда приходит каждый день или три раза в неделю четко, а у нас – другая ситуация. Мы не можем так часто играть, потому что концерт – он концептуальный. Нам и не надо. Зачем? От этого очень устаешь тоже. Это, действительно, такая работа, это – халтура, чаще всего. Многие к этому так относятся: 'Ай, там кабак, ну.' Это – не творчество, это – зарабатывание денег. И поэтому для таких музыкантов, может быть, удобнее уехать в Москву, конечно. Именно работать. В Финляндию многие уезжают." (Translation: p. 129)

C.19   Константин Кинчев

(Riabov and Lubenskii 2008)

"Я за великую светлую Русь со столицей в Киеве. Столица должна быть здесь, а страна должна называться 'Русь'" (Translation: p. 218)

(Shugailo 2007)

"Вообще я вижу будущее России в симфонии властей: власть светская на все решения должна получать благословение от духовенства, президент должен идти рука об руку с патриархом, тогда будет и держава крепнуть. В общем-то сейчас хорошие позиции занимает Путин." (Translation: p. 217)

C.20   Виктор Културов

(Kultashov 2006)

Витя: "Ты с мелодией разберешься, не проблема. Короче [imitates trumpet] этого не надо [...]"
David-Emil: "Ты сам это показал."

Витя: "Я никогда не пел [imitates trumpet]. Как это, знаешь... Такая русская мелодия была в самый первый раз. Играй, как есть. Вот это вот [imitates trumpet] тоже, а не 'гррр'." (Translation: p. 41)

"Мелодии и аккорды, которые используются в этой музыке, они, мне кажется, никогда не использовались в русском роке и то, что использовалось в русском роке, не используется в нашем проекте, все вот эти мелодии привычные. Наверное, джазовым звучанием мы как раз и отличаемся. Оно не джазовое, как брать джаз, который – импровизации джазовые, соло – нет. Вот именно какие-то аккорды, какие-то ноты – джазовые." (Translation: p. 41)

"Но они когда-то были частью России. Мне кажется, от того, что они отделились от нас, они не стали какой-то там другой, отличающейся от нас страной. Мне кажется, они стали, вот частью нас, но которая не хочет признавать это." (Translation: p. 177)

"Стиль, возможно, чуть-чуть поменялся. Из русского рока вот он превратился в какой-то такой панк. Потом он перешел в Ска-панк с трубами там. Местами даже регги присутствует." (Translation: p. 191)

C.21 Билли Новик

(Novik 2005)

"Мне кажется, что во многих песнях у меня есть строчки про какие-то улицы, это – конкретные улицы. Есть, например, улица Малая Морская где-то, где-то про Купчино песня. Когда употребляешь в песнях конкретные названия, определенные названия, которые существуют реально, то это, мне кажется, делает эти все истории более правдоподобными [...]. И в Питере у меня есть такая возможность, поскольку я знаю, я представляю, например, что такое перекресток Невского и Малой Морской. Если я буду об этом петь, и те люди, которые тоже это понимают, они будут четко понимать, о чем я пою." (Translation: p. 150)

C.22   Вячеслав Петкун

(Kozyrev and Barabanov 2007b, 56)
"Если говорить именно о музыке, – то никакого московского рока на фоне питерского просто не было. Питер – это 'Кино', 'Аквариум', 'Алиса', 'ДДТ'. А Москва – это что? Замечательная группа 'Центр' и, конечно, 'Звуки Му'. Вот и все." (Translation: p. 127)

(Kozyrev and Barabanov 2007b, 63)
"Я, приехав из Питера, понял, что антагонизм москвичей к питерцам гораздо слабее, чем питерцев к москвичам. Потому что помимо Питера у москвичей в число антагонистов входит еще вся остальная Россия. А Питеру в этом смысле попроще." (Translation: p. 132)

C.23   Александр Руденко

(Rudenko n.d.)
"В начале 2005 года в группу приходит Дэвид-Эмиль Викстрем – труба / подданный Австрии и США, приехал изучать русскую, а, попав в SVOБOДУ, также украинскую современную музыку" (Translation: p. 79)

"вторым трубачом и эксклюзивным представителем гр. SVOБOДА в Европе." (Translation: p. 79)

(Rudenko 2006)
"Да, поп-рок – это вот эти команды, которые Сплин, Би-2, 7Б, Смысловые галлюцинации, ну вся вот эта седьмая волна или восьмая, я их путаю сейчас, ну не важно. [talks about next wave] Попса у нас – это Меладзе, Орбакайте – вот эта вся компания." (Translation: p. 122)

"И мне здесь понравилось. Я понял, что музыкой лучше здесь заниматься, чем в Москве. Здесь как-то, ну я поначалу не верил, говорят какая здесь атмосфера, здесь да, здесь как-то спокойнее, здесь город более музыкальный. Не зря же здесь, ну можно сказать, все лучшие группы отсюда, из Питера, кого мы не возьмем. Ну есть и в Москве тоже, но меньше. И здесь как-то уютнее. Здесь мало места. Здесь все как-то друг друга знают. А Москва – она огромная. Эх!... Не, хороший город. Но у меня как-то не сложилось там. Не получилось. [...] Поэтому музыкой, мне кажется, лучше заниматься, по крайней мере, поначалу. Москва, не знаю, на меня все-таки давит. Москва – это город, там очень сильно чувствуются конфликты маленького человека и мегаполиса. В Питере это как-то не так ощущается. Здесь и народ подобрее, что самое ценное, помягче как-то. Там в Москве очень много негатива, как мне показалось. Я просто от этого уехал." (Translation: p. 130)

"потому что русский рок – это больше уклон на текст идет, а поп-рок – это уклон на музыку, претензия на музыку, я бы сказал. Это когда мозгов, мне кажется, не хватает, то тогда говорят, что: 'А у нас поп-рок'. Когда хорошего текста не могут написать." (Translation: p. 136)

"При этом юморить на грани вообще какой-то истерии, какого-то безумия, какого-то шутовства безумного, вот это вот есть Ленинград, что, в принципе, мне нравится в них, и что я как раз в своем творчестве тоже пытаюсь сделать. Чтобы там была какая-то пляска, такое безумное веселье, такое нет, сумашествие, вот. Что как бы, мне кажется, и есть свобода, освобождение от этих проблем, комплексов, которые у людей есть." (Translation: p. 171)

"Океан Ельзи пишет серьезные песни на украинском языке, потому что они живут во Львове. Я их очень люблю. [sarcastic laughter] У нас ближе к Воплям Видоплясова - такая веселая энергичная музыка, такая 'Хей, Хей, Братан.'" (Translation: p. 181)

"Панк-ска с элементами гранжа [...] С украинскими текстами, с украинскими и русскими такими. Больше даже не чисто украинскими, а на суржике на таком, чтобы понятно и в России, и на Украине там, и в Белоруссии. Ну это, в основном – такие веселые песни – серьезные песни, они вот на русском языке." (Translation: p. 183)

"А что там остальные песни тоже больше стилизация идет под украинский фольклор [...] Мне просто нравится украинская народная - это тоже, меня, видишь, я подумал, что это в какой-то степени от ностальгии, вот когда пожил в Москве там с 95-ого года." (Translation: p. 183)

"Которые ближе к фольклору, да, или та же самая 'Ла-ла'. Она по словам такая, [...] И вот 'Село моє пусте, Неначе вимерло' – это уже и есть какой-то тоже украинский фольклор, потому что фольклора больше всего, это – в украинских деревнях. Это – хаты-мазанки, [...] сало, горилка. Я стараюсь штампы не брать: 'сало, горилка' – основной штамп. [...] Да, можно сказать, и 'Ла-ла' туда относится." (Translation: p. 187)

"'Чоботи', конечно, самый главный фольклор. Такая же песня есть даже. Вот в этом году мы были на Украине и зашли в магазины, взяли вот эти свадебные песни украинские, да. А мне говорили раньше, что есть такая песня 'Чоботи': я слышал такую фразу просто 'Чоботи з бугая, Не боятся холода нічого.' Ну и решил я написать такую песню. А потом вот мне говорили: 'Да есть же такая песня, это вообще – народная.' Фомич мне все время говорил. [...] смотрим 'чоботи', поставили, мы послушали – ну да, там только 'Чоботи, чоботи з бугая, Не боятся холода нічого. Чоботи, чоботи ви мої, Наробили клопоту ви мої [should be мені].' Это тоже откуда-то из украинского фольклора, там очень много тоже песен вот таких вот. Потому что украинские свадебные – это тоже собиралось из фольклора в этой области." (Translation: p. 187)

"Или вот Маруся. Это 'Маруся раз, два, три, калина', это же – 'Розпрягайте, хлопці', это вот что ни на есть самая украинская народная песня, которую пели очень давно как бы и поют до сих пор за столами, на свадьбах, везде. Вот это есть Украинский колорит." (Translation: p. 188)

(Svoboda n.d.)

"Музыка – это свобода, а музыка SVOБOДы – это смесь ска, реггей, фолка, мелодичных гуцульских напевов и взрывного панка." (Translation: p. 181)

(Svoboda 2008)

"Скоро пройдут концерты группы SVOБOДA, приуроченные ко Дню рождения легендарного борца за свободу Батьки Махно. Тем более, что лидер группы родом из тех же мест. Первый концерт – 26 октября в Roks club, где Вы попадете на театрализованное шоу 'Махноград': горилка, шампанское, украинские песни, слэм и много дыма." (Translation: p. 181)

C.24 Олег Скрипка

(Chernin 2006, 515)

"Ни для кого не секрет, что для русского уха украинский язык звучит смешно. Это такая смешная версия русского языка. Но по-доброму смешная." (Translation: p. 177)

C.25   Евгений Федров

(Fedrov 2006)

"Ну вот атмосфера, которая здесь, культура, которая здесь есть, она очень традиционная, не такая авангардная, как в Москве. [...] Конечно, это имеет значение. Мы здесь живем. Если бы не имело значения, мы бы поехали в Москву и стали бы богатыми людьми. Там много денег, в Москве. Здесь нет, но зато здесь есть люди, которые думают больше об искусстве, нежели о деньгах." (Translation: p. 125)

C.26   Дмитрий Храмцов

(Khramtsov 2005)

"Во-первых, как я уже сказал, такую музыку, как мы играем, она как бы здесь чужая немножко. Это с одной стороны хорошо, потому что у нас нет конкуренции. Мы одни только здесь. А с другой стороны это плохо, потому что у нас нету как-бы такого, ну, среды, в которой мы могли бы существовать как вот. [...] Вот, ну и то есть в плане заработки не очень, ну, в принципе, нормально. [...] То есть по сравнению с рок-музыкантами, которые собирают в клубах столько людей сколько мы собираем, по-моему, лучше. Потому что у нас еще варианты другие: мы играем на фестивалях каких-то, на корпоративных мероприятиях, на которые не зовут этих музыкантов, потому то что они играют там альтернативную музыку, которая только в клубах там для, не знаю, для панков. Ну в этом отношении, конечно, есть на что пожаловаться, но вообщем-то у нас есть заработок. Мы музыкой зарабатываем, то есть какие-то деньги и вообщем-то неплохо, нормально, хорошо. Можно лучше конечно, ждем когда... тоже вот диски продаются наши." (Translation: p. 107)

"В том смысле, что мы как бы, не широко известная группа такая, то есть нас не крутят по радио, по телевизору, в этом свойстве мы – андеграунд. То есть у нас нет какой-то задачи там кому-то противостоять или там, я не знаю, как бы есть какая-то официальная культура, мы – неофициальная. У нас какие-то свои ценности там, то есть мы любим эту музыку, ее играем, она немножко отличается как бы от поп-музыки или от какой-то там, которую знают. Ну большинство людей слышит, и в этом смысле, может быть – андеграунд. То есть мы себя сознательно не хотим находиться в андеграунде, потому что мы такие там нонконформисты там, не знаю, просто мы играем в клубах в небольших – в этом смысле андеграунд. Потому, что вот такая музыка 'world music' в России не очень развита, то есть не очень большой рынок, и поэтому она так немножко стоит как бы рядом с какой-то андеграундной музыкой." (Translation: p. 121)

"Про Питер говорят, что он – творческий город: 'Питер. Вот мы приехали в Питер. Там стремились...' Мне сложно сказать, потому что я отсюда родом и для меня тут ничего особенного, я все здесь знаю, то есть для меня это все – будничное. Питер – всегда так было, и ничего такого я не вижу здесь особенного. То есть по сравнению с Москвой, так я в Москву езжу только раз в месяц поиграть и не могу сказать, что Питер лучше Москвы в чем-то, что в Москве творчества нет, только все в Питере." (Translation: p. 130)

С.27 Сергей Чернов

(Chernov 2006a)

"Русский рок – это группа ДДТ, группа Чиж и компания. Трудно сформулировать. Как бы такой мессианский немножко, который больше, чем музыка, который с какими-нибудь религиозными идеями, или такая довольно примитивная музыка и с каким-то обязательным моментом русского фольклора или русского чего-то. Чайф группа: просто все его [...], когда ТаМтАм устроил клуб, вот у него было правило, что не должно там быть русского рока вообще. Я считал, что русский рок – это группа Аквариум, группа Гражданская оборона и еще какая-то группа. Просто разные виды его. ТаМтАма идея, мне кажется, она – чисто такая интернациональная, что там нет такой провинциальности. Идея еще русского рока в том, что они – не хуже западных групп, и что у нас есть своя идея какая-то русская и много людей, наверное, много поклонников у них. И много людей, наверное, так думает, но это не очень интересно, мне кажется." (Translation: p. 138)

C.28 Татьяна Яценко

(Iatsenko 2006)

"Я часто же с Бони Немом езжу в Москву и мне приходилось общаться очень часто с москвичами, и 'Москва и марихуана' – это несколько саркастичная песня, потому что москвичи, они очень слепо следуют моде, то есть у них там: 'О, мода на кокаин' – все нюхают. 'О, мода на марихуану' – все покупают, курят просто в безумных количествах. И вот весь мой сарказм по поводу Москвы вылился в эту песню. Ну а вообще, марихуана там продается лучше и лучшего качества, чем у нас." (Translation: p. 125)

"Потому что у нас так получилось, что у нас вышел первый альбом, и у нас все песни так или иначе связаны с городом. Я вообще очень люблю город и даже песня 'Санкт-Петербург', она хоть и на немецком языке, но написана о нашем городе. Наверное, я – фанатка Питера." (Translation: p. 149)

"Мы берем за основу регги-традиции, то есть, допустим, регги-барабаны, регги-бас, но, допустим, бас-гитара звучит более плотно, барабаны звучат более разнообразно, рагамафины у нас звучат более жестко. Вообще вся музыка звучит более жестко за счет гитары, которая играет с фуззом, но, как мне кажется, и еще за счет того, что у нас, особенно на концертах, у нас – более эмоциональное исполнение. То есть, если взять, например, ямайский roots-регги, то под эту музыку хорошо лежать на пляжике, и это может быть фоновой музыкой. Мне кажется, что наша музыка может нравиться и не нравиться, но как фоновая она вряд ли будет восприниматься." (Translation: p. 160)

"Мне кажется, во-первых, регги-музыка, она – очень мудрая, все-таки она идет из корней, мы от них не отказываемся, не смотря на то, что это урбан-регги и, благодаря своей мудрости, к регги можно подключить и джаз и немножко блюза, немножечко посмешивать это все. То есть, она может впитать в себя другие еще стили из-за своей вот этой мудрости." (Translation: p. 161)

APPENDIX C. QUOTES IN THEIR ORIGINAL LANGUAGE   333

C.29   N.N.

(Kulturportal Russland n.d.)

"Barbarenlounge mit Dj Nata (Nowosibirsk) (Propeller Barbie Dance: Ska, Ragga, Gypsie, Polka, Electro, Turbo, Folk und mehr aus Russland)". (their orthography) (Translation: p. 231)

Jingle on Nashe Radio St. Petersburg during 2005 and 2006

"Самая полная коллекция рок-н-ролла и все модное в нашей музыке сегодня. Наша музыка! Наше радио! Сделано в России!" (Translation: p. 211)

(Misteriia Zvuka n.d.)

"Под 'русский рок' подпадают и такие альбомные проекты компании 'Мистерия Паблишинг' как 'Воплі Відоплясова', 'Океан Эльзи', Чиж, Запрещенные барабанщики, Ва-Банкъ, Ария, Сергей Шнуров." (Translation: p. 212)

(OST * Klub n.d.)

"Es ist wie ein Orkan, der mit Vollgas vom Osten kommend auf einen zurast und einen packt. Gnadenlos. Was hinter diesem 'Naturphänomen' steckt, ist nichts anderes als die Gruppe RUSSKAJA. Ein irres Ensemble mit sieben irren Musikern aus Russland und Österreich, die wie ein Sturm aufspielen, einen mitreißen und das Publikum ekstatisch zum Tanzen bringen. Denn Ska wird von RUSSKAJA so kraftvoll russisch interpretiert, dass man glaubt, man sei an einer wodkagefüllten Sputnikrakete festgeschnallt und durchbräche damit die Schallmauer. Und weil der Wodka bei den Konzerten von RUSSKAJA auch mit Vollgas rinnt, kann spätestens bei der Zugabe jeder fließend Russisch und weiß, was es bedeutet am Roten Platz Pogo zu tanzen." (Translation: p. 277)

(FM n.d.)

"Радио Русский Берлин – это новые и старые хиты из России. [...] Радиостанция стремится поддержать своих слушателей в сохранении их культурных корней, создавая одновременно связь между немецкой и русской культурами." (Translation: p. 241)

References

Bibliography

007-berlin.de. n.d. Berlin für Russen, Russen für Berlin / Berlin dlia russkikh, russkie dlia Berlina. 007-berlin.de. http://www.007-berlin.de/ (accessed 02.04.2009).

Alekseenko, Larisa, and Oksana Prokhorova. 2008. Krizis lishil artistov deneg. *Trud*, 12.12., http://www.trud.ru/issue/article.php?id=200812122340801 (accessed 18.12.2008).

Alleyne, Mike. 2000. White reggae: Cultural dilution in the record industry. *Popular Music and Society* 24 (1): 15-30, http://www.informaworld.com/openurl?genre=article&issn=0300%2d7766&volume=24&issue=1&spage=15 (accessed 01.03.2010).

Anderson, Benedict. 1991. *Imagined Communities – Reflections on the Origin and Spread of Nationalism*. Revised ed. London, New York: Verso.

Appadurai, Arjun. 1996. *Modernity at Large: Cultural Dimensions of Globalization*. Minneapolis, London: University of Minnesota Press.

Arte. 2008. Haydamaky. http://www.arte.tv/de/kunst-musik/tracks/Diese-Woche/navigation/2026100.html (accessed 10.09.2008).

Bahry, Romana. 1994. Rock Culture and Rock Music in Ukraine. In *Rocking the State – Rock Music and Politics in Eastern Europe and Russia*, edited by Sabrina Petra Ramet, 243-96. Boulder, San Francisco, Oxford: Westview Press.

Baily, John. 2001. Learning to Perform as a Research Technique in Ethnomusicology. *British Journal of Ethnomusicology* 10 (2): 85-98, http://www.jstor.org/stable/3060663 (accessed 08.01.2014).

Barrow, Steve, and Peter Dalton. 1997. *Reggae – The Rough Guide*. London: The Rough Guides.

Barth, Fredrik. 1998. Introduction. In *Ethnic Groups and Boundaries – The Social Organization of Culture Difference*, edited by Fredrik Barth, 9-38. Long

Grove: Waveland Press. Original edition, 1969.

Beck, Ulrich. 1997. *Was ist Globalisierung?* Frankfurt am Main: Suhrkamp.

Bennet, Andy. 2004. Consolidating the music scenes perspective. *Poetics* 32: 223-34.

Berlin.de – Der Beauftragte für Integration und Migration. 2008. Zuwanderer und Einwohner Berlins nach Staatsangehörigkeit. http://www.berlin.de/lb/intmig/statistik/demografie/einwohner_staatsangehoerigkeit.html (accessed 12.03.2010).

Beumers, Birgit. 2005. *Pop Culture Russia! Media, Arts, and Lifestyle.* Santa Barbara, Denver, Oxford: ABC-Clio.

Bhabha, Homi K. 1990. The Third Space. In *Identity: Community, Culture, Difference*, edited by Jonathan Rutherford, 207-21. London: Lawrence and Wishart.

Bhabha, Homi K. 1994. *The Location of Culture.* London: Routledge.

Biddle, Ian, and Vanessa Knights, eds. 2007. *Music, National Identity and the Politics of Location – Between the Global and the Local.* Hampshire, Burlington: Ashgate.

Bilaniuk, Laada. 2005. *Contested Tongues – Language Politics and Cultural Correction in Ukraine.* Ithaca, London: Cornell University Press.

Billy's Band. 2003a. Ofitsial'nyi sait. http://www.billysband.ru/ (accessed 10.02.2009).

Born, Georgina, and David Hesmondhalgh. 2000a. Introduction: On Difference, Representation, and Appropriation in Music. In *Western Music and its Others: Difference, Representation and Appropriation in Music*, edited by Georgina Born, and David Hesmondhalgh, 1-58. Berkeley, Los Angeles: University of California Press.

Born, Georgina, and David Hesmondhalgh, eds. 2000b. *Western Music and its Others: Difference, Representation and Appropriation in Music.* Berkeley, Los Angeles: University of California Press.

Bottà, Giacomo. 2006a. Interculturalism and New Russians in Berlin. *CLCWeb: Comparative Literature and Culture* 8 (2), http://docs.lib.purdue.edu/clcweb/vol8/iss2/5/ (accessed 17.06.2007).

Bottà, Giacomo. 2006b. Pop Music, Cultural Sensibilities and Places: Manchester 1976–1997. Paper read at ESF-LiU Conference. Cities and Media: Cultural

Perspectives on Urban Identities in a Mediatized World, Vadstena, Sweden, 25–29 October 2006, at Linköping.

Boym, Svetlana. 2001. *The Future of Nostalgia*. New York: Basic Books.

Bratersky, Alexander. 2006. Children of the Revolution. *Russia Profile*, 24.07., http://www.russiaprofile.org/page.php?pageid=Culture+%26+Living&articleid=672 (accessed 28.03.2008).

Brusila, Johannes. 2003. *Local Music, not from here – The Discourse of World Music examined through three Zimbabwean case studies: The Bhundu Boys, Virginia Mukwesha and Sunduza*. Helsinki: Finnish Society for Ethnomusicology Publications.

Bundesverwaltungsamt. 2007. Spätaussiedler und Angehörige – Herkunftsstaaten 2007. Bundesverwaltungsamt. http://www.bva.bund.de/nn_376892/DE/Aufgaben/Abt__III/Spaetaussiedler/statistik/07SpaetaussiedlerundAngehoerigeHerkunftsl2007.html (accessed 24.03.2010).

Bundesverwaltungsamt. 2008. Spätaussiedler und Angehörige – Herkunftsstaaten 2008. Bundesverwaltungsamt. http://www.bva.bund.de/nn_376892/DE/Aufgaben/Abt__III/Spaetaussiedler/statistik/08SpaetaussiedlerundAngehoerigeHerkunftsl2008.html (accessed 24.03.2010).

Bundesverwaltungsamt. 2009. Spätaussiedler und Angehörige – Herkunftsstaaten 2009. Bundesverwaltungsamt. http://www.bva.bund.de/nn_376892/DE/Aufgaben/Abt__III/Spaetaussiedler/statistik/09SpaetaussiedlerundAngehoerigeHerkunftsl2009.html (accessed 24.03.2010).

Burlaka, Andrei. 2007a. *Aleksandr Bashlachev*. In *Rok Entsiklopediia – Populiarnaia muzyka v Leningrade-Peterburge 1965-2005 – 1*, 134-36. St. Petersburg: Amfora.

Burlaka, Andrei. 2007b. *Reggistan*. In *Rok Entsiklopediia – Populiarnaia muzyka v Leningrade-Peterburge 1965-2005 – 3*, 133-35. St. Petersburg: Amfora.

Burlaka, Andrei. 2007c. *Rok Entsiklopediia – Populiarnaia muzyka v Leningrade-Peterburge 1965-2005*. Vol. 1-3, St. Petersburg: Amfora.

Burlaka, Andrei. 2007d. *Strannye Igry*. In *Rok Entsiklopediia – Populiarnaia muzyka v Leningrade-Peterburge 1965-2005* – 3, 309-14. St. Petersburg: Amfora.

Butler, Kim D. 2001. Defining Diaspora, Refining a Discourse. *Diaspora* 10 (2): 189-219.

Chang, Kevin O'Brien, Robert Witmer, and Len McCarthy. 2005. Jamaica. In *Caribbean and Latin America*, edited by John Shepherd, David Horn, and Dave Laing, 60-74. London, New York: Continuum.

Chernin, Anton. 2006. *Nasha Muzyka: Pervaia polnaia istoriia russkogo roka, rasskazannaia im samim*. St. Petersburg: Amfora.

Chernov, Sergey. 2003. Berlin still has a russian zone. *The St. Petersburg Times*, 29.05., http://www.sptimesrussia.com/index.php?action_id=2&story_id=10137 (accessed 29.05.2003).

Chernov, Sergey. 2005a. 'Orange Plague' Kills Concert. *The St. Petersburg Times*, 01.04., http://www.sptimes.ru/index.php?action_id=2&story_id=3155 (accessed 05.02.2008).

Chernov, Sergey. 2005b. Tank warfare. *The St. Petersburg Times*, 23.09., http://www.sptimes.ru/story/15642 (accessed 23.09.2005).

Chernov, Sergey. 2006b. Chernov's choice. *The St. Petersburg Times*, 28.04., http://www.sptimes.ru/index.php?action_id=2&story_id=17480 (accessed 13.02.2008).

Chernov, Sergey. 2006c. Taking a stand. *The St. Petersburg Times*, 18.08., http://www.sptimes.ru/index.php?action_id=100&story_id=18591 (accessed 13.02.2008).

Chernov, Sergey. 2007. Rock in a hard place. *The St. Petersburg Times*, 16.03., http://www.sptimes.ru/index.php?action_id=2&story_id=21020 (accessed 13.02.2008).

Chernov, Sergey. 2008a. Chernov's choice. *The St. Petersburg Times*, 19.12., http://www.sptimes.ru/story/27887 (accessed 19.12.2008).

Chernov, Sergey. 2008b. Chernov's choice. *The St. Petersburg Times*, 17.10, ii, http://www.sptimes.ru/story/27404 (accessed 17.10.2008).

Clifford, James. 1986. Introduction: Partial Truths. In *Writing Culture – The Poetics and Politics of Ethnography*, edited by James Clifford, and George E. Marcus, 3-26. Berkeley, Los Angeles, London: University of California Press.

Clifford, James. 1994. Diasporas. *Cultural Anthropology* 9 (3): 302-38.
Cloonan, Martin. 1999. Pop and the Nation-State: Towards a Theorisation. *Popular Music* 18 (2): 193-207.
Cohen, Sara. 1997. Identity, Place and the 'Liverpool Sound'. In *Ethnicity, Identity and Music – The Musical Construction of Place*, edited by Martin Stokes, 117-34. Oxford, New York: Berg Publishers. Original edition, 1994.
Cohen, Sara. 1999. Scenes. In *Key Terms in Popular Music and Culture*, edited by Bruce Horner, and Thomas Swiss, 239-50. Malden, Oxford, Carlton: Blackwell Publishing.
Cohen, Sara. 2001. *Rock Culture in Liverpool – Popular Music in the Making*. Reprint ed. Oxford: Oxford University Press. Original edition, 1991.
Cooley, Timothy J. 1997. Casting Shadows in the Field. In *Shadows in the Field – New Perspectives for Fieldwork in Ethnomusicology*, edited by Gregory F. Barz, and Timothy J. Cooley, 3-19. New York, Oxford: Oxford University Press.
Cooley, Timothy J., and Gregory Barz. 2008. *Casting Shadows: Fieldwork Is Dead! Long Live Fieldwork! Introduction*. In *Shadows in the Field – New Perspectives for Fieldwork in Ethnomusicology*, edited by Gregory F. Barz, and Timothy J. Cooley, 3-24. New York, Oxford: Oxford University Press. 2nd revised edition.
coverinfo.de. n.d. Cover-Versionen- und Musikzitate-Datenbank. http://www.coverinfo.de (accessed 04.06.2008).
Cushman, Thomas. 1995. *Notes from Underground – Rock Music Counterculture in Russia*. Albany: State University of New York Press.
Dahlhaus, Carl. 1980. *Die Musik des 19. Jahrhunderts*. Edited by Carl Dahlhaus. Vol. 6, *Neues Handbuch der Musikwissenschaft*. Wiesbaden: Akademische Verlagsgesellschaft Athenaion.
Darieva, Tsypylma. 2004. *Russkij Berlin – Migranten und Medien in Berlin und London*. Münster: Lit Verlag.
Davis, Stephen. n.d. Reggae. Grove Music Online. http://www.oxfordmusiconline.com/subscriber/article/grove/music/23065 (accessed 08.09.2008).
Deep Sound Underground Club. n.d. Deep Sound Underground Club. http://www.deepsoundclub.com/index.html (accessed 22.10.2005).

DeNora, Tia. 2000. *Music in Everyday Life*. Cambridge, New York: Cambridge University Press.

Diehl, Keila. 2002. *Echoes from Dharamsala: Music in the Life of a Tibetan Refugee Community*. Berkeley, Los Angeles, London: University of California Press.

Dietz, Barbara. 2000. German and Jewish migration from the former Soviet Union to Germany: background, trends and implications. *Journal of Ethnic and Migration Studies* 26 (4): 635-52.

Dockwray, Ruth. 2005. "Deconstructing the Rock Anthem: Textual Form, Participation and Collectivity." Dissertation, Institute of Popular Music, University of Liverpool, Liverpool.

Domanskii, Iurii. 2010. *Russkaia rok-poeziia: tekst i kontekst*. Moscow: Intrada – Izdatel'stvo Kulaginoi.

Eastblok Music. n.d. Eastblok Music Shop. http://www.eastblok.de/catalog/ (accessed 04.12.2008).

Eastblok Music. n.d. Haydamaky Artist Page. http://eastblok.de/ebm/index.php?option=com_content&task=view&id=6 (accessed 02.11.2007).

Eriomin, E. M. 2011. *Tsarskaia rybalka, ili Strategii osvoeniia bibleiskogo teksta v russkoi rok-poezii: Sluchai B. Grebenshchikova*. Blagoveshchensk: Izdatel'stvo BGPU.

Erlmann, Veit. 1999. *Music, Modernity, and the Global Imagination: South Africa and the West*. Oxford: Oxford University Press.

Eurasia Group. 2009. Fat Tails in an Uncertain World. http://docs.eurasiagroup.net/fattails2009.pdf (accessed 07.05.2009).

Everett, Walter. 1999. *The Beatles as Musicians – Revolver through the Anthology*. New York, Oxford: Oxford University Press.

Fawkes, Helen. 2004. Ukraine drive to keep Russian off buses. *BBC News*, 18.06., http://news.bbc.co.uk/go/pr/fr/-/2/hi/europe/3783353.stm (accessed 04.09.2007).

Federal Ministry of the Interior. 2005. *Immigration Law and Policy*. Berlin: Federal Ministry of the Interior.

Feld, Steven. 1994a. Communication, Music, and Speech about Music. In *Music Grooves*, edited by Steven Feld, and Charles Keil, 77 – 95. Chicago: The University of Chicago Press.

Feld, Steven. 1994b. *From schizophonia to schismogenesis: on the discourses and *commodification practices of 'world music' and 'world beat'*. In *Music Grooves: Essays And Dialogues*, edited by Steven Feld, and Charles Keil, 257-89. Chicago: The University of Chicago Press.

Feld, Steven. 2000a. A Sweet Lullaby for World Music. *Public Culture* 12 (1): 145-71.

Feld, Steven. 2000b. *The poetics and politics of Pygmy Pop*. In *Western Music and its Others: Difference, Representation and Appropriation in Music*, edited by Georgina Born, and David Hesmondhalgh, 280-304. Berkeley, Los Angeles: University of California Press.

Feoktistova, Svetlana. 2008. Vakkhanaliia rassypletsia. *Vzgliad*, 02.12., http://www.vz.ru/culture/2008/12/2/234816.html (accessed 11.12.2008).

Frith, Simon. 2000. *The Discourse of World Music*. In *Western Music and its Others: Difference, Representation and Appropriation in Music*, edited by Georgina Born, and David Hesmondhalgh, 305-22. Berkeley, Los Angeles, London: University of California Press.

Frolova-Walker, Marina. 2007. *Russian Music and Nationalism – From Glinka to Stalin*. New Haven, London: Yale University Press.

Frolova-Walker, Marina, Jonathan Powell, Rosamund Bartlett, Izaly Zemtsovsky, Mark Slobin, Jarkko Niemi, and Yuri Sheikin. n.d. Russian Federation. Grove Music Online. http://www.oxfordmusiconline.com/subscriber/article/grove/music/40456pg2 (accessed 11.03.2009).

Gates, Henry Louis Jr. 1988. *The Signifying Monkey: A Theory of African-American Literary Criticism*. New York, Oxford: Oxford University Press.

Gavrikov, V. A. 2007. *Mifopoetika v tvorchestve Aleksandra Bashlacheva*. Briansk: Ladomir.

Gavrikov, V. A. 2011. *Russkaia pesennaia poeziia XX veka kak tekst*. Briansk: Brianskoe SRP VOG.

Geertz, Clifford. 1973. *The Interpretation of Cultures*. New York: Basic Books.

Gemba, Holger. 2007. Ruslana – Interkulturelles Marketing aus den Karpaten. *Osteuropa* 57 (5): 137-49.

Giddens, Anthony. 2000. *The Consequences of Modernity*. Cambridge, Oxford: Polity. Original edition, 1990.

Gift Music. n.d. WOMEX & WMCE Award 2006. http://www.giftmusic.de/womexwmceaward/womexwmceaward2006/index.html (accessed

05.12.2008).
Gogol, Nikolai. 1985. *The Complete Tales of Nikolai Gogol*. Edited by Leonard J. Kent. Vol. 1, Chicago, London: The University of Chicago Press.
Gololobov, Ivan. 2013. There are no Atheists in Trenches under Fire: Orthodox Christianity in Russian Punk. *Punk and Post-Punk* 1 (3): 305-21.
Gololobov, Ivan, Hilary Pilkington, and Yngvar Bordewich Steinholt. 2014. *Punk in Russia: Cultural mutation from the 'useless' to the 'moronic'*. New York, London: Routledge.
Gololobov, Ivan, and Yngvar Bordewich Steinholt. 2013. The Elephant in the Room? 'Post-Socialist Punk' and the Pussy Riot Phenomenon. *Punk and Post-Punk* 1 (3): 249-51.
Gorenberg, Gershom. 2008. How Do You Prove You're a Jew? *The New York Times*, 02.03, http://www.nytimes.com/2008/03/02/magazine/02jewishness-t.html (accessed 04.03.2008).
Gramota. n.d. Gramota.Ru – spravochno-informatsionnyi internet-portal 'Russkii iazyk'. http://www.gramota.ru/ (accessed 28.02.2008).
Grossberg, Lawrence. 1994. *Is Anybody Listening? Does Anybody Care? On Talking about 'The State of Rock'*. In *Microphone Fiends: Youth Music and Youth Culture*, edited by Tricia Rose, and Andrew Ross, 41-58. New York, London: Routledge.
Guilbault, Jocelyne. 2001. World music. In *The Cambridge Companion to Pop and Rock*, edited by Simon Frith, Will Straw, and John Street, 176-92. Cambridge, New York: Cambridge University Press.
Gupta, Akhil, and James Ferguson, eds. 1997. *Anthropological Locations – Boundaries and Grounds of a Field Science*. Berkeley, Los Angeles, London: University of California Press.
Hall, Stuart. 1990. Cultural Identity and Diaspora. In *Identity: Community, Culture, Difference*, edited by Jonathan Rutherford, 222-37. London: Lawrence & Wishart.
Hall, Stuart. 1996. Introduction: Who Needs 'Identity'? In *Questions of Cultural Identity*, edited by Stuart Hall, and Paul Du Gay, 1-17. London, Thousand Oaks, New Delhi: Sage Publications.
Hannerz, Ulf. 1992. *Cultural Complexity – Studies in the Social Organization of Meaning*. New York: Columbia University Press.

Hannerz, Ulf. 1996. *Transnational Connections – Culture, People, Places*. London, New York: Routledge.

Hannerz, Ulf. 2000. Flows, boundaries and hybrids: keywords in transnational anthropology. *Transnational Communities Programme – Working Paper Series* WPTC-2K-02, http://www.transcomm.ox.ac.uk/working%20papers/hannerz.pdf (accessed 15.05.2009).

Harlamov, Yury. 2005. Schum radio program about russian music – Radio Corax – Halle, Germany. Yahoo! Groups – Russian popular music. http://launch.groups.yahoo.com/group/russian_popular_music/message/32 (accessed 04.12.2008).

Hastrup, Kirsten. 1999. *Viljen til Viden – En humanistisk grundbog*. Copenhagen: Gyldendalske Boghandel.

Hebdige, Dick. 1987. *Cut 'n' Mix – Culture, Identity and Caribbean Music*. London, New York: Comedia.

Hebdige, Dick. 1993. *Subculture – The meaning of style*. Reprint ed. London, New York: Routledge.

Helbig, Adriana. 2006. The Cyberpolitics of Music in Ukraine's 2004 Orange Revolution. *Current Musicology* 82: 81-101.

Helbig, Adriana. 2014. *Hip Hop Ukraine: Music, Race, and African Migration*. Bloomington: Indiana University Press.

Hellier-Tinoco, Ruth. 2003. Experiencing people: relationships, responsibility and reciprocity. *British Journal of Ethnomusicology* 12 (1 Fieldwork impact): 19-34, http://www.jstor.org/stable/30036867.

Hesmondhalgh, David. 2005. Subcultures, Scenes or Tribes? None of the Above. *Journal of Youth Studies* 8 (1): 21-40.

Hill, Juniper. 2007. 'Global Folk Music' Fusions: The Reification of Transnational Relationships and the Ethics of Cross-Cultural Appropriations in Finnish Contemporary Folk Music. *Yearbook for Traditional Music* 39: 50-83.

Hitzler, Ronald, Thomas Bucher, and Arne Niederbacher. 2005. *Leben in Szenen: Formen jugendlicher Vergemeinschaftung heute*. Edited by Winfried Gebhardt, Ronald Hitzler, and Franz Liebl. 2nd, revised ed. Vol. 3, *Erlebniswelten*. Wiesbaden: VS Verlag für Sozialwissenschaften.

Hrytsa, Sophia. n.d. Ukraine, §II: Traditional music, 3. Music of the Carpathians. Grove Music Online. http://www.grovemusic.com/shared/views/

article.html?section=music.40470.2.3 (accessed 10.09.2007).

Hufen, Uli. 2010. *Das Regime und die Dandys: Russische Gaunerchansons von Lenin bis Putin*. Berlin: Rogner & Bernhard.

Hylland Eriksen, Thomas. 2003. Introduction. In *Globalisation – Studies in Anthropology*, edited by Thomas Hylland Eriksen, 1-17. London, Sterling: Pluto Press.

International Intellectual Property Alliance. n.d. Country Reports. http://www.iipa.com/countryreports.html (accessed 19.02.2014).

Ivanova, Julia. 2008. METRO Extensions. *Neva News*, 26.04., http://nevanews.com/index.php?id_article=179&section=7 (accessed 21.08.2008).

Jakobson, Roman. 1981. Linguistics and Poetics. In *Roman Jakobson Selected Writings: Poetry of Grammar and Grammar of Poetry*, edited by Stephen Rudy, 18-51. The Hague, Paris, New York: Mouton Publishers.

Kaffee Burger. n.d. Willkommen! http://www.kaffeeburger.de (accessed 02.12.2008).

Kaminer, Wladimir. 2000. *Russendisko*. München: Manhattan.

Kaminer, Wladimir. 2006. News: Gute Nachrichten von Kaminer. Rodina Club Berlin. http://www.rodina-club.de/?page=news (accessed 02.01.2007).

Kappeler, Andreas. 1992. *Russland als Vielvölkerreich – Entstehung, Geschichte, Zerfall*. München: C.H. Beck.

Kappeler, Andreas. 2003. *Der schwierige Weg zur Nation – Beiträge zur neueren Geschichte der Ukraine*. Wien, Köln, Weimar: Böhlau Verlag.

Kappeler, Andreas. 2005. *Russische Geschichte*. 4. revised ed. München: C.H. Beck.

Keightley, Keir. 2001. Reconsidering rock. In *The Cambridge Companion to Pop and Rock*, edited by Simon Frith, Will Straw, and John Street, 109-42. Cambridge, New York: Cambridge University Press.

Khinkulova, Kateryna. 2006. Ukraine rock battles Russian pop. *BBC News*, 08.05, http://news.bbc.co.uk/go/pr/fr/-/2/hi/europe/4984184.stm (accessed 03.09.2007).

King, Stephen A. 1998. International reggae, democratic socialism, and the secularization of the Rastafarian movement, 1972-1980. *Popular Music and Society* 22 (3): 39 — 60, http://www.informaworld.com/openurl?genre=article&issn=0300%2d7766&volume=22&issue=3&spage=3

9 (accessed 01.03.2010).
King, Stephen A. 2002. *Reggae, Rastafari, and the Rhetoric of Social Control*. Jackson: University Press of Mississippi.
Kiss, Antje, and Harald Lederer. 2006. *Migration, Asyl und Integration in Zahlen*. 14 ed. Nürnberg: Bundesamt für Migration und Flüchtlinge.
Kiss, Antje, and Harald Lederer. 2009. *Ausländerzahlen 2008*. Nürnberg: Bundesamt für Migration und Flüchtlinge.
Klid, Bohdan. 2007. Rock, Pop and Politics in Ukraine's 2004 Presidential Campaign and Orange Revolution. *Journal of Communist Studies and Transition Politics* 23 (1): 118-37.
Koning, Jos. 1980. The Fieldworker as Performer: Fieldwork Objectives and Social Roles in County Clare, Ireland. *Ethnomusicology* 24 (3): 417-29, http://www.jstor.org/stable/851151 (accessed 29.01.2010).
Kormil'tsev, Il'ia. 2006a. Velikoe rok-n-roll'noe naduvatel'stvo-2. Chast' pervaia. *Agentstvo politicheskikh novostei*, 20.06., http://www.apn.ru/publications/article9874.htm (accessed 14.02.2008).
Kormil'tsev, Il'ia. 2006b. Velikoe rok-n-roll'noe naduvatel'stvo-2. Chast' tret'ia. *Agentstvo politicheskikh novostei*, 20.07., http://www.apn.ru/publications/article10053.htm (accessed 14.02.2008).
Kovalev, Roman K. 2004. Chastushka. In *Encyclopedia of Russian History*, edited by James R. Millar, 230. New York: Macmillan Reference USA.
Kozyrev, Mikhail, and Boris Barabanov. 2007a. *Moi Rock-n-Roll – Black book*. Vol. 1, Moscow: Gaiatri.
Kozyrev, Mikhail, and Boris Barabanov. 2007b. *Moi Rock-n-Roll – Red book*. Vol. 3, Moscow: Gaiatri.
Kozyrev, Mikhail, and Boris Barabanov. 2007c. *Moi Rock-n-Roll – White book*. Vol. 2, Moscow: Gaiatri.
Kucher, Katharina. 2007. Vom Flüchtlingslager in die Konzertsäle: Die Geschichte des Don Kosaken Chores. *Osteuropa* 57 (5): 57-68.
Kulturportal Russland. n.d. Kulturportal Russland. http://www.kulturportal-russland.de (accessed 03.10.2005).
Laitin, David D. 2004. The De-cosmopolitanization of the Russian Diaspora: A View from Brooklyn in the 'Far Abroad'. *Diaspora* 13 (1): 5-35.
Lehmann, Dieter. 2008. Kazachok. Grove Music Online. http://

/www.grovemusic.com/shared/views/article.html?section=music.14801 (accessed 03.06.2008).

Library of Congress. 1997. ALA-LC Romanization Tables: Transliteration Schemes for Non-Roman Scripts. http://www.loc.gov/catdir/cpso/roman.html (accessed 29.04.2008).

Lipsitz, George. 1994. *Dangerous Crossroads: Popular Music, Postmodernism and the Poetics of Place*. London, New York: Verso Books.

Livingston, Tamara E. 1999. Music Revivals: Towards a General Theory. *Ethnomusicology* 43 (1): 66-85, http://www.jstor.org/stable/852694 (accessed 07.02.2014).

Lohr, Eric. 2004. Immigration and Emigration. In *Encyclopedia of Russian History*, edited by James R. Millar, 654-56. New York: Macmillan Reference USA.

Loomba, Ania. 2005. *Colonialism / Postcolonialism*. 2nd ed. London, New York: Routledge. Original edition, 1998.

Loriia, Elena. 2007. Lider gruppy 'Akvarium' Boris Grebenshchikov: 'Ia moliu Boga, chtoby vypravlenie Rossii prodolzhalos'. *Izvestiia*, 13.11., http://www.izvestia.ru/person/article3110205/index.html (accessed 13.02.2008).

Lundberg, Dan, Krister Malm, and Owe Ronström. 2003. *Music Media Multiculture – Changing Musicscapes*. Translated by Radford, Kristina, and Andrew Coulthard. Stockholm: Svenskt visarkiv.

MacFadyen, David. 2001. *Red Stars: Personality and the Soviet Popular Song, 1955-1991*. Montreal, Kingston, London, Ithaca: McGill-Queen's University Press.

MacFadyen, David. 2002. *Estrada?! Grand Narratives and the Philosophy of the Russian Popular Song since Perestroika*. Montreal, Kingston, London, Ithaca: McGill-Queen's University Press.

MacFadyen, David. 2003. *Songs for Fat People: Affect, Emotion, and Celebrity in the Russian Popular Song, 1900-1955*. Montreal, Kingston, London, Ithaca: McGill-Queen's University Press.

MacFadyen, David. 2008. Navigation: Establishing a Mainstream. *Far from Moscow*. http://www.moscow.ucla.edu/?p=2673 (accessed 01.12.2008).

Manuel, Peter. 1988. *Popular Musics of the Non-Western World – An Introductory Survey*. New York, Oxford: Oxford University Press.

Mazzanti, Sergio. 2007. Il concetto di 'russkij rok' tra storia e mito. In *Percorsi della memoria (Testo arti metodologia ricerca)*, edited by Alessandro Cifariello, and Claudio Cadeddu, p. 281-300. Rome: Azimut.

McClary, Susan. 2000. *Conventional Wisdom – The Content of Musical Form.* Berkeley, Los Angeles: University of California Press.

McMichael, Polly. 2009. Prehistories and Afterlives: The Packaging and Repackaging of Soviet Rock. *Popular Music and Society* 32 (3 Popular Music in the Post-Soviet Space): 331 – 350, http://www.informaworld.com/openurl?genre=article&issn=0300%2d7766&volume=32&issue=3&spage=3 31 (accessed 30.07.2009).

McMichael, Polly. 2013. Defining Pussy Riot Musically: Performance and Authenticity in New Media. *Digital Icons* 9: 99-113, http://www.digitalicons.org/issue09/files/2013/06/DI_9_6_McMichael.pdf (accessed 29.09.2013).

Merriam-Webster Online Dictionary. n.d. Migrant. Merriam-Webster Online. http://www.m-w.com/dictionary/migrant (accessed 24.11.2008).

Misteriia Zvuka. n.d. O Kompanii. http://www.mystery.msk.ru/company.phtml?id=mp (accessed 14.02.2008).

Mitchell, Tony. 1996. *Popular Music and Local Identity: Rock, Pop and Rap in Europe and Oceania.* London, New York: Leicester University Press.

Monson, Ingrid. 1999. Riffs, Repetition, and Theories of Globalization. *Ethnomusicology* 43 (1): 31-65, http://www.jstor.org/stable/852693 (accessed 07.02.2014).

Moore, Allan. 2002. Authenticity as authentication. *Popular Music* 21 (02): 209-23, http://www.journals.cambridge.org/abstract_S0261143002002131 (accessed 12.06.2013).

Moore, David Chioni. 2001. Is the Post- in Postcolonial the Post- in Post-Soviet? Toward a Global Postcolonial Critique. *PMLA* 116 (1): 111-28.

Morley, David, and Kevin Robins. 1990. No Place like Heimat: Images of Home(land) in European Culture. *New Formations* 12: 1-23.

Muzykal'nyi klub Moloko. n.d. Andegraundnyi muzykal'nyi klub. http://moloko-club.spb.ru/about (accessed 23.092008).

Nashe.ru. n.d. Vse o NASHEI rok-muzyike. http://www.nashe.ru/ (accessed 26.01.2009).

Neumann, Patrick T. 2007. Grand Prix: Der Osten rockt den Grand Prix. *Der*

Tagesspiegel online, 11.05., http://www.tagesspiegel.de/weltspiegel/nachrichten/grand-prix-osteuropa-dj-bobo/102465.asp (accessed 12.05.2007).

Nikitina, Ol'ga Eduardovna. 2011. *Biograficheskie mify o russkikh rok-poetakh*. St. Petersburg: Izdatel'skii Tsentr "Gumanitarnaia Akademiia".

Noll, William. 2000. *Ukraine*. In *Europe*., edited by Timothy Rice, James Porter, and Chris Goertzen, 806-25. New York, London: Garland Publishing.

Ofitsial'nyi portal Administratsii Sankt-Peterburga. 2008. Naselenie. http://gov.spb.ru/day/people (accessed 22.08.2008).

Ohliger, Rainer, and Ulrich Raiser. 2005. *Integration und Migration in Berlin. Zahlen – Daten – Fakten*. Berlin: Der Beauftragte des Senats von Berlin für Integration und Migration.

Oliphant, Roland. 2009. Of Lyrics, Nationalism, and Gay Pride. *Russia Profile*, 11.03., http://www.russiaprofile.org/page.php?pageid=Culture+%26+Living&articleid=a1236790641 (accessed 11.03.2009).

Olson, Mark J. V. 1998. 'Everybody Loves Our Town': Scenes, Spatiality, Migrancy. In *Mapping the Beat – Popular Music and Contemporary Theory*, edited by Thomas Swiss, John Sloop, and Andrew Herman, 269-89. Malden, Oxford: Blackwell Publishers.

Ong, Aihwa. 1999. *Flexible Citizenship – The Cultural Logics of Transnationality*. Durham, London: Duke University Press.

OST * Klub. n.d. Programm – RUSSKAJA: 'Vollgas' auf Russisch! http://www.ost-klub.at/programm.php?id=65&lang=1&m=11&y=2005 (accessed 12.12.2005).

Peck, Jeffrey M. 1992. Rac(e)ing the Nation: Is There a German 'Home'? *New Formations* 17: 75-84.

Pilkington, Hilary. 1994. *Russia's youth and its culture: a nation's constructors and constructed*. London, New York: Routledge.

Pilkington, Hilary, Elena Omel'chenko, Moya Flynn, Ul'iana Bliudina, and Elena Starkova, eds. 2002. *Looking West? Cultural globalization and Russian Youth Cultures*. University Park: The Pennsylvania State University Press.

Postgarage. n.d. Russian Style Discoteka. http://www.postgarage.at/event677-1.htm (accessed 03.12.2008).

Putin, Vladimir Vladimirovich. 2005. Poslanie Federal'nomu Sobraniiu Rossiiskoi Federatsii. http://www.kremlin.ru/appears/2005/04/25/1223_type63372type63374type82634_87049.shtml (accessed 11.08.2008).

Putin, Vladimir Vladimirovich, and Dmitrii Medvedev. 2008. Obrashcheniia Vladimira Putina i Dmitriia Medvedeva k sobravshimsia na kontserte posle zaversheniia golosovaniia na vyborakh Prezidenta Rosii. http://kremlin.ru/appears/2008/03/02/2334_type63374type82634_161461.shtml (accessed 11.03.2008).

Radio Rossii. 2007. Programma B. Grebenshchikova 'Aerostat'. http://www.radiorus.ru/section.html?rid=3172 (accessed 02.02.2009).

FM, Radio Russkii Berlin 97.2. n.d. Profil' radiostantsii. http://www.radio-rb.de/page/senderportrait.html (accessed 16.11.2012).

radiomultikulti. n.d. Russendisko Club mit Wladimir Kaminer und Yuriy Gurzhy. http://www.multikulti.de/_/beitrag_jsp/key=beitrag_43858.html (accessed 04.01.2007).

Radke, Evelyn. 2002. "Russische Rockmusik: Zur Funktion einer Subkultur in den 70er und 80er Jahren." Magisterarbeit im Fach Slavistik / Literaturwissenschaft, Fakultät für Sprach- und Literaturwissenschaften, Institut für Slavistik, Technischen Universität Dresden, Dresden.

Radke, Evelyn. 2008. *Rock in Russland – Zur Spezifik der Liedtexte einer Subkultur in der späten Sowjetzeit*. Saarbrücken: VDM Verlag Dr. Müller.

Ramet, Sabrina Petra. 1994. *Rocking the State: Rock Music and Politics in Eastern Europe and Russia*. Boulder, San Francisco, Oxford: Westview Press.

Real Records. n.d. O kompanii. http://www.realrec.ru/about.php (accessed 14.10.2008).

Reggistan. n.d. History. http://www.reggaestan.ru/pages/stan02e.html (accessed 27.08.2005).

Riabov, Mikhail, and Andrei Lubenskii. 2008. Kinchev prizval vydat' dochek Putina za britanskikh printsev i vossozdat' stolitsu Rusi v Kieve. *Novyi Region – Kiev*, 23.02., http://www.nr2.ru/kiev/165835.html (accessed 28.03.2008).

Rudenko, Aleksandr. n.d. Istoria. http://svoboda.ikso.net/hist_ru.php (accessed 06.06.2006).

Ruslana. 2008. Grafik. Ruslana. http://www.ruslana.ua/ru/show.php (accessed 18.10.2013).

Ruslana. n.d. Hutsulian Project: In the rhythm of mountains – to reach the summit. The Carpathians. The Hutsulia. http://www.ruslana.com.ua/main_eng.html (accessed 12.06.2007).

Ruslana. n.d. Kolomiyka. http://www.ruslana.com.ua/pages/clipeng_kolomyika.html (accessed 21.09.2007).

Russia.ru. 2008. Skol'ko deneg prinosit popsa v krizise. http://www.russia.ru/video/troitskiypopsa/ (accessed 11.12.2008).

Russian Rock Club of America. n.d. U Nas Byli. http://www.russianrock.net/newsite/reports/reports.shtml (accessed 20.11.2008).

Russkaia Germaniia. 2008. Rusmedia – Russische Medien in Deutschland. http://www.rg-rb.de/win/Mediadaten_2008_a5.indd.pdf (accessed 20.11.2008).

Russophobie. n.d. Bald. http://www.russophobie.de (accessed 26.01.2007).

Rutten, Ellen. 2007. Tanz um den roten Stern – Die Russendisko zwischen Ostalgie und SozArt. *Osteuropa* 57 (5): 109-24.

Ryback, Timothy W. 1990. *Rock around the bloc – A history of Rock Music in Eastern Europe and the Soviet Union*. New York, Oxford: Oxford University Press.

Said, Edward W. 1994. *Orientalism: Western Conceptions of the Orient*. New York: Vintage Books. Original edition, 1979.

Scherbakova, Anna. 2006. City Rich In Expectations, Proclamations. *The St. Petersburg Times*, 10.01., http://www.sptimes.ru/index.php?action_id=2&story_id=16521 (accessed 23.10.2008).

Schiller, Nina Glick, Linda Basch, and Cristina Szanton Blanc. 1995. From Immigrant to Transmigrant: Theorizing Transnational Migration. *Anthropological Quarterly* 68 (1): 48-63.

Schlögel, Karl. 1994. Berlin: 'Stiefmutter unter den russischen Städten'. In *Der große Exodus: Die russische Emigration und ihre Zentren 1917 bis 1941*, edited by Karl Schlögel, 234-59. München: C.H. Beck.

Scholze-Stubenrecht, Werner, and Matthias Wermke, eds. 1996. *Duden – Rechtschreibung der deutschen Sprache*. 21 revised ed. 12 vols. Vol. 1, Mannheim, Leipzig, Wien, Zürich: Dudenverlag.

Schröder, Stephan Michael. 1996. *Auf Jagd nach Schnarks. Einleitende*

Bemerkungen zur (skandinavischen) Identitätsforschung. In *XII. Arbeitstagung der deutschsprachigen Skandinavistik,* edited by Walter Baumgartner, and Hans Fix, 576-86. Wien: Fassbaender.

Schuepp, Chris. 2008. Letter from Videostan. Transitions Online. http://www.tol.cz/look/TOL/article_single.tpl?IdLanguage=1&IdPublication=4&NrIssue=297&NrSection=3&NrArticle=20224&ST1=ad&ST_T1=job&ST_AS1=1&ST2=body&ST_T2=letter&ST_AS2=1&ST3=text&ST_T3=aatol&ST_AS3=1&ST_max=3 (accessed 28.11.2008).

Schum. n.d. Diskothek. http://www.newchance.de/schum/index.php?menue=diskothek (accessed 26.01.2007).

Schum. n.d. Radiosendung. http://www.newchance.de/schum/index.php?menue=radio (accessed 18.11.2008).

Shank, Barry. 1994. *Dissonant Identities – The Rock'n'Roll Scene in Austin, Texas.* Hanover, London: Wesleyan University Press.

Sharapova, Olga. 2008. Salaries Present Mixed Picture. *The St. Petersburg Times,* 28.10., http://www.sptimes.ru/story/27494 (accessed 28.10.2008).

Shaw, Claire. 2013. 'Fashion Attack': The Style of Pussy Riot. *Digital Icons* 9: 115-28, http://www.digitalicons.org/issue09/files/2013/06/DI_9_7_Shaw.pdf (accessed 29.09.2013).

Shelemay, Kay Kaufman. 2008. The Ethnomusicologist, Ethnographic Method, and the Transmission of Tradition. In *Shadows in the Field – New Perspectives for Fieldwork in Ethnomusicology,* edited by Gregory F. Barz, and Timothy J. Cooley, 141-56. New York, Oxford: Oxford University Press. 2nd revised edition. Original edition, 1997.

Shergina, Natal'ia. 2009. Rok-muzykant Sergei Shnurov: 'Ne dumaiu, chto ia isportil pokolenie'. *Novye Izvestiia,* 27.03., http://www.newizv.ru/news/2009-03-27/107195 (accessed 01.04.2009).

Shmeleva, Elena, and Aleksei Shmelev. 2002. *Russkii anekdot: Tekst i rechevoi zhanr.* Moscow: Iazyki Slavianskoi Kul'tury.

Shohat, Ella. 1992. Notes on the 'Post-Colonial'. *Social Text* 31/32 Third World and Post-Colonial Issues): 99-113, http://www.jstor.org/stable/466220 (accessed 07.02.2014).

Shtetl Superstars Orchestra. n.d. Shtetl Superstars Orchestra. Myspace. http:/

/www.myspace.com/shtetlsuperstarssoundsystem (accessed 18.11.2008).
Shugailo, Tat'iana. 2007. Kinchev trebuet rasstrelivat' gomoseksualistov: ekskliuzivnoe interv'iu lidera gruppy 'Alisa'. *Ezhednevnye Novosti*, 22.02., http://novostivl.ru/old.php?sstring=&year=&f=ct&t=070222ct05 (accessed 14.05.2009).
Shumady, N.S., and Z.Y. Vasylenko. 1969. *Kolomyiky*. Kiev: Naukova Dumka.
Shvedov, Sergei. 2007. Grustnyi prazdnik den' Rozhdeniia. http://www.makhno.ru/forum/showthread.php?p=3671 (accessed 05.09.2008).
Slobin, Mark. 1993. *Subcultural Sounds: Micromusics of the West*. Hanover, NH: Wesleyan University Press.
Slobin, Mark. 2003. The Destiny of 'Diaspora' in Ethnomusicology. In *The Cultural Study of Music – A critical Introduction*, edited by Martin Clayton, Trevor Herbert, and Richard Middleton, 284-96. New York, London: Routledge.
Smirnov, Il'ia. 1994. *Vremiia Kolokol'chikov – Zhizn' i smert' russkogo roka*. Moscow: INTO.
Smith, Anthony D. 2003. *Nationalisme – Teori, ideologi, historie*. Translated by Nygaard, Anders. København: Hans Reitzels Forlag.
SOK. n.d. O gruppe. http://sokmusic.ru/Aboutgroup/ (accessed 02.04.2009).
Solomon, Thomas. 2003. 'Bu Vatan Bizim' ['This Land is Ours']: Nationalism in Turkish Rap in Diaspora and in the Homeland. Paper read at 12th Biannual IASPM Conference, at Montreal, Quebec.
Solomon, Thomas. 2004. The local and the global in Turkish rap music – a view from Istanbul. Paper read at 2nd Media and Cultural Studies Conference, at Istanbul.
Solomon, Thomas. 2006. Whose Hybridity? Whose Diaspora? Agency and Identity in Transnational Musics. Paper read at ICTM-colloquium "Emerging Musical Identities", at Wesleyan University.
Solomon, Thomas. 2007. Articulating the Historical Moment: Turkey, Europe, and Eurovision 2003. In *A Song for Europe: Popular Music and Politics in the Eurovision Song Contest*, edited by Ivan Raykoff, and Robert Tobin, 135-45. Aldershot: Ashgate.
Solomon, Thomas. 2008. Diverse Diasporas: Multiple Identities in 'Turkish Rap' in Germany. In *Music from Turkey in the Diaspora*, edited by Ursula Hemetek, and Hande Sağlam, 77-88. Wien: Institut für Volksmusikforschung und

Ethnomusikologie.

Sonevytsky, Maria. 2006. Leather, Metal, Wild Dances: Ukrainian Pop's Victory at the 2004 Eurovision Song Contest and the Politics of Auto-Exoticism. Paper read at US Branch of the International Association for the Study of Popular Music, at Nashville (TN).

Staff Writer. 2005. Governor Matviyenko Paints Rosy Picture. *The St. Petersburg Times*, 01.04., http://www.sptimes.ru/index.php?action_id=2&story_id=3150 (accessed 23.10.2008).

Starovoitova, I.A. 2008. *Russkaia leksika v zadaniiakh i krossvordakh – Gorod*. Vol. 3, *Uchebnoe posobie dlia izuchaiushchikh russkii iazyk kak vtoroi*. St. Petersburg: Zlatoust.

Statistisches Bundesamt. 2012. *Bevölkerung und Erwerbstätigkeit – Ausländische Bevölkerung Ergebnisse des Ausländerzentralregisters 2011*. Online ed. Fachserie 1 Reihe 2. Wiesbaden: Statistisches Bundesamt.

Statistisches Bundesamt. 2006. *Ausländische Bevölkerung – Ergebnisse des Ausländerzentralregisters 2005. Bevölkerung und Erwerbstätigkeit*. Wiesbaden: Statistisches Bundesamt.

Steinholt, Yngvar Bordewich. 2005. *Rock in the Reservation: Songs from the Leningrad Rock Club 1981-1986*. Larchmont: The Mass Media Music Scholars' Press.

Steinholt, Yngvar Bordewich. 2013. Kitten Heresy: Lost Contexts of Pussy Riot's Punk Prayer. *Popular Music and Society* 36 (1): 120-24.

Steinholt, Yngvar Bordewich. in press. Russian Rock / Russkiy rok. In *The Continuum Encyclopedia of Popular Music of the World*, edited by John Shepherd, David Horn, and Dave Laing.

Steinholt, Yngvar Bordewich. in press. Soviet rock (Vocal-instrumental ensembles – VIA). In *The Continuum Encyclopedia of Popular Music of the World*, edited by John Shepherd, David Horn, and Dave Laing.

Steinholt, Yngvar Bordewich, and David-Emil Wickström. 2008. Ensretting, segmentering og unnvikende strategier: Tendenser i det 'nye' Russlands populærkultur. *Den Jyske Historiker* 117-118 (Rusland efter Sovjet: Nye rammer – nye skel): 120-38.

Stites, Richard. 1992. *Russian Popular Culture – Entertainment and society since 1900*. Cambridge, New York: Cambridge University Press.

Stokes, Martin, ed. 1997a. *Ethnicity, Identity, and Music: The Musical Construction of Place*. Oxford, New York: Berg Publishers. Original edition, 1994.

Stokes, Martin. 1997b. Introduction: Ethnicity, Identity and Music. In *Ethnicity, Identity and Music – The Musical Construction of Place*, edited by Martin Stokes, 1-27. Oxford, New York: Berg Publishers. Original edition, 1994.

Stokes, Martin. 2004. Music and the Global Order. *Annual Review of Anthropology* 33: 47-72.

Stolyarova, Galina. 2005. Police to Step Up Patrols to Protect Foreigners. *The St. Petersburg Times*, 24.06., http://www.sptimes.ru/index.php?action_id=2&story_id=59 (accessed 22.08.2008).

Straw, Will. 1991. Systems of Articulation, Logics of Change: Communities and Scenes in Popular Music. *Cultural Studies* 5 (3): 368-88.

Straw, Will. 2004. Cultural Scenes. *Society and Leisure* 27 (2): 411-22.

Strukov, Vlad. 2013. From Local Appropriation to Global Documentation, or Contesting the Media System. *Digital Icons* 9: 87-97, http://www.digitalicons.org/issue09/files/2013/06/DI_9_5_Strukov.pdf (accessed 29.09.2013).

Stupnikov, Denis. 2006. Lazareva subbota russkogo roka. *Pravaia.ru – pravoslavno-analiticheskii sait*, 19.04., http://www.pravaya.ru/dailynews/7420 (accessed 12.02.2008).

Sugarman, Jane C. 2004. *Diasporic Dialogues: Mediated Musics and the Albanian Transnation*. In *Identity and the Arts in Diaspora Communities*, edited by Thomas Turino, and James Lea, 21-38. Warren, Michigan: Harmonie Park Press.

Summit, Jeffrey A. 2000. *The Lord's song in a strange land – Music and Identity in Contemporary Jewish Worship*. Oxford, New York.

Survilla, Maria Paula. 2002. *Of Mermaids and Rock Singers – Placing the Self and Constructing the Nation Through Belarusan Contemporary Music*. New York, London: Routledge.

Svoboda. 2008. Sait gruppy 'Svoboda' – Novosti. http://skasvoboda.ucoz.ru/index/0-10 (accessed 05.01.2009).

Svoboda. n.d. Ofitsial'nyi sait gruppy SVOBODA – Glavnaia. http://www.svobodamuz.spb.ru/ (accessed 18.092008).

Tagg, Philip. 1999. Introductory notes to the Semiotics of Music – Version 3.

http://tagg.org/xpdfs/semiotug.pdf (accessed 23.02.2007).

Taruskin, Richard. 1997. *Defining Russia Musically – Historical and Hermeneutical Essays*. Princeton, Oxford: Princeton University Press.

Taylor Nelson Sofres (TNS). n.d. TNS. http://www.tns-global.ru (accessed 22.02.2008).

Taylor, Timothy D. 1997. *Global Pop: World Music, World Markets*. New York, London: Routledge.

Tochka, Nicholas. 2013. Pussy Riot, freedom of expression, and popular music studies after the Cold War. *Popular Music* 32 (02): 303-11, http://www.journals.cambridge.org/abstract_S026114301300007X (accessed 07.02.2014).

Tölölyan, Khachig. 1996. Rethinking Diaspora(s): Stateless Power in the Transnational Moment. *Diaspora* 5 (1): 3-36.

Tonereise. n.d. English Info. http://www.tonereise.com/index-filer/page0007.htm (accessed 05.03.2009).

Trofimov, Aleksandr, ed. 2003. *Russkii rok entsiklopediia*. Moscow: A.T. Publishing.

Troitsky, Artemy. 1987. *Back in the USSR – The True Story of Rock in Russia*. Boston, London: Faber amd Faber.

Turino, Thomas. 2003. Are we global yet? Globalist discourse, cultural formations and the study of Zimbabwean popular music. *British Journal of Ethnomusicology* 12 (2): 51-79, http://www.jstor.org/stable/30036849 (accessed 07.02.2014).

Turino, Thomas. 2004. Introduction: Identity and the Arts in Diaspora Communities. In *Identity and the Arts in Diaspora Communities*, edited by Thomas Turino, and James Lea, 3-19. Warren, Michigan: Harmonie Park Press.

Tverskoi gosudarstvennyi universitet. n.d. Izdaniia. http://poetics.nm.ru/ (accessed 02.06.2009).

Urban, Michael, and Andrei Evdokimov. 2004. *Russia gets the Blues – Music, Culture, and Community in Unsettled Times*. Ithaca, London: Cornell University Press.

Vasmer, Maks. 1996. *Etimologicheskii Slovar' Russkogo Iazyka – V chetyrekh tomakh*. Edited by B. A. Larina. Vol. 1, St. Petersburg: Azbuka.

Virtual'nyi muzei ::: Kommunal'naia kvartira. n.d. Ekspozitsiia. http:/
/www.kommunalka.spb.ru/expo.htm (accessed 05.03.2009).

Voronina, Olga G. 2013. Pussy Riot Steal the Stage in the Moscow Cathedral of Christ the Saviour: Punk Prayer on Trial Online and in Court. *Digital Icons* 9: 69-85, http://www.digitalicons.org/issue09/files/2013/06/DI_9_4_Voronina.pdf (accessed 29.09.2013).

Wadada. n.d. Pesnia Den'gi v ispolnenii gruppy Marksheider Kunst. http:/
/wadada.net/kunst/dengi.htm (accessed 09.09.2008).

Wallis, Roger, and Krister Malm. 1984. *Big sounds from small peoples – The music industry in small countries*. London: Constable.

Wanner, Adrian. 2005. Wladimir Kaminer: A Russian Picaro Conquers Germany. *The Russian Review* 64: 590-604.

Wanner, Catherine. 1996. Nationalism on Stage: Music and Change in Soviet Ukraine. In *Retuning Culture – Musical Changes in Central and Eastern Europe*, edited by Mark Slobin, 136-55. Durham, London: Duke University Press.

Wayback Machine. n.d. Internet Archive: Wayback Machine. http:/
/www.archive.org/web/web.php (accessed 03.12.2007).

Webb, Peter. 2007. *Exploring the Networked Worlds of Popular Music – Milieu Cultures*. New York, London: Routledge.

Weisethaunet, Hans, and Ulf Lindberg. 2010. Authenticity Revisited: The Rock Critic and the Changing Real. *Popular Music and Society* 33 (4): 465-85, http://www.tandfonline.com/doi/abs/10.1080/03007761003694225 (accessed 12.06.2013).

Wickström, David-Emil. 2009a. Who are 'die Russen' currently living in Germany? dew's blog. http://www.ikso.net/~dew/blog/?p=114 (accessed 12.03.2009).

Wickström, David-Emil. 2003. "Signifyin' Vigdal – Aspects of the Ragnar Vigdal Tradition and the Revival of Norwegian Vocal Folk Music." Master's Thesis in Ethnomusicology, Grieg Academy – Department of Music, University of Bergen, Bergen.

Wickström, David-Emil. 2007. Marusia visits Berlin – Cultural flows surrounding the Russendisko. *Musik og Forskning* 31: 65-84, http:/
/kunstogkulturvidenskab.ku.dk/forskning/publikationer/musik_forskning/

publikationer/musikogforskning31_2008_wickstrom.pdf (accessed 07.02.2014).

Wickström, David-Emil. 2008. 'Drive-ethno-dance' and 'Hutzul Punk' – Ukrainian popular music and strategies of localization in a Post-Soviet context. *Yearbook for Traditional Music* 40: 60-88.

Wickström, David-Emil. 2011. *Okna otkroi! – Open the windows! Scenes, transcultural flows, and identity politics in popular music from Post-Soviet St. Petersburg. Soviet and Post-Soviet Politics and Society*. Stuttgart: ibidem-Verlag.

Wickström, David-Emil. 2013. post-soviet popular music literature. dew's blog. http://pspm-bibliography.d-ew.info (accessed 10.12.2013).

Wickström, David-Emil. 2009b. Eurovision as a new battlefield in the Russian-Georgian war. dew's blog. http://www.ikso.net/~dew/blog/?p=75 (accessed 02.03.2009).

Wickström, David-Emil, and Yngvar Bordewich Steinholt. 2009. Visions of the (holy) Motherland in contemporary Russian popular music: Nostalgia, patriotism, religion and russkii rok. *Popular Music and Society* 32 (3 Popular Music in the Post-Soviet Space): 313-30, http://www.informaworld.com/openurl?genre=article&issn=0300%2d7766&volume=32&issue=3&spage=313 (accessed 30.07.2009).

Wieck, Cordula. 2008. Positionen: Nicht die fünfte Kolonne Putins. *Der Tagesspiegel Online*, 09.09., http://www.tagesspiegel.de/meinung/kommentare/Kaukasus-Russland;art141,2610288 (accessed 09.09.2008).

World Music Central. 2006. World Music Labels Receive WOMEX & WMCE Awards. http://worldmusiccentral.org/article.php/2006090522290671 (accessed 05.12.2008).

Yarotsky, Yury. 2002. Show Business 1991-2000. *Kommersant'*, 12.02., http://www.kommersant.com/tree.asp?rubric=3&node=41&doc_id=310116 (accessed 05.09.2006).

Yekelchyk, Serhy. 2010. What Is Ukrainian about Ukraine's Pop Culture? The Strange Case of Verka Serduchka. *Canadian-American Slavic Studies* 44.

Yurchak, Alexei. 2006. *Everything was forever, until it was no more – The last Soviet generation*. Princeton, Oxford: Princeton University Press.

Zaytseva, Anna. 2006. Rock in Leningrad/Sankt-Petersburg: vom Leben vor und nach dem Tod. *kultura*. *Russland-Kulturanalysen* 2 (5): 3-10, http://www.forschungsstelle.uni-bremen.de/images/stories/pdf/kultura/kultura_5_2006.pdf (accessed 04.02.2008).

Zhuk, Sergei I. 2010. *Rock and Roll in the Rocket City: The West, Identity, and Ideology in Soviet Dniepropetrovsk, 1960-1985*. Washington, D.C., Baltimore: Woodrow Wilson Center and Johns Hopkins University Press.

Zotov, Mikhail, and Svetlana Bogdanova. 2007. Radio v virtual'noi srede: metamorfozy traditsionnogo media. *Broadcasting. Televidenie i radioveshchanie*, http://www.broadcasting.ru/articles2/econandmen/radio_v_virtualn_srede_metamorfozy_tradicion_media (accessed 14.05.2009).

Discography

Ackee Ma-Ma u.r.b. 2005. *Urban*. Misteriia zvuka / Silver Records Slvr 070-2. CD.
Akvarium. 2002a. *Treugol'nik*. Soiuz Szcd 1456-02. CD.
Akvarium. 2002b. *Deti dekabria*. Soiuz Szcd 1822-02. CD.
Akvarium. 2005. *Reggae*. Soiuz Szcd 3276-05. CD.
Akvarium. 2006. *Bespechnyi russkii brodiaga*. Misteriia zvuka MZ 332-2. CD.
Akvarium. 2008. *Loshad' Belaia*. Misteriia Zvuka. MP3.
Alisa. 1986. *Energiia*. Melodiia 26733. LP.
Alisa. 2000. *Solntsevorot*. CD-Land CDL217-00. CD.
Alisa. 2003. *Seichas pozdnee, chem ty dumaesh'*. Moroz M'iuzik. CD.
Alisa. 2005. *Izgoi*. Real Records RR-311-CD. CD.
Alisa. 2007b. *Stat' Severa*. Grand Records GRP CD-03. CD.
Alisa. 2008. *Puls' Khranitelia Dverei Labirinta*. CD-Maximum. CD.
Apparatschik. 1994. *Apparatschik*. Weltwunder CD WW 201-2. CD.
Bashlachev, Aleksandr. 1999. *Bashlachev I*. Otdelenie Vykhod 003. CD.
Billy's Band. 2003b. *Parizhskie Sezony*. Billy's band. CD.
Billy's Band. 2005. *Otorviomsia Po-Piterski*. Grand Rekords GR CD-417. CD.
Boney M. 1978. *Nightflight to Venus*. Hansa 26 026 OT. LP.
Brigadnyi podriad. 2003. *Nasilie i sex*. Sparc CD-P 16. CD.
Clash, The. 1979. *London Calling*. CBS Records. LP.

Con Brio. 2006. *Demo*. CD.
Crossing. 2007. *Chast' Zhizni*. mp3.
Crossing. 2009. *Ia ne Gagarin*. mp3.
Dr. I-Bolit & Tribal Roots. 2004. *Go Rastaman Go*. Antrop ATR 04168. CD.
Dschinghis Khan. 1979. *Dschinghis Khan*. Jupiter-Records. LP.
EAV. 1997. *Im Himmel ist die Hölle los*. EMI Electrola. CD.
Gazmanov, Oleg. 2005. *Sdelan v SSSR*. Grand Rekords. CD.
Grazhdanskaia Oborona. 1988. *Vse idet po planu*. GrOb Records / Misterii Zvuka Khor 009. MC / CD.
Haidamaky. 2005. *Perverziia*. Comp Music Ltd. CD.
Haydamaky. 2006. *Ukraine Calling*. Eastblok Music EBM 005. CD.
Haydamaky. 2008. *Kobzar*. Eastblok Music EBM 010. CD.
Kino. 1986. *Noch'*. Melodiia 26795. CD.
Kino. 1988. *Gruppa krovi*. Moroz Records dMR 01998 CD. CD.
Kurylev, Vadim. 2003. *Ekvilibrium*. Antrop ATR 03144. CD.
La Minor. 2009. *Oboroty*. Eastblok Music EBM014. CD.
Leningrad. 2000. *Dachniki*. Gala Records GL 10253. CD.
Leningrad. 2002. *Piraty XXI veka*. Gala Records GL 10286. CD.
Leningrad. 2003. *Dlia millionov*. Misteriia zvuka MZ 100-2. CD.
Leningrad. 2006. *Hleb*. Eastblok Music EBM 006. CD.
Leningrad & the Tiger Lillies. 2004. *H.YA*. ShnurOK / Misteriia Zvuka Shnurok-007 / MZ 300-2/9. CD.
Little Cow. 2007. *I'm in Love with Every Lady*. Eastblok Music EBM 008. CD.
Lyapis Trubetskoy. 2010. *Agitpop*. Eastblok Music EBM019. CD.
Markscheider Kunst. 2001. *Krasivo sleva*. Gala Records. CD.
Markscheider Kunst. 2004. *St. Petersburg – Kinshasa Tranzit*. Gala Records GL 10334. CD.
Markscheider Kunst. 2008. *Cafe Babalu*. Gala Records GL10510. CD.
Markscheider Kunst. 2010. *Utopia*. Eastblok Music EBM018. CD.
Nirvana. 1991. *Nevermind*. Geffen GED 24425. CD.
NOM. 2002. *NOM-15*. SoLyd Records SLR 0319. CD.
Okean El'zy. 2003. *Supersymetriia*. Lavina music. CD.
Piligrim. 2007. *Slava Rossii*. CD-Maksimum CDM 0607-2724. CD.
Reggistan. 1999. *Reggi-Reggi-Reggei*. Demo. CD.

Rok-gruppa. 2003. *Popsa*. Nikitin. CD.
Ruslana. 2003. *Dyki Tantsi*. Comp Music Ltd 571612 2. CD.
Russkaja. 2008. *Kasatchok Superstar*. Chat Chapeau CCR015-2. CD.
Sex Pistols. 1993. *Never Mind the Bollocks Here's the Sex Pistols*. Virgin. CD.
Shazalakazoo. 2011. *Karton City Boom*. Eastblok Music EBM021. CD.
Shukar Collective. 2007. *Romatek*. Eastblok Music EBM 009. CD.
SkaZka Orchestra. 2012. *Kalamburage*. Eastblok Music EBM024. CD.
Suzirya. 2000. *Songs and Dances of the Ukraine*. ARC Music EUCD 1604. CD.
Svoboda. 2005. *Demo*. CD.
Svoboda. 2007. *Demo*. MP3.
Svoboda. 2009b. *Pervak*. Antrop ATR 09777. CD.
Televizor. 2001. *Otechestvo illiuzii*. Caravan. CD.
The Offspring. 1994. *Smash*. Epitaph 86432. CD.
Various Artists. 2000. *KINOproby – Tribute Viktor Tsoi*. Real Records. CD.
Various Artists. 2003a. *My iz Pitera – Obzor piterskogo roka*. Sparc. CD.
Various Artists. 2003b. *Russendisko-Hits*. Trikont US-0308. CD.
Various Artists. 2003c. *Trib'iut Borisu Grebenshchikovu 50 – Nebo*. Antrop ATR 03152. CD.
Various Artists. 2003d. *Trib'iut Borisu Grebenshchikovu 50 – Zemlia*. Antrop ATR 03162. CD.
Various Artists. 2004a. *Pomaranchevi pisni*. Comp Music Ltd. CD.
Various Artists. 2004b. *Russendisko Hits 2*. Russendisko Records Buschfunk 15862. CD.
Various Artists. 2004c. *Russensoul*. Trikont US-0318. CD.
Various Artists. 2004d. *Russkie narodnye Pesni – Pervyi vypusk*. Megalainer Rekordz MLSZ-0411. CD.
Various Artists. 2005a. *BalkanBeats Vol.1*. Eastblok Music EBM 003. CD.
Various Artists. 2005b. *Café Sputnik – Electronic Exotica from Russia*. Eastblok Music EBM 004. CD.
Various Artists. 2005c. *Radio Russendisko*. Russendisko Records RD 002. CD.
Various Artists. 2005d. *Uezdnyi gorod N – 20 let spustia*. Antrop ATR 05267. CD.
Various Artists. 2005e. *Ukraina – Songs of the Orange Revolution*. Eastblok Music EBM 002. CD.
Various Artists. 2006a. *BalkanBeats Vol.2*. Eastblok Music EBM 007. CD.

REFERENCES   361

Various Artists. 2006b. *Russkii Andegraund Volume 1*. Antrop ATR 06329. CD.
Various Artists. 2006c. *Shtetl Superstars*. Trikont 4555. CD.
Various Artists. 2007a. *Beginner's Guide to Eastern Europe*. Nascente NSBOX 032. CD.
Various Artists. 2007b. *Muzyka NEsoglasnykh*. Realmusic. MP3.
Various Artists. 2007c. *Ost Klub Kapitel 2*. Chat chapeau CCR014-2. CD.
Various Artists. 2008a. *BalkanBeats Vol.3*. Eastblok Music EBM 011. CD.
Various Artists. 2008b. *Dzha do it*. Salon AV CDSAV08081. CD.
Various Artists. 2008c. *Ukraine do Amerika*. Russendisko Records LC: 09340. CD.
Various Artists. 2012a. *Luna Park*. Eastblok Music EBM023. CD.
Various Artists. 2012b. *Russendisko (Soundtrack)*. Polydor. CD.
Various Artists. 2013. *Die Lieblingslieder der deutschen Taxifahrer*. GMO – The Label GMO 017-2. CD.
Various Artists. n.d. *Pi-Rock Zona V.01*. Pi-Rock Records. CD.
VIA Volga-Volga. 2008. *PESNYA.RY*. Volga-Volga. MP3.

Videography

Akvarium, and NOM. 2008. Bespechnyi russkii brodiaga. Youtube. http://www.youtube.com/watch?v=GwgYSsM6TvM (added by victorpuzo, 30.10.2008; accessed 02.02.2009).
Alisa. 2007a. Rok [sic]-en [sic]-rol Krest. Youtube. http://www.youtube.com/watch?v=WnsqwQJ_ZBE (added by d61lda7, 03.10.2007; accessed 02.02.2009).
Alisa. 2008. The sky of Slavs. Youtube. http://www.youtube.com/watch?v=L7CEiSa_6vw (added by alisachannel, 09.02.2008; accessed 02.02.2009).
Gazmanov, Oleg. n.d. Prosmotr video-rolika 'Sdelan v SSSR'. http://www.gazmanov.ru/media/clips/clips_17.html (accessed 26.09.2008).
Gruppa Piligrim. n.d. Klipy gruppy 'Piligrim'. http://www.piligrim-rock.ru/ru/item487 (accessed 05.02.2009).
Gruppa Piligrim. n.d. Zapis' na festivale 'Slava Rossii! Slava Moskve! 2006'. http://www.piligrim-rock.ru/ru/video/item471/item472 (accessed 05.02.2009).
Haydamaky. 2007. HAYDAMAKY kohania. Youtube. http://www.youtube.com/

watch?v=UXWMFspdKZk (added by Armin Siebert, 24.01.2007; accessed 09.10.2007).

NOM. 2007. Nina. Youtube. http://www.youtube.com/watch?v=IzO0nfXuO8s (added by ormfdmrush, 07.01.2007; accessed 09.02.2009).

Ruslana. 2006a. Kolomyjka – Ruslana. Youtube. http://www.youtube.com/watch?v=c3sTkRHziKI (added by natalyaa, 06.04.2006; accessed 20.06.2007).

Ruslana. 2006b. Dance with the Wolves. Youtube. http://www.youtube.com/watch?v=wszR8RffR6w (added by Cora Angel, 11.06.2006; accessed 18.10.2013).

Svoboda. 2009a. Svoboda at Okna otkroi! 2005 (02.07.2005). Youtube. http://www.youtube.com/watch?v=L-76kzf__No (added by damil78, 04.11.2009; accessed 05.11.2009).

Tagg, Philip. 2007. God, Queen, Jude and Nation. Youtube. http://uk.youtube.com/watch?v=F8mloXf07-I (added by etymophony, 18.07.2007; accessed 26.01.2009).

Interviews

Angerer, Matthias. 13.07.2007. Vienna (Austria). Interviewed by David-Emil Wickström.

Baburin, Dmitrij, Sergej Fiedler, Nikolaj Leinweber, and Sergej Stehr. 07.12.2009. Berlin (Germany). Interviewed by David-Emil Wickström.

Burlaka, Andrei. 22.03.2005. St. Petersburg (Russia). Interviewed by David-Emil Wickström.

Chernov, Sergey. 03.07.2006a. St. Petersburg (Russia). Interviewed by David-Emil Wickström.

Con Brio, and Viktor Kultashov. 27.08.2005. Rehearsal with Con Brio. St. Petersburg (Russia). Interviewed by David-Emil Wickström.

Danilova, Elena. 21.06.2006. St. Petersburg (Russia). Interviewed by David-Emil Wickström.

Efremenko, Sergei "Efr". 25.05. & 26.05.2005. St. Petersburg (Russia). Interviewed by David-Emil Wickström.

Fedorova, Ekaterina, Elena Novikova, and Elena Zhornik. 28.03.2005a. St.

Petersburg (Russia). Interviewed by David-Emil Wickström.

Fedorova, Ekaterina, Elena Novikova, Elena Zhornik, Anastasia Postnikova, and Inka Lishenkevich. 12.03.2005b. St. Petersburg (Russia). Interviewed by David-Emil Wickström.

Fedrov, Evgenii. 08.02.2006. St. Petersburg (Russia). Interviewed by David-Emil Wickström.

Feinshtein-Vasil'ev, Mikhail. 11.06.2002. St. Petersburg Rock Interviews 6: Mikhail Feinshtein-Vasil'ev. St. Petersburg (Russia). Interviewed by Yngvar Bordewich Steinholt. Transcript at http://www.hum.uit.no/a/steinholt/fanvasilev.pdf (accessed 23.03.2009).

Gornung, Anton. 08.12.2009. Berlin (Germany). Interviewed by David-Emil Wickström.

Gurzhy, Yuriy. 05.10.2005. Berlin (Germany). Interviewed by David-Emil Wickström.

Iatsenko, Tat'iana. 30.01.2006. St. Petersburg (Russia). Interviewed by David-Emil Wickström.

Ivanov, Andrei. 20.12.2004. St. Petersburg (Russia). Interviewed by David-Emil Wickström.

Ivanov, Dimitrii. 25.09.2005. St. Petersburg (Russia). Interviewed by David-Emil Wickström.

Kagadeev, Andrei. 06.12.2004. St. Petersburg (Russia). Interviewed by David-Emil Wickström.

Kasparov, Alexander, and Armin Siebert. 11.10.2005. Berlin (Germany). Interviewed by David-Emil Wickström.

Kasparov, Alexander, and Armin Siebert. 19.07.2006. Berlin (Germany). Interviewed by David-Emil Wickström.

Khramtsov, Dmitrii. 18.04.2005. St. Petersburg (Russia). Interviewed by David-Emil Wickström.

Kiselev, Evgenii. 30.01.2006. St. Petersburg (Russia). Interviewed by David-Emil Wickström.

Kopeikin, Nikolai. 02.06.2005. St. Petersburg (Russia). Interviewed by David-Emil Wickström.

Kopeikin, Nikolai, Andrei Kagadeev, and Ivan N. Turist. 26.10.2001. St. Petersburg Rock Interviews 4: N.O.M.Zhir. St. Petersburg (Russia). Interviewed by

Yngvar Bordewich Steinholt. Transcript at http://www.hum.uit.no/a/steinholt/nom.pdf (accessed 14.05.2009).

Kultashov, Viktor. 12.02.2006. St. Petersburg (Russia). Interviewed by David-Emil Wickström.

Loseva, Svetlana. 06.09.2005. St. Petersburg (Russia). Interviewed by David-Emil Wickström.

Novik, Billy. 24.03.2005. St. Petersburg (Russia). Interviewed by David-Emil Wickström.

Opitz, Olaf. 21.07.2006. Berlin (Germany). Interviewed by David-Emil Wickström.

Parygin, Roman. 23.06.2006. St. Petersburg (Russia). Interviewed by David-Emil Wickström.

Rudenko, Aleksandr. 09.01. & 15.01.2006. St. Petersburg (Russia). Interviewed by David-Emil Wickström.

Tropillo, Andrei. 23.05.2005. St. Petersburg (Russia). Interviewed by David-Emil Wickström.

Vashkevich, Denis, and Anton Lukanin. 30.01.2006. St. Petersburg (Russia). Interviewed by David-Emil Wickström.

Vladimirov, Aleksandr. 22.12.2005. St. Petersburg (Russia). Interviewed by David-Emil Wickström.

Yaroshevskiy, Mikhail. 03.08.2007. New York (USA). Interviewed by David-Emil Wickström.

SOVIET AND POST-SOVIET POLITICS AND SOCIETY

Edited by Dr. Andreas Umland

ISSN 1614-3515

1   Андреас Умланд (ред.)
    Воплощение Европейской
    конвенции по правам человека в
    России
    Философские, юридические и
    эмпирические исследования
    ISBN 3-89821-387-0

2   *Christian Wipperfürth*
    Russland – ein vertrauenswürdiger
    Partner?
    Grundlagen, Hintergründe und Praxis
    gegenwärtiger russischer Außenpolitik
    Mit einem Vorwort von Heinz Timmermann
    ISBN 3-89821-401-X

3   *Manja Hussner*
    Die Übernahme internationalen Rechts
    in die russische und deutsche
    Rechtsordnung
    Eine vergleichende Analyse zur
    Völkerrechtsfreundlichkeit der Verfassungen
    der Russländischen Föderation und der
    Bundesrepublik Deutschland
    Mit einem Vorwort von Rainer Arnold
    ISBN 3-89821-438-9

4   *Matthew Tejada*
    Bulgaria's Democratic Consolidation
    and the Kozloduy Nuclear Power Plant
    (KNPP)
    The Unattainability of Closure
    With a foreword by Richard J. Crampton
    ISBN 3-89821-439-7

5   Марк Григорьевич Меерович
    Квадратные метры, определяющие
    сознание
    Государственная жилищная политика в
    СССР. 1921 – 1941 гг
    ISBN 3-89821-474-5

6   *Andrei P. Tsygankov, Pavel
    A. Tsygankov (Eds.)*
    New Directions in Russian
    International Studies
    ISBN 3-89821-422-2

7   Марк Григорьевич Меерович
    Как власть народ к труду приучала
    Жилище в СССР – средство управления
    людьми. 1917 – 1941 гг.
    С предисловием Елены Осокиной
    ISBN 3-89821-495-8

8   *David J. Galbreath*
    Nation-Building and Minority Politics
    in Post-Socialist States
    Interests, Influence and Identities in Estonia
    and Latvia
    With a foreword by David J. Smith
    ISBN 3-89821-467-2

9   Алексей Юрьевич Безугольный
    Народы Кавказа в Вооруженных
    силах СССР в годы Великой
    Отечественной войны 1941-1945 гг.
    С предисловием Николая Бугая
    ISBN 3-89821-475-3

10 Вячеслав Лихачев и Владимир
    Прибыловский (ред.)
    Русское Национальное Единство,
    1990-2000. В 2-х томах
    ISBN 3-89821-523-7

11 Николай Бугай (ред.)
    Народы стран Балтии в условиях
    сталинизма (1940-е – 1950-е годы)
    Документированная история
    ISBN 3-89821-525-3

12 *Ingmar Bredies (Hrsg.)*
    Zur Anatomie der Orange Revolution
    in der Ukraine
    Wechsel des Elitenregimes oder Triumph des
    Parlamentarismus?
    ISBN 3-89821-524-5

13 *Anastasia V. Mitrofanova*
    The Politicization of Russian
    Orthodoxy
    Actors and Ideas
    With a foreword by William C. Gay
    ISBN 3-89821-481-8

14   Nathan D. Larson
     Alexander Solzhenitsyn and the
     Russo-Jewish Question
     ISBN 3-89821-483-4

15   Guido Houben
     Kulturpolitik und Ethnizität
     Staatliche Kunstförderung im Russland der
     neunziger Jahre
     Mit einem Vorwort von Gert Weisskirchen
     ISBN 3-89821-542-3

16   Leonid Luks
     Der russische „Sonderweg"?
     Aufsätze zur neuesten Geschichte Russlands
     im europäischen Kontext
     ISBN 3-89821-496-6

17   Евгений Мороз
     История «Мёртвой воды» – от
     страшной сказки к большой
     политике
     Политическое неоязычество в
     постсоветской России
     ISBN 3-89821-551-2

18   Александр Верховский и Галина
     Кожевникова (ред.)
     Этническая и религиозная
     интолерантность в российских СМИ
     Результаты мониторинга 2001-2004 гг.
     ISBN 3-89821-569-5

19   Christian Ganzer
     Sowjetisches Erbe und ukrainische
     Nation
     Das Museum der Geschichte des Zaporoger
     Kosakentums auf der Insel Chortycja
     Mit einem Vorwort von Frank Golczewski
     ISBN 3-89821-504-0

20   Эльза-Баир Гучинова
     Помнить нельзя забыть
     Антропология депортационной травмы
     калмыков
     С предисловием Кэролайн Хамфри
     ISBN 3-89821-506-7

21   Юлия Лидерман
     Мотивы «проверки» и «испытания»
     в постсоветской культуре
     Советское прошлое в российском
     кинематографе 1990-х годов
     С предисловием Евгения Марголита
     ISBN 3-89821-511-3

22   Tanya Lokshina, Ray Thomas, Mary
     Mayer (Eds.)
     The Imposition of a Fake Political
     Settlement in the Northern Caucasus
     The 2003 Chechen Presidential Election
     ISBN 3-89821-436-2

23   Timothy McCajor Hall, Rosie Read
     (Eds.)
     Changes in the Heart of Europe
     Recent Ethnographies of Czechs, Slovaks,
     Roma, and Sorbs
     With an afterword by Zdeněk Salzmann
     ISBN 3-89821-606-3

24   Christian Autengruber
     Die politischen Parteien in Bulgarien
     und Rumänien
     Eine vergleichende Analyse seit Beginn der
     90er Jahre
     Mit einem Vorwort von Dorothée de Nève
     ISBN 3-89821-476-1

25   Annette Freyberg-Inan with Radu
     Cristescu
     The Ghosts in Our Classrooms, or:
     John Dewey Meets Ceauşescu
     The Promise and the Failures of Civic
     Education in Romania
     ISBN 3-89821-416-8

26   John B. Dunlop
     The 2002 Dubrovka and 2004 Beslan
     Hostage Crises
     A Critique of Russian Counter-Terrorism
     With a foreword by Donald N. Jensen
     ISBN 3-89821-608-X

27   Peter Koller
     Das touristische Potenzial von
     Kam"janec'–Podil's'kyj
     Eine fremdenverkehrsgeographische
     Untersuchung der Zukunftsperspektiven und
     Maßnahmenplanung zur
     Destinationsentwicklung des „ukrainischen
     Rothenburg"
     Mit einem Vorwort von Kristiane Klemm
     ISBN 3-89821-640-3

28   Françoise Daucé, Elisabeth Sieca-
     Kozlowski (Eds.)
     Dedovshchina in the Post-Soviet
     Military
     Hazing of Russian Army Conscripts in a
     Comparative Perspective
     With a foreword by Dale Herspring
     ISBN 3-89821-616-0

29 *Florian Strasser*
    Zivilgesellschaftliche Einflüsse auf die
    Orange Revolution
    Die gewaltlose Massenbewegung und die
    ukrainische Wahlkrise 2004
    Mit einem Vorwort von Egbert Jahn
    ISBN 3-89821-648-9

30 *Rebecca S. Katz*
    The Georgian Regime Crisis of 2003-
    2004
    A Case Study in Post-Soviet Media
    Representation of Politics, Crime and
    Corruption
    ISBN 3-89821-413-3

31 *Vladimir Kantor*
    Willkür oder Freiheit
    Beiträge zur russischen Geschichtsphilosophie
    Ediert von Dagmar Herrmann sowie mit
    einem Vorwort versehen von Leonid Luks
    ISBN 3-89821-589-X

32 *Laura A. Victoir*
    The Russian Land Estate Today
    A Case Study of Cultural Politics in Post-
    Soviet Russia
    With a foreword by Priscilla Roosevelt
    ISBN 3-89821-426-5

33 *Ivan Katchanovski*
    Cleft Countries
    Regional Political Divisions and Cultures in
    Post-Soviet Ukraine and Moldova
    With a foreword by Francis Fukuyama
    ISBN 3-89821-558-X

34 *Florian Mühlfried*
    Postsowjetische Feiern
    Das Georgische Bankett im Wandel
    Mit einem Vorwort von Kevin Tuite
    ISBN 3-89821-601-2

35 *Roger Griffin, Werner Loh, Andreas
    Umland (Eds.)*
    Fascism Past and Present, West and
    East
    An International Debate on Concepts and
    Cases in the Comparative Study of the
    Extreme Right
    With an afterword by Walter Laqueur
    ISBN 3-89821-674-8

36 *Sebastian Schlegel*
    Der „Weiße Archipel"
    Sowjetische Atomstädte 1945-1991
    Mit einem Geleitwort von Thomas Bohn
    ISBN 3-89821-679-9

37 *Vyacheslav Likhachev*
    Political Anti-Semitism in Post-Soviet
    Russia
    Actors and Ideas in 1991-2003
    Edited and translated from Russian by Eugene
    Veklerov
    ISBN 3-89821-529-6

38 *Josette Baer (Ed.)*
    Preparing Liberty in Central Europe
    Political Texts from the Spring of Nations
    1848 to the Spring of Prague 1968
    With a foreword by Zdeněk V. David
    ISBN 3-89821-546-6

39 *Михаил Лукьянов*
    Российский консерватизм и
    реформа, 1907-1914
    С предисловием Марка Д. Стейнберга
    ISBN 3-89821-503-2

40 *Nicola Melloni*
    Market Without Economy
    The 1998 Russian Financial Crisis
    With a foreword by Eiji Furukawa
    ISBN 3-89821-407-9

41 *Dmitrij Chmelnizki*
    Die Architektur Stalins
    Bd. 1: Studien zu Ideologie und Stil
    Bd. 2: Bilddokumentation
    Mit einem Vorwort von Bruno Flierl
    ISBN 3-89821-515-6

42 *Katja Yafimava*
    Post-Soviet Russian-Belarussian
    Relationships
    The Role of Gas Transit Pipelines
    With a foreword by Jonathan P. Stern
    ISBN 3-89821-655-1

43 *Boris Chavkin*
    Verflechtungen der deutschen und
    russischen Zeitgeschichte
    Aufsätze und Archivfunde zu den
    Beziehungen Deutschlands und der
    Sowjetunion von 1917 bis 1991
    Ediert von Markus Edlinger sowie mit einem
    Vorwort versehen von Leonid Luks
    ISBN 3-89821-756-6

44   Anastasija Grynenko in
     Zusammenarbeit mit Claudia Dathe
     Die Terminologie des Gerichtswesens
     der Ukraine und Deutschlands im
     Vergleich
     Eine übersetzungswissenschaftliche Analyse
     juristischer Fachbegriffe im Deutschen,
     Ukrainischen und Russischen
     Mit einem Vorwort von Ulrich Hartmann
     ISBN 3-89821-691-8

45   Anton Burkov
     The Impact of the European
     Convention on Human Rights on
     Russian Law
     Legislation and Application in 1996-2006
     With a foreword by Françoise Hampson
     ISBN 978-3-89821-639-5

46   Stina Torjesen, Indra Overland (Eds.)
     International Election Observers in
     Post-Soviet Azerbaijan
     Geopolitical Pawns or Agents of Change?
     ISBN 978-3-89821-743-9

47   Taras Kuzio
     Ukraine – Crimea – Russia
     Triangle of Conflict
     ISBN 978-3-89821-761-3

48   Claudia Šabić
     "Ich erinnere mich nicht, aber L'viv!"
     Zur Funktion kultureller Faktoren für die
     Institutionalisierung und Entwicklung einer
     ukrainischen Region
     Mit einem Vorwort von Melanie Tatur
     ISBN 978-3-89821-752-1

49   Marlies Bilz
     Tatarstan in der Transformation
     Nationaler Diskurs und Politische Praxis
     1988-1994
     Mit einem Vorwort von Frank Golczewski
     ISBN 978-3-89821-722-4

50   Марлен Ларюэль (ред.)
     Современные интерпретации
     русского национализма
     ISBN 978-3-89821-795-8

51   Sonja Schüler
     Die ethnische Dimension der Armut
     Roma im postsozialistischen Rumänien
     Mit einem Vorwort von Anton Sterbling
     ISBN 978-3-89821-776-7

52   Галина Кожевникова
     Радикальный национализм в России
     и противодействие ему
     Сборник докладов Центра «Сова» за 2004-
     2007 гг.
     С предисловием Александра Верховского
     ISBN 978-3-89821-721-7

53   Галина Кожевникова и Владимир
     Прибыловский
     Российская власть в биографиях I
     Высшие должностные лица РФ в 2004 г.
     ISBN 978-3-89821-796-5

54   Галина Кожевникова и Владимир
     Прибыловский
     Российская власть в биографиях II
     Члены Правительства РФ в 2004 г.
     ISBN 978-3-89821-797-2

55   Галина Кожевникова и Владимир
     Прибыловский
     Российская власть в биографиях III
     Руководители федеральных служб и
     агентств РФ в 2004 г.
     ISBN 978-3-89821-798-9

56   Ileana Petroniu
     Privatisierung in
     Transformationsökonomien
     Determinanten der Restrukturierungs-
     Bereitschaft am Beispiel Polens, Rumäniens
     und der Ukraine
     Mit einem Vorwort von Rainer W. Schäfer
     ISBN 978-3-89821-790-3

57   Christian Wipperfürth
     Russland und seine GUS-Nachbarn
     Hintergründe, aktuelle Entwicklungen und
     Konflikte in einer ressourcenreichen Region
     ISBN 978-3-89821-801-6

58   Togzhan Kassenova
     From Antagonism to Partnership
     The Uneasy Path of the U.S.-Russian
     Cooperative Threat Reduction
     With a foreword by Christoph Bluth
     ISBN 978-3-89821-707-1

59   Alexander Höllwerth
     Das sakrale eurasische Imperium des
     Aleksandr Dugin
     Eine Diskursanalyse zum postsowjetischen
     russischen Rechtsextremismus
     Mit einem Vorwort von Dirk Uffelmann
     ISBN 978-3-89821-813-9

60 Олег Рябов
    «Россия-Матушка»
    Национализм, гендер и война в России XX века
    С предисловием Елены Гощило
    ISBN 978-3-89821-487-2

61 Ivan Maistrenko
    Borot'bism
    A Chapter in the History of the Ukrainian Revolution
    With a new introduction by Chris Ford
    Translated by George S. N. Luckyj with the assistance of Ivan L. Rudnytsky
    ISBN 978-3-89821-697-5

62 Maryna Romanets
    Anamorphosic Texts and Reconfigured Visions
    Improvised Traditions in Contemporary Ukrainian and Irish Literature
    ISBN 978-3-89821-576-3

63 Paul D'Anieri and Taras Kuzio (Eds.)
    Aspects of the Orange Revolution I
    Democratization and Elections in Post-Communist Ukraine
    ISBN 978-3-89821-698-2

64 Bohdan Harasymiw in collaboration with Oleh S. Ilnytzkyj (Eds.)
    Aspects of the Orange Revolution II
    Information and Manipulation Strategies in the 2004 Ukrainian Presidential Elections
    ISBN 978-3-89821-699-9

65 Ingmar Bredies, Andreas Umland and Valentin Yakushik (Eds.)
    Aspects of the Orange Revolution III
    The Context and Dynamics of the 2004 Ukrainian Presidential Elections
    ISBN 978-3-89821-803-0

66 Ingmar Bredies, Andreas Umland and Valentin Yakushik (Eds.)
    Aspects of the Orange Revolution IV
    Foreign Assistance and Civic Action in the 2004 Ukrainian Presidential Elections
    ISBN 978-3-89821-808-5

67 Ingmar Bredies, Andreas Umland and Valentin Yakushik (Eds.)
    Aspects of the Orange Revolution V
    Institutional Observation Reports on the 2004 Ukrainian Presidential Elections
    ISBN 978-3-89821-809-2

68 Taras Kuzio (Ed.)
    Aspects of the Orange Revolution VI
    Post-Communist Democratic Revolutions in Comparative Perspective
    ISBN 978-3-89821-820-7

69 Tim Bohse
    Autoritarismus statt Selbstverwaltung
    Die Transformation der kommunalen Politik in der Stadt Kaliningrad 1990-2005
    Mit einem Geleitwort von Stefan Troebst
    ISBN 978-3-89821-782-8

70 David Rupp
    Die Rußländische Föderation und die russischsprachige Minderheit in Lettland
    Eine Fallstudie zur Anwaltspolitik Moskaus gegenüber den russophonen Minderheiten im „Nahen Ausland" von 1991 bis 2002
    Mit einem Vorwort von Helmut Wagner
    ISBN 978-3-89821-778-1

71 Taras Kuzio
    Theoretical and Comparative Perspectives on Nationalism
    New Directions in Cross-Cultural and Post-Communist Studies
    With a foreword by Paul Robert Magocsi
    ISBN 978-3-89821-815-3

72 Christine Teichmann
    Die Hochschultransformation im heutigen Osteuropa
    Kontinuität und Wandel bei der Entwicklung des postkommunistischen Universitätswesens
    Mit einem Vorwort von Oskar Anweiler
    ISBN 978-3-89821-842-9

73 Julia Kusznir
    Der politische Einfluss von Wirtschaftseliten in russischen Regionen
    Eine Analyse am Beispiel der Erdöl- und Erdgasindustrie, 1992-2005
    Mit einem Vorwort von Wolfgang Eichwede
    ISBN 978-3-89821-821-4

74 Alena Vysotskaya
    Russland, Belarus und die EU-Osterweiterung
    Zur Minderheitenfrage und zum Problem der Freizügigkeit des Personenverkehrs
    Mit einem Vorwort von Katlijn Malfliet
    ISBN 978-3-89821-822-1

75   Heiko Pleines (Hrsg.)
     Corporate Governance in post-
     sozialistischen Volkswirtschaften
     ISBN 978-3-89821-766-8

76   Stefan Ihrig
     Wer sind die Moldawier?
     Rumänismus versus Moldowanismus in
     Historiographie und Schulbüchern der
     Republik Moldova, 1991-2006
     Mit einem Vorwort von Holm Sundhaussen
     ISBN 978-3-89821-466-7

77   Galina Kozhevnikova in collaboration
     with Alexander Verkhovsky and
     Eugene Veklerov
     Ultra-Nationalism and Hate Crimes in
     Contemporary Russia
     The 2004-2006 Annual Reports of Moscow's
     SOVA Center
     With a foreword by Stephen D. Shenfield
     ISBN 978-3-89821-868-9

78   Florian Küchler
     The Role of the European Union in
     Moldova's Transnistria Conflict
     With a foreword by Christopher Hill
     ISBN 978-3-89821-850-4

79   Bernd Rechel
     The Long Way Back to Europe
     Minority Protection in Bulgaria
     With a foreword by Richard Crampton
     ISBN 978-3-89821-863-4

80   Peter W. Rodgers
     Nation, Region and History in Post-
     Communist Transitions
     Identity Politics in Ukraine, 1991-2006
     With a foreword by Vera Tolz
     ISBN 978-3-89821-903-7

81   Stephanie Solywoda
     The Life and Work of
     Semen L. Frank
     A Study of Russian Religious Philosophy
     With a foreword by Philip Walters
     ISBN 978-3-89821-457-5

82   Vera Sokolova
     Cultural Politics of Ethnicity
     Discourses on Roma in Communist
     Czechoslovakia
     ISBN 978-3-89821-864-1

83   Natalya Shevchik Ketenci
     Kazakhstani Enterprises in Transition
     The Role of Historical Regional Development
     in Kazakhstan's Post-Soviet Economic
     Transformation
     ISBN 978-3-89821-831-3

84   Martin Malek, Anna Schor-
     Tschudnowskaja (Hrsg.)
     Europa im Tschetschenienkrieg
     Zwischen politischer Ohnmacht und
     Gleichgültigkeit
     Mit einem Vorwort von Lipchan Basajewa
     ISBN 978-3-89821-676-0

85   Stefan Meister
     Das postsowjetische Universitätswesen
     zwischen nationalem und
     internationalem Wandel
     Die Entwicklung der regionalen Hochschule
     in Russland als Gradmesser der
     Systemtransformation
     Mit einem Vorwort von Joan DeBardeleben
     ISBN 978-3-89821-891-7

86   Konstantin Sheiko in collaboration
     with Stephen Brown
     Nationalist Imaginings of the
     Russian Past
     Anatolii Fomenko and the Rise of Alternative
     History in Post-Communist Russia
     With a foreword by Donald Ostrowski
     ISBN 978-3-89821-915-0

87   Sabine Jenni
     Wie stark ist das „Einige Russland"?
     Zur Parteibindung der Eliten und zum
     Wahlerfolg der Machtpartei
     im Dezember 2007
     Mit einem Vorwort von Klaus Armingeon
     ISBN 978-3-89821-961-7

88   Thomas Borén
     Meeting-Places of Transformation
     Urban Identity, Spatial Representations and
     Local Politics in Post-Soviet St Petersburg
     ISBN 978-3-89821-739-2

89   Aygul Ashirova
     Stalinismus und Stalin-Kult in
     Zentralasien
     Turkmenistan 1924-1953
     Mit einem Vorwort von Leonid Luks
     ISBN 978-3-89821-987-7

90 Leonid Luks
    Freiheit oder imperiale Größe?
    Essays zu einem russischen Dilemma
    ISBN 978-3-8382-0011-8

91 Christopher Gilley
    The 'Change of Signposts' in the
    Ukrainian Emigration
    A Contribution to the History of
    Sovietophilism in the 1920s
    With a foreword by Frank Golczewski
    ISBN 978-3-89821-965-5

92 Philipp Casula, Jeronim Perovic
    (Eds.)
    Identities and Politics
    During the Putin Presidency
    The Discursive Foundations of Russia's
    Stability
    With a foreword by Heiko Haumann
    ISBN 978-3-8382-0015-6

93 Marcel Viëtor
    Europa und die Frage
    nach seinen Grenzen im Osten
    Zur Konstruktion ‚europäischer Identität' in
    Geschichte und Gegenwart
    Mit einem Vorwort von Albrecht Lehmann
    ISBN 978-3-8382-0045-3

94 Ben Hellman, Andrei Rogachevskii
    Filming the Unfilmable
    Casper Wrede's 'One Day in the Life
    of Ivan Denisovich'
    Second, Revised and Expanded Edition
    ISBN 978-3-8382-0044-6

95 Eva Fuchslocher
    Vaterland, Sprache, Glaube
    Orthodoxie und Nationenbildung
    am Beispiel Georgiens
    Mit einem Vorwort von Christina von Braun
    ISBN 978-3-89821-884-9

96 Vladimir Kantor
    Das Westlertum und der Weg
    Russlands
    Zur Entwicklung der russischen Literatur und
    Philosophie
    Ediert von Dagmar Herrmann
    Mit einem Beitrag von Nikolaus Lobkowicz
    ISBN 978-3-8382-0102-3

97 Kamran Musayev
    Die postsowjetische Transformation
    im Baltikum und Südkaukasus
    Eine vergleichende Untersuchung der
    politischen Entwicklung Lettlands und
    Aserbaidschans 1985-2009
    Mit einem Vorwort von Leonid Luks
    Ediert von Sandro Henschel
    ISBN 978-3-8382-0103-0

98 Tatiana Zhurzhenko
    Borderlands into Bordered Lands
    Geopolitics of Identity in Post-Soviet Ukraine
    With a foreword by Dieter Segert
    ISBN 978-3-8382-0042-2

99 Кирилл Галушко, Лидия Смола
    (ред.)
    Пределы падения – варианты
    украинского будущего
    Аналитико-прогностические исследования
    ISBN 978-3-8382-0148-1

100 Michael Minkenberg (ed.)
    Historical Legacies and the Radical
    Right in Post-Cold War Central and
    Eastern Europe
    With an afterword by Sabrina P. Ramet
    ISBN 978-3-8382-0124-5

101 David-Emil Wickström
    Rocking St. Petersburg
    Transcultural Flows and Identity Politics in
    the St. Petersburg Popular Music Scene
    With a foreword by Yngvar B. Steinholt
    Second, Revised and Expanded Edition
    ISBN 978-3-8382-0100-9

102 Eva Zabka
    Eine neue „Zeit der Wirren"?
    Der spät- und postsowjetische Systemwandel
    1985-2000 im Spiegel russischer
    gesellschaftspolitischer Diskurse
    Mit einem Vorwort von Margareta Mommsen
    ISBN 978-3-8382-0161-0

103 Ulrike Ziemer
    Ethnic Belonging, Gender and
    Cultural Practices
    Youth Identitites in Contemporary Russia
    With a foreword by Anoop Nayak
    ISBN 978-3-8382-0152-8

104 Ksenia Chepikova
     ‚Einiges Russland' - eine zweite
     KPdSU?
     Aspekte der Identitätskonstruktion einer
     postsowjetischen „Partei der Macht"
     Mit einem Vorwort von Torsten Oppelland
     ISBN 978-3-8382-0311-9

105 Леонид Люкс
     Западничество или евразийство?
     Демократия или идеократия?
     Сборник статей об исторических дилеммах
     России
     С предисловием Владимира Кантора
     ISBN 978-3-8382-0211-2

106 Anna Dost
     Das russische Verfassungsrecht auf dem
     Weg zum Föderalismus und zurück
     Zum Konflikt von Rechtsnormen und
     -wirklichkeit in der Russländischen
     Föderation von 1991 bis 2009
     Mit einem Vorwort von Alexander Blankenagel
     ISBN 978-3-8382-0292-1

107 Philipp Herzog
     Sozialistische Völkerfreundschaft,
     nationaler Widerstand oder harmloser
     Zeitvertreib?
     Zur politischen Funktion der Volkskunst
     im sowjetischen Estland
     Mit einem Vorwort von Andreas Kappeler
     ISBN 978-3-8382-0216-7

108 Marlène Laruelle (ed.)
     Russian Nationalism, Foreign Policy,
     and Identity Debates in Putin's Russia
     New Ideological Patterns after the Orange
     Revolution
     ISBN 978-3-8382-0325-6

109 Michail Logvinov
     Russlands Kampf gegen den
     internationalen Terrorismus
     Eine kritische Bestandsaufnahme des
     Bekämpfungsansatzes
     Mit einem Geleitwort von
     Hans-Henning Schröder
     und einem Vorwort von Eckhard Jesse
     ISBN 978-3-8382-0329-4

110 John B. Dunlop
     The Moscow Bombings
     of September 1999
     Examinations of Russian Terrorist Attacks
     at the Onset of Vladimir Putin's Rule
     Second, Revised and Expanded Edition
     ISBN 978-3-8382-0388-1

111 Андрей А. Ковалёв
     Свидетельство из-за кулис
     российской политики I
     Можно ли делать добро из зла?
     (Воспоминания и размышления о
     последних советских и первых
     послесоветских годах)
     With a foreword by Peter Reddaway
     ISBN 978-3-8382-0302-7

112 Андрей А. Ковалёв
     Свидетельство из-за кулис
     российской политики II
     Угроза для себя и окружающих
     (Наблюдения и предостережения
     относительно происходящего после 2000 г.)
     ISBN 978-3-8382-0303-4

113 Bernd Kappenberg
     Zeichen setzen für Europa
     Der Gebrauch europäischer lateinischer
     Sonderzeichen in der deutschen Öffentlichkeit
     Mit einem Vorwort von Peter Schlobinski
     ISBN 978-3-89821-749-1

114 Ivo Mijnssen
     The Quest for an Ideal Youth in
     Putin's Russia I
     Back to Our Future! History, Modernity, and
     Patriotism according to Nashi, 2005-2013
     With a foreword by Jeronim Perović
     Second, Revised and Expanded Edition
     ISBN 978-3-8382-0368-3

115 Jussi Lassila
     The Quest for an Ideal Youth in
     Putin's Russia II
     The Search for Distinctive Conformism in the
     Political Communication of Nashi, 2005-2009
     With a foreword by Kirill Postoutenko
     Second, Revised and Expanded Edition
     ISBN 978-3-8382-0415-4

116 Valerio Trabandt
     Neue Nachbarn, gute Nachbarschaft?
     Die EU als internationaler Akteur am Beispiel
     ihrer Demokratieförderung in Belarus und der
     Ukraine 2004-2009
     Mit einem Vorwort von Jutta Joachim
     ISBN 978-3-8382-0437-6

117   Fabian Pfeiffer
      Estlands Außen- und Sicherheitspolitik I
      Der estnische Atlantizismus nach der
      wiedererlangten Unabhängigkeit 1991-2004
      Mit einem Vorwort von Helmut Hubel
      ISBN 978-3-8382-0127-6

118   Jana Podßuweit
      Estlands Außen- und Sicherheitspolitik II
      Handlungsoptionen eines Kleinstaates im
      Rahmen seiner EU-Mitgliedschaft (2004-2008)
      Mit einem Vorwort von Helmut Hubel
      ISBN 978-3-8382-0440-6

119   Karin Pointner
      Estlands Außen- und Sicherheitspolitik III
      Eine gedächtnispolitische Analyse estnischer
      Entwicklungskooperation 2006-2010
      Mit einem Vorwort von Karin Liebhart
      ISBN 978-3-8382-0435-2

120   Ruslana Vovk
      Die Offenheit der ukrainischen
      Verfassung für das Völkerrecht und
      die europäische Integration
      Mit einem Vorwort von Alexander
      Blankenagel
      ISBN 978-3-8382-0481-9

121   Mykhaylo Banakh
      Die Relevanz der Zivilgesellschaft
      bei den postkommunistischen
      Transformationsprozessen in mittel-
      und osteuropäischen Ländern
      Das Beispiel der spät- und postsowjetischen
      Ukraine 1986-2009
      Mit einem Vorwort von Gerhard Simon
      ISBN 978-3-8382-0499-4

122   Michael Moser
      Language Policy and the Discourse on
      Languages in Ukraine under President
      Viktor Yanukovych (25 February
      2010–28 October 2012)
      ISBN 978-3-8382-0497-0 (Paperback edition)
      ISBN 978-3-8382-0507-6 (Hardcover edition)

123   Nicole Krome
      Russischer Netzwerkkapitalismus
      Restrukturierungsprozesse in der
      Russischen Föderation am Beispiel des
      Luftfahrtunternehmens "Aviastar"
      Mit einem Vorwort von Petra Stykow
      ISBN 978-3-8382-0534-2

124   David R. Marples
      'Our Glorious Past'
      Lukashenka's Belarus and
      the Great Patriotic War
      ISBN 978-3-8382-0574-8 (Paperback edition)
      ISBN 978-3-8382-0675-2 (Hardcover edition)

125   Ulf Walther
      Russlands "neuer Adel"
      Die Macht des Geheimdienstes von
      Gorbatschow bis Putin
      Mit einem Vorwort von Hans-Georg Wieck
      ISBN 978-3-8382-0584-7

126   Simon Geissbühler (Hrsg.)
      Die Revolution 3.0
      Der Umbruch 2013/14 und die Perspektiven
      der Ukraine
      ISBN 978-3-8382-0581-6 (Paperback edition)
      ISBN 978-3-8382-0681-3 (Hardcover edition)

127   Andrey Makarychev
      Russia and the EU
      in a Multipolar World
      Discourses, Identities, Norms
      ISBN 978-3-8382-0629-5

128   Roland Scharff
      Kasachstan als postsowjetischer
      Wohlfahrtsstaat
      Die Transformation des sozialen
      Schutzsystems
      Mit einem Vorwort von Joachim Ahrens
      ISBN 978-3-8382-0622-6

ibidem-Verlag

Melchiorstr. 15

D-70439 Stuttgart

info@ibidem-verlag.de

www.ibidem-verlag.de
www.ibidem.eu
www.edition-noema.de
www.autorenbetreuung.de